D0536174

An Introduction to the Sociology of Religion

This book fills a niche by giving equal weight to the classical sociological tradition and to the sociology of contemporary religion. It looks not only at sociologists of religion, but at wider sociological theories with a bearing on religion. All of which makes it one of the most wide-ranging textbooks on the market. Clearly written and concise, the authors convey even the most complex theories with a minimum of fuss. A valuable textbook for students.
    Linda Woodhead, Professor of Sociology of Religion, Lancaster University, UK

Is it true that religion is weakening in modern times, or are we facing religious resurgence? What is fundamentalism? How does it emerge and grow? What role does religion play in ethnic and national conflicts? Is religion a fundamental driving force or do political leaders use religion for their own purposes? Do all religions oppress women? These are some of the questions addressed in this book.

An Introduction to the Sociology of Religion provides an overview of sociological theories of contemporary religious life. Some chapters are organized according to topic. Others offer brief presentations of classical and contemporary sociologists from Karl Marx to Zygmunt Bauman and their perspectives on social life, including religion. Throughout the book, illustrations and examples are taken from several religious traditions.

An Introduction to the Sociology of Religion

Classical and Contemporary Perspectives

Inger Furseth

KIFO Centre for Church Research, Norway and University of
Southern California, USA

and

Pål Repstad

Agder University College, Norway

Routledge
Taylor & Francis Group

LONDON AND NEW YORK

First published 2006 by Ashgate publishing

Published 2016 by Routledge
2 Park Square, Milton Park, Abingdon, Oxon OX14 4RN
711 Third Avenue, New York, NY 10017, USA

Routledge is an imprint of the Taylor & Francis Group, an informa business

British Library Cataloguing in Publication Data
Furseth, Inger
  An introduction to the sociology of religion:classical
  and contemporary perspectives
  1.Religion and sociology
  I.Title II.Repstad, Pål
  306.6

Library of Congress Cataloging-in-Publication Data
Furseth, Inger.
  An introduction to the sociology of religion: classical and contemporary
  perspectives / Inger Furseth and Pål Repstad.
    p. cm.
  Includes bibliographical references (p.   ) and index.
  ISBN 0-7546-5653-5 (hardcover: alk. paper) – ISBN 0-7546-5658-6 (pbk.: alk.
  paper) 1. Sociology and religion. I. Repstad, Pål. II. Title.

BL60.F84 2006
306.6–dc22

2005031990

ISBN 13: 978-0-7546-5658-6 (pbk)
ISBN 13: 978-0-7546-5653-1 (hbk)

Typeset by IML Typographers, Birkenhead, Merseyside.

Contents

List of tables

Foreword

What is fundamentalism? How does it emerge? What role does religion play in ethnic conflicts today? Is religion a fundamental force or do political leaders use religion to promote other interests? Do all religions oppress women or do some religions empower women?

These are only a few examples of questions posed frequently today. Indeed, sociology in its early phase demonstrated a high degree of interest in religion. During the latter half of the twentieth century, general sociology and the sociology of religion developed along separate paths. This book gives an introduction to sociological theories of religion. We believe that anyone with an interest in religion or the social sciences will benefit from reading it. A growing number of students and scholars of theology, religious studies and church history have begun to use social scientific perspectives. Sociologists have also found a new interest in cultural analysis. The aim of this book is to provide the reader with an overview of existing sociological theories of religion. If we do have an implicit aim, it is to prevent the sociology of religion from becoming an isolated field within sociology. We firmly believe that the sociology of religion constitutes an integrated part of general sociology.

Several chapters in this book are organized according to topic. Two chapters give a brief overview of classical and contemporary theory. They look not only at sociologists of religion, but at wider sociological theories with a bearing on religion. We believe that this book will be useful for upper-level undergraduate students within the social sciences, religious studies and theology. However, the book can also be used by graduate students who are new to the sociology of religion.

We are grateful that KIFO Centre for Church Research and Agder University College provided us with the opportunity to work on this book. Inger Furseth also owes appreciation to the Norwegian Non-Fiction Writers' and Translators' Association (NFF) for a grant. We are also grateful to Line Nyhagen Predelli and Willy Guneriussen, who read drafts and commented. Most of all, we are grateful to each other. Writing can be a relatively solitary venture, but we have had fun and learnt from each other. Inger Furseth has written the first draft to Chapters 3, 4, 6, 9, 10 and 11, and Pål Repstad has done the same for Chapters 1, 2, 5, 7, 8 and 12. However, we have commented on each other's work to such a degree that we both are responsible for the entire book.

Inger Furseth and Pål Repstad
Oslo/Kristiansand, May 2006

1

Sociological perspectives on religion

1.1 What is sociology?

It is hardly possible to state briefly and irrefutably what sociology is. We may say that sociology is the study of human social life, in groups and in communities, but such a statement does not offer an adequate distinction between sociology and other disciplines, for example, history. Our aim is not to make strict distinctions between different disciplines. Such distinctions do not descend from the sky: they are the result of an obscure mixture of specific differences, professional interests, academic and political power structures, and historical coincidences. Even so, highlighting some key characteristics that are commonly used to describe sociology as a discipline can be useful. This issue will be dealt with here and then we will continue by considering the differences between the sociology of religion and other fields of sociology – and between the sociology of religion and other disciplines that study religion. Along the way, a few themes and perspectives will be introduced, to which we will return throughout the book.

French philosopher Auguste Comte formulated the concept of sociology more than a hundred years ago. Since then, sociology has been taught at universities across the world, and as an academic discipline has witnessed an exceptional growth in the last fifty years or so. The word "sociology" is a combination of Greek and Latin and simply means civic studies. Of course, sociology is civic studies characterized by its own specific perspectives.

In describing sociology, we may say that this discipline has the explanation and the understanding of human action as its core interest. Why do human beings act the way they do? When using the expression "sociological explanation," strict explanations of causality are not implied. The expression is used in a wider sense, meaning all contributions that provide new information regarding a specific phenomenon. In order to explain human actions, then, we will distinguish between explanations of personal quality, of social relations, and of social systems.

An explanation of personal quality states that an event takes place due to the qualities of the individual, which are viewed as relatively stable. This is an explanation "from within." To illustrate, if a person commits a crime, the criminal act is explained by the defendant's criminal character. Or when an individual demonstrates a deep religious involvement, an explanation of quality states that this individual has a religious personality. Explanations of personal quality tend to contain an element of moral praise or condemnation: "You cannot expect anything good from such a depraved person" or "she is kind through and through." Explanations of personal quality usually point to characteristics of entire groups or categories. Such explanations have been prolific through the ages, not least regarding explanations based on gender or race: "Women are not cut out to be leaders" or "Black people are not fit for this kind of work." Explanations of personal quality are frequently found in popular language, and they also appear in the sciences from time to time. For example, a psychologist may maintain that a given behavior can only be explained through a deep-seated character trait.

The social sciences offer several arguments against explanations of personal quality. One argument is that such explanations tend to be the result of tautologies: people are involved in religion because they are deeply religious. Sociologists will, however, take this issue further and ask *why* people become religious. In answering this question, they frequently rely on relational explanations: a fact or an event must be understood through the social relations in which people engage. Explanations of relations – also called social explanations – are by some found to be the best explanations in the social sciences (Wadel 1990). Such explanations provide information as to why we act the way we do by demonstrating how we are affected by our interpersonal relationships. We take other people into consideration when we act; we "respond" to other people's actions. Taking other people's actions into consideration does not necessarily mean that we subject ourselves to them. We may learn from others and adjust our behavior to them, but we may also find them irritating, object to them, try to deceive them, or consciously ignore them. In all of these situations – and thousands more – we constantly interact with other people.

The word "relations" may signal a certain modicum of permanence in personal relationships. Yet, even in casual meetings something social may be activated. If two men, unknown to each other, pass in the street, we may relatively safely assume that one will pull in his stomach and the other will stop picking his nose as they are passing. Social conventions appear even in such short-term relations. Furthermore, we act and think not only in direct social contact with others, but we also act based on memories of previous social relations. It is not even necessary to have experienced everything ourselves. We know that a burned child dreads the fire. Yet even a child who has never experienced what it is like to be burned has learned to handle matches with caution, having learned from parents' warnings or from children's programs on TV. Social relations are not always direct; they can be indirect or mediated: passed on through mass media, such as film or TV. This issue points to a contemporary debate within sociology. Some sociologists will maintain that mass media and the new technological forms of communication are to the forefront in ways not seen before, and this demonstrates that we live in a new era. Others will object by arguing that direct social relations constitute the major contributing factor in forming our social lives and understanding ourselves, even today.

The third type of explanation mentioned here is the system or structural explanation. This form of explanation can be found in everyday life, too, as for example when people speak of "development" or "society" as formative powers that affect our lives. Some sociologists speak of "social laws." In all of these cases, there is an underlying notion that specific patterns or built-in regularities in society affect people whether they like it or not.

Several contemporary social scientists object to an extensive use of system explanations. Such explanations tend to conceal the fact that societal structures are, after all, human-made. Some have pointed out that system explanations tend to form a so-called self-fulfilling prophecy: if everybody thinks that a system is unchangeable, so it is. In the sociology of religion, some have used the notion of "secularization" – meaning a weakening of the importance of religion – as if it were an inexorable force of nature. Most sociologists today would disagree with the idea that society evolves through inevitable social laws that operate completely independently of human action. At the same time, several sociologists remain firm in their belief that it is useful to speak of social forces that affect individuals and social relations. However, there is disagreement as to whether these forces are stable, or strong, or whether they have the ability to control human action. Schematically speaking, a major trend in contemporary sociology will emphasize how social actors interpret the world and act accordingly. Some "structuralists" criticize the actor-oriented approach for underrating the importance of external factors that affect people's lives, especially technological and economic factors. In other words, some sociologists stress society when explaining social life, whereas others focus on the human agent.

A major focus in sociology is the study of the interactions that take place between individuals and societal forms. The term "societal form" is here used in a wide sense. It includes "frozen" societal structures as well as more dynamic patterns found in social relations, which mutually affect one another. On the one hand, individuals are capable of changing societal forms, especially when they are acting within a goal-oriented and coordinated organization. On the other hand, individuals are also born into a pre-existing society that affects them in various ways.

Societal forms are material and non-material. Once a bridge is built across a beautiful fjord, most people will prefer to use it rather than swim or cross by boat, even if they initially opposed its construction. In other words, once a technology has been introduced, it is difficult to imagine its non-existence. Material and social factors reinforce each other, as when a religious elite expresses its power and significance through spectacular buildings and splendid garments. These material artifacts do not have a meaning in and of themselves, but individuals interpret them and give them meaning. For example, the pyramids of Giza made people awestruck thousands of years ago. Yet, for today's blasé tourist, the same pyramids only represent a "must," a visit that is briefly mentioned in social conversation.

Although non-material societal forms are invisible, they still have an impact on individuals. In a religious context, for example, traditions that are perceived as morally true and right are often experienced as being as strong as a brick wall. Seen from a sociological perspective, traditions are created by individuals and they are objects of change, at least in principle. However, they are difficult to change in everyday life, especially if an individual stands alone.

This book presents several sociological theories of religion. Some theories complement each other and can be combined, whereas others are more or less mutually exclusive. Here, we will briefly introduce the most common schools found in contemporary sociology. We mentioned above that sociology tends primarily to be either actor-oriented or structure-oriented. Some sociologists emphasize the human actor's ability to act and change social structures. These theorists focus on how individuals create society (sociology "from below"). Other theorists argue that society forms the individual (sociology "from above"). These two positions also appear in the sociology of religion. A current issue is, for example, how anchored or disembedded individuals are in relation to established religious traditions.

Furthermore, a common distinction is found between an idealistic and a materialistic perspective. This debate centers on the question as to which social conditions are fundamental and determinate for individuals and society. Two classical sociologists represent relatively opposite views on this issue: in danger of becoming too schematic, we may say that Karl Marx saw the development of religion largely as a reflection of economic conditions, whereas Max Weber attempted to demonstrate that religion in itself could determine the economic development in a given historical context (see Chapter 3). We must add, however, that both of them also included the mutual interdependence of material and ideal factors in their analyses.

Furthermore, a few sociological theories tend to be oriented towards a harmonic view of society, whereas other theories focus on social conflict. Several theories belong in the middle, as they attempt to combine the two perspectives. Karl Marx is often described as a theorist of social conflict, although he had an extensive interest in solidarity and community. Talcott Parsons (Section 3.7) is frequently characterized as a harmony-oriented classical sociologist. Indeed, Parsons argued that religion contributes to social integration. Yet he was far from blind to the possibility that religion also can represent a source of conflict. In spite of these modifications, the distinction between harmony- and conflict-oriented sociology continues to be meaningful, because sociologists tend to disagree on the fundamental nature of conflict in society. Conflict theorists will view order and harmony as superficial entities. They maintain that underneath a surface of apparent harmony, there is a form of balance of power or oppression of the weaker party. Whereas harmony theorists view conflict as undesirable, conflict theorists look at existing social conditions with suspicion.

Because sociologists are reluctant to embrace explanations of personal quality, there is a rivalry between, on the one hand, sociological explanations of human action and, on the other hand, biological and genetic explanations. Having to choose between hereditary and environmental factors, the sociologist will tend to choose the latter. In more ways than one, sociology has constituted a significant part of the trend in modern thought towards viewing social phenomena as human-made and socially determined, rather than ingrained qualities given by birth, nature, or God. A striking example is the transformation of the understanding of gender roles. Whereas women's and men's roles in society previously were interpreted as inherent traits based on the nature of women and men, they are now seen as a result of traditions and power relations (see Chapter 11). In other words, there has been a shift in sociology away from an essentialistic understanding of reality, where the phenomena in question are regarded as stable with fixed essential properties, to a constructivist understanding, where reality is seen as a human construction to which individuals give meaning. Sociologists like to add that reality is socially constructed in the sense that it is formed by individuals in interaction, individuals who "negotiate" with each other in order to create a shared perception of the world. Yet the idea that something is socially constructed does not exclude the fact that it is real in everyday life. For example, even if gender roles are socially constructed, they are experienced in a very real sense in the lives of women and men.

The idea that human phenomena are socially constructed and therefore in principle changeable constitutes a major trend in contemporary sociology. However, other trends are also present. In the media, there is a growing tendency to present popular research that attempts to prove that women's and men's behavior is determined by genetic and biological factors. One example, taken from the Norwegian newspaper *Vårt Land* (March 25, 2003), is a report from a scientist concluding from his research on twins that there is a moderate degree of genetic influence on people's religiosity. We must mention, however, that another geneticist described this scientific hunt for a "faith gene" as sheer nonsense.

We cannot take for granted that social and environmental explanations will continue to have a high status in the future. If genetic and biological explanations achieve more prominence, this may in fact have moral implications. The sociological approach of interpreting human life and social conditions as human-made and changeable carries an inherent moral potential that can be used to criticize and change society. In contrast, explanations referring to a God-given or innate nature have throughout history been used to legitimate discrimination as well as injustice.

It is hardly possible to make a definite statement about the role of sociology in contemporary society. On the one hand, sociology tends to be critical towards society. On the other, the sociological understanding of the complexity of society represents a corrective to social engineering. When it comes to the role of religion in society, sociology has – along with other modern disciplines – contributed to a decreasing validity of religion. The reason is that sociology searches for human, and not religious, explanations. In other words, sociology has in itself a secularizing effect. This is an issue to which we will return in Chapter 12, which discusses the relationship between sociology and religious faith.

1.2 The sociology of religion and general sociology

It is important to know that the sociology of religion does not inherently differ from general sociology. Sociology of religion has as its subject the study of religion in its social context, but it applies the same theories and methods that are used to study economics, politics and other social phenomena.

Generally, sociologists of religion have an interest in religion's effect on society and society's influence on religious life. This book will attempt to demonstrate that there is interdependence between general sociology and the sociology of religion. The tendency for the sociology of religion to become relatively isolated from general sociology may in part be due to the fact that contemporary sociology, in contrast to its classical roots, has given little attention to religion. In academic circles, religion has largely been viewed as a phenomenon of diminishing importance. The British sociologist James A. Beckford (2000) points out that general sociology in its early phase demonstrated a high degree of interest in religion, Max Weber and Émile Durkheim being classical examples. Later, general sociology and the sociology of religion developed along separate paths. After the Second World War, several

Western countries experienced a demand for a sociology that could contribute to rebuilding society through economic and political development, which led to a neglect of sociology of culture and religion. In contemporary society, Beckford argues, general sociology and the sociology of religion demonstrate a shared interest in several themes. Examples are gender, language, and meaning, but also the body, as for instance bodily expressions in rituals. Globalization is another common theme and this is, in fact, an area where sociologists of religion have made major contributions to general sociology. The debate on rational choice theory has proved to be significant in both fields of sociology. All of these themes are only mentioned briefly here without further explanation. However, they will be discussed in more detail later.

The gap between the sociology of religion and general sociology may also be due to the fact that sociologists of religion have tended to focus on internal church matters. The reason is that much sociology of religion has been conducted in close relationship with established churches. Thus, not only religion is affected by its social context, but also the sociology of religion. This book attempts to combine the sociology of religion with general sociology. Some chapters are organized according to theme, while others offer brief presentations of contemporary sociologists and their perspectives on social life, including religion. We have made an effort to include sociologists who do not necessarily deal with religion as a major theme. Our hope is that these sections will inspire the reader to consider how religion can be studied from a variety of sociological perspectives, including those that are more rarely found in the sociology of religion.

1.3 Sociology as science

The claim that sociology is an empirical science is based on the idea that there must be consistency between systematically collected and analysed data and the conclusions. This idea does not imply that sociology is objective in the sense that only one conclusion is possible and correct. This issue raises complicated questions debated by theorists of science, which we will not pursue in great detail here. However, our view is that sociology is largely a form of interpretation. We do not believe that sociologists will produce an unambiguous and definite sociological truth, even if they are given abundant resources to refine their instruments and conduct endless studies. The idea that sociology will produce one truth about society is frequently called positivistic. It implies an optimistic and ambitious view of sociology and its possibilities which is commonly found among the classical sociologists.

Positivism has been subjected to severe attacks during the past forty years, with the result that few believe in an objective sociology today. A common argument is that society is changing, and analytical tools that proved to be useful a few decades ago are of little help in trying to understand contemporary society. Also, individuals are able to set goals and act according to that which is meaningful to them. On this basis, several theorists of science will argue that human beings constitute a far more complicated object of study than mechanical systems. Furthermore, human consciousness and the ability to formulate aims imply that the humanities and the social sciences are qualitatively different than the natural sciences. To illustrate, the humanities and the social sciences are not capable of providing exact predictions about the future. It is possible to give an outline of a development that took place in the past and prolong it into the future, but there is always the possibility that something new may appear. For example, even with the knowledge of African and European musical traditions, jazz was not foreseen. Moreover, even if we know a lot about European religion, we are unable to predict whether the European Union will have one common religion in the year 2050 – or if the EU will continue to exist, for that matter.

Furthermore, scientists too are members of society and they have their own personal, religious and political sympathies and frameworks for interpretation. When scholars focus on some issues, other issues remain in the dark. On this basis, it is too simplistic to argue that theology and ethics are normative and subjective disciplines whereas the social sciences are descriptive and objective. Although a sociologist may be open-minded, nobody is able totally to break away from their background and pre-conceived notions. It is easier to detect such pre-conceived beliefs in other scholars than in oneself. Therefore, research must be available to the public, thus facilitating mutual criticism and learning.

Today, the academic world tends to harbor a relatively critical view of the sciences. Some go extremely far in their critique, nearly dissolving all forms of knowledge. Most sociologists attempt to find a middle position between the old positivistic view and the new critical relativism. Many will agree with our argument that sociology is a form of interpretation. However, few are fully prepared to accept the postmodern view that one interpretation is of equal value to any other. We will claim that there are common norms and requirements viable for all sciences. One requirement is that a comprehensive discussion should be included. Another requirement is that arguments against one's own position must be presented and discussed in a way that is fair and acceptable to the opponents. In addition, all scientists must describe their procedures in ways that enable other scientists to check the validity and reliability of their work. Furthermore, the arguments must be stringent, so that the conclusions are clearly stated and logically tenable. Based on the notion mentioned above that no scholar escapes their own pre-conceived ideas, it is also reasonable to ask every scholar to formulate their position and its possible effect on their research.

An additional requirement is that the empirical data must support the scholar's conclusions. This does not imply a naïve notion that empirical data are unambiguous entities that can be taken from a reality "out there" as final proofs. Data are measured and analysed in different ways, and they too must be interpreted. Nevertheless, sociology is an empirical science, which means that researchers must be willing to revise their beliefs and theories in light of new data. Researchers must be open for new surprising information that leads to a reconsideration of their preconceptions. Sociologists who never put themselves in a situation where they risk being corrected by new information are not good sociologists. This is a cause for concern in contemporary sociology: for a long time, there seems to have been a development towards a division of labor between theorists and empiricists. Some theorists tend to write essays on general developments in society, essays that are well formulated, charming and interesting. Yet they are frequently based on rather vague and unsystematic empirical evidence. On the other hand, several sociologists earn their living by processing large amounts of empirical data without attempting to use theory or place their data within a larger frame of interpretation.

This book deals mostly with sociological theories of religious life. This may lead the reader to believe that our sympathy primarily lies with the theorists, but this is not necessarily true. An important goal in the development of sociology is to keep the theorists and the empiricists together. The criticism we direct against theories does not deal only with possible built-in logical weaknesses but also with the ability of theories to stand up against empirical data.

Nevertheless, this book does not provide a systematic presentation of updated empirical data about religious life throughout the world but offers only examples and illustrations. Even if we have tried to include material from several religious traditions, this book has a Western profile, and the majority of our examples are taken from the encounter between Christianity and modernity. In this way, this book is colored and limited by the context within which we do our research.

Little information about sociological methods is included here. This is partly due to the size of this book but also because there is no distinct method for the sociology of religion. We must rely on the same methods as the sociologists who study economy, love, or the outdoors. The main methods are observation and fieldwork, interviews, questionnaires, and analysis of written material.

Although there are no distinctive methods in the sociology of religion, sociologists who study religion will, at times, face a distinctive set of challenges. The study of religious minorities may, for example, offer challenges in relation to achieving access and trust by the group under scrutiny. The researcher may find it difficult to decide which informants to believe, since members and former members often will present strikingly different pictures of reality. Another challenge is information derived from opinion polls. Lately, there has been a discussion about their reliability regarding religious practice. Bluntly put, some sociologists maintain that people tend to exaggerate church attendance, especially if they live in communities where church attendance is viewed as proper behavior. Indeed, some American sociologists suggest that the exaggerations on an average reach 50 per cent when they compare surveys with other records (Hadaway et al. 1993).

These methodological problems do not differ dramatically from other branches of sociology. Sociologists from various fields engage in the debate on advantages and disadvantages in quantitative and qualitative methods. Quantitative methods are distinguished by extensive use of measurements, for example, in wide-ranging surveys based on representative samples from the entire population. Such methods are well suited to provide an overview of the diffusion of a phenomenon. At the same time, they have a tendency to be superficial and fragmentary because they collect fragments of single features from numerous individuals. If the purpose of the study is to explore qualities – meaning peculiarities and nuances in social phenomena – then qualitative methods are more useful, as these methods collect richer and more varied data. Qualitative methods are also useful if the aim is to follow a development closely over a period of time. Due to practical limitations, the use of qualitative methods usually implies the study of relatively small groups that are not representative of a larger population. For that reason, conclusions in qualitative studies are often tentative. Our view is a rather practical one: select the appropriate method according to the purpose of your study. Moreover, it is possible to combine different methods in the same research project. Such an approach enables comparisons between different sets of data, which strengthens the conclusions.

1.4 The sociology of religion versus other disciplines that study religion

As we attempt to pinpoint the distinctive sociological approach to religion, it may be useful to consider the similarities and differences between the sociology of religion and other disciplines that study religion. Indeed, religion is an object of study within several disciplines, such as pedagogy, theology, philosophy, psychology, social anthropology, history, and religious studies. As noted, the borders between the different disciplines are not absolute, but fluid and changing. Several different scholars, such as sociologists, philosophers, theologians, and historians of religion, share an interest in the same theories. Some scholars also interact more frequently with those from other disciplines who share the same area of interest than they do with scholars from their own discipline. For example, those who study the family come from several disciplines. The same is true for those with an interest in ritual studies or gender studies. In spite of such interdisciplinary interaction and cooperation, this section briefly comments on the relationship between the sociology of religion and other disciplines that study religion.

A rather common observation is that sociology has a more general sphere of study than other social sciences, which tend to focus on specific sections of society. For example, political science has the study of politics as its subject, and pedagogy has the study of education and learning. When it comes to the pedagogy of religion, this field developed as churches experienced a need to know how best to teach their theology. For that reason, pedagogy of religion has been perceived as an applied theological discipline. On the one hand, it is clearly normative, because its aim is to find out how religion should be taught. On the other, pedagogy of religion has increasingly become an empirical science without attachments to specific religious traditions. When doing empirical research, scholars within this field apply the same sociological and historical methods as other scholars. Nevertheless, they still tend to offer advice as to how a church or a government agent should act, which sociologists of religion seldom do.

A profound distinction is found between theology and the social sciences. Theology is often labeled a normative science, because it attempts to prescribe how human beings should act. In contrast, the social sciences are perceived to be descriptive, because they give information as to how humans actually are. Although useful at times, such a distinction is too simplistic. First of all, several areas within theology make use of empirical methods, examples being linguistics and the historical methods that experienced a breakthrough in the study of biblical texts in the nineteenth century. More recently, social science methods have been applied in biblical research, especially in the study of the New Testament life-world. In spite of the obvious methodological problem in applying recent theories on ancient Christianity, the sociological interpretations of various early Christian groups have proven useful (Gager 1975; Meeks 1983; Dutcher-Walls 1999).

Church history has become a rather secularized theological discipline, in the sense that religious explanations no longer are used to analyse historical events. Even in academic institutions with close ties to churches and conservative religious groups, it is rare to find explanations of the type: "The Holy Spirit moved people so that ... happened." The explanatory factors are social, economic and cultural; in short, secular. Within the area of systematic and practical theology, theology becomes explicitly normative and offers advice as to how people should think. Nevertheless, even in normative, constructive sciences, such as theology and law, there are norms for scientific behavior to which these scholars must adhere. One example is the norm of impartiality. Moreover, we mentioned above that the social sciences are not purely objective and descriptive. One major difference between theology and the social sciences lies, perhaps, in how explicitly normative these sciences are. The normative nature of the social sciences tends to be more hidden behind vaguely formulated conclusions as to what people should do. The social sciences operate with several implied premises regarding notions about the common good, about normalcy and abnormalcy, and about possibilities for change.

A simplistic description of the difference between the sociology of religion and the psychology of religion will state that psychologists of religion focus on questions related to the individual's religious life, whereas sociologists emphasize the role of religion in society. Yet these boundaries are fluid and the common area of interest seems to be growing. Few, if any, psychologists today use only intrapsychic explanations. Instead, they combine this approach with a focus on social relations and social environments. On the other hand, there seems to be a growing interest in the individual in contemporary sociology. This is evident in the increasing number of sociological studies that attempt to explain how the individual or groups of individuals shape their identity and their self-image.

Since the nineteenth century, social anthropology has viewed religion as an important part of the culture in pre-industrial societies. Yet there used to be a geographical division of labor between sociologists and social anthropologists. When sociological theory was formulated in the nineteenth century, the aim was to understand the development of industrial society and its consequences, for example, the effect of modernization on social integration. Quantitative sociological methods were frequently seen as appropriate to study modern societies because they require a certain level of literacy. In contrast, social anthropologists tended to study small-scale pre-modern societies, and the most common method was long-term participation in the community to be studied. Today, several social anthropologists have directed their attention towards Western local communities. The growing pluralism brought about through immigration of non-Westerners to the West has created a growing interest in social anthropology. The cultural diversity has also resulted in a more intense dialogue between sociologists and anthropologists, including scholars of religion. This does not, however, represent an entirely new development. Émile Durkheim is considered a classical theorist within both disciplines, and several scholars discussed in this book are social anthropologists, for example, Mary Douglas.

Scientific theory distinguishes between idiographic and nomothetic sciences. Whereas an idiographic science seeks knowledge of that which is unique and exceptional, a nomothetic science attempts to detect general laws and regularity. Previously, history was commonly described as an idiographic science, and sociology was considered a nomothetic science. These are, at best, half-truths. Throughout the history of the sciences, these two disciplines have directed critique against each other. Historians have criticized sociologists for their use of sweeping generalizations and claimed that they are suppressed by "model tyranny." Their argument is that historical events have qualities that are so unusual that history does not repeat itself. Likewise, sociologists have criticized historians and stated that they are suppressed by "detail tyranny." Sociologists have pointed out that historians do, indeed, harbor ideas about human behavior which they do not explicitly state. During the last few decades, historians and sociologists have, however, demonstrated that they share an interest in some of the same phenomena and that they are willing to make use of the other discipline. Contemporary sociologists tend to be less ambitious than their predecessors, as they do not describe human and social life in terms of "social laws." They will admit that their findings and conclusions must be contextualized, that is, be situated in a local and historical context. Historians, on the other hand, have come to realize that they are unable to capture all of reality in their historical narratives and that they must make the reader aware of the limitations of their approach. By using explanations and models taken from sociology, they often address a wider audience. The confrontation and challenge that specific historical data offer will also frequently lead to revisions of sociological models.

The last discipline considered here is the history of religion or religious studies. Generally, the approach taken within the history of religion focuses in more detail upon the history of world religions and its content than does the sociology of religion. This does not mean that the sociology of religion lacks an interest in the content of religious ideas, rituals and other religious practices. However, sociologists tend to have an interest in the content of religious ideas, as long as they contribute to an understanding of the interdependence between religious life and its social context, while leaving the description of religious dogmas, customs, and institutions to the scholar of religion.

Historically, historians of religion viewed their own field as scientific and objective, in contrast to theology, which they defined as obdurate and dogmatic. The history of religion was largely shaped as a science in the nineteenth century by Christian theologians who ran into difficulties in achieving permanent positions at the theological faculties due to their view on various theological issues. The more recent critique of positivistic sciences has, however, reached the various religious studies departments, so scholars within this discipline will also admit that their work is affected by their interpretations.

Religious studies have undergone change in more ways than one over the past few decades. Schematically speaking, the focus has shifted from ancient texts to modern individuals, from elite to popular religion, from the study of specific religious systems and institutions to the search for religious signs everywhere in society. Although parts of religious studies have been moving closer to the sociology of religion, the features of the two disciplines are quite different. Religious studies harbors a stronger emphasis on a historical perspective and more interest in describing the contents of religion than does the sociology of religion. The laborious linguistic qualifications are perhaps less important today than they used to be, although they still represent a requirement to enter the discipline, just as fieldwork does to the social anthropologist, knowledge of Greek to the theologian, and an understanding of a statistical fourfold table to the sociologist.

1.5 Classical sociology – a comment

In a book that deals mainly with contemporary religion, some readers may object that too much attention is given to classical sociologists, whose work was largely published a century or more ago. More recent sociology has, however, a tendency to debate with its founders. On this basis, one may conclude that sociology as a discipline is not properly established. This might be true, if one believes that a science should be cumulative, in the sense that knowledge is built gradually whereby new findings either add to or adjust old findings. Other theories of science, as represented by Thomas Kuhn (1970), paint the picture of the development of the sciences as a conflictual drama, as a series of scientific revolutions. Kuhn argues that when an established paradigm or fundamental system of thought no longer functions as a frame of interpretation for new findings, a revolutionary change of paradigm occurs, whereby the established sciences break down and a new generation of scientists establishes new scientific standards. A classic example of changing paradigms is the transition from a geocentric to a heliocentric world-view within the natural sciences, a transition that was painful for the Church, for politicians, and for scientists alike.

Some will maintain that sociology is still not an established science with one common paradigm. Rather, it is a multi-paradigmatic science where fundamentally different assumptions about individual and society compete for status and attention. Without doubt, there are several schools of thought within sociology, and this might explain the continued desire to debate with the predecessors. This is particularly true for the sociology of religion, where references to "the founding fathers" occur quite frequently.

Canadian sociologist of religion Roger O'Toole speaks of classical sociology as having an ambiguous legacy (2001). It is possible to argue that a strong focus on classical sociology restrains the cumulative aspect of the science. Another argument is that the work of classical sociologists is irrelevant, merely due to developments that have taken place since their time. Indeed, a fundamental premise in sociology is that individuals and society are changing. Some sociologists continue to claim that there are universal constants in human beings, although most contemporary sociologists have relatively modest ambitions regarding their ability to develop generalizations. Instead, sociology today tends to emphasize context, as it relates to both time and place.

O'Toole has several objections to the frequent use of classical sociology. He claims that instead of countering the opponent's argument in a debate, some will invoke the classical sociologists as mere authorities. Furthermore, continued discussions of "what Weber really means" are hardly suitable to achieve an understanding of the forces that shape contemporary society. Finally, some claim that any use of the classical scholars today represents a superficial representation, at worst a distortion, of their views. An objection to the latter argument is that the classical thinkers can be made relevant by letting their texts function as a source of inspiration. In this case, it is of less importance if our interpretations correspond fully with the authors' hundred-year-old intentions (however we would uncover them). The important issue is that their texts are used as we are confronted with new empirical data. Hopefully, they will contribute to a debate regarding the most adequate interpretations of social life, says O'Toole.

On this basis, we will argue that the sociology of religion should give ample room to the classics and at the same time include contemporary theory. We are aware that the combination of a hundred-year-old classical tradition and the variety of theories, as represented in this book, signals that sociology is a complex discipline – individuals and society are changing and living human beings constitute part of the object of study. The same is true for the sociology of religion. As religion undergoes change, the sociology of religion also develops along new trends. The scholars who preceded us have reflected upon the issues of religion and society, and the fact that their work may be fruitful to our studies should fill us with a sense of humility – a suitable virtue for sociologists of religion, who are hardly able to explain everything about their object of study.

2

Religion as a phenomenon – definitions and dimensions

2.1 Defining religion – not just an academic issue

We often use the word "religion," perhaps without thinking much about the way we define it. What is religious and what is non-religious? This chapter will show that scholars who study religion disagree on this issue. If we want to detect the meaning of the word, there is not much help in looking at its derivation, either. The word "religion" has Latin roots, but even in classical Rome it was interpreted in various ways. Sometimes it meant "to re-read" and sometimes "to bind together." It is possible, of course, to imagine that religion is something that is repeated, in the form of rituals, or something that binds gods and human beings together. Yet this does not provide us much help in defining the word. The Danish sociologist of religion, Ole Riis (1996: 10), is right when he says: "In spite of the efforts of the Latin teachers, the word triggers other ideas in modern readers."

All disciplines that study religion debate how the phenomenon should be defined. In empirically based disciplines such as the sociology of religion, the discussion does not center on questions of religious truth. Sociologists and psychologists tend to focus on how fruitful the definition is, meaning how well suited it is to detect the characteristic features of the object of study. Their concern is also that a good definition should be a tool for formulating exciting and relevant scientific problems. However, the past few decades have revealed that seemingly academic questions of definition have a practical and political side, too.

Several contemporary organizations and movements are engaged in a process to obtain legal status as a religion, due to the benefits that such a status provides. One example is Scientology (Aldridge 2000: 13–16), which was introduced about a century ago. As an alleged scientifically based therapeutic movement, Scientology promises its adherents more control in their lives. Within this organization, a process of increasing ritualization has taken place, accompanied by the formulation of creeds, the use of "church" as a term to describe the organization, a more pronounced pastoral effort, and even sanctions against heretics. One goal within Scientology has been to obtain legal status as a religion, and it has succeeded in several countries. Critics maintain, though, that the organization is primarily a commercial project that entices naïve followers to pay large sums of money.

Several countries provide legal benefits to religious communities, such as legal protection, the right to plead religious freedom, and tax-exemption. Some countries, such as Germany, offer help to religious communities in collecting membership fees.

In societies where religion is highly valued, religious communities will also receive a certain amount of prestige and respect just because they are seen as carriers of religious values. However, not every movement benefits from being defined as a religious movement. In intellectual, rationalistic circles, for example, religion is often considered to be synonymous with naïvety or fanaticism. In some instances, religious movements see an advantage in downplaying their religious profile, especially in situations facing restrictions or legal sanctions. Missionary societies have, for example, frequently defined themselves as relief organizations rather than evangelical organizations. Another example is Transcendental Meditation, which refused any attempt to be defined as a religion in the United States. As a result, TM could be taught in schools and military academies as a nondenominational method that promises mental well-being (Barker 1995).

The ways in which we define religion will actually affect a country's legal codes and public policy. More intangible, but no less important, various definitions of religion will influence groups differently, especially when the definitions have an ethnocentric form, that is, when they are based on local standards for what is considered to be religious. For example, when a definition of religion describes a country's dominant religious tradition as the norm, other forms of religion will appear to be foreign and divergent phenomena that must be explained and perhaps even controlled. We will later discuss how difficult it is to avoid ethnocentrism in definitions of religion.

The argument that definition of religion is more than just an academic issue could lead the reader to believe that academic debates are of little value. A detailed debate on definitions will definitely create a desire for more substantial knowledge. However, discussing definitions is more than sophistry. Indeed, it helps to clarify and pinpoint the object of study. Therefore, debates that conclude with constructive proposals for specific definitions are important, and so is the critique that is directed towards them. Besides, such debates are not just found in sociology. Most textbooks in the history of religion, psychology of religion, and sociology of religion include similar debates. They usually have the form of presenting two or more types of definitions, which are analysed according to their strengths and weaknesses, a procedure that also will be used here. In the sociology of religion, this debate often takes the form of a discussion between *substantive* and *functional* definitions of religion.

Substantive definitions include characteristics of the content (or substance) of religion. This content is usually based on the human belief in extraordinary phenomena, that which we cannot experience with our senses or grasp with our intellect. Functional definitions describe the utility or the effect that religion is supposed to have for individuals and/or society. For example, some functional definitions define religion as all human activity that gives meaning to life. Simply stated: substantive definitions tell us what religion *is*; functional definitions what religion *does*.

2.2 Substantive definitions: The common content of all religions

In several encyclopedias, Edward Tylor (1832–1917) is described as the founder of

British social anthropology. He presented a substantive definition of religion as "a belief in spiritual beings." Tylor's (1903) theory is that human beings develop religious beliefs in order to explain dreams, visions, unconsciousness and death. Historically, the belief that all men have souls developed into a belief in spirits, gods, devils and other spiritual beings. In an intermediary stage, such spiritual forces were connected to specific places and objects; later they became more detached.

Tylor's theory of religion was later criticized as naïvely evolutionary and ethnocentric. He attempted to find a common denominator for all religions and to detect the relationship between religious belief in primitive and modern man. At the same time, he distinguished quite definitely between primitive and modern religiosity, for instance, by maintaining that the "lower" forms of animism were without the ethical content he found in the religion of "the educated modern mind." Naturally, Tylor has been accused of introducing an all-too-cognitive and intellectual definition of religion. For him, religion has to do with belief, and he explains the origin of religion as a result of man's inquiry into the existence of dreams, unconsciousness and death. Perhaps this objection to Tylor's theory does not take into consideration that people's inquiry about death is not necessarily an intellectual activity characterized only by distance, but also by sadness. Nevertheless, it seems reasonable to include religious practice in a definition of religion, not only belief. The British historian of religion, R.R. Marrett (1914: xxxi), clearly criticized Tylor's intellectualism when he stated, "native religion is something that is not so much thought out as danced out."

Substantive definitions tend to specify the object of people's faith, although this object is described in various ways. "Belief in divine beings" is a possibility. Such a definition has the advantage of being relatively similar to ordinary people's idea of religion. However, this definition is clearly ethnocentric, because it excludes significant Eastern traditions from the religious sphere, for example, parts of Buddhism, Hinduism and Confucianism. Émile Durkheim (1982/1912) pointed out this weakness in Tylor's definition. Popular Buddhism is often combined with a multiplicity of gods and spiritual beings, but to the monks who feel they are continuing the tradition of Buddha, the absence of desire for contact with the divine is a significant issue. At the same time, features in Buddhism and Confucianism exceed a Western, rationalistic world-view, which will lead some to include them in the category of a religion. The phrase "belief in something supernatural" appears frequently in definitions of religion. Yet such a statement also points to the issue of ethnocentrism. Émile Durkheim (1982/1912) claimed that the distinction between the natural and the supernatural is a Western distinction that presupposes the rationalism of the Age of Enlightenment.

The American sociologist Roland Robertson (1970: 47) proposes a substantive definition of religion by using the concept "supra-empirical." For Robertson, religious culture and religious actions arise out of "a distinction between an empirical and a supra-empirical, transcendent reality." A similar definition is found in Michael Hill's introduction to the sociology of religion. According to him, religion is:

> The set of beliefs which postulate and seek to regulate the distinction between an empirical reality and a related and significant supra-empirical segment of reality; the

language and symbols which are used in relation to this distinction; and the activities and institutions which are concerned with its regulation. (Hill 1973: 42–3)

The word "empirical" is often defined by that which is based on experience, and in some instances, based solely on the experience of the senses. However, the distinction between an empirical and a supra-empirical reality is also inspired by the West and is similar to the distinction between the natural and the supernatural. A distinction between the empirical and the supra-empirical will yield little meaning in a culture where all of existence is permeated by what the West calls the supra-empirical, that is, a culture where everyday experiences are impregnated by forces and powers. On the other hand, Western intellectuals will recognize such a definition as a familiar way of thought. Indeed, much Christian theology is centered on a clarification of the relationship between the two dimensions of reality. They are not clearly separated in religions of the Western world either, but they often appear in mixed forms. When facing challenges and problems, most Christians will tend to combine prayer and rational behavior. Christian theology also describes how God acts through people who are touched by religion.

The advantage of Hill's definition is that he includes beliefs, language, symbols, practice and institutions. In this way, he escapes any critique that his definition is too intellectual. Hill avoids ranking the two types of realities, as Robertson does when he claims that empirical reality is "subordinated in significance to the non-empirical" (1970: 47). Robertson's definition is somewhat problematic. In several religions, the hereafter is ascribed more importance than the here-and-now. However, human religious life demonstrates that life on earth has a major impact on the ways in which religion is practiced. The role of religion in a person's life should, therefore, be a topic for empirical research, not a premise in a definition.

Several scholars of religion have attempted to avoid ethnocentrism in their definitions. The American scholar of religion, Melford Spiro (1966), has taken a somewhat different route. He defines religion as "an institution consisting of culturally patterned interaction with culturally postulated superhuman beings" (Spiro 1966: 96). Spiro continues by defining "superhuman beings" as beings believed to possess "power greater than man." According to him, such beings can affect man and man affects them. By using the concept of interaction, Spiro points to an important aspect of several religions, namely the communication between the religious person and the religious "being." On the one hand, Spiro's definition does not presuppose a sharp division between the natural and the supernatural, inherited from the Age of Enlightenment. On the other hand, the question is whether his notion of superhuman beings also includes every human being who has made an impact on history. It sounds reasonable that the historical Jesus, Buddha and Muhammad are included in this category. The question is whether historical figures such as the Roman emperors, Napoleon and Hitler are as well.

Moreover, there is a long tradition of including the concept of the sacred as a core concept in substantive definitions of religion. Indeed, Émile Durkheim's classic definition has substantive and functional elements: "a unified system of beliefs and practices relative to sacred things, that is to say, things set apart and forbidden – beliefs and practices which unite into one single moral community called a Church, all those who adhere to them" (Durkheim 1982/1912: 47). The substantive elements in Durkheim's definition are systems of beliefs, practice, sacred things that are set apart and forbidden, and a church. The functional element lies in the claim that religion produces integration in a moral community. Durkheim uses the French words *séparées* and *interdites* to explain the implication of the word sacred (*sacrées*). A reasonable interpretation is that the sacred is a powerful entity which compels respect and cannot be approached in an ordinary way. In *The Sacred Canopy*, Peter L. Berger (1967) defines religion as man's relationship to "a sacred cosmos." When he attempts to define the content of the sacred, he relies on the concept proposed by Rudolf Otto, the German theologian and scholar of religion. According to Otto (1958/1917), the sacred fills people with awe and fascination; it is *mysterium tremendum et fascinosum.*

The concept of the sacred may be useful. A division between the natural and the supernatural points to qualities in the object of worship. A division between the sacred and the profane points to the attitudes of the practitioner of religion: the sacred is that which is met by awe. Thus the concept of the sacred comprises more than "the supernatural." For example, most Danes have a deferential respect for their flag without believing the story that their flag fell from heaven to mark the birth of the Danish nation.

However, we are still unable to escape accusations of ethnocentricity. The concept of the sacred also has a Western source. Seen from a historical perspective, this concept appeared in the nineteenth-century context, which emphasized religious experience as the core of religion. The focus on the sacred was an attempt, particularly by liberal Protestantism, to carve out a place for religion in a situation where the natural sciences, psychology, and a secular historical research threatened traditional Christian cosmologies.

The concept of the sacred is relatively wide. Consequently, a definition that has the sacred as its core concept is difficult to use in empirical research on religion. Some will argue that if a distinction between sacred sites such as St. Peter's Basilica, Mecca, the Taj Mahal, Wembley Stadium, and Elvis Presley's home Graceland is impossible, significant nuances are lost. Others will maintain that an inclusive definition of religion will stimulate research because it leads to the discovery of religion in areas where it is otherwise neglected. This is the argument of the American sociologist Meredith McGuire (1997), who favors relatively broad definitions. She claims that they inspire theoretical questions and encourage the use of perspectives taken from the sociology of religion to analyse several different types of phenomena. No doubt various forms of contemporary religion have relatively loose ties to established religious institutions but, in this situation, broad definitions can be used as "sensitising concepts" (Blumer 1969) that provide scientists with ideas in their search for new religious forms in new contexts. Hardly any contemporary sociologist of religion will argue that religion only includes events and practices that take place in churches, mosques, and temples. However, if the concept of religion is so broad and inclusive that every world-view and devoted human commitment is identified as religion, the concept becomes obscure and useless. For example, it is difficult to speak of secularization if every world-view and interpretation of life is regarded as religious. It is not necessary for scholars to include in their definition of religion every phenomenon that constitutes a possible object of research. Some scholars have, for example, an interest in the study of religion and politics, which offers an opportunity to create an analytical distinction between a religious and a political commitment.

Some scholars who use substantive concepts of religion tend to characterize phenomena that are similar to religion as quasi-religions or religious surrogates. Communism, fervent nationalism, and hooliganism are often described by such concepts. Words such as quasi-religion, pseudo-religion, and semi-religion have a negative bias, which in turn might affect religion as such, because they create associations to fanaticism and irrationality. This is a reminder that language and concepts are often suffused with values. It is more important to point out similar substantive traits than give the object of study value-loaded prefixes such as quasi and pseudo.

As we are discussing the complicated relationship between definitions of religion and their implicit values and normativity, we will refer to an old distinction between religion and magic, introduced by the pioneer of social anthropology, Bronislav Malinowski (1974/1925). According to him, magic is practiced in order to obtain something else, whereas religious practice is a goal in itself. However, he admits that in real life religion and magic tend to appear in mixed forms, a fact that is not always recognized in popular science. Here, religion is frequently described in positive terms, such as piety and devotion, whereas magic is portrayed as manipulating, technical, and selfish. The use of concepts such as superstition demonstrates even more ethnocentricity, especially when one's own religion is described as belief and the religion of others is described as superstition. Such statements are clearly normative, whether they come from the mouth of a Christian or a humanist. Today, the concept of superstition is hardly used by scientists.

Syncretism is a concept that previously was used in religious studies, but is now criticized for its ideological and ethnocentric implications. Critics maintain that syncretism presupposes the idea that some religions are pure (meaning superior), whereas other religions are mixed (meaning inferior). A sociologist will argue that every religion is affected by its context and therefore appears in hybrid forms, especially in a modern situation characterized by cultural communication and exchange. From a sociological point of view, the idea of a "pure" religion is an ideological, and often a theological, construct.

2.3 Functional definitions: The effect of religion on individuals and/or societies

As noted, functional definitions define religion according to the utility or effects that religion is supposed to have for the individual and/or society. Several functional definitions are based on a view that religion is a human attempt to create meaning and identity. The German sociologist Thomas Luckmann uses an extremely wide functional definition in his book, *The Invisible Religion* (1967). Here, Luckmann defines religion as "the transcendence of biological nature by the human organism" (1967: 49). He refers to the formation of the self as a religious process. Human beings develop their understanding of self by placing themselves in a meaningful totality where they are creating a frame of reference for interpreting reality. On this basis, Luckmann distinguishes between religion in a broad sense, which is a human constant, and social, institutionalized forms of church-related religion, which are declining in modern societies. In his book, he gives an outline of the universes of meaning or frames of reference that are created in modern societies. When it comes to definitions of religion, Luckmann differs from his collaborator Peter L. Berger. Whereas Berger (1967) adopts a substantive definition by describing religion as the formation of a sacred cosmos, Luckmann views every "cosmos-creation" that forms meaning and identity as religious.

Another and somewhat narrower functional definition stems from the American scholar of religion, Milton Yinger, who defines religion as "a system of beliefs and practices by means of which a group of people struggles with the ultimate problems of human life" (Yinger 1970: 7). He lists several problems that find their attempted solution in religion: How do we relate to death? Is there meaning in life, despite suffering, disappointments, and tragedies? How can we bring our hostility and self-centeredness under control? Definitions of this kind tend to relate religion to functions such as creating meaning, empowerment, and courage. In several functional definitions, religion's presumed ability to provide integration is also emphasized. Religion's integrative functions appear in Yinger's list of religious questions in a way that reminds us of Sigmund Freud's view of religion: religion is a bulwark against the suppressed urges of the individual (see Section 3.5).

Several functional definitions are so inclusive that they conceal the differences between that which we in everyday language will term religious and non-religious world-views. On the other hand, many argue that functional definitions are not ethnocentric because they do not make claims on the content of religion. All attempts at creating meaning are included. Yet not all functional definitions are actually that inclusive. By taking a closer look at the definition developed by Yinger, we find that its specifications of the "ultimate problems" that human beings struggle with are not self-evident. In addition, the functions that religion is supposed to have, according to this definition, are overwhelmingly positive. This may lead to a biased form of research, where religion's negative effects are neglected.

The critique can be taken further: is it true that religion always deals with "the deepest questions"? Of course, religious people in several different traditions have dealt with serious questions of an existential nature. The many ascetic revivalist traditions have focused on these issues and incorporated them as part of their lifestyles. However, an empirical scholar with an interest in contemporary religion will admit that religious practice can also take the form of fun, entertainment, play and consumption. Yet another critique of functional definitions claims that definitions should not include empirical questions. One empirical question is, for example, whether religions actually have the functions of creating meaning and integration. By including these functions into the definition itself, these aspects of religion are presupposed and excluded from empirical analysis.

Some maintain that functional definitions are reductionist, which means that they reduce religion to something other than religion; they explain the existence of religion by referring to its alleged functions. If religion is, for example, defined as an attempt to find meaning in the face of death and suffering, religion is seen as a result of the fear of death. This approach will not lead a scholar to interpret religion from the inside, but to view it from the perspective of its more or less recognized functions. The issue at stake here is not whether religion originates in fear of death, although one should be cautious with such sweeping generalizations, but that phenomena are included into the definition when they should constitute objects of study.

2.4 Broad or narrow definitions of religion?

We argued above that broad definitions of religion will stimulate the study of religion in contexts that are not ordinarily considered to be religious. On the other hand, sweeping definitions that include different phenomena tend to conceal those differences. Another argument against broad definitions is that scientific definitions should not deviate too much from everyday language. In spite of our statements regarding ethnocentrism, people in large parts of the world will use a substantive definition of religion. One may object that science should provide new perspectives, which contrast and challenge ordinary people's ideas. Nevertheless, if terms used in everyday language are given a totally different meaning in science, the ability of the humanities and the social sciences to communicate with the outside world will be increasingly complicated.

The use of broad definitions also has ethical implications. The approach taken by some to label humanism a religion, for example, can be described as a form of concept-imperialism, because this is hardly the understanding that humanists have of themselves. We are not arguing that scientists should only reproduce people's subjective self-understanding. However, if the scientific reinterpretation becomes too rigid, it will create a definite communication problem between the parties involved.

Some think that substantive definitions are narrow whereas functional definitions are not, which is often the case. However, broad and inclusive definitions of religion are not necessarily functional. In fact, some functional definitions include a relatively narrow spectrum of functions that are perceived to be religious. In addition, some substantive definitions are wide. One example is a definition that includes every world-view or interpretation of life and every practice related to such views. This definition does not include functions that these views are perceived to have. Nevertheless, such a vague and generalized substantive definition will be difficult to use in empirical research. Wherein lies the distinction between that which is included in a world-view and that which is excluded? Some argue that a world-view is characterized by a certain modicum of reflection and systematization. On the basis of this argument, a statement claiming that the human race is sinful will be defined as a world-view, whereas a spontaneous utterance of disgust from a disappointed human being will not. However, the transitions are fluid, and a demand for systematization and reflection can be criticized for favoring intellectualism over spontaneous commitment.

Furthermore, some functional definitions are narrow. One example is a definition that only includes world-views that contribute to the integration of society. On the one hand, one may say that this is a broad definition of religion since many phenomena can contribute to unity in society. On the other hand, the definition is also narrow, because it excludes every religion that creates strife and conflict in society.

Recently, there have been attempts at distinguishing between religion and religiosity, and between world-views and interpretations of life. The idea is that religions and world-views are established and institutionalized traditions, whereas religiosity and interpretations of life describe the individual effort to find meaning in life. Several scholars of religion will maintain that in modern or postmodern societies, the search for life interpretations draws on established religions and traditional world-views. Interpretations of life are, then, based on several established traditions, which are combined with the individual's own interpretations.

Some have also attempted to distinguish between religion and spirituality. The word "spirituality" is often used in a wider sense than "religion." It refers to a search for meaning and an interpretation of life which are relatively free of established religious traditions. The distinction between religion and spirituality can be useful in some research. However, a normative ranking between the two concepts is often implied, where religion is viewed as a rigid phenomenon devoid of spirit, whereas spirituality is perceived as a phenomenon that provides life and empowerment.

2.5 Do we need definitions of religion?

In our deliberations so far, we have discussed several quite different definitions of religion. Some are too general and vague, some are ethnocentric and biased, and some are reductionist. A viable question is whether we should try to develop a definition that has universal validity. More contemporary theories of science tend to view religious and scientific entities as social and contextual constructions. Seen from this perspective, the search for the essential in religion appears to be a rather static and ahistorical enterprise. Indeed, the classical sociologist Max Weber can be used to support such a statement. Weber claimed that his aim was not to find "the essence of religion," but to study the conditions for and the effects of a specific type of social action. Weber begins his sociology of religion, which was first published in 1922, with the following statement: "To define 'religion,' to say what it *is*, is not possible at the start of a presentation such as this. Definition can be attempted, if at all, only at the conclusion of the study" (Weber 1964/1922: 1). Weber's dislike of definitions is an easy target of critique. After all, he discusses specific topics within the sociology of religion, where he includes certain phenomena and excludes others. Indeed, no one is completely inductive; the selected material does not grow organically from the ground and into the text. Therefore, Weber must have used some form of implicit definition, which could very well have been clarified for the reader. Nevertheless, there is a sympathetic aspect of Weber's respect for empirical variety, even if he never completed his comprehensive studies of religious life nor developed a final, authoritative definition of religion.

Some argue that every attempt at developing general definitions of religion conceal that which is unique, dynamic, and contextual in each religious tradition. This form of argumentation is similar to the critique that is directed against ethnocentricity. The phenomenology of religion is the discipline that has taken the systematization of religion based on common characteristics the furthest. For that reason, it has frequently been met by critique: is it possible to claim that Christian prayer and Islamic prayer "really" are one and the same? This questioning has also been used within each religious tradition: what are the actual common characteristics of prayers during a Christian charismatic meeting and the quiet prayer of a monk in his cell?

Sociology is more modest today than just two or three generations ago, as it relates to the belief that this discipline can reveal or formulate laws for social life. In a postmodern perspective, the formulation of universally valid definitions appears to be somewhat modern and authoritarian. However, a total rejection of the comparative approach that attempts to find common characteristics and develop categories would dissolve all forms of science. A possible middle position is the argument that research must relax its claims to universally valid definitions and be satisfied with definitions that are useful within limited time and space. A substantive definition that is fruitful in studies of religion in Norway, Sweden, and Britain should perhaps be exchanged for other definitions in other contexts.

Recently, some scholars have drawn upon the philosopher Ludwig Wittgenstein's reflections on definitions (Wittgenstein 1958; see, for example, Aldridge 2000). Wittgenstein uses sports as an example in his discussion. There are numerous forms of sport and it is difficult to find a definition that will include all of them. The element that all sport activities share is not a set of common characteristics, but a "family likeness," which enables us to recognize them as sports. The analogy is that we are able to recognize some family features in each member of a family even if every member does not share all features. In this way, the significance often attached to the development of precise definitions is defused. We may use them and discuss them, all the time knowing that we will, most likely, never reach an authoritative and uncontroversial definition, in sports, in family, or in religion.

2.6 The dimensions of religion

Scholars within the sociology of religion and other related disciplines distinguish between different dimensions of religion. To formulate new dimensions can be seen as attempts at developing and amplifying definitions of religion. Some of the same dimensions are found among several scholars, although they also operate with different ones. In the late 1960s, the historian of religion Ninian Smart (1968) presented a set of classifications based on six dimensions. Three dimensions are labeled para-historical, meaning that they transcend the borders of history, as Smart says, with a somewhat ethnocentric formulation. These are the dogmatic dimension, the mythological dimension, and the ethical dimension. Then, three historical dimensions follow: the ritual dimension, the experiential dimension, and the social dimension. Another historian of religion, Eric J. Sharpe, has criticized Smart's classification and argued that the mythological and ritual dimensions can be excluded. They do not belong to "the intrinsic part of the structure of religion" that must be included to understand the phenomenon (Sharpe 1983: 94). Sharpe admits that mythology and rituals frequently occur in religious life, but so do regulations, music, and symbols. He concludes that religion has four modes: the existential, the intellectual, the institutional, and the ethical.

Based on our discussion of the definitions above, we now know that we no longer have to engage in a debate on the core of religion. As sociologists, we also want to avoid essentialist debates on the most fundamental dimensions of religion. However, we will discuss one classification of religious dimensions frequently used in sociology. In the introduction to a study of American piety, the sociologists Rodney Stark and Charles Glock (1968) describe five dimensions of religious commitment. An important motivation for these scholars is to contribute towards a more precise usage of terms in debates on the role of religion in society. Stark and Glock argue that the word "religious" has a plurality of meanings. This ambiguity might explain the basis for a debate that took place when their book was published, where some argued that religion was flourishing in the United States whereas others saw a religious decline. Stark and Glock claim that beneath the plurality in religious expression, five dimensions of religiosity are manifested: the belief dimension, religious practice, the experience dimension, the knowledge dimension, and the consequential dimension.

The belief dimension includes more or less systematized ideas that the religious person believes and holds to be true. Perhaps a better solution would have been to label this dimension content of faith or the dogmatic dimension, since it emphasizes *what* a person believes, not just *that* they believe.

Religious practice includes two forms, ritual and devotion. Rituals are specific formalized religious actions that the adherents of a religion are expected to perform. Rituals within Christianity include church services, baptism, and Holy Communion. Stark and Glock point out that devotion, or affection and worship, is less formalized and public than rituals. Examples of Christian devotion are private prayers and reading of the Scriptures. Several intermediate forms exist. An ordinary Christian church service is, for example, open to the public and it gives room for silent prayers. Parts of the service tend to be formalized through liturgies, but the sermon is open for more improvisations and spontaneity.

The experience dimension has to do with subjective religious experiences, for example, a feeling of divine presence. The knowledge dimension constitutes the knowledge that religious people are expected to have about dogmas, rituals, and religious texts. Finally, the consequential dimension includes the effects that religion has in the lives of individuals, in their everyday life, if you will.

Several aspects of this classification are debatable, for example, the authors' claim of universality. Some have also pointed out that it is too individualistic. The classification is related to individual religiosity, not religious communities or the role of religion in society. Therefore, it should not be interpreted as a complete list of viable topics within the sociology of religion. If church–state relationship is of interest, this classification is useless. Stark and Glock only meant for it to be used in studies on individual religion. Even so, some will maintain that a social dimension should be included that deals with the various forms of religious communities where individuals participate.

In spite of these objections, let us take a look at some of the ways in which this classification can be used. As noted, the authors hoped to increase the level of precision in debates on religion. Here, we will return to the question whether the concept of religion is general and universal. By using this classification, we might approach this question empirically. For example, is there a tendency in empirical studies that the participants have a high score on all five religious dimensions? If so, this could be interpreted as some sort of empirical support for the argument that religion is a meaningful and unified concept, particularly if several studies in different contexts reach the same conclusion.

However, on the basis of empirical studies, it is impossible to draw definite conclusions regarding the issue of religion as a unified phenomenon. Not enough studies are conducted, and existing studies differ on critical issues, which make comparisons difficult. In the early 1970s, Richard Clayton (1971) criticized the idea of multi-dimensionality. He conducted a statistical analysis, a so-called factor analysis, of data on religion among Americans. Clayton found that the belief dimension formed a basis for all the other dimensions. Religious belief led to a higher score on the other dimensions. Yet Clayton's conclusion can hardly be seen as a universally valid conclusion, even if religious belief is important for ritual practice and other forms of involvement. First of all, it is likely that the relationship between these dimensions runs both ways. Belief reinforces ritual practice, which again reinforces belief, and so forth. Second, religious communities vary regarding the significance that they attach to dogma.

The Swedish sociologist Göran Gustafsson (1997) outlined some empirical findings based on survey data from Sweden where Stark and Glock's dimensions were used. These studies found that the knowledge dimension and the consequential dimension showed the lowest statistical correlation with the other dimensions. In other words, detailed religious knowledge does not necessarily lead to religious commitment or religious experiences. Such a finding supports general observations: a highly specialized professor of religion does not necessarily share its faith or participate in its rituals. The low correlation between the consequential dimension and the belief dimension can be interpreted in several ways. One possible interpretation is that in a society permeated by Christian traditions, the whole society is affected by the Christian culture in such a way that the active believers do not stand out. Another possibility is that in a relatively secularized and religiously diverse society, the active believers do not demonstrate a different lifestyle, but live like everyone else, because they are all affected by modernity.

The most closely integrated dimensions of religion are then religious belief, religious practice, and religious experience. This too should be qualified. Several individuals, not least in northern Europe, believe in elements of the Christian tradition without participating in religious activities on a regular basis. They are what is commonly called "private Christians" who practice "believing without belonging," as termed by the British sociologist of religion Grace Davie (1990). In a situation of religious individualism, perhaps it is true that religious experience tends to be separated from institutional belief and practice. At the same time, the level of individualization should not be exaggerated. Even in relatively secularized societies, individuals develop their religious universes of meaning in communication with the institutionalized religious traditions. This is an issue to which we will return in Section 7.7.

Religious dimensions can also be a useful tool to describe religious communities and their distinctive features. Various communities place a different emphasis on each of the dimensions discussed here. The world religions do not give the same importance to faith, doctrine, a religious life, rituals, and experience. For example, Catholicism is generally said to be more ritual-oriented than Protestantism, and Islam is frequently described as a religion that emphasizes rituals and lifestyle. By comparing dimensions of religiosity in different traditions, common features can be found. One example is Christianity, where different dogmatic traditions such as Pietism and Liberal Protestantism share an affinity for religious fervor and emotion. In contemporary Western societies, new religious movements and Christian charismatic communities stress the experience dimension. In fact, Stark and Glock provide some suggestions regarding the use of these dimensions. They claim that the belief dimension is of major importance in Christianity, followed by religious practice. The Christian mystical tradition and what they (not completely without a normative slant) call "some extreme Protestant sects" tend to emphasize religious practice.

Furthermore, these dimensions can be used to identify and discuss tensions, both within and between religious movements. Tensions frequently occur between dogmatic and more expressive forms of religion. In some instances, such tensions appear in different religious roles. A classic distinction exists between the priest and the prophet. The priest is usually identified as a person who has a correct belief, correct rites, and a high degree of knowledge. The prophet is described as a person who stresses religious experiences that tend to shatter religious traditions, and she or he practices an ascetic and demanding lifestyle.

These dimensions are not useful in all situations. In some instances, they are unable to detect unique differences. An illustrative example is two different religious traditions that both emphasize religious experience. In one case, the religious elite claims authority on the basis of experience only they can access. This tradition excludes the large majority. In another case, lay people claim that their religious experiences are equal to those of the clergy. This tradition has a democratizing effect. In spite of the fact that both traditions stress religious experience, they are quite different. By using Stark and Glock's religious dimensions as tools for analysis, we would only detect the similarity between the two traditions, not their differences.

For a sociologist, an analysis of a particular religion should not focus exclusively on formal organizations. The analyses must also produce information about informal social variations and possible changes over time. A few illustrative examples: the emphasis on systematic content of belief has varied through the ages. By taking a look at the Christian tradition, we find that the institutionalization of theology at the universities in the twelfth century resulted in an increasing emphasis on dogma. Today, we observe that expressivity and experience are religious dimensions of great importance, often at the cost of dogmatic content. The difference between women's and men's religiosity can also be interpreted as one of different emphases on dimensions, although it is easy to end up in essentialistic stereotypes in this area.

Sociologists will often interpret religion in a different way than the participants. Good sociology will move between an accurate report of the participants' understanding and a more external reductionist view of religion. Good sociologists will tend to have a sense of irony on behalf of history and society. Faced with a mystic who believes that his experiences derive directly from God, the sociologist will look for socially constructed metaphors and discourses that affect their experiences, as well as the different ways in which these experiences are communicated. Another example: some religious traditions view formalized rituals as "dead ceremonies." Such a view is premised on a certain level of individualism and ideals of personal devotion and authenticity. A sociologist will be happy to point out that these religious groups, too, have institutionalized rituals in their meetings. Charismatic groups that cherish spontaneity tend, for example, to have informal norms about when it is proper to speak in tongues and when it represents disorder and chaos.

In this chapter, we have presented and discussed numerous definitions of religion. Yet we will not end by proposing a concluding definition. Our hope is that we have succeeded in demonstrating that definitions and concepts are fruitful and productive for research when they are objects of critique and reflection, not of subservient acceptance.

3

Classical sociologists and their theories of religion

The aim of this chapter is to give an introduction to the classical sociologists and their theories of religion. Although Freud was a psychologist, he is included here because his theory of religion had a major impact on the sociology of religion. The chapter is organized chronologically and covers from 1850 to around 1950 – even if a few of the writers lived and wrote beyond 1950. We have attempted to organize each subsection by using a consistent scheme. After a brief presentation of a particular theorist, we describe his theory of individual and society, before we take a look at religion and refer to some of the critique that has been raised. We also attempt to offer suggestions as to how different theories may be used in empirical studies of religion.

In this chapter and the following, we will in some instances look at possible connections between the context of the theorist under consideration, his *Sitz im Leben*, and his sociological interpretations. It should be noted that our review of sociologists only includes men: sociology of religion has, until recently, been a massively masculine affair. Towards the end of the chapter, we will attempt to relate the theorists to each other. In particular, focus is directed on the distinction between structural and actor-oriented theories and its consequences for the view of religion.

3.1 Karl Marx: Religion as projection and illusion

Karl Marx (1818–83) was born the son of a lawyer in Trier, Germany. His parents were Jewish, although his father later converted to Protestantism. In 1841 Marx finished his doctorate in philosophy at the University of Berlin. During the following decade, he moved between Cologne, Brussels, Berlin, and Paris. In Paris, he and Friedrich Engels participated in revolutionary groups. The Communist Manifesto was published here in 1848. Marx had to flee the following year, and he settled in London, where he lived the rest of his life. Through his writings, Marx introduced into social theory the concepts of historical materialism and social class theory, an emphasis on the significance of technology, the theory of human alienation, and the idea that collective actors can achieve control of nature and social relations. Though there is no systematic treatment of religion in Marx's writings, it is possible to detect his view of religion by taking a look at his general social theory and his theory of alienation.

In his analysis of the political economy, Marx emphasizes the distinction between productive forces and production relations. Productive forces consist of tools, technical organization of work, and machines. Production relations are about the relations between immediate producers. In the capitalist society Marx sees emerging at his time, production relations have to do with the relations between the capitalists and the members of the working class. The important issue here is who owns and governs the means of production. Marx believes that change in productive forces results in change in production relations, which calls forth change in the producers. In other words, new machinery will change the relations between the owners and the workers, and this will bring about a change in the workers as well as the owners. The formation of a capitalist economy is, in this way, an outcome of a historical process. Capitalism is founded upon a class division between the proletariat, or the working class, on the one hand, and the bourgeoisie, or the capitalist class, on the other. These classes are in endemic conflict regarding the distribution of the fruits of industrial production.

In his analysis of alienation in *Economic and Philosophical Manuscripts* (Marx 1975/1844), Marx emphasizes that in capitalist societies the worker himself is treated as a commodity or an object. Because Marx views labor and production as a part of the human being, he believes that everything that disturbs this relationship contributes to alienation. The alienation of the workers from their products has a number of dimensions: they do not own the means of production, they do not govern the products, and their labor has become a commodity. Workers in modern society are also physically under the control of the mechanical machinery of the factories. Alienation is, thereby, related to a lack of control of the societal conditions for human development. Because the alienated person has lost their true identity, they turn to religion to achieve an understanding of the world and perhaps find hope for better existence in this or the coming world. In *Contribution to the Critique of Hegel's Philosophy of Right* (1955/1844), Marx argues that religion represents a false picture of reality, that religion is an illusion which asserts that neither individuals nor collectives have control of their own conditions, but are subject to forces they do not understand, forces that are interpreted in different ways in religion.

Analyses of Marx's theory of religion tend to distinguish between his theory of religion as superstructure and religion as ideology. We will first discuss his theory of religion as superstructure. In *German Ideology* (1955/1845–46), Marx and Engels outline that the basic structure of society consists of productive forces and production relations. Resting upon this basic foundation is a structure of politics, legal codes, morality, metaphysics, and religion. This superstructure is based on and affected by the foundation. Religion is one facet of the whole superstructure that mainly adapts to the changes in the mode of production. According to Marx, consciousness cannot obtain total freedom from its social basis. This view appears in the first volume of *Capital* (1983/1867), where he gives an outline of the roots of religion. Here, he claims that in the earlier stages of human development, religion was the result of primitive man's helplessness in the face of natural forces. In bourgeois society, which is based on the production of commodities, Protestant Christianity and its individualism is the most appropriate form of religion. Marx concludes, "the religious world is but the reflex of the real world" (Marx 1983: 83).

Marx's theory of religion and its relationship to the social basis varies in his work. In *Theses on Feuerbach* (1955/1845), his emphasis is on the dialectical conception of the relationship between social praxis and consciousness. In *German Ideology* and *Capital*, he seems to end with a more deterministic view of religion. Here, religion is treated as a social product, a result of external forces and a reflection of the world.

In Marx's theory, religion is also viewed as ideology. In *German Ideology* (1955/1945–46), Marx and Engels claim that the human consciousness is rooted in social praxis. From this general notion follows the theory of the role of ideology in class societies. Briefly stated, this theory argues that in class societies, the ruling ideas of any historical period are the ideas of the ruling class. These ideas are a tool for the manipulation and oppression of the subordinate class in society. The prevalent ideas at any given time, including religion, provide legitimation of the interests of the dominant class. It should be noted that the ruling class also is a victim of the same type of illusion as the working class. They interpret social and historical forces as an expression of something transcendent, because they are alienated, too.

In his *Contribution to the Critique of Hegel's Philosophy of Right* (1955/1844), Marx argues that man creates religion and that religion paints a false picture of reality. For that reason, the struggle against religion is indirectly a struggle against the world which this religion depicts. Religion is simultaneously an instrument of those imposing injustice and an attitude of protest against that injustice. Religion is a popular reaction to oppression. A critique of religion is, therefore, a critique of those who need religion.

Marx's analysis of religion has been met by critique. Here, the discussion centers around three issues, namely the content of religion, religious variation, and religious change. Regarding the content of religion, Marx stresses that religion is illusory because it reflects a reality that is based on social class relationships while it attempts to hide class interests. In this way, he dismisses the reasons with which the believers themselves justify their actions. He assumes a position where he decides which ideology represents the truth. Marx also concludes with a reductionistic argument, where religion is merely the reflection of societal forces. The second topic pertains to religious variation. In Marx's view, religion is a collective phenomenon, shared by virtually all members of a particular class and with seemingly the same intensity. Since people's ideas and actions are products of external forces, the relationship between ideology and social class becomes deterministic. The third issue concerns the explanation for religious change. According to Marx, historical materialism represents a development that will cause the displacement of religion by the worker's true consciousness of reality. Because ideology is deduced from social or economic changes, his theory cannot account for the introduction of new ideology into society. The reason is that religious innovation represents a deviation from the pre-existing social order.

Marx had a profound effect on the development of sociology and on certain aspects of the sociology of religion. His materialistic interpretation of history was new and innovative at a time when the dominating intellectual climate was idealistic, in the sense that human thoughts and ideas were considered to have decisive effects for the development of society. His idea that religion fulfills the needs of those near the bottom of the social hierarchy, and that they compensate by searching for alternative goals, for example in religion, is often called deprivation theory (see Section 7.1). Deprivation theory came to have a profound effect on the studies of working-class religion (Halévy 1949; Thompson 1965) and the analysis of religious movements (Davis 1948–49; Glock and Stark 1965; Wilson 1967, 1970). Furthermore, the influence from Marx is found in the works of Jürgen Habermas, Pierre Bourdieu, and Michel Foucault, as well as in the writings on the sociology of religion conducted by Peter L. Berger, Thomas Luckmann, and Bryan S. Turner (1991). Marx's theories can be applied in studies of how groups use religion to legitimate their own interests, and in analyses of religion used as power to support specific groups.

3.2 Émile Durkheim: Religion as integration

Émile Durkheim (1858–1917) was born in Lorraine, France and was raised in an orthodox, traditional Jewish family. In 1893 he delivered a doctoral dissertation entitled *The Division of Labor in Society* (1893), which became a classic in sociology. He also wrote *The Rules of Sociological Method* (1966/1895) and *Suicide* (1897). In 1906 Durkheim became a professor at the Sorbonne and in 1912 produced his final book, *The Elementary Forms of the Religious Life*, where he develops his theory of religion. The contribution of Durkheim's theory lies in his emphasis on the normative basis for social integration, the dangers of individualism and anomie, and the significance of the collective.

Durkheim belongs to the French sociological tradition, which was concerned with questions about social disintegration and social unity. The notion that society forms an integrated unity was prominent in Germany and France at the end of the nineteenth century, and it achieved great significance for Durkheim. Within this tradition, society is viewed as an integrated unity that, in some sense, is comparable to that of a living organism. Whereas the biological organism is governed by a material relation, society is bound together by the ties of ideas and social unity. This tradition points to two key themes in the writings of Durkheim: morality and social solidarity.

Durkheim explains social solidarity by means of structural and moral factors. In his book *The Division of Labor in Society* (1984/1893), he distinguishes between the form of social solidarity resulting from commonality, and the form of solidarity resulting from specialization. These types of social solidarity are related to the degree of specialization and mutual dependence in society. Like many of his contemporaries, Durkheim assumes that society has undergone a fundamental structural change from primitive to modern society. However, he believes that the nature of society is unchanged. Society, in its primitive and modern form, is a moral reality *sui generis*, and moral and religious representations adjust according to social change.

Durkheim believes that simple and primitive societies are characterized by a minimal degree of division of labor, resulting in a high degree of commonality – individuality is almost non-existent. In these types of society, moral solidarity is based on commonality. This collective consciousness connects the individual directly to society and gives society a strong moral consensus. Durkheim calls this form of solidarity "mechanical" solidarity. As the division of labor increases, another type of solidarity develops: "organic" solidarity. The relations between members of this type of society are characterized by mutuality and dependence, and as a result of specialization, a form of solidarity develops. The baker, the butcher, the police officer, and everyone else are mutually dependent upon each other, and they are aware of this dependence. In this type of society, individuality is developed. The collective conscience or consciousness (*la conscience collective*) weakens and becomes more vague, and members of such a society share fewer common ideas.

Apart from structural factors, moral factors, such as religion, may also contribute to social solidarity. This brings us to Durkheim's sociology of religion. In his book *Suicide* (1997/1897), Durkheim points out the statistical relationship between suicide rates and religious denomination in several Western European countries. Predominantly Protestant countries everywhere seem to have higher suicide rates than those that are mainly Catholic. Since both denominations prohibit suicide with equal stringency, the explanation must be sought in differences rooted in the two denominations. Durkheim argues that each Protestant is left alone before God, whereas each Catholic is integrated into a set of social practices, such as confession, mass, obligatory doctrine, and so forth. For that reason, Protestant churches are less integrated than the Catholic churches. They offer less protection against the types of suicides that are caused by a low level of integration (egoistic suicide) than the Catholic churches do. Durkheim's study suggests that the degree of integration in other sectors of society is related to suicide rates in a comparable way. This means that an integrated religion is not the only protection against suicide. These early books introduce a recurring theme in Durkheim's works, namely the diminishing role of traditional religion in modern societies.

Durkheim's conviction is that all forms of religion essentially are the same. To study religion more closely, he wanted to examine the simplest and most primitive religion known, presuming it must represent the basic pattern for all religions. *The Elementary Forms of the Religious Life* (1982/1912) is based on existing studies of the religious life of the Australian Aboriginals. In this book, Durkheim categorized all religious phenomena into beliefs and rites. Religious beliefs consist of conceptions, and religious rites of specific actions. Religious belief presupposes a classification of all things into two groups, the sacred and the profane, with religion embodying the sacred. Durkheim wants to interpret the meaning of religious beliefs and rites and conclude that when members of society participate in a religious rite, they are actually worshiping society. Society controls its members according to their physical strength, and gives them respect for a moral authority. Men get the idea that outside themselves exist one or several powers, which they worship in religion. These powers are symbolic expressions of a moral reality, namely society.

According to Durkheim, all religious rituals have the same function, no matter where and when they take place (Durkheim 1982: 427). In this way, religion is both indispensable and universal. In his discussion of the role of religion in modern societies, this idea is evident. Here, he claims that traditional religion will not be able to fulfill its function in specialized societies, and that there will be a functional alternative. For Durkheim, function expresses a form of utility, which points to society and its needs. He describes religion in modern society, which he believes will be rational and will express the sacred values of society and its unity. Faith will be based on reason, and justice will be one of its core values. In this religion, man will be the object for a new cult. Durkheim refers to this new religion as individualism or moral individualism; as the cult of the man or the cult of the individual or, finally, as the human personality cult (Pickering 1984: 485). Since the cult of the individual represents the highest moral ideal of society, the state should organize the cult and be its head. Durkheim's humanistic religion is not totally united with the state, but it transcends the state as well as the nation. It is also universalistic in a fundamental way, since it refers to humanity as a moral subject and object.

Durkheim's sociology of religion was met with criticism when it first appeared. In the more empirically oriented critiques, questions were asked about the validity of Durkheim's work, especially related to his book on the elementary forms of the religious life. In this book, Durkheim based his analyses on collected ethnographic material on totemism in Australia, material that is considered insufficient by today's standards. Furthermore, Durkheim's use of the material is criticized, or the fact that he emphasized the probably untypical Australian case (Nielsen 1998: 148). Questions have also been raised if it is possible to extend the definition of the function of religion in a pre-modern society in Australia to the function of religion everywhere else in the world, and at all times.

The theoretical critique has primarily been directed against Durkheim's theory of society. As mentioned above, Durkheim was influenced by his contemporaries' view of society as an organism. According to this idea, society was perceived as an organic system where each part has functions that contribute to the maintenance of the system. It is difficult to explain such functions without including a conscious purpose. In this way, Durkheim's theory ends in teleology, where he presumes the existence of some form of higher intelligence that creates aspects of society that will serve some form of purpose.

Durkheim's system perspective also affects his views on the origin and acceptance of religion. In contrast to Marx, who interprets a dominant religion to be the outcome of social struggle, Durkheim sees religion as a phenomenon that has an a priori meaning or social function. In this way, Durkheim's approach does not invite studies of how one particular religion is able to achieve a position of dominance. Instead, religion becomes a presupposition for society.

Many of Durkheim's central ideas came to have a profound effect on general sociology as well as the sociology of religion. Durkheim belongs to the school of early functionalism and he considered sociology to be the science of social integration. His insistence on the social dimension of religion has continued to inspire sociological and anthropological reflection on religion, as found in the works of Thomas Luckmann, Mary Douglas, and Danièle Hervieu-Léger.

3.3 Max Weber: Social action, rationality, and religion as legitimation

Max Weber (1864–1920) was born in Thuringia, Germany. In 1869, the family moved to Berlin, where his father became a National–Liberal politician in the Germany of Bismarck. In 1889, he obtained his Ph.D. in jurisprudence, whereas his interests thereafter turned in a more economic direction. After a few years as a *Privatdozent* at the University of Berlin, Weber became full professor of economics at Freiburg University in 1894, and accepted a position at the University of Heidelberg in 1896. In 1904 to 1905, *The Protestant Ethic and the Spirit of*

Capitalism was published. Many of his writings appeared posthumously, among them his vast systematization of the social sciences, *Wirtschaft und Gesellschaft* (Economy and Society) (1968/1925).

Although Weber lived at approximately the same time as Durkheim, he belonged to a different intellectual tradition. Germany did not have a positivistic tradition like France's, but the dominating school was historicism. Historicism argued that human action was of such a kind that one could not apply the research methods used in the natural sciences to study human phenomena – one must use intuition. Weber agreed that human action does not exist in the subject-matter treated by the natural sciences, but he pointed out that causal analysis and objectivity cannot be replaced by intuition (Giddens 1985: 134). His aim was to understand human action, which is rational and predictable. For him, the individual is the atom of sociology. This means that although it is necessary in the social sciences to use concepts that refer to collectivities, such as states, classes, and groups, references to a collective implies references to individual action.

Weber is concerned with religious action as a particular type of social action. To achieve an understanding of social action, he looks at it from the viewpoint of the meaning that the action has. He believes that the reason that ordinary men are influenced by religion is related to their mundane expectations, namely the hope for a good life in this world. Religious action is, therefore, meaningfully oriented toward ordinary ends. Furthermore, religiously motivated action is relatively rational (Weber 1964: 1). In his theory of social action, Weber distinguishes between two different kinds of rationality. Action that has a calculable character is motivated by purposive rationality, whereas action which is meaningful in itself is motivated by value rationality (see Section 7.4 for more information on Weber's action theory). He attempts to interpret religious action by understanding the motives of the actor from a subjective point of view. He postulates a basic drive for meaning and discusses the problem of meaning. According to the American historian Arthur Mitzman (1971: 220), Weber seems to relate the development of modernity to the problem of theodicy, that is, the justification of God's existence in the face of human suffering. Weber believes (1964: 138) that the historical quest for a theological answer to the problem of suffering is the beginning of philosophy and rational thought. In this way, the world's monotheistic religions have created the basis for a rational world-view.

In his *Sociology of Religion* (1964/1922), Weber describes the evolution of religion. Religion began with individual magical efforts at controlling the supernatural, and it has continued with increasingly rational attempts at understanding the relationship of the gods to nature. There is a line of development of religious forms that can be characterized by rationalization and *Entzäuberung der Welt* (a disenchantment of the world). In his *Collected Essays in the Sociology of Religion*, which was published in 1920, Weber claims that through the process of rationalization religion has been shifted into the realm of the non-rational. He describes the modern world as "a world robbed of gods" (Weber 1979: 281–2). There is an underlying romantic notion in his thinking. For him, the primitive world is a world of unity, where everything was magic. At some point of time in history, this unity was broken and split into rational cognition, on the one hand, and mystic experience, on the other.

A consistent theme in Weber's work is to define and explain the distinguishing characteristics of Western civilization. *The Protestant Ethic* was to serve as an introduction to this major theme (2001/1904–05). Here, Weber specifies the interrelation of religious ideas and economic conduct. His thesis is that Puritan ideas influenced the development of capitalism. Weber begins by arguing that economic conduct seems to possess an ethical content of its own. He defines the concept "spirit of capitalism" as the idea of hard work as a duty that carries its own intrinsic reward. He proceeds to look for its origin in the religious ideas of the Reformation. Although the Reformers did not intend to promote "the spirit of capitalism," their doctrines contained implicit incentives in this direction, especially the Calvinist doctrine of predestination. Perhaps one might think that a dogma stating that God has pre-determined all things, including eternal salvation and damnation, would lead to apathy. However, in a popular version of Calvinism, each individual was inspired to look for signs that one was among the chosen few. Such signs were, most significantly, to be found in economic success. Weber's essays on Protestantism gave rise to an intellectual controversy, in part because it challenged Marx's interpretation of history and his theory of historical materialism (Bendix 1977: 50). Many have misunderstood Weber in the sense that they have believed that he was only concerned with the world-shaping significance of ideal forces. Weber claimed, however, that they constitute only one of several parts of the problems that were at the center of the development of capitalism.

The fact that Weber connects religion to social classes and status groups is evident in his sociology of religion (Weber 1964/1922). Here, he examines the religious propensities of different social groups whose material interests might give rise to divergent religious beliefs (1964: 80–117). Weber distinguishes between groups that depend upon agriculture, commerce, industry, and handicraft. Economically and politically advantaged groups, as he describes them, use religion to legitimate their own life pattern and situation in the world. Underprivileged groups are more inclined toward religious ideas that promise rewards for one's own good deeds and punishment for the other's injustice. Furthermore, peasants have a general tendency to magic and animistic magic (animism), and bureaucrats are generally carriers of a rational religion. The middle classes are inclined to embrace rational, ethical, inner-worldly religious ideas, and the working class is characterized by indifference to or rejection of religions common to the modern bourgeoisie (see Section 7.6).

In this way, Weber emphasizes the material conditions and status situations of various social groups, which he thinks, in turn, give rise to different lifestyles to which some religious ideas correspond. However, historical conditions can change the relationship between status groups and systems of belief. Because ideas are more than adjustments to the social situation, intellectual leaders are important in the development of religious ideas. The relationship between ideas and given historical conditions is the result of individual choices. These choices are, again, affected by what the members of the various status groups find congenial to their interests.

In our assessment of Weber's sociology of religion, we will focus on the content of religion, religious variation, and religious change. Regarding the content of religion, Weber expresses that religious systems are human values and that they are the outcome of historical processes. On the one hand, he frequently points to instances where ideas express material interests in a direct way. On the other, he also identifies situations where ideology influences or initiates social change. Although Weber attempts to provide a correction to the materialism of Marx, it is not his aim to substitute a one-sided materialistic causal explanation for an equally one-sided spiritualistic explanation. Religion is not reduced to a simple product of external factors, but is related to intentionally motivated individuals who have specific purposes, and the material and the ideal conditions under which they live. For that reason, the content of religion and the believers' perceptions of their beliefs and practices are important.

Regarding religious variation, Weber studies group formation on the basis of shared religious ideas. In contrast to Durkheim, who viewed religion as an expression of the consciousness of the whole society, Weber thinks that ideas can have integrative functions for a group. Nevertheless, he makes a similar point to that of Marx, asserting that there is a relationship between the content of an ideology and the social position of the group who functions as its carriers. Yet this relationship is not deterministic. In contrast to Marx, Weber thinks that one ideology is usually not limited to members of one social stratum only. Nor will all members of one social stratum adhere to the same religion.

When it comes to explanations for religious change, there is no logical historical development or evolution in Weber's theory. Although the main theme in his sociology is that the process of rationalization is a major changing force in Western civilization, he does not see rationalization as a unilinear development toward a new social order. Instead, it represents a "paradox of unintended consequences" (Weber 1979: 54). Weber's theory also includes an understanding of religious innovation. Indeed, his study of Judaism shows, for example, how the old prophets broke with the existing customs and established an ideology that became dominant for a whole society.

The popularity of Max Weber's sociology has waxed and waned among various groups of sociologists (see Swatos et al. 1998). Weber did not form a school in sociology, as did Marx and Durkheim. However, his contribution was carried further within other disciplines, such as economics, political science, and religious studies. In the English-speaking world, Talcott Parsons' translation of *The Protestant Ethic* brought Weber to the attention of American sociologists in the 1930s, where he had been more or less "unknown." The Frankfurt School of sociology and Jürgen Habermas also focused on topics discussed by Weber, such as the hermeneutical approach within the theory of science, and the role of various forms of rationality in modern societies. Weber's sociology of religion has also greatly affected the works of Peter L. Berger. Since the 1980s, there has been a growing interest in Weber, especially in areas having to do with historical sociology and social theory.

3.4 Georg Simmel: Individuality, sociability, and religion

Whereas the previous sections deal with the historical processes of modernization in the Western world, one classical sociologist stands out, namely Georg Simmel (1858–1918), whose work centers on the individual. Simmel was a German-Jewish sociologist and philosopher who was born in Berlin and remained there until 1914, when he attained a full professorship at the University of Strasbourg. Simmel wrote more than two dozen books and well over two hundred articles, which dealt with a number of issues, among them philosophy, literature, art, the personality, and religion. The unique character of his work is his emphasis on experience and emotions, the relationship between the inner self and the outer, modern culture, as well as the tension between subjectivity and objectivity.

A consistent theme in all of Simmel's work is the theory of social forms. Simmel operates with a fundamental distinction between form and content. He thinks that the social world consists of forms, whose task is to create connections between contents. Contents are those aspects of existence that are determined in themselves but cannot immediately be perceived by us. Forms are thereby synthesizing principles that organize experience and shape contents. An illustrative example of the distinction between form and content is marriage. According to Simmel, marriage is a form of sociability that exists across the world. However, the content of the marriage form varies. For example, in contemporary society, weddings can take place in church, or in the town hall. There are also common-law marriages and registered partnerships. In spite of these variations, no couple by themselves have invented the form "marriage" – this is regulated by society, and transferred historically by society from one generation to another. Although forms are structuring principles, they are not fixed, but develop and change, and sometimes disappear.

Simmel's theory of personality is also based on the distinction between form and content. His focus is on how the various psychic contents form a unified personality (Simmel 1971: 252). In his image of the human being, he emphasizes creativity, fragmentation, and conflict. Human beings are not passive receptors, but active in creating their own categories to enable cognition. Furthermore, Simmel believes that man seldom experiences wholeness in his life, because the structure of social interaction demonstrates a plurality of claims on the individual (1971: 10). The human experience is permeated by innumerable conflicts, of which some are positive and constructive, and some are costly and tragic.

On the basis of his theory of social forms, Simmel develops a theory of cultural evolution. He claims that at an early stage in development the forms are fragmentary and preliminary, and they are connected to practical purposes. As soon as these elements of culture have been created, they become objectified, and traditions are formed. At the second level of cultural development, the forms become autonomous objects of cultivation. For example, moral rules now become ethical principles. On the third level, the forms become a "world," meaning an irreducible world of experience, such as the worlds of art, science, and others.

In his study of the metropolis, Simmel describes the development of modern culture from the idea that the objective spirit, meaning the intellect, predominates the subjective spirit, or the individual's emotions (Simmel 1971: 337). The overgrowth of objective culture reduces the individual to purely objective existence, and the isolated urban dwellers respond through a "blasé outlook," indifference, and sometimes aversion. On the basis of his analysis of early industrialism, Simmel expected that the gap between objective and subjective culture would widen and that the individual's experience of isolation would intensify. To find a solution to the dilemma of modernity, he turned to culture, hoping that art, scholarship, and religion would be a source of relief.

Religion played a relatively minor role in Simmel's work, although he devoted a considerable part of his writing to this topic during the last two decades of his life. In 1898 he published an essay, "A Contribution to the Sociology of Religion," and in 1906 came his book, *Religion* (a new edition was published in 1912). Both were translated into English in 1997. In both essay and book, Simmel presents a theory of the historical origin of religion. A fundamental premise is the idea that "man projects himself into his gods" (Simmel 1997: 112, 181). The gods do not exist as the idealization of individual characteristics, but the relationships that exist between individuals have a tendency to influence religious ideas and images. For example, loving relationships create the idea of a loving deity. Once such ideas are formed, they become independent. In this way, religion is secondary to the original interpersonal relations.

As elsewhere in his work, Simmel also uses the distinction between form and content in his theory of religion. Here, he makes a distinction between religion and religiosity, where he defines religiosity as "a state or a spiritual rhythm lacking any object" (1997: 165). Religiosity may develop so far as to create its own transcendent forms, such as gods and doctrines of faith. In this way, religiosity, meaning content, may create an objective world for itself, or the form religion.

There is an integrative potential in religion (1997: 207). Religious inspiration is drawn from the fact that the sum of the individuals is more than just a sum. Individuals develop powers that cannot be traced within the individual alone, and a greater unity, a deity, grows from these units. On the other hand, there is a conflict between the individual's search for independence and meaning by focusing on their own inner life, and the longing for being part of the group (1997: 182).

Simmel does not find religion able to fulfill the spiritual need of his time. The major problem is that his contemporaries look at religion as a set of claims. Religion has become a large, bureaucratic system that does not give room for the sincerity, subjectivity, and the expressive need that seems to accompany the new type of modern individuality. Simmel represents a romantic trend and emphasizes symbols, meaning, the unique, and subjective sincerity. He suggests a radical reconstruction of the spiritual life. One must fully grasp the meaning of the idea that religion is not a set of beliefs but an "an attitude of the soul" (1997: 9) or a perspective, a way of looking at the world. Simmel shares the skepticism towards dogma, which was prevalent at his time, where the idea is that faith itself is more important than the object of faith. For him, reality is divided between the subjective and the objective, and a third realm is created by the interaction of human beings that may serve as a bridge between the two. In this way, religion is a reality capable of bridging the rift between the subjective and the objective (Helle 1997: xii–xiii). One may say that Simmel suggests an objectless religion, although he would hardly characterize it as a secular religion, which Victoria Lee Erickson (2001: 114) does. The reason is that secular religion clings to a specific content (Simmel 1997: 22), which Simmel rejects.

Simmel places the focal point of theoretical concern on individual selves in interaction. Society is a "web of interactions." In many ways, he represents a middle ground between Durkheim's notion of society as *sui generis* and Weber's understanding of society as an aggregate of social action. For all this, there remain strong functionalist and evolutionary overtones in his sociology, which can be clearly seen in his theory of the historical origin of religion. There are also several similarities between Durkheim and Simmel: both believe that religion emerges in social relations, and the individual transfers his or her relation to a deity to the collectivity. Simmel views religion as a fundamental aspect of human relations, and, therefore, religion will always exist as a way of being.

Simmel's extensive writings and lectures have ensured his place as one of the classical sociologists. After his death, Simmel's work was promoted by several Chicago School sociologists. His influence is also found in the work of Erving Goffman and Peter L. Berger. Simmel's distinction between religion and religiosity can be used in studies of the religious life in modern societies, and his idea that there is a relationship between social interactions and religious images can be useful in analyses of religious life stories.

3.5 Sigmund Freud: Religion as parental dependence and instinct control

Sigmund Freud (1856–1939) grew up in Austria in a Jewish family. Towards the end of his life, the difficult conditions for Jews in his home country led him to emigrate to Britain. Freud began his scientific career in physiology and anatomy, and gradually developed an interest in human psychology. Freud is a towering and controversial figure in the history of psychology. Since his theories of religion had such an impact on the sociology of religion, he is included here. The new and original aspect of Freud's work is his radical break with the well-established optimistic and rationalistic view of human nature.

Freud is known as the founding father of psychoanalysis. He pictures man as a being with strong biological instincts, especially sexual instincts. Even the little child is a sexual being. Freud believes that unacceptable social instincts to a certain degree can be sublimated into artistic, religious or other energy-demanding activities. Such socially illegitimate instincts are, metaphorically speaking, pushed into the subconscious, and the individual does not openly acknowledge this process. However, the subconscious material will strike back upon the individual's conscious life and actions, for instance in the form of slips of the tongue, dreams, neuroses, and compulsive thoughts. Psychoanalysis is not only an analysis; it is also a program for action. According to Freud, experienced psychoanalysts can uncover unreleased and unconscious conflicts through conversations with patients and their uncensored associations. By lifting this conflictual information from the subconscious, the information can be approached and handled in a rational way. Thereby, individuals can achieve a more harmonious life, more governed by reason. Freud continued to refine his psychoanalytical program throughout his life. His first comprehensive presentation was published in 1901, entitled *The Psychopathology of Everyday Life* (1953–74/1901).

Freud's concept of religion is extremely critical and reductionist. He had a strong antagonism towards the Catholic hierarchy, an antagonism that has been related to his feelings of discrimination as a scientist, discrimination which he attributed in part to the widespread anti-Semitism that dominated the Christian Austria (Isbister 1985: 208). In 1913, a breach appeared between Freud and the psychologist Carl Gustaf Jung, who had been his primary disciple for a long time. Their different views on religion were a key element in this breach. Nevertheless, Freud was not consistently anti-religious in his private life; for example, he had a lengthy and humorous correspondence with Oskar Pfister, a Swiss pastor and a strong admirer (Freud and Meng 1963). In several publications, Pfister attempted to uphold the main ideas of psychoanalysis, while at the same time toning down the critique of religion. For him, psychoanalysis was useful in Christian pastoral care. The major issue was to bring everything up from the deep waters of the soul, analyse it, and then live a life in Christian freedom.

In some instances, Freud voices a relatively functionalist explanation of religion, as in *Civilization and its Discontents* (1953–74/1930). Here, the existence of religion is partly explained by its contribution to tame man's natural aggressive instinct. Religion supports morality and prevents society from disintegrating into a dog-eat-dog existence. However, Freud's dominant view of religion is negative. Religion emerges as a psychological necessity, but the religious attitude is infantile, imprisoned, and immature. Early in his academic production, Freud reached the conclusion that religious concepts were solely projections of the inner psyche. In 1901 he wrote, "I think that a great part of the mythological world-view, stretching far into most of the modern religions, is nothing but psychology projected into the outer world" (Freud 1953–74/1901: 259). In the same place, he writes that psychic factors and conditions in the unconscious are "reflected in the construction of a supernatural reality."

Freud's discussion of religion appears in three books: *Totem and Taboo* (1960/1913), *The Future of An Illusion* (1928/1921), and *Moses and Monotheism* (1964/1938). In many ways, he draws parallels between religion and neurotic suffering. Magicians and participants in religious rituals are compelled to act in fixed ways, because they are governed by compulsive ideas. Thereby, the origin of religion is psychological. God is an exaggerated father figure, and religion is an attempt to handle frustrations created in the relations between the little child and its parents, especially the father. As the child is both afraid of and dependent upon its parents, religious man is dependent on God. In *Totem and Taboo*, Freud includes in his explanation of religion a "narrative of origin," of a horde killing their father to access their mother. In *Moses and Monotheism*, he develops a narrative with the same structure in order to explain the Jewish religion and its descendant, Christianity. According to Freud, Moses was an Egyptian who forced his religion upon the Jews. This resulted in conflict, as the Jews wanted to believe in their tribal god Jahweh. The conflict culminated in the Jews murdering Moses on the mountain just outside the Promised Land. These events caused a sense of guilt, which created the need for salvation in generation after generation of Jews and Christians.

Freud's theories of the origin of religion are, of course, extremely speculative. He was aware of this weakness and admitted that they were based on psychological probabilities, and that objective proof was impossible to obtain (1964/1938). At the same time, he stated that it was scientifically validated that unconscious ideas can be transmitted from generation to generation, which is a highly controversial proposition as well.

Sigmund Freud's theory of psychoanalysis has always been controversial. The critique has pointed out that it is too deterministic. Freud is a distinctive representative of the belief, which was prevalent at his time, that the human and the social sciences could uncover laws of the mind in the same way as the natural sciences could detect laws of nature. The critique has also argued that he exaggerated the significance of sexuality in human life. In the philosophy of science, psychoanalysis has been criticized for presenting propositions and conclusions that are impossible to validate empirically. Despite the Freudians' strong rhetorical emphasis on science, it opens up the way for unscientific speculation (Hamilton 2001). Critique has also been directed against Freud's sweeping generalizations. Based on a limited number of treatments of bourgeois women from Vienna, he draws general conclusions about humankind. Furthermore, his descriptions of religion are too general, as his theory actually is closely connected to a strict version of Christianity.

Nevertheless, Freud was extremely important for the twentieth century's concept of man. The image of a thoroughly rational and conscious human being is difficult to maintain after Freud. As it relates to religion, Freud's theory of religion has no significant support today, with the exception of the idea that the individual's concept of God can be coloured by childhood impressions (Spiro 1965).

3.6 George Herbert Mead: The social basis of identity formation

George Herbert Mead (1863–1931) grew up in Ohio; he was the son of a Protestant clergyman who taught theology at Oberlin College. Mead studied at Oberlin before he enrolled at Harvard University in 1887 to study philosophy. In 1888, Mead went to study in Berlin, where he became interested in social psychology. He also studied under Simmel. Upon his return to the US in 1891, Mead became an instructor at the University of Michigan and later at the University of Chicago, where he remained for the rest of his life. His main works, collected essays and lectures, all published after his death, are *Mind, Self, and Society* (1934), *The Philosophy of the Act* (1938), and *The Philosophy of the Present* (1959).

In *Mind, Self, and Society* (1962/1934), Mead analyses the conscious mind and the self-awareness of social actors. From German idealism, he adopted the idea that the development of the self needs reflexivity, that is, the ability of an individual to be an object to himself by "taking the role of the other" (Mead 1962: 153). He discussed gestures as signs and symbolic communication, using the example of a dog-fight to illustrate the "conversation of gestures" (Mead 1962: 43), in which each dog's action is a stimulus for the other dog. Gestures become significant when there is an attitude behind them, as for example, if someone is shaking a fist. In this case, we would assume that the gesture indicates not only a possible attack, but that the person has some motive behind it. When the gesture has a meaning behind it, and when it arouses that meaning in the other individual, we have a significant symbol. The conversation of gestures can be external, between different individuals, or internal, "between a given individual and himself" (1962: 47).

Mead claims that human beings only become human in social interaction or when a reflective mind takes the self as an object. The self emerges from social interaction in which human beings, in "taking the role of the other," internalize the attitudes of real and imagined others. The capacity of taking the role of others develops in two stages: play and game. In play, children take the role of a few significant others, such as parents or teachers. Here, one role at a time is played. The fundamental difference between play and game is that in the game "the child must have the attitude of all the others involved in that game" (1962: 154). At this stage, the child must understand the rules of the game and that their actions are determined by their assumption of the action of the others (1962: 164). In the game, the attitudes of the other players organize into a sort of unit, which controls the response of the individual. Mead terms this unit or social group "the generalized other." The game implies the ability to take the role of the generalized other. The generalized other "gives to the individual his unity of self" (1962: 154).

The generalized other also exerts social control over the individual, which ensures social stability. However, this control is not complete. Individuals can act spontaneously, a notion Mead upholds by distinguishing between the "I" and the "me." Mead postulates that the "me" (the self that emerged from taking the attitude of others) is involved in a continual interaction with the "I" (the creative part of the self). The "I" and the "me" are separated and yet belong together. Taken together they constitute a personality (1962: 178). Due to the constant interactions of the "I" and the "me," society is never static but always changing.

Because of Mead's focus on the development of the self and mind, there has been a tendency to overlook his views on the nature of society. He proposes a dialectical relationship between the individual and society. Mind and self only develop in society, and society is changed by individuals. The interdependence between individual and society is based on communications whereby the individual takes on the role of other individuals. Taking on the role of the other integrates the individual in the social process and organizes the conduct of a group (1962: 254–5).

Mead discusses religion in his work, although it does not constitute a significant part of his theory. During his studies at Harvard, he read Darwin, which informed a growing distance he felt from the religiosity of his father and the religious atmosphere at Oberlin. However, Adams and Sydie (2002a: 319) claim that the Christian principles Mead was taught by his parents remained an influence throughout his life.

According to Mead, several institutions of human life, such as language, the economy, and religion, involve a process of role-assumption. At the same time, they involve an extension of that process. The economic role is based on the idea of passing over that which one does not need, and the religious role is based on the pattern of helpfulness in family relations. Both the religious and the economic roles are potentially universal, and they have organizing power in the human community. Mead thinks that Christianity paved the way for social progress in the modern world, when it comes to politics, science, and economics (1962: 293), because the Christian notion of an abstract universal society gradually lost its religious significance and transformed into a concept of a rational universal human society. This in turn became the premise for the idea of social progress. In spite of the fact that economic and religious principles are often seen in opposition to each other, both of them are integrative. They are premised on the ability to take on the role of the other, and, therefore, they bring groups closer together through the process of communication. They are also universal in their character in the sense that they tend to build a common universal community (1962: 297).

In this sense, the capacity to adopt the role of the other to a greater degree by more and more people implies a development towards democracy (1962: 286). The ideal that every individual should stand on the same level with everyone else was first expressed in the idea of a universal religion. From there, this ideal was carried over into the political sphere, as expressed in the French Revolution and the writings of Rousseau. In this way, what applies to individuals also applies to institutions in society, and to the international society. In his introduction to Mead's book *Mind, Self, and Society*, Charles W. Morris (1962: xxxiv) writes that Mead is an internationalist, who constantly refers to the League of Nations, to which nations reach towards the wider society of which they feel a part.

In his introduction to Mead's social psychology, Anselm Strauss (1965: xviii) claims that Mead's devotion to reason prevented him from going the way of many Darwinians at the time, who interpreted collective action as an irrational phenomenon. In spite of this, he does tend to see *some* forms of collective action as irrational phenomena. For example, he describes collective religious behavior as a situation where there is a "fusion of the "I" and the "me," which leads to "intense emotional experiences" (1962: 274). In this way, collective religious behavior becomes an abnormality that stands in contrast to ordinary social life.

Nevertheless, several concepts in Mead's theory can be useful in sociological studies of religion. His concept of the generalized other can be connected to personal conceptions of God, a connection Mead surprisingly does not make (Morris 1962: xxiv). His approach can also give insight into the socialization of selves into a faith community, and the learning of religious language, symbols, and gestures. Mead also offers concepts for analysis of the formation of a religious self, a religious identity.

After Mead's death, his perspectives were defined by the term "symbolic interactionism," a sociological approach that is characterized by the attempt to explain action and interaction as results of the meaning that the actors give to objects and to social action. For Mead, interaction based on communication through the use of symbols is important. His perspective came to represent an opposition to the approach that emphasized the socialized and norm-ruled individual, as seen in the works of Talcott Parsons. Mead's work became important to various sociologists, such as Ervin Goffman and Peter L. Berger. This approach came to represent competition to the dominant school in American sociology in the 1950s and 1960s, namely structural functionalism.

3.7 Talcott Parsons: The individual and social functions of religion

After Durkheim, functionalism had continued to dominate social anthropology, but it lost much of its significance within sociology as early as the 1920s. It was Talcott Parsons (1902–79) who renewed sociological functionalism. Parsons, who grew up in a Protestant home as the son of a minister, discovered German sociology, especially Max Weber, during a stay in Europe. He also studied the work of the British economist Alfred Marshall, the Italian economist and sociologist Vilfredo Pareto, and Émile Durkheim. Parsons spent most of his career as professor of sociology at Harvard University. His most important works include *The Structure of Social Action* (1937), *The Social System* (1951), and, together with Edward A. Shils, *Towards a General Theory of Action* (1951). Parsons developed a general, voluntaristic theory of action, which he applied to a wide variety of issues. The novel aspect of his perspective was his functionalist vision and his view of modern society as a system. Although he seldom wrote specifically on religion, much of what he wrote is relevant for the understanding of religion.

In *The Structure of Social Action* (1949/1937), Parsons claims that social action is human behavior which is motivated and directed by the meaning the actor discerns in the external world. The actor in question can be an individual, a group, an organization, a region, a total society, or a civilization. Action always takes place in a situation. The individual actor's environment consists of physical surroundings, the actor's own biological organism, and other actors, as well as cultural and symbolic objects. Action and interaction take place within a symbolic universe, from which each action acquires a meaning both for the actor and for others. Norms and values guide the actor in the orientation of each action.

In *The Social System* (1979/1951), Parsons argues that human action cannot be considered in isolation, but it is always related to other actions. In this way, action becomes part of a larger whole, an action system. Three conditions must be fulfilled for a social system to survive: structural conditions, conditions of change, and functional conditions. Parsons defines the function of any living system as activities directed toward meeting the needs of the system qua system. A social phenomenon is explained by pointing out that this phenomenon is functional for society. Function is here the same as cause. At this point, Parsons can be distinguished from Durkheim, because Durkheim distinguishes between cause and function (Østerberg 1988).

According to Parsons, Bales, and Shils, there are four functions that must be present in any system of action (Parsons et al. 1953). These are adapting to given conditions in the environment (Adaptation), the achievement of collective goals (Goal-attainment), integrating the actions of members into society (Integration); and maintaining the values in society (Latency). Altogether these somewhat complicated terms are abbreviated into the so-called AGIL schema. The last function, to maintain the values in society, is related to motivation in the action system. This function becomes the point of contact between systems of action and the symbolic and cultural universe. Religion is part of this universe. It becomes particularly important for the action system in that it, as the rest of the culture, supplies symbols and ideas that are necessary for the creation of motivation in the action system.

Parsons insists that social action consists of three systems: personality, culture, and the social system. Later, he added a fourth system: biological organism. Like Durkheim, Parsons sees an analogy between society and the living organism. However, Parsons borrows from cybernetics. He asserts that a system of action, like all other functioning systems, is characterized by a constant circulation of energy and information. The organism is the sub-system that is highest in energy and lowest in information, whereas culture is the sub-system most abundant in information and most lacking in energy. A hierarchy of control is established between the four sub-systems. This means that the cultural system, including religion, controls the social system, the personality, and the organism (Rocher 1974: 28–51).

Parsons assumes that religion has several functions in society. First, religion helps members of society to deal with unforeseeable and uncontrollable events, such as an early death. Second, through rituals religion enables individuals to live with uncertainty. Religion also gives meaning to life and explains phenomena that otherwise would seem meaningless, such as suffering and the problem of evil. In this way, religion calms tensions that otherwise would disturb the social order, and helps to maintain social stability.

Parsons argues that religion will continue to be important in modern societies. He developed a theory of "the religion of love" (Parsons 1974). On the basis of what he observed within the American counter-culture in the 1970s, he assumes the development of a new and significant religious movement. The American counter-culture resembled early Christianity in its emphasis on the theme of love. The new movement was focused on a this-worldly rather than a transcendental level, and it idealized a society free of economic and power interests, free of coercion and even of rationally oriented discipline, achieving spontaneous solidarity in ways often governed by the imperative of love. The American counter-culture in the 1960s and 1970s was a reaction against certain aspects of rationalistic and utilitarian individualism, and the new movement would reinforce the affective solidarity in society. Because the new religion of love would be a secular religion, it would provide a new level of integration with the secular society in which the new religiosity also comes to be institutionalized.

In Parsons' sociology, religion has a vital function. Religion becomes, to a large degree, a presupposition for the maintenance of society. However, religion is not functional for society only, as Durkheim asserts; it is functional for the individual as well. Parsons claims that religion will always exist, although it might take a secular form. For him, unbelief is impossible in modern society, and for that reason, religion will also continue to be important in the future (Parsons 1971).

Many aspects of Parsons' theory have been questioned. One difficult area is his causal explanation of social action. Although Parsons explains behavior in terms of reasons for action, individuals are more or less governed by the norms in the value system, so that action is actually presented in terms of effects. In this way, social action ends up being ruled by norms, and thus it is a reactive phenomenon. Parsons is criticized for making a direct connection between norms and actions. The issue is that material and economic conditions can be just as important for action as are norms. In addition, Parsons' functionalist explanations are criticized. While he explains the existence of a phenomenon by pointing to its necessary functions in society, it is difficult to explain such functions without ending in an understanding of society as a collective being with its own consciousness, will, and needs.

Parsons is concerned with the positive contributions of religion to society. With the emphasis on harmony, integration, and solidarity, he tends to neglect the many situations where religion can be a source of conflict and disruption of the social order (see Section 9.2). Since the role of religion is to establish stability, Parsons' theory cannot account for religion as a source of social innovations or change.

Parsons trained a number of scholars, such as Robert N. Bellah and Clifford Geertz, who became influential in the study of religion. Although he was a very influential scholar in the mid-twentieth century, his influence is more limited and diffuse today. One reason is that during the political radicalization in the 1960s and 1970s, Parsons and other functionalists were criticized for overlooking conflictual interests in society. Another reason is that sociology in general has turned to a more action-oriented approach and there is a widespread skepticism towards the claim that one single theory will be able to explain all social phenomena.

3.8 Between structures and actors

In this chapter, we have taken a brief look at some of the most important classical sociologists and their theories of religion. Finally, we will address some of the commonalities and differences that are to be found between the various theories. There are several ways to compare and discuss classical sociological theories, although a more fundamental distinction is found in their sociological approaches, namely the distinction between structural and actor-oriented theories.

Structural theories can be described as those that view specific supra-individual arrangements (social structures, systems, developments) as the most fundamental factors in society. They provide frameworks and tend to determine the individual's thinking, action, and social life. Structures can be material, as with Marx, or material and moral, as with Durkheim, material and normative, as with Parsons, or instinctual, as with Freud. In some theories, society is characterized by conflict (Marx and Freud), whereas others emphasize harmony (Durkheim and Parsons). The weakness in many structural theories is that they often represent generalizations at a higher level, and they tend to ignore the individual actor and the contexts within which the social action takes place. In this way, social phenomena are understood as products of external forces. Actor-oriented theories, on the other hand, tend to explain social reality by referring to purposive social action. This perspective is seen in the works of Weber, Simmel, and Mead. This perspective is concerned with the conditions for social action, and the social actor is viewed as rational and oriented towards clearly defined goals. Social phenomena are here not reduced to social class interests or psychological states of frustration or deprivation, but are interpreted as rational reactions to societal conditions.

The distinction between structural and actor-oriented theories has consequences for the interpretation of religion. Structural theories tend to view religion as a result of large-scale societal transformations. In Marx's theory, for example, religion is a result of historical development, a development which will also result in the disappearance of religion. Many structural theories tend to emphasize the significance religion holds for society's needs. Freud argues that religion helps to diminish the human inclination to hurt others. Durkheim believes that religion has the function of creating social solidarity and stability. Likewise, Parsons claims that religion is a necessity both for the individual and the social system by ensuring motivation and stability. In this way, religion is a phenomenon that is an effect of external conditions, and that exists because it fulfills some type of societal purpose.

Structural theory tends largely to ignore the individual's motives for participation in religious rituals or groups. To the degree that the individual's motives are included, they are often meant to be frustration and deprivation.

Within action theory, the purpose is to understand the actor's action. For Weber, for example, religion is related to the individual's need for meaning, not to society's need for maintenance. According to Simmel and Mead, religion originates in social interaction. Here, religion is not a product of a linear historical development, a social consciousness or the system's tendency towards equilibrium. It is a product of specific individuals who lived in a given historical context. Religion has, furthermore, no a priori meaning, which means that its social role can vary in various societies, at different times and places. Action-oriented theories tend to emphasize the individual's motives for religious action. These may vary from a search for meaning in life to more self-centered motives, such as improving one's economic prospects.

The distinction between structural and actor-oriented theories is not clear-cut, which is evident when we look at the classical sociologists. Simmel explains religion, for example, on the basis of the social actor's actions and interactions, on the one hand, whereas he is similar to Durkheim by giving religion an a priori role, on the other hand. Likewise, Mead's premise is that the actor is rational, but he ends up interpreting religious collective action as a more irrational phenomenon, a position usually taken by structural theorists.

We have seen that classical sociology does not provide an unambiguous answer to the question of the relationship between individual and society. Whereas some theorists approach the problem from the side of the individual, others approach it from the side of society. The relationship between individual and society is not unambiguous, either. Whereas societal frames may give strict control in some situations, the individual's freedom to act is larger in other situations. Although there are fundamental differences in these approaches, different theories can be used in different types of contexts. In the following chapter, we will see how contemporary sociological theory represents an attempt to combine structural and actor-oriented theories.

4

Religion in contemporary sociology and cultural analysis

This chapter gives an introduction to some perspectives on religion found in contemporary sociology and cultural analysis. It has been common to distinguish between classical and contemporary sociology, although this distinction is often vague and fluid. The period we are discussing here begins around 1960. All the theorists included were born before the Second World War, although their theories became significant in the 1960s and have remained so until the present. We have tried to present the most important theorists who are frequently debated within contemporary sociology and cultural analysis, and we have included the notion of cultural analysis because some of these theorists are important in fields outside sociology. For example, Habermas, Bauman, and Foucault have made significant contributions within philosophy, ethics, and cultural critique.

Many theorists presented here have not written extensively on the topic of religion. Nevertheless, we decided to include them for two reasons. First, we want to accentuate what they actually have said about religion, since this might represent new information for many. Second, we want to demonstrate how their general perspectives can be used in analyses of religion.

We begin this chapter by introducing the theorists who are oriented towards system analyses: Jürgen Habermas and Niklas Luhmann. Then follows micro-sociological analyses, as we find them in the writings of Erving Goffman, Peter L. Berger, and Thomas Luckmann. Finally, we will discuss some theorists who focus on the relationship between structure and action: Pierre Bourdieu, Michel Foucault, Anthony Giddens, and Zygmunt Bauman. Each subsection is structured in more or less the same way. We first take a look at more general theories regarding the individual and society, before we present the theorist's view on religion, followed by critique. Towards the end, we outline some common themes and issues.

4.1 Jürgen Habermas: The place of religion in rational dialogue

Jürgen Habermas' (b. 1929) combination of critical analysis of the work of others with an elaboration of his own systematic social theory has been widely influential. Since the mid-1950s, Habermas was connected to the Frankfurt School of critical theory, a neo-Marxist tradition in sociology, and in the 1960s and 1970s he engaged in the critique that intellectuals directed against inequality and domination. Habermas deals with a wide range of issues, although he has had a consistent focus on the relation between reason, modernity, and democracy with the aim of providing an outline of an emancipated, rational society. In his work, Habermas also discusses religion, sometimes directly and explicitly, and sometimes more implicitly, for example in *Reason and Rationality*, a collection of articles published in 2002.

Throughout his work, Habermas attempts to reconstruct Weber's theory of the rationalization of society. In *The Structural Transformation of the Public Sphere* (1989/1962), he explores the origin, the potential, and the decline of the bourgeois public sphere that developed in the eighteenth century. This public forum of rational debate was distinct from the state and the economy, and it helped make parliamentary democracy possible. It also promoted the Enlightenment's ideals of equality, justice, and human rights. Habermas found in these institutions the origin of the modern public sphere. He argues, however, that the public sphere relatively quickly began to decline due to growing industrialization and the rise of popular mass media. In spite of its decline, Harbermas argues that this public sphere became a historical example of a public culture guided by reason.

Habermas follows Weber's theory of the inevitability of rationalization and secularization in many ways. For example, his theory of religion is related to his understanding of the dual structure of society, which comprises both system and life-world. He sees the life-world as a "finite province of meaning" and as a public sphere of communicative action. His premise is that individuals need personal integration, identity, or meaning, and that meaning is dependent upon integrating cultural norms created by society. Here, Habermas draws upon Émile Durkheim and Peter L. Berger (Habermas 1980: 117–18). Thereby, traditions, values, and religion constitute part of the life-world on which the communicative competence is based.

In his book about the legitimation crisis of late capitalism, which was published in 1973, Habermas (1980) points out how the "meaning" promised by religion has changed during different stages of cultural evolution. In primitive stages of social development, the natural world was part of the mythical world. In archaic societies, religion became a source of personal integration, giving a unified understanding of the life of the group and the individual's place in society. At this time, religion had a double function. On the one hand, religion provided the individual with knowledge that their existence was part of a larger totality, and in this way, religion functioned as a solution to cognitive doubt. On the other hand, religion presented a comfort when faced with the fact that existence is accidental. Habermas agrees with Weber that modernization has had a profound effect on traditional religion. With social development, humans achieved increased control over nature, and secular knowledge became an independent sphere, while religion became limited to questions about meaning and purpose. In this way, science and religion were separated, and they exist within two separate cultural spheres in modern society (1980: 119–20).

Habermas claims that the social sciences to a large degree have influenced the function of modern religion. Advanced capitalism has created a number of problems that the social sciences have attempted to solve by producing technical knowledge about the social world. Thereby, the social sciences have invaded the sphere of religion, which has to do with values and social integration. Furthermore, the social sciences have undermined the faith in traditional religion by pointing out the relative character of all cultural phenomena and thus they have challenged religion's claim to absolute truth.

In modern societies, the life-world is threatened by reification due to trespassing by the noncommunicative media of money and power. The rational potential of the life-world is realized when formal processes of communicative action, *discourses*, are institutionalized. Habermas' aim is to preserve the life-world and bring out its fundamental communicative core, which is to serve the normative self-regulation of society. For him, the emergence of undistorted communication is a fulfillment of the Enlightenment ideal. Religion is a phenomenon that is bound to abdicate to the force of rationality and retreat to a private sphere set apart from science and politics. Habermas believes that a reconstruction of traditional religious world-views will not have any convincing effects or meaning in modern societies (Wuthnow et al. 1987: 231).

However, there is one exception where religion may have a function, and this is in the communication process. Habermas argues that in some theological discussions (for example, Wolfgang Pannenberg, Jürgen Moltmann, Dorothea Sölle) the idea of God is transformed into an abstraction that shares those characteristic traits that Habermas believes describe the ideal communication. The concept of God symbolizes the process that binds a community of individuals together that strives for emancipation (Habermas 1980: 121).

In his *Theory of Communicative Action* (1984–87), Habermas develops his sociology of religion further. Here, his view on religion is based on a theory of the "linguistification of the sacred," a developmental process whereby that which has been perceived as a referent set apart, God, comes to be known immanently as a communicative structure (Habermas 1987: 77–111). Habermas believes that mythical views of the world involve little or no differentiation between culture and nature, or between language and world. Since mythical world-views hinder a clear demarcation of a domain of subjectivity, full communication is not possible under the conditions of religion (1984: 49–52). It seems that Habermas believes that discourses can include talk about the truth and rightfulness of religion, but that religion will not serve the emancipated communicative action in any fundamental way. In order to achieve cultural modernity, science, morality, and art must be split off from traditional world-interpretation (Habermas 1982: 251). Thus it seems that religion has little relevance for the communicative competence.

Critique has been directed against Habermas' perspective on the development of public debate and political participation in Western societies. This critique has become particularly relevant in discussions on multicultural society and the rights of religious minorities, such as Muslims in the Western world. In an article entitled "Religious Traditions in the Public Sphere: Habermas, MacIntyre and the Representation of Religious Minorities" David Herbert (1996) argues that Habermas' ideal-speech community assumes a singular public sphere rather than a multiplicity of public spheres. In practice, not all voices are heard equally. For example, the voices of several groups in society, such as women, gay activists, and religious and ethnic minorities, have often been excluded from formal political structures of discourse and dialogue. As a result, the principle of decision by quality of argument alone is undermined. Herbert also argues that Habermas overemphasizes the importance of consensus as the outcome of rational discussion. Instead, he calls for a theory that includes the relationship between different and often competing public spheres.

Furthermore, American sociologist Craig Calhoun (1992: 34–5) has pointed out that Habermas seems to ignore phenomena such as nationalism, feminism, and gay, ethnic, and youth consciousness, which often imply important redefinitions of issues and identities as these groups are involved in political struggles. Habermas treats identities and interests as settled within the private world and then brought fully formed into the public sphere. However, one of the key changes in the public sphere since the classical era has been an increasing prominence of what may be called "identity politics" (Warner 1992). Contemporary social movements have increasingly focused on the personal identity formation of minority groups and presented appeals for respect for their difference.

In the early 1990s, the philosopher Charles Taylor, known as a multicultural theorist, addressed the claims made by ethnic groups to maintain a distinctive identity and engage in "the politics of recognition" (Taylor 1992; 2003). The idea is to preserve their ethnic identities and achieve a public recognition of their uniqueness. Herein lies the inspiration to a "politics of difference," which is contrary to the idea of assimilation (see Chapter 10). Habermas has been criticized for his inadequate analysis of the problem of difference in contemporary society. However, he has conceded that the "politics of recognition" has become a chief concern of public culture and provides some opportunity for the discussion of matters of universal concern. The question Taylor raises is whether it is possible to organize a society around a strong collective definition without limiting the basic rights of people who do not share this definition. For example, is it possible to continue to organize liberal societies around the idea that the public sphere is secular and separated from the private sphere, which may be religious, when there are Muslim minorities who believe that politics and religion cannot be separated?

Habermas' reply to Taylor is that the social glue in complex societies is related to consensus about procedures for legality and exercise of political power. He believes that political integration excludes fundamentalist ideas of the fusion of religion and politics. According to Habermas, "all that needs to be expected of immigrants is the willingness to enter the political culture of their new homeland, without having to give up the cultural form of life of their origins by doing so" (Habermas 1994: 139). He does not believe that this will take place until the children of immigrants have grown to maturity. For Habermas, fundamentalism represents a false answer. He believes that it is the burden of the faithful to "endure the secularization of knowledge and the pluralism of world pictures regardless of the religious truths they hold" (Habermas 2002: 151).

In his introduction to the collection of Habermas' work on religion, the philosopher Eduardo Mendieta (2002) admits that Habermas certainly is a secularist, although he believes that it is a misconception that Habermas is anti-religion. Instead, Habermas acknowledges the role that religion has played in the identity of the West. In Habermas' view, "religion without philosophy is speechless, philosophy without religion is contentless; both remain irreducible as along as we must face our anthropological vulnerability without consolation, without ultimate guarantees" (Mendieta 2002: 28).

4.2 Niklas Luhmann: Religion as function

Niklas Luhmann (1927–98) was a German sociologist who studied under Talcott Parsons in the 1960s. In his sociology, he drew on formal logic, cybernetics, and biology. Through his numerous publications, some of which are translated into English, Luhmann developed a system theory.

Luhmann's most important theoretical interests are centered on two issues: a general theory of social systems and a theory of modern society (Luhmann 1982: xi–xii). In his general theory, social systems are perceived largely as communication networks: social systems are based on shared meaning and shared meanings are always the result of communication. Luhmann follows Durkheim and Parsons in arguing that society is differentiated into various functional systems, such as the legal system, economics, science, religion, and so forth. However, in contrast to Parsons, who emphasizes the necessity of shared value commitments in modern society, Luhmann believes that modern society has maintained order without relying on society-wide consensus (Holmes and Larmore 1982: xvii). Thus Luhmann does not believe, as did Parsons, that there is one single overarching and integrated system striving for equilibrium.

In his analysis of modern societies, Luhmann emphasizes two elements: the dramatic range of societal complexities and the differentiation of societal systems. The first element implies that there is no key institution in society that is formative for all other institutions. Whereas Marx claims that the economic institution affects all other institutions in society, Luhmann argues that there is no central one. The differentiation of modern society implies that there are several systems (Adams and Sydie 2002b: 37–8). All systems, social as well as psychic, are self-organized and self-referential or self-conscious (autopoietic) entities based on meaning. This means that one system observes the behavior taking place in another system, but can only interpret or understand that behavior according to its own definitions. For example, the religious system will interpret behavior in other systems in terms of the distinction between sacred and profane, the legal system in terms of the distinction between legal and illegal, and the scientific system in terms of the distinction between truth and falsity. Each system observes and reacts to the others based on its own specific categories and interpretations of the world, and there is never any direct transfer from one system to another.

Some sociologists (Calhoun et al. 2002: 136) have argued that Luhmann's theory has drastic implications for how one system can affect another. Since each system does not have access to the interpretation of other systems, it is ignorant of the ways in which it affects them. Luhmann believes that modern society is characterized by a high degree of interdependence. In comparison to pre-industrial and early industrial society, modern societies demonstrate less consensual and social solidarity (Adams and Sydie 2002b: 38).

Under the umbrella of system theory, Luhmann introduces an analysis on trust, risk, and power in modern societies. People put their trust "in the self-evident matter-of-fact 'nature' of the world and of human nature every day" (Luhmann 1979: 4). For example, we trust that technological inventions, such as the phone, the Internet, or a car, will function correctly. The more complex a society is, the more trust is necessary. But living in modern society not only requires trust, but also risk-taking. However, we seek safety and security, and therefore we seek to reduce risk (Luhmann 1993). For Luhmann, life in the modern world means that we trust those persons or organizations with power, so that we can reduce risk (Adams and Sydie 2002b: 41).

Within this framework, Luhmann interprets religion, especially in a Western context, agreeing with Talcott Parsons, Peter L. Berger, and Thomas Luckmann that modern society is characterized by institutional differentiation and pluralistic individual identities. In *The Differentiation of Society* (1982), he argues that one of the many forms of differentiation that takes place in modern societies is the privatization of religion. Secularization is the consequence of the differentiation process whereby systems in society have become relative, independent from religious norms, values, and legitimations. Religion not only retreats from important sectors of social life, but comes under pressure to develop its own specialized system.

Luhmann distinguishes between "professional" and "complementary" roles, which are critical for structuring the relationship individuals have to major institutional domains. In past societies, individuals belonged to specific status groups. This belonging determined "the profession" a person could follow. Modern societies have developed complementary social roles, where one person can be a doctor and a patient, or a politician and a voter at the same time. This functional interference threatens the relative independence of the major functional systems. In order to uphold the independence of the systems, a distinction is made between "private" and "public." A consequence of this distinction is that the individual decision-making process has become privatized in Western societies. Thereby, decision-making regarding religious convictions and practice has also become private. A person may or may not attend church; they may or not pray.

At the same time, a corresponding professionalization of public action is taking place. The rise of the expert leads to a situation where professionals become the public representatives of societal systems. In this way, the privatization of religion implies that the individual's decisions regarding religion have become privatized, at the same time as the representatives of the religious system, that is, the religious leaders, experience a decline in public influence (Beyer 1990: 374–8). Luhmann's view of religion implies that religion has a minimal influence upon other systems.

Nevertheless, religion does have specific functions. Religion deals with the questions that other systems raise. The systems of art and science produce questions that religion addresses. Furthermore, religion reduces insecurity. Luhmann believes that if religion is becoming increasingly privatized, a possible solution lies in finding effective ways where religion can have far-reaching implications outside the strictly religious realm. One example here is the public role that religion has played in Latin America, where religio-political movements such as liberation theology have tried to assert that religious norms and values are binding for everyone.

Luhmann (1995) distinguishes between how a system relates to the society as a whole and how it relates to other systems. He analyses the former in terms of function and the latter in terms of performance. Whereas function refers to "sacred" communication about the transcendent and the aspects that religious institutions claim for themselves, performance refers to situations where religion is applied to problems that originate in other systems (Luhmann 1982: 238–42). Through performance, religion demonstrates its importance for other secular aspects of life. However, a result of this process may be that non-religious concerns impinge upon religiosity, so that other social concerns limit the autonomy of religion (Beyer 1990: 378–9).

The most common critique against Luhmann is directed against the abstract aspects of his work. He never tried to reduce the complexity of his work in order to make it more accessible. However, his system theory becomes so abstract that both actors and societies are ignored. Indeed, Luhmann's theory postulates everything as systems. Also, he overemphasizes the fragmentation of individual and society. If society and individuals are as fragmented as he claims, they would more or less fall apart. Thus Luhmann's work has been perceived as abstractions that have little root in reality. Nevertheless, some of the topics Luhmann addresses are found in Anthony Giddens' work, as well as in the Canadian sociologist of religion Peter Beyer's theories of religion and globalization (1944) (see Chapter 5).

4.3 Erving Goffman: Everyday life as drama and rituals

Erving Goffman (1922–82) is one of the most widely read interpretative sociologists. Born in Canada, he worked in the United States, at the universities of Chicago, Berkeley, and Pennsylvania. Goffman studied natural sciences, and was involved in documentary film-making in Canada, before he turned to sociology. His interest in documentary film is evident in his sociology, as his major interest lies in the rules and order that are present in everyday social interaction.

Goffman studied sociology at the University of Chicago. He was inspired by Herbert Blumer and other sociologists who belonged to "the Chicago School" of sociology. Their aim was to study social interaction in various contexts. The Chicago School focused on the mental, interpretative, and creative processes of individual human beings rather than the structural frameworks of macro-society. The following statement from Blumer is representative for this sociological paradigm, often called "symbolic interactionism": "… group or collective action consists of the aligning of individual actions, brought about by the individuals' interpreting or taking into account each other's actions" (Blumer 1962: 184). A vivid academic debate has questioned whether Erving Goffman can be considered a symbolic interactionist. On the one hand, he shares this school's interest in micro-sociology and close, direct, social interactions. On the other hand, his interpretation of society is more structuralist: in his writing, Goffman demonstrates how social interaction is formed by rules and order and can be interpreted as rituals. Influenced by Durkheim, he also speaks of interaction as something that gives us a sense of social embeddedness and a type of sacred quality as human beings (Goffman 1967). While he shares the symbolic interactionists' view on human creativity, he believes that social interaction follows relatively firmly established rules. If the individual breaks these rules, society will be torn apart.

Goffman wrote many books, and his early works were exceptionally popular. Some of the most well known are *The Presentation of Self in Everyday Life* (1959),

Asylums (1961), *Stigma* (1963), *Interaction Ritual* (1967), and *Frame Analysis* (1974). Although Goffman never systematized his ideas into one comprehensive theory, some recurrent themes occur in his work. Goffman sees society as a theater stage. Social interactions possess a dramaturgical quality where the individuals act according to their roles. However, all actors have a "role distance;" that is, they are not stage actors who act according to a written script, but they create their own script during the performance. Human beings have a multi-faceted ego, able to display or hide different parts of themselves to make a favorable impression and avoid embarrassing and awkward situations. We are always more than we reveal in our encounters with others. We show something different "back stage" than we do "front stage." One illustrative example is how health workers tend to relax physically and emotionally in the absence of patients. They can even engage in condescending conversations about patients in order to create a sense of unity among professionals (Goffman 1961). Many observations made by Goffman deal with an individual's creative, but quite predictable, "management of impression" in social situations where people meet without knowing each other.

In addition to metaphors from the stage, Goffman uses the concept of ritual, expanding Durkheim's description of rituals to include everyday encounters. Rituals intensify common sentiments, thereby strengthening a sense of community among people. Conversational topics and forms of talk are respected through ritual confirmations and responses. Embarrassing instances of breaking the rules of the game are politely ignored as long as possible, and people distinguish between jokes and seriousness, all in order to maintain "the order of interaction" (Goffman 1967).

Goffman's understanding of roles is not deterministic. People enter and leave roles, and give them a particular form, in order to obtain something. Even in so-called "total institutions" like prisons or traditional asylums, individuals have a certain freedom of action, despite the strict frames of these institutions. Goffman's term "total institution" is presented in his study of a large mental hospital in the US, *Asylums* (1961). A total institution is a place for habitation and work where people in the same situation are cut off from contact with society for a considerable period of time. The inhabitants live in a closed and formally administered setting. The managers have extensive power, for example, to check and control. In total institutions, symbolic and ritual markings take place, for instance, to ensure that the inhabitants rid themselves of the identities they had before they entered the institution. This process is called "mortification." Nameplates are uncommon, the patients' own clothes are replaced with uniforms. However, even in such a regulated situation, Goffman's major interest is to demonstrate how people take on roles in order to secure freedom of action and show their own subjective identity. Just by transcending the demands of the total institution, patients and prisoners succeed at least to some extent in showing their difference, their humanity.

Critique has been directed against Goffman for his view of human beings as extremely cynical and selfish. Some also argue that he tends to generalize on the basis of a blasé and polite Western middle class with few boundaries and plenty of room for action (Baert 1998: 80). Nevertheless, Goffman's model of man is strikingly different than the atomistic "economic man" of rational choice theory (see Section 9.3). As noted, Goffman's primary interest lies in the patterns and the order of the interactions. In his world, individuals help each other through complicated patterns of interaction in order to maintain trust and a sense of community in micro-relations.

As many micro-oriented sociologists, Goffman has been criticized for directing little attention to the structures of society, such as the effects of social class on micro-relations. Goffman rarely responded to his critics, yet he argued that his aim was to study direct face-to-face interactions. Such relations had their own order, he said. He did not deny that there might be macro-structures that should be studied. However, such macro-structures are only loosely related to direct individual interactions (Goffman 1983). It has been said that Goffman viewed macro-sociology as boring (Strong 1988: 245), but this should not be taken to mean that Goffman was indifferent to normative social questions. Even if his prose is funny, easy-going, and non-moralistic, a sense of indignation often appears in his texts. One example is his book *Stigma*, where he describes how disabled people are expected to endure their disabilities with a sense of humor and refrain from complaints. They are expected to see themselves as human beings who are like anyone else, but they are also expected not to press their luck and participate socially in areas of contact that others feel are not their proper place, such as the dance floor or a particular restaurant.

Even if religion is a rather marginal topic in Goffman's writing, his focus on everyday ritualized interactions can be seen as a bridge to the sociology of religion. His concepts and perspectives represent possible tools for analyzing organized religious life. One example is his distinction between "front stage" and "back stage." Another example is his descriptions of informal rules when people meet. Finally, his interpretations of people's struggle to maintain distinction, creativity, and human dignity, also in the face of difficult situations, are important in an era of increasing individualism, including religious individualism.

4.4 Peter L. Berger and Thomas Luckmann: Religion as social construction

Peter L. Berger (b. 1929) was born in Vienna, Austria. He has been a professor at Boston University and written extensively on sociology and the sociology of religion. His works include *The Sacred Canopy* (1967), *A Rumor of Angels* (1969), *The Heretical Imperative* (1979), and *The Desecularization of the World* (1999). Berger has further demonstrated an interest in economic development in his book, *The Capitalist Revolution* (1986). Inspired by Weber, he has argued that the Pentecostal movement has been crucial for the socio-economic development in Latin America. In 1966 Berger co-authored *The Social Construction of Reality* with Thomas Luckmann (b. 1927), professor of sociology at the University of Konstanz in Germany, as well as *Modernity, Pluralism and the Crisis of Meaning* (1995). In addition to the books co-authored with Berger, Luckmann has written several books on sociology and the sociology of religion, among others, *The Invisible Religion* (1967) and *Life-World and Social Realities* (1983). Luckmann also edited *The Changing Face of Religion* (1989) with the British sociologist of religion, James A. Beckford. Berger and Luckmann were key figures in the sociology of religion in the 1960s and 1970s. In the following, we first examine the books they have written together, before we examine each individual's works.

The Social Construction of Reality (1981/1966) was written at a time when functionalism and structuralism dominated sociology. In this book, Berger and Luckmann argue for an understanding of human reality as a social construction. They believe that everyday reality, which is understood to be an ordered reality, is taken for granted. Everyday reality is also unproblematic, because it is shared with others in an interaction that takes place according to a specific pattern.

Berger and Luckmann have a dialectic view of reality. They claim "Society is a human product. Society is an objective reality. Man is a social product" (1981: 79). When they argue that society is a human product, they mean that human beings continually express themselves through various activities whereby they create objects. Berger and Luckmann label this process "externalization." Society is an objective reality. When human beings create an object, for example building a house or composing music, these objects obtain an independent character, existing independent of the human beings who created them. The house or the music becomes products that appear to be given. Berger and Luckmann label this process "objectification." Finally, they claim that human beings are a product of society. The objectified relations that human beings have created constitute frames for human activity, which in turn affect the human beings who created them. People are affected by the architecture and the function of the house or the music. This process is labeled "internalization." According to Berger and Luckmann, externalization, objectification, and internalization constitute a continuous process. It is within this dialectic that they view society as a human product at the same time as human beings are a product of society.

Berger and Luckmann's project is to bridge the gap between macro-sociology and micro-sociology, or between structuralism and interactionism. They draw on several theoretical traditions. One source of inspiration is the German philosopher Alfred Schütz (1899–1959), who attempts to explain how individuals construct common-sense knowledge. Agreeing with structuralism, Berger and Luckmann claim that social reality exists independently of and reacts to human subjects. There is an objective social reality, which Durkheim also claims. In addition, Berger and Luckmann are influenced by George Herbert Mead and other symbolic interactionists in their assumption that the human subjective relationship to the world gives the objective world meaning. Berger and Luckmann's book became influential within both the sociology of knowledge and the sociology of religion. Whereas sociology in the 1950s and 1960s had a tendency to paint a relatively reductionist picture of the individual, Berger and Luckmann provided a new focus on the human being as a social actor (Martin 2001: 159).

Berger and Luckmann's book *Modernity, Pluralism and the Crisis of Meaning* (1995) is an analysis of the mechanisms leading to what they believe is a crisis of meaning in modern societies. The development in modern societies leads to a situation where shared meaning is difficult to maintain for large groups of individuals. Therefore, patterns of meaning can only be shared and maintained in smaller groups. On this basis, the authors suggest that intermediate institutions, such as environmental groups, local churches, local political party organizations, and other voluntary organizations, can mediate between the individual and society.

One theme that appears both in Berger and Luckmann's collaborative publications as well as in much of Berger's work is that of order and consistency. For Berger and Luckmann, society is a world-building enterprise. *Nomos* is the opposite of *anomie* or lawlessness. If anomie represents a breakdown of the social order, nomos represents order and its normative regulations. When Berger and Luckmann discuss society's symbolic universe, they are concerned with its nomic or ordering function. They believe that the symbolic universe creates legitimation for the institutional order, as well as helping the individual put things in their right place and order the different phases of his or her own biography (Berger and Luckmann 1981: 113). When pluralism becomes widespread, most people will experience uncertainty and feel lost in a confusing world (Berger and Luckmann 1995: 40–41).

Shortly after his first book with Thomas Luckmann was published, Peter L. Berger wrote *The Sacred Canopy* (1967). Here, he uses the perspective on religion that was developed with Luckmann. Berger's theme continues to be that order is the most basic human need (Dorrien 2001: 32). For him, the important cultural concepts in a society can only be maintained if the members of society internalize them. In this regard, Berger outlines how the role of religion has changed in modern societies. In pre-modern societies religion formed an overarching sacred canopy that created an overall perspective for the whole society. This protective canopy provided legitimation, meaning, and order to the vulnerable construction that society calls reality. As society became differentiated, several societal institutions became separated from religion. In such a situation, religion lost what Berger calls a plausibility structure. In order to be plausible for the individual, knowledge requires a social structure, a plausibility structure, to support it. The differentiation of society led to a situation where traditional knowledge dissolved and was no longer taken for granted. The consequence of this secularization process was pluralization of the world: in place of an overall universe were now several limited, often competing, universes (see Section 5.8). Furthermore, religion was pushed out of the public sphere and into the private sphere.

In *The Sacred Canopy*, Berger gives a relatively unilinear outline of the development of increasing secularization in modern societies. However, Berger (1999) has rather humorously admitted that he was wrong at this point. He argues that it is impossible in modern societies to believe in the same way as in pre-modern societies. Yet he admits that people are able to hold on to religious beliefs even if they are no longer taken for granted. People continue to be religious in most societies, perhaps with the exception of Europe. However, people are religious in a new way, which is true even in situations where people argue that they have returned to the old religion. Other sociologists have contested Berger's assumption that Europe constitutes an exceptional case with its widespread secularization. British sociologist of religion Grace Davie (2001) claims that institutional religion continues to play an important part in many European countries, and French sociologist of religion Danièle Hervieu-Léger (2001) argues that in spite of *laïcité* or secularization in France, Catholicism continues to be a pervasive influence in contemporary French culture.

In *The Invisible Religion* (1967), Thomas Luckmann agrees with Berger that the social structure has been secularized. He argues that traditional institutional religion is weakening in modern industrial societies. Nevertheless, other universes of meaning are created in this situation. The early Berger claimed that secularization left an empty space, a conclusion with which Luckmann disagrees. His argument is that secularization facilitates the growth of non-institutional religion outside the established religious institutions, a so-called "invisible religion." Within the invisible religion, the individual constructs their personal identity and their own meaning system. Based on this interpretation, religion may constitute several different phenomena, such as a national day celebration, experiences in nature, or experiences of fellowship at, for example, a football game or a rock concert.

Luckmann's theory of invisible religion is related to his understanding of religion as an anthropological phenomenon. He claims that human beings transcend their biological nature by building objective, morally binding and all-encompassing meaning systems. Nearly everything human is thereby religious. This view has been met with criticism. Many have argued, among them Berger, that if everything human is religious, the distinction between religion and non-religion falls apart (Berger 1967).

Several aspects of Berger and Luckmann's theories have been met by critique. First, their emphasis on order: Berger acknowledges that the social order is vulnerable. However, he says in *Facing up to Modernity*, "order is the primary imperative in social life" (1977: xv). In a functionalist way, he perceives social institutions as phenomena that tend toward equilibrium and order. It seems as though Berger and Luckmann propound a form of cognitive balance theory, where they assume that individuals cannot live with contradictions and inconsistencies between different forms of knowledge and thus attempt to create balance, meaning, harmony, and integration. This perspective does not account for the fact that human beings vary regarding their acceptance of inconsistencies in their lives.

Berger and Luckmann's perspective has also been criticized for being too intellectual. Whereas some desire intellectually advanced meaning systems, others are satisfied with relatively simple ones. Some have also argued that not everyone has a need to find meaning in all aspects of their lives (McGuire 1997: 29; see also the discussion on Bauman in Section 4.9). Others claim that Berger and Luckmann are too focused on harmonization and, as a result, do not analyse how meaning systems serve powerful interests. To what degree does the symbolic universe, for example, protect the interests of specific social groups and classes? (Horrell 2001: 150).

Berger characterizes his own theoretical orientation as a type of "conservative humanism" (Poloma 1979: 202). On this basis, he is skeptical towards theories that promote rapid social change, because he is fundamentally suspicious towards those visions that are presented as alternative to the status quo. This might imply that Berger is negative to social change. In many ways, he represents a longing for an orderly past, as he sees it.

4.5 Pierre Bourdieu: Religion and social practice

Pierre Bourdieu (1930–2002) was a dominant figure in French social sciences who became influential internationally. From the 1950s onward, he conducted a number of research projects and wrote more than thirty books. He was initially trained as an anthropologist within the structuralist tradition; later he was associated with Erving Goffman (Postone et al. 1993: 2). Bourdieu was the son of a postman in a village in southern France, and his upbringing in a country characterized by its sharp social class and urban/rural divisions has often been used to explain his desire to detect the strategies used by the dominant classes to sustain their power and prestige. Bourdieu studied domination in several different contexts. His project was to overcome the oppositions in classical social theory between structuralism and phenomenology. For him, social life must be understood in terms of the objective material, social, and cultural structures, as well as the constituting practices and experiences of groups and individuals.

The topic of religion is integrated into Bourdieu's general work. He also published a few articles in French where he analyses religious domination (see Dobbelaere 1998a: 61), of which one is translated to English (Bourdieu 1987). In 1979, his most influential work, *Distinction*, was published. Here, he analyses the differences in taste between various social classes revealed in the varied preferences regarding art, music, food, home furnishing – and religion. For example, Bourdieu claims in this book that individuals or social groups who experience downward social mobility will adopt a traditional religion that emphasizes a celebration of the past, because this supports a return to the old social order and re-establishes their social being (Bourdieu 1986: 111).

Three fundamental concepts are central in Bourdieu's work: "habitus," "capital," and "field." The notion of habitus refers to principles that produce and reproduce the practices of a social class or class fraction. Bourdieu believes that social structures and embodied knowledge of the same structures produce enduring orientations to action, which are constitutive of social structures (Bourdieu 1986: 170). The habitus does not reflect individual experiences, but collective experiences that function on an unconscious plane and become important determinants in each individual's life.

Bourdieu's notion of capital is related to the capacity to exert control over one's own future and that of others. He focuses on the interplay of social, cultural, and economic capital. Economic capital is the most efficient form of capital, whereas symbolic capital will mask the economic domination of the dominant class and the socially legitimate hierarchy. A dominant class can also use its cultural capital – its language, culture, and artefacts – to establish hegemony. According to Bourdieu, the school system is a key institution whereby social order is maintained, because the language, values, assumptions, and models of success and failure adopted in the school belong to the dominant class.

Finally, the concept of field is used to give an account of the multi-dimensional space of positions and the position-taking agents. The social structure can be described as being composed of different "fields." The process within each field takes the form of a competition over positions and advancements. An example of a field is that of art. The art field has its own internal struggles over acknowledgement, power, and capital. In this way, each field is a site of struggle. On the basis of these three concepts, Bourdieu interprets social practice in terms of the relationship between current capital and class habitus, which is realized within a specific field.

Using his notion of field, Bourdieu analyses Max Weber's theory of religious power. He focuses on the interaction between differentiating categories of lay persons and various religious agents, such as prophets and priests. According to Bourdieu, the symbolic interactions that take place in the religious field are a result of the religious interests that are in play. These interests consist, in turn, of justifications of a person's or group's existence. Competition for religious power has to do with competition for religious legitimacy, that is, the legitimate power to modify the practice and world-view of lay people by imposing on them a religious habitus. Religious legitimacy reflects the religious power relations at the time and is also related to the degree to which an agent has control over what Bourdieu terms "material and symbolic weapons of religious violence" (Bourdieu 1987: 128). An example of such a weapon would be the excommunication of a priest. For Bourdieu, religious power and domination has to do with a domination of the categories of perception. These perceptions always favor those who are in power, which means that those who are dominated tend to diminish themselves and their perceptions. This is a condition Bourdieu describes as symbolic violence. In this way, religious violence is another form of symbolic violence.

According to Bourdieu, the prophet and the priest engage in a competition for lay followers. However, in a class-divided society lay people do not constitute a single entity, but consist of differentiating categories, who have diverse and contradictory religious interests. The priest and the prophet must adjust their preaching and their pastoral activities to these different interest grous, changing the content of their message to suit their audience. In this way, the religious field influences the interactions between the audience, the religious agent, and the message of the agent. Although Bourdieu analyses religious power, he does not end with a reductionist view of religion. Yet, if religious power is revealed, he also believes that the power of religious legitimation is diminished.

As noted, power and domination have to do with a domination of the categories of perception. To analyse symbolic power, Bourdieu (1994) looks at different ways in which power is exercised through classifications and name-giving, which may take place in more or less formalized rituals. He analyses the French elite schools that are rich in rituals related to the initiation of new students. Bourdieu believes that by studying these rites of initiation, he is able to grasp some characteristic traits shared by a whole class of rites. The rites of initiation are symbolically significant because they have the power to affect reality. For example, rites of initiation "consecrate difference" between a man and a woman. First, they transform the perceptions others have of a person and the behavior they adopt towards him or her. For example, a person is often given a new title during a rite. Second, the rites transform the representation that people have of themselves, and the behavior they feel obliged to adopt in order to conform to that representation. The initiated person achieves a right to speak and act on behalf of the category that is preached through the initiation. Thus rituals emphasize that a person really is what he or she presents him- or herself to be, that the person's social identity is not just based on personal faith or false pretenses. Bourdieu's view on ritual implies that it is a social practice, which includes the possibility to construct and maintain power, and his approach has been used in studies of religious rituals and ritual practice (Bell 1992).

Bourdieu's notions of habitus, capital, and field can be useful in analyses of religious domination, and so can his notions of "doxa" and "orthodoxy" (Bourdieu 1977). Doxa refers to knowledge that is taken for granted without deliberate considerations, for example, the power hidden in language, and in concepts and classifications. Traditional knowledge and relations of domination are maintained until someone begins to question them. At this point, those who want to maintain traditional knowledge and social relations must defend them, or become orthodox. Bourdieu's notions of doxa and orthodoxy have proven useful in analyses of religious power. His nuanced analysis of social class, particularly the distinction between cultural and economic capital, can be fruitful in an analysis of social class and religion.

We have mentioned that Bourdieu attempts to break out of the conflict between structures versus agency that tends to polarize much social theorizing. He embarks on a search for a thoroughgoing relationalism that grasps both objective and subjective reality. However, criticism has been directed towards Bourdieu for tending to end in a type of structuralism, where the concept of habitus has associations with mechanistic notions of power and a deterministic view of human agency (Wacquant 1993: 238). He has also been criticized for exaggerating the conflictual aspect of social life.

4.6 Michel Foucault: Spirituality, corporality, and politics

Michel Foucault (1926–84) is a major figure in French philosophical discourse on topics related to reason, language, knowledge, and power. Inspired by Karl Marx, Sigmund Freud, and Friedrich Nietzsche, Foucault is often labeled a post-structuralist in the sense that he wants to discover the non-rational framework of reason, but without any commitment to either an underlying order or a finally determinant power in the construction. His project is to detect the different discursive practices that exert power over human bodies. According to Foucault, knowledge does not necessarily lead to liberation. Instead, he sees knowledge more often as the basis of new means of social control. Foucault's work ranges over a number of disciplines, such as history, criminology, psychiatry, philosophy, as well as sociology. His work on madness, imprisonment, and sexuality has particularly been of great interest for sociologists.

Foucault was an atheist and he did not offer any systematic examination of religious themes. Nevertheless, he looked at Christianity as an important shaping force in the Western world. From his earliest references in the 1950s and 1960s, which discuss the role of religious institutions in the history of madness, to his examination of confession from 1976 until his death, there are underlying religious questions embedded in much of his work (Carrette 1999).

Foucault delivered a critique of religion in several different ways. From his early work in the 1950s and 1960s, he focused on the repressive nature of religion. He was also engaged in the "death of God" discourse, which was prevalent at the time (Foucault 1999: 85–6). During this period, he was engaged in examining the "discursive structures" or the way ideas about specific areas of life, such as madness or medical practice, are formed through discourse. This idea of discourse is important in his work as it demonstrates the temporality and constructedness of ideas. In *Madness and Civilization* (1967/1961) Foucault maps the cultural contours of madness, while in *The Birth of the Clinic* (1973/1963) he focuses on medical practice at the end of the eighteenth century. Although Foucault does not analyse religion in great detail in these two books, he sees religion as a part of the culture that influences and determines how madness and medicine have been understood in the West.

In *The Order of Things* (1970/1966), Foucault addresses cultural change by examining how knowledge is reconstituted in different historical periods. Foucault calls these particular knowledge forms *epistemes*, which means sets of presuppositions that organize what counts as knowledge, reality, and truth, and indicate how these matters can be discussed. For example, since the eighteenth century the modern *episteme* has focused on the idea of the autonomous, rational subject – man – as the subject and the object of discourses about life and labor. The idea that time and space determine an individual's thoughts and action is prevalent in Foucault's work. Knowledge and myths are considered to be productions of a specific time. In this way, the value of religion for individuals and groups does not have a set function or role but changes in relation to everything else (Wuthnow et al. 1987: 156, 162).

In the early 1970s, Foucault began to explore how a discourse was formed. He extends his analysis from examining the "conditions of possibility" for a discourse in isolation to examining an "apparatus" of knowledge. Thereby, he includes non-discursive as well as discursive practices. In *Discipline and Punish: The Birth of the Prison* (1977a/1975), he analyses the transition in the eighteenth century from the use of corporal punishment to incarceration and discipline. Here, he examines how power and knowledge are bound up in a complex "network of relations." Punishment became more "gentle," but it also became more thorough, the goal being to transform the prisoner into an obedient subject. The prisoner was therefore subjected to a strict discipline of rules, order, habits, and authority that was exercised continually around him and upon him. Discipline was reinforced by the use of surveillance that would constantly "see" and monitor the behavior of the prisoner. All prisoners were conscious of their permanent visibility, which assured the automatic functioning of power. The prisoners knew that they could be seen, but never when they were being seen. As a result, they disciplined themselves in case they were being observed. This "gaze" eliminated the need for physical violence and material constraints. Every prisoner became his own overseer. Foucault also demonstrates how different models of punishment had a religious basis, especially in developing a concern for the soul (Carrette 2000: 19).

In the multi-volume *History of Sexuality* (1976–84), Foucault's critique of religion focuses on religious authority in the demand for confession. He engages in an explicit discussion of Christianity by examining confession and the ethics of self. Foucault had a Catholic background and this religious heritage influenced his work; indeed, one can hardly imagine that he would conduct a study of confession unless he came from a Catholic tradition. In the first volume (1986), Foucault's central argument is that sexuality is not a given but something that is historically constructed. He shows, for example, in the later volumes, how early notions about restraint and the art of living in relation to sexual pleasure, as found in the Greco-Roman world, were modified in Christianity and its ideas about "finitude, the Fall and evil" (Foucault 1988: 239). He attempts to show how this change came about, claiming that the sexual discourse in the eighteenth and nineteenth centuries to a large extent was established by the practice of confession within Christianity. In the confession, sex was linked to the truth of the individual. Later, the techniques of confession were eventually adopted by the practices of medicine, psychiatry, and pedagogy. In this way, Foucault suggests that Freud's articulation of his "talking cure" originated in the techniques and mechanisms of confession.

According to Jeremy R. Carrette (2000: 143–51), a lecturer in religious studies in Scotland who has written extensively on Foucault and religion, Foucault's critique of religion operates on the basis of five interrelated factors that are found in his wider work. The first factor Carrette mentions is that religion and culture are integrated in Foucault's work. When Foucault examines the history of madness, medicine, prisons, and sexuality in the West, he analyses their roots in the discourses and practices of Christianity. Foucault also had an interest in Buddhism (Foucault 1999: 110–14) and Islam. For him, religion is a central part of culture and that includes several different religious traditions. Second, Foucault believes that religious discourse is framed and positioned in and through the human process of power/knowledge.

The third factor has to do with the embodiment of belief. We have seen that Foucault focused on sexuality and the body in his work. For him, the body was marked by history. In spite of the fact that the body and sexuality formed part of the historical processes that were concealed and denied within religion, Foucault argues that religion actually is always about sexuality and the body because discourses about religious practice and belief center around the body and are always concerned with what people do with their bodies. The fourth factor on which Foucault's critique of religion is based has to do with the analysis of mechanisms of power. Power for Foucault is a "multiplicity of force relations" in any given context. Power is everywhere and comes from everywhere. Since religion is a part of the wider culture, it exists as a manifestation of power. Religion is a system of power, as it orders life through a set of force relations.

The final factor Carrette mentions is the religious government of the self. Foucault points out that there is a mutual act of disclosure and renunciation in the practice of confession. In this process, the self is formed and shaped. Through religious practice individuals can transform and modify themselves. Religious discourse not only governs the self at an individual level but also at an institutional level, as the religious self is always part of a history that produces and maintains the self. Discipline, which previously was external and consisted of techniques of surveillance that monitored the behavior of the prison inmate, has in modern society become internalized. In this society, people discipline themselves as good citizens and diligent workers. Foucault does not envision a future of increasing liberation; that is, he does not believe that if religion is left behind, the liberated man will emerge. Rather, Foucault's critique of religion implies a critique of all regimes of knowledge.

Criticism has been directed towards Foucault for focusing on a white, male, Western tradition. He is not concerned with the effect that power has on dominated groups, such as women and ethnic minorities. In addition, his analysis of discourses of power, truth, sexuality, and religion is a masculine analysis. Since he operates with a gender-neutral analysis of power, it is easy to overlook the power exercised over women. Furthermore, Foucault's notion of power being everywhere and coming from everywhere has been criticized for reducing everything to power. The fact that power is viewed not as the possession of specific groups or individuals, but that it is all-pervasive diffuses power. It also makes resistance impossible. Nevertheless, Foucault's work has been used in analyses of religion and power, religion and culture, and religion and the body (see Carrette 2000). His notion of discourse has also been used in connection with different forms of discourse in modern society, such as nationalism (Calhoun 1997).

4.7 Anthony Giddens: Religion in late modernity

Anthony Giddens (b. 1938) is a leading British sociologist who has now published more than thirty-one books and is well known in most of the scholarly world. Giddens first established himself as an interpreter of classical sociological theory (Giddens 1985/1971) and a contributor to modern analysis of social class and stratification (Giddens 1989/1973). With the formulation of his own structuration theory, Giddens became a sociological theorist in his own right. In *The Constitution of Society* (1984), Giddens developed an interpretation of structure and agency. His most recent stage of research centers on modernity and politics, where he has examined the impact of modernity on social and personal life. In the 1990s, Giddens became a political actor in Britain and, among others, contributed to the modernization of the British Labour Party, which is revealed in his book, *The Third Way* (1998). Although Giddens has not examined religion in great detail, his works on modernity, such as *Consequences of Modernity* (1990) and *Modernity and Self-Identity* (1991), are particularly relevant for studies of religion in modern or late modern societies.

Giddens' project is to bridge the gap between structure and agency that has affected much of sociological theory (Giddens 1984). In his structuration theory, he sees social relations structured in time and space as the outcome of the operation of a "duality of structure." This means that people make society and, at the same time, they are constrained by it. Giddens argues that although action and structure usually are seen as opposing concepts, they cannot be analysed separately. On the one hand, he places great emphasis on individual action or the rational deciding actor. On the other, he emphasizes that an individual cannot act in any meaningful way without drawing upon existing collective interpretative schemes.

When Giddens speaks about structure, he refers to the "rules and resources" that act as common interpretative schemes. Language is an example of what Giddens means by structure. Language organizes practices, but language is also reproduced by practices. Giddens' notion of structure emphasizes that structure not only constrains social action, but also enables action. By providing common interpretative schemes, structure allows new action to take place. Giddens' intention is that neither agency nor structure be given primacy in his theory. However, some (Bryant and Jary 1991) have questioned whether he has been successful in achieving his goal or whether his work continues to demonstrate a bias toward individual agency.

In *The Consequences of Modernity* (1990), Giddens is concerned with the characteristic traits in our current historical era. In dealing with this question, he enters into a debate whether notions of postmodernity represent a new phenomenon or whether they are just a continuation of modernism (see Section 5.2). Giddens argues that there are definite changes that mark the current era, but he suggests that they should be thought of in terms of "radicalized modernity" rather than postmodernity. The reason is that these changes are produced by the same forces that produced the modern age.

According to Giddens, the current age offers unparalleled opportunities but also unexpected dangers. Since individuals in late modern societies have access to information about the world and each other, that information enables them to reflect on the causes and consequences of their actions. Reflexivity in modern social life consists of the fact that social practices are constantly examined and reformed in light of new information. Thereby, the character of these practices changes. Such a revision of conventions is applied to all aspects of human life. In this way, the modern world is a world that is constituted through reflective applied knowledge, but at the same time we cannot be sure that any given element of that knowledge will not be revised later (Giddens 1990: 38–9).

In his book on self-identity (1991), Giddens discusses the connections between modern life and the individual. The individual exists within a structure, but is also an agent, which means that the self must be created. Giddens claims that the construction of the self as a reflexive project is an important part of the reflexivity of modernity. The identity is not something given, but it is achieved through negotiated and reflexive use of the resources that each life offers. Identity is created and chosen by the individual. One element in self-creation is self-actualization, which is the effort of the individual to make oneself into what one wants to be. The self has become a project for which each individual is responsible. This can be both liberating and troubling. To have a choice over your identity implies having some anxiety over deciding your "real" self or "true" identity. It also implies a lot of work to monitor your actions so that they are consistent with your "true" identity.

Like Luhmann, Giddens refers to concepts of trust and risk. He agrees with Luhmann that there is a need for trust in the modern world because we know so little about the systems with which we have to deal. At the same time, we are faced with dangers because we do not know the unintended consequences of our actions. We are also faced with dangers because we trust the experts of knowledge we do not have, and we rely on the working of systems we do not understand.

Giddens distinguishes between the environment of trust and risk in pre-modern and modern societies (Giddens 1990: 100–11). When examining traditional societies, Giddens places religious cosmologies as modes of belief and ritual practice in the environment of trust. The reason is that they gave moral and practical interpretations of personal and social life and of nature. Religion also played a role in the environment of risk in traditional societies. It could be a source of anxiety, because the threats of dangers of nature often were experienced through religious codes and symbols, and it could also be a source of existential anxiety. When examining modern societies, Giddens emphasizes that most situations in modern life are incompatible with religion as a pervasive influence on day-to-day life. In modern societies, religious cosmology is replaced by knowledge that is governed by logical thought and empirical observation, which are focused upon material technology. Here, Giddens presents a relatively traditional view on the role of religion in modern societies, where religion is perceived to have a reduced significance (see Section 5.5 about secularization theory). For Giddens, religion and tradition are closely connected, and he believes that modern life undermines both of them, although more so tradition than religion.

Giddens argues that high modernity generates new moral problems. The doubt and insecurity inherent in our time favor a resurgence of religion (Giddens 1991: 185). This resurgence of interest in religion takes place during important life events, such as birth, marriage, and death. It is not only confined to traditional forms of religion, but results in the formation of "new forms of religious sensibility and spiritual endeavour" (1991: 207). This resurgence has to do with fundamental traits of late modernity. Giddens argues that high modernity has reached its limit, so that religion now thrusts itself "back to centre-stage" (1991: 208). In this way, survival of religion is a consequence of high modernity.

Giddens' view of religion has been critiqued. Let us first examine his notion of the loss of tradition. Giddens claims, "In conditions of high modernity, in many areas of social life – including the domain of the self – there are no determinate authorities" (Giddens 1991: 194). He also states, "The loss of anchoring reference points deriving from the development of internally referential systems creates moral disquiet that individuals can never fully overcome" (Giddens 1990: 185). British professor of religion Paul Heelas (1999: 201, 216) is among those who believe that Giddens exaggerates the weakening of tradition in late modern societies. Heelas also believes that traditions change; that is, they constantly emerge and recede, are maintained, constructed and reconstructed.

Second, Giddens' account of religion in high modernity also has its weaknesses. British sociologist of religion James A. Beckford (1999: 36–7) has pointed out that Giddens seems to use a functionalist type of explanation. According to his theory of high modernity, religion's chances of survival are extremely slim. At the same time, Giddens uses precisely high modernity as the explanation for resurgence of religion. Furthermore, Giddens looks at religion in terms of individual response to moral dilemmas. Thereby, he presents a narrowly individualized and rationalized picture of religion, which does not take into account its collective aspects.

4.8 Zygmunt Bauman: Liquid postmodernity

The sociologist Zygmunt Bauman (b. 1925) has lived a dramatic life. He was born in Poland of Jewish parents, and upon Hitler's attack on Poland, the family fled to the Soviet Union. As a Communist, Bauman participated on the Soviet side in the battle of Berlin in 1945. He made an academic career as a sociologist in Warsaw, but became increasingly critical towards the Communist regime. Upon his defection from the Communist Party in 1968, he was fired from his position as a professor. After a short stay in Israel, he became professor of sociology in Leeds in Britain, and this city has functioned as his home base as he travels extensively to give lectures (Smith 1999).

Bauman's biography can be traced in his numerous books. He has kept a strong commitment to social equality, even if he is almost allergic to any form of authoritarian and dogmatic thinking. He is allied with those social theorists who combine sociology with ethics. Yet he tends to emphasize the ambiguities that various perspectives represent. Bauman cannot easily be categorized in his relation to classical sociology. He rejects Durkheim and Parsons' image of society as a "programmed" phenomenon. His premise is that man is an active being. He believes that human beings are oriented toward collectives as they attempt to create order and meaning. At the same time, he describes stifling social structures, especially economic structures. He always depicts such structures as manmade, as he reminds us that "things could have been different" (Varcoe 2003: 39).

Bauman is primarily known for his critique of modernity. As a sociologist and ethicist, he is open to the possibilities that a postmodern, relativistic culture offers in developing an ethical consciousness "from below" (for a general discussion of modernity and postmodernity, see Section 5.1). In his more recent books, such as *Globalization: The Human Consequences* (1998a) and *Work, Consumerism and the New Poor* (1998b), the focus is, however, less on postmodernity. Instead, he has renewed his old interest in the critique of social, political, and economic inequality and injustice.

Bauman's sharpest critique of modernity is found in *Modernity and the Holocaust* (1989). Here he claims that the Holocaust, or the Nazi project of Jewish extinction, is not a proof of human irrationality. It is not a demonstration of the breakdown of modernity and the regression to pre-modern, primitive forms of culture, either. He argues that emotional, aggressive, and irrational sentiments are unable to arrange systematic extinction programs in the form of Holocaust: "Rage and anger are very primitive and inefficient tools for mass extinction. They usually run into the sand before the job is finished" (1989: 90). For Bauman, the Holocaust was possible because it was a consequence of the modern project, which aims at order, tidiness, and control. Modernity is intolerant of the foreign and the "slimy," as it demands purity in the name of reason. A common feature of the modern, as found in Communism, Nazism, as well as Social Darwinism, is the persecution of deviants. An important instrument has been bureaucracy. A key expression of modernity, bureaucracy is not a neutral tool but has built-in characteristics that may lead to inhuman forms of practice. Bureaucracy implies an extensive division of labor and a fragmentation of tasks: because the bureaucrats have a technical responsibility for small tasks only, their moral responsibility is pulverized. Bauman believes that the consequences of brutality will tend to provoke contempt, particularly when they are visible and appear in close proximity. However, there are several degrees of separation between the actors in a bureaucracy who take the initiatives and the final results of their actions. Thereby, the victims have no face and moral commitment is weakened.

According to Bauman, modernity and bureaucracy do not necessarily lead to devastation and horror. He points out two conditions that made the Holocaust possible. One was the situation of war, which implied demands for loyalty on the part of the German citizens. The other was the passivity of common German citizens towards the Nazi authorities during the early phase. However, modern bureaucracy also constituted an important condition for the process of social engineering that took place, with the extinction of all Jews as the final aim.

In several texts from around 1990, Bauman admits that he finds positive options in a postmodern, playful, individualist culture. In *Postmodern Ethics* (1993), he describes the postmodern as a more self-critical and modest type of modernity with a more relaxed attitude toward order and purity. There is also an element of hope in some of these texts. He suggests that man's moral commitment to close relationships can gradually expand to an inclusive universal morality of compassion and care. He voices faith in spontaneous communities and their ability to soften rigid and powerful institutions. Nevertheless, even his earlier books direct criticism against post-modernity, indifference, and lack of community and solidarity. This critique seems to have increased lately, for example in *Liquid Modernity* (2000) and *Community: Seeking Safety in an Insecure World* (2001). Bauman's critique of modernity and bureaucracy has, in some instances, been used as an argument for the deconstruction of the public sector and for a romantic view of private welfare solutions. This is a misunderstanding. Indeed, Bauman has strengthened his critique of international capitalism in his recent writings.

Bauman's discussion of the sociology of love in *Postmodern Ethics* (1993) is a good example of his sense of complexity and ambiguity. He argues that love can be affected by that which is fixed and firmly established. In this case, the couple has a common codex that defines the frames of their relationship. Their relationship is not dependent upon the mood at any specific moment. Both of them know they can enjoy the other without having to continually give more. This liquid love is more dynamic, but it is also more calculating and frail. Both parties calculate gains and losses in each given situation. Neither of them invests energy or emotion without making sure they will get something in return. Whereas fixation tends to result in a relationship characterized by duty and routine, liquid love tends to result in instability, insecurity, and threat, particularly for the weaker partner. Perhaps it is necessary to create a certain fixation as a bulwark for love, Bauman suggests (1993: 123).

Bauman has focused more on ethics than on religion. He seems to follow a rather common view in sociology that modernity has weakened the role of religion in society. The metaphysical roots of social community have disappeared. Seduction has replaced oppression and common religious references as the basis for social integration. The happy consumer has fulfilled his or her needs and the system is upheld, he writes in *Intimations of Postmodernity* (1992).

Postmodern man is oriented towards the here-and-now and is an ardent consumer of experiences. However, this quest for experience has little to do with religion, Bauman says in the article "Postmodern religion?" (1998b). In contrast to some sociologists who use a wider definition of religion, Bauman is unable to find any religious dimension in postmodern man's quest for self-realization and happiness. He seems to use a substantive concept of religion, as he relates religion to people's understanding of themselves as insufficient beings who are dependent upon divine intervention and help. In this article, he also rejects the view that human beings have a fundamental need to understand existential issues. There is little in the busy routines of everyday life that stimulates questions of the ultimate meaning of existence: the cattle must be fed, the crops taken into the barn, the taxes paid, the dinner cooked, the appointments kept, the video machines repaired, and so forth.

Bauman seems to reach a similar conclusion to Foucault, namely that religious leaders produce their own consumers. Historically, religious leaders have had the power to "inflict" religious topics on people. Religion has been introduced from above rather than grown from an inner human nature. In postmodern societies, religious organizations will face difficulties in eliciting a response, because the postmodern mentality seeks happiness and pleasure, not the traditional religious focus on human limitation and sadness.

However, Bauman argues that one form of religion, fundamentalism, is related to postmodern society. For him, fundamentalist religion (and fundamentalism in general, including politics) is a product of postmodern society's focus on the perfect ideal and the happy consumer, who continually searches for pleasure and experience. Fundamentalism is a refuge offered to the unsuccessful consumer, that is, someone who harbors a fear of all the choices one must make in life and the fact that one only can trust oneself. Fundamentalism is not a pre-modern relic. Instead, it is a safe haven for those who are afraid in a culture where every single individual must build his or her own identity and defend his or her own choices. On this premise, Bauman predicts that postmodern society will continue to have large groups of religious individuals.

Several historians and sociologists have argued that the basis for Bauman's critique of modernity is more related to the situation in Germany before and during the Second World War than to modernity as such (Varcoe 1998). When it comes to his view on religion, it is possible to maintain that Bauman tends to identify religion with fundamentalism. Based on his descriptions of a postmodern openness towards a new and warmer morality, some sociologists have indeed claimed that postmodern society is more open to religion than modernity is (see Section 12.5).

4.9 Some common themes and issues

This chapter has presented some of the most important theorists within contemporary sociology and cultural analysis. Here, the idea is to analyse a few issues they have discussed and consider possible implications that their theories may have for religion.

All the theorists included here have been concerned with the relationship between individual and society. We saw in the previous chapter how Talcott Parsons' theory of structural functionalism dominated sociology in the 1950s. Erving Goffman was only a few years younger than Parsons, but he changed the understanding of human interaction in sociology. Inspired by Mead, Goffman looked at ritual and strategies as an integrated part of the interaction in everyday life, and his perspective became important in the 1960s. On the one hand, he interpreted society as a theater, where people cannot do exactly what they like, because they have roles to play. On the other hand, all interaction is characterized by an element of improvisation. People are not only ruled by the roles given to them. As we have seen, much of contemporary sociology represents different attempts at combining structure- and actor-oriented theories.

The sociologists discussed here analyse the relationship between individual and society in different ways. Many draw upon earlier classical theory. A common theme, however, seems to be their emphasis on a tension between individual and society. They agree that "pure individuality" does not exist outside society, but that personalities are developed in social interaction. This perspective is clearly demonstrated by Goffman, Berger, and Luckmann. At the same time, the individual's desires and preferences do not originate inside each individual, but are socially produced. Some stress structures so that the actors disappear. This criticism has particularly been directed against Luhmann. Many also present a view on the relationship between individual and society that is characterized by lack of harmony. Most stress that people often experience the structures as limiting factors for the individual. This is evident in Bourdieu's and Foucault's works. In this area, Giddens has attempted to argue that structures also facilitate action by providing resources and the power to act. The debate on the relationship between individual and society has lately appeared in connection with the debate on the development of identity. Whereas all the theorists argue that individual identity is socially constructed, Giddens is the theorist who has gone the furthest in claiming that identity is created and chosen by the individual. On the other hand, Bourdieu has signaled through his concept of habitus that individuals tend to carry cultural luggage of which they are unaware.

The theorists' ideas on individual and society have consequences for their views on religion. According to Berger and Luckmann, religion is a phenomenon that is produced in everyday interaction. Giddens argues that social actors create religion, but that this production is related to the larger social development. Religion is, to a much larger degree, a product of structures in Habermas, Luhmann, Bourdieu, and Foucault.

The second theme shared by several theorists is the social and cultural construction of knowledge. In their analysis of the social construction of knowledge, Berger and Luckmann focus on everyday interaction. They draw on Mead, who represented an alternative approach to the dominant functionalism. Mead emphasizes that all knowledge is based on practical experience and communication, and not just a mirror of objective reality. This implies a view that perceptions of religion and reality will vary among various individuals and groups. The result is the idea that various cultures and historical periods will develop different religious forms.

The question of the social construction of knowledge has been one of the major themes within sociology and cultural analysis since the 1960s. There are several theorists who have attempted to understand history and multicultural diversity in new ways. Many theorists discussed in this chapter focus on the changes within Western culture. Berger points out how the changes in the plausibility structures have led to fragmentation of the traditional religious canopy in modern societies. Whereas religion previously gave legitimation, meaning, and order to social reality, religion will only have this function for a limited universe in pluralistic societies, where different world-views are competing. Michel Foucault attempts to uncover the different characteristic approaches to knowledge in various historical periods. He is one of the most important theorists within so-called "structuralism" and later "post-structuralism." Structuralism has its roots in Durkheim's sociology, especially in his emphasis on the social roots of knowledge. Foucault's concern is how power and historical change form knowledge. According to him, religion is purely a product of a specific time period. It does not have an a priori social role or function. Another post-structuralist sociologist, Bourdieu, emphasizes the struggle over classifications and symbolic violence. He argues that culture and religion in a given society are not factors that unify people, which is Berger and Luckmann's argument, but that the culture dominates them. According to Bourdieu, the use of classifications such as race, gender, social class, sexual orientation, taste, and religious orientation is a means by which social hierarchies are maintained.

This leads us to the third theme, which centers on inequality, power, and difference. In the 1950s, sociological theory was concerned with social integration, consensus, and other factors that were meant to hold society together. This changed in the 1960s. Focus was directed onto issues such as social class, race, ethnicity, gender, and sexual orientation. The classical theorists of sociology had been concerned with social inequality and social difference, but as a new generation of sociologists began to draw upon Marx, they began to stress inequality and difference. Within this tradition, common themes are conflict and struggle, and consensus is seen as a result of power relations and the use of power. For example, Habermas discusses hegemonic ideology to explain why the oppressed have accepted inequality. For him, secularity, and not religion, represents liberation. Berger and Luckmann also analyse how religion legitimates political power and existing social relations. Furthermore, Foucault points out how the confessional practice within the Church represents a discipline of the self and the body. Bourdieu views religious power as power over perception. Thereby, religion constitutes one aspect of symbolic violence. In addition, Luhmann explains power as a system and as a personal trait. Common for Luhmann, Habermas, and Foucault is that power requires communication.

The last theme mentioned here is these theorists' view on modernity and its consequences for religion. Sociological modernization theories have, for the most part, been based on social conditions that exist in the Western world. On this basis, models of the process of modernization have been made with the expectation that the rest of the world would eventually follow them. In this area, several sociologists have more or less automatically drawn upon secularization theories as they were presented by, among others, Weber. One has assumed that it was only a matter of time before the rest of the world would follow the pattern found in Western Europe, namely a unilinear development towards religious disintegration and privatization. This view is evident in the works of the early Berger and Habermas. Foucault also argues that Christianity previously played a significant role in Western culture, but that religion is no longer important. Giddens claims, on the one hand, that a high degree of modernity has forced out religion, and on the other hand, that a high degree of modernity facilitates religious resurgence. Bauman is the theorist with the most critical view of modernity. He seems to favor various social reform movements, although religion does not play a major role in them. He also seems to relate religion to fundamentalism.

In the 1960s, critique was raised against theories of modernization, where unilinear concepts of social change were rejected. Today some theorists argue that there might be several versions of modernity and many different modernization projects. We will also see that criticism has been directed against unilinear secularization theories. These are topics we will discuss later. For example, we will take a look at various interpretations of new religious movements and so-called fundamentalism. Are all religious conservatives anti-modern or do they represent alternative versions of modernity? The world is characterized by globalization, expansion of the economic market, and a growing international migration. This book attempts to discuss the significance that this development will have for religion.

5

The great narratives: Modernity, postmodernity, globalization, and secularization

A major part of the sociological debate centers on how we should characterize fundamental features of contemporary society. For empirically oriented sociologists, these debates may become *too* grand and reach too far afield. Many sociologists remain skeptical as to whether it is feasible to capture "the spirit of the time" by using terms such as modernity or postmodernity. In trying to capture an entire era with one all-encompassing concept, we have no choice but to gloss over vast differences between and within societies. This chapter will give an outline of the debates on modernity, postmodernity, and the relationship between these two concepts. We will also briefly discuss globalization. These debates are not limited to the sociology of religion, but are present in general sociology, history, and a number of other academic fields. A more specific element in the sociology of religion is the debate on secularization. We will present some principal features of secularization theories, that is, theories propounding that religion has diminished in importance. Towards the end, the critique of such theories is addressed.

5.1 The characteristic traits of modernity

To simplify, one may say that modern societies and modern projects have been dominated by five fundamental ideas (Schaanning 1992):

- Belief in truth and method
- Belief in final instances
- Belief in disclosure strategies
- Belief in progress
- Belief in liberty.

The belief that there are certain fundamental truths is, needless to say, older than modernity. What characterizes the modern project is that scientific methods are developed to reach the truth. The truth produced by using scientific methodology is called a truth in the final instance, that is, some fundamental elements upon which truth rests. In pre-modern society, truth normally rested in the final instance on transcendental elements outside the field of human experience. The fundamental truth was often placed in a religious field. Modernity puts the final instances closer to man, as it argues that human reason and/or experience constitutes the basis of truth.

Belief in disclosure strategies points to the importance in modernity to disclose and remove prejudices and superstition. Marx, Nietzsche, and Freud interpreted contemporary ideologies and religions with suspicion. Nevertheless, in order to disclose the truth, they had to determine their own final presuppositions, whether they were beliefs in economic and technological developments or subconscious instincts. Armed with disclosure strategies and scientific methods, the proponents of modernity attempted to increase man's freedom.

The Latin term *modernus* can be traced back to the fifth century AD, where it was used to distinguish between the old heathen and the new Christian epoch. Thus, linguistically, "modern" means nothing but the new time, in contrast to the old time (Smart 1990). When, then, does modernity begin as an era? Some date the cradle of modernity to the intellectuals of the late 1800s. Several scholars go back even further, even all the way back to Augustine's individualism and philosophy of progress (Kroker and Cook 1988). Many scholars appear to follow historian Arnold Toynbee (1954), who places the beginning of "the modern epoch in the history of the West" at the end of the fifteenth century, in societies along the European Atlantic coast, where a technological conquest of the seven seas was initiated. Max Weber can be labeled a sociologist of modernity. Through his analysis of Protestantism and its effect on the emergence of a disciplined instrumental attitude (Weber 2001/1904–05), he places the beginning of modernity in the sixteenth century. Several scholars also link the emergence of modernity – not least its critique of tradition, belief in reason, and desire for freedom – to the Age of Enlightenment in the eighteenth century and the French Revolution. It is impossible to give a definitive answer to the question of when modernity began. Perhaps the question is not even of interest for a sociologist. Sociologists are generally more preoccupied with the distribution and social role of ideas and practices than with who initiated them. It is also likely that the critique of tradition that characterizes modernity was only important to the intellectual elite at first, and that it gained acceptance in the general population much later.

Inspired by Weber, sociologist Bryan S. Turner (1990) has provided a description of a modern society. According to him, the following features characterize modern society:

- Ascetic discipline
- Secularization
- Belief that instrumental, focused reason has universal validity
- Differentiation of the various spheres of the life-world
- Bureaucratization of economic, political, and military practices
- Increasing monetization of values.

We shall return to several of these features when we examine secularization theories. Here, we just point out that Turner emphasizes some significant historical and geographical milestones in the early development of modernity. In particular, modernity is expressed through Western imperialism in the sixteenth century, the dominance of capitalism in Britain, Holland, and Flanders from the seventeenth century, the new natural science research methods developed in the seventeenth century, and the institutionalization of Calvinist-inspired attitudes and practices in Northern Europe in the centuries following the Reformation. In the nineteenth century, the modernization processes may be seen in the separation of family from kinship, household from the economy, and the establishment of motherhood as an institution. Turner claims that even if the idea of the individual citizen can be traced back to ancient Greece through the autonomous Italian city-states, the idea of the citizen as an abstract carrier of universal rights is a clearly modern notion.

It is common among scholars to relate modernization to the emergence of a rational way of thought. Some feel that this is too simplistic and that the modern epoch has consisted of numerous tensions between reason on the one hand, and Romanticism on the other (Guneriussen 1999). This tension can be traced in the works of the classical sociologists, at least in their concern with vanished forms of community, for example, the Romantic roots of Durkheim's ideas on community and solidarity. Indeed, the postmodern critique of modernity that we examine below may be seen as a radicalization of Romantic trends within modernity.

5.2 From modernity to postmodernity?

In contemporary society, several principal ideas of modernity based on reason are met by suspicion and doubt. Trust in scientific truth was stronger a century ago than it is today. At the realization that historical contexts and power relations in a society affect science, people experienced a loss of faith in a "pure" search for truth. Several factors, such as the awareness of media, language, power, and historical contexts, have eroded the confidence in reason and experience as final instances that constitute the foundation of truth. Those who exposed prejudices and superstition have themselves been exposed, and the norms of modernity have been criticized. The critique has been directed at scientific theory as well as at ethical assumptions.

Scientifically based knowledge has been accused of promoting an inhuman tyranny of normality. The belief in progress and in humanity's never-ending search for freedom has also come under scrutiny. So has the modern notion of the integrated, relatively autonomous subject. The subject is no longer a stable and unified entity. Indeed, this is a theme that always has appeared in sociology, which has maintained that human beings are affected by their social contexts. The problematization of the human subject tends to be connected with a growing awareness of language as a medium. According to contemporary thought, language uses man as much as man uses language. The idea that language represents reality in a direct way has become highly problematic in several academic fields. One of the early explorers and presenters of postmodern thought, Jean Baudrillard (1983), argues that with the new media technology, aggressive mass media, and a growing recreational industry, we witness innumerable simulations of reality. All the signs that surround us contribute to undermining our sense of reality.

The concept of modernity has been under attack, and intellectuals have responded by using the concept of postmodernity to describe contemporary society and culture. Before we turn to this debate, we will take a brief look at a few other terms frequently used by sociologists. In the 1970s, sociologists debated if we were moving in the direction of a postindustrial society. In his book *The Coming of Postindustrial Society* (1973), American sociologist Daniel Bell examines the rising living standard in the Western world following the Second World War. Since people no longer need to spend as much money on basic material necessities such as food, housing, and clothing, new needs arise within education, research, health, recreation, business, finance, and transportation. These new needs are generally satisfied by the emerging service sector. Science has become an important production force. The postindustrial society is to a great extent a knowledge and information society. Bell emphasizes that capitalist as well as non-capitalist societies may be postindustrial.

Within sociology, Bell contributed to the weakening of the functionalist idea that societies over time will develop into a harmonious unity, where each part contributes in different ways. In his book *The Cultural Contradictions of Capitalism* (1976), Bell developed a theory inspired by Weber based on the idea that tensions and conflicts between culture, economy, and politics are embedded in society. While politics regulates the division of power and interests, the economy creates and supplies goods, and the culture establishes meaning through experiences, symbols, and expressions. Each area is controlled by its basic principle: self-realization in culture, equality in politics, and efficiency and rationality in the economy. Bell claims that a conflict appears between culture and economy if culture turns its back on the efficiency of economy in favor of an irrational hedonistic rejection of traditions and established institutions. Bell predicts a trend toward a consumer culture based on games, exhibitionism, and critique of authority. At the same time, he appears to believe that the order of the postindustrial society will be preserved because experts will constitute a powerful and socially responsible "knowledge class."

"Post-materialism" is another term primarily used by the social scientist Ronald Inglehart to characterize the new features of modern society. In several publications (1977, 1990), he asserts that major value changes are occurring in the Western world. As people have attained a reasonable level of financial security and affluence, they turn towards what Inglehart labels "post-materialist values," such as aesthetics, self-realization, and environmental awareness. In the religious field, Inglehart believes that this general value shift will lead to less interest in organized, conventional religious traditions, but a renewed interest in spirituality and "the sacred."

Terms such as "postmodern" and "postmodernity" are popular, although they tend to lack precision. They derive from art theory and architecture, and over the course of twenty years or so they have been adopted by the humanities and the social sciences. Sociologist of religion James Beckford (1992: 19) has captured some features often linked to postmodernity:

1   A refusal to regard positivistic, rationalistic, instrumental criteria as the sole or exclusive standards of worthwhile knowledge
2   A willingness to combine symbols from disparate codes or frameworks of meanings, even at the cost of disjunctions and eclecticism
3   A celebration of spontaneity, fragmentation, superficiality, irony and playfulness
4   A willingness to abandon the search for overarching or triumphalist myths, narratives or frameworks of knowledge.

Here, postmodernity is contrasted to modernity and its belief in scientifically based knowledge, whereby the strict application of methods will disclose how the world really is and how it functions. Clearly the Enlightenment's belief in progress and scientific optimism is attacked by postmodern thought. "So-called postmodernity is nothing but the 'de-mystification' of the sanctity the Enlightenment conferred on reason. It is the secularization of secularism," sociologists William H. Swatos Jr. and Kevin Christiano (1999: 225) contend, consciously alluding to Max Weber's statement that modernization implies *die Entzauberung der Welt* (the disenchantment of the world).

Some scholars outline profound contrasts between modernity and postmodernity. Others draw attention to the continuity between modernity and postmodernity: the modern project also embodies skepticism of traditions and inherent notions. In *The Persistence of Modernity* (1991), the German Albrecht Wellmer writes about this continuity: the postmodern is a wiser and more modest form of modernity, characterized by experiences of war, nationalism, and totalitarian movements. Postmodernity is a continuation of the heritage of the Enlightenment, but with less utopianism and belief in science.

This debate is, needless to say, extremely relevant for questions on the destiny of religion in contemporary society. In postmodernity, criticism is leveled not only at religious absolutism, but also at the new scientifically based "truths", and the quotation marks are important. In the words of Peter L. Berger: the relativizers will themselves be relativized (1969).

The idea of postmodernism as a special feature of our time has, needless to say, also been critiqued. Some scholars have pointed to geographical and social limitations. A postmodern mentality may be considered an elite phenomenon constrained by social class, perhaps most prominent in social strata characterized by cultural capital, to use Bourdieu's term. It is likely that postmodernity is found more among journalists and artists than among farmers and pensioners. Another argument is that the use of characteristics of entire epochs or societies tends to neglect social differences and conflicts. Steve Bruce (2002) maintains that the overriding social institutions – politics, the economy, and technology – continue to be highly controlled by modern logic and rationality rather than postmodern logic and rationality. Bureaucratic rationality has hardly lost its power as a social factor since Weber wrote on bureaucracy and rationalization. It is not by random chance that the concept of postmodernity has gained more popularity among culture and media sociologists than among economic and political sociologists. Most people in the Western hemisphere are still engaged in numerous sub-projects of modernity. Whether the "I" and the personality of the individual have, for some, been theoretically "de-centered" or dissolved, it is still part of our operative everyday knowledge that we perform as individual actors. It may even be so for many postmodernists when they leave the auditorium or go home from the café. In general, people have a somewhat less problematic relationship to language and subject than literary science has. Many social and technical legitimizations of modernity continue to be useful in everyday life, including the perception of the human being as a controller, master, and creator in relation to nature, and the human quest for wealth and welfare. Therefore, if we must use definitive labels for our epoch, we would prefer late modern to postmodern.

5.3 Globalization

Globalization has to do with the processes that have led the world to become a single worldwide socio-cultural system or an institutionalized world order (Robertson 1991: 51). Traditionally, sociologists assumed that modernization was a unilinear process that took place within the boundaries of the nation-state. In the 1960s, the awareness emerged that societies were becoming highly interdependent. Many sociologists realized that the processes and problems that interested them had an inherently global dimension. Sociologists J.P. Nettl and Roland Robertson (1968) claimed that modernization was not a process that took place in similar ways across the world, but that modernization was a result of the attempts of societal elites to place their society in a global hierarchy. Immanuel Wallerstein (1974) argued that this hierarchy, which divided the world into dominant, industrial, capitalist countries and weaker Third World countries in terms of economy and politics, was a result of long-term changes in the capitalist world economy. He believed that this development brought about a global division of labor and a dominant world culture. This world culture or "global culture" became the primary concern of Mike Featherstone (1990), who pointed to trans-societal cultural processes, which give rise to communication processes which gain some autonomy on a global level.

In the sociology of religion, globalization theories are often associated with Roland Robertson, who began in the 1990s to analyse the religious aspect of global change. He challenged the conventional view that the world system was caused by economic forces and made up of economic structures. Instead, he claims that religion is an integral part of the process of globalization and a crucial domain in which conflicts over alternative directions are played out. According to Robertson (1991), the processes of globalization began and were set in rapid motion during the period 1880–1925. Four major reference points were established as far as "international society" was concerned: societies, individuals, international relations, and humankind. The second phase of globalization, which began in the 1960s, involves the reconstruction and problematization of these four reference points. Therefore, the following features characterize the late twentieth century: national cultures are called into question, and so is the need to declare one's identity. Since a large number of religious organizations and movements are multinational, they often end up in a tense relationship with national governments. Widespread church–state tensions around the world illustrate this phenomenon, says Robertson (1987). In addition, because globalization calls into question the identities of societies and individuals and brings different civilizations into one public square, religious traditions can become powerful sources of new images of world order. In response to unsettling global changes, Robertson (1991) found a general nostalgia or an appetite for images of the past. This leads religious groups and movements to return to fundamentals as a way to root the individual in a nation's religious culture and to reshape the world order. Religious leaders also become global actors, engaged in global debates (Robertson 1992). Although religion will not determine the direction of global-ization, Robertson argues that religion will help to influence the definition of the global situation.

Robertson called attention to the importance of the religious reaction to the globalization process, brought forth by the tensions it has produced. Peter L Beyer (1994) also focuses on the religious reaction to globalization. He distinguishes between religious movements that react against globalization and religious movements that celebrate diversity. The first category includes various forms of fundamentalist movements that react against global trends that threaten old identities. The second category includes liberal movements, such as religious environmentalism, that attempt to give the world culture itself ultimate meaning. According to Beyer (1990), the globalization of society may provide a fertile ground for the renewed public influence of religion. Yet he believes that religious actors and beliefs will have a more prominent role in the discourse about the global situation than in the institutions that shape global relations.

Other sociologists of religion have also analysed the religious reaction to globalization. Frank J. Lechner (1993: 27–8) noted that global culture has become the target of several fundamentalist movements (see Chapter 9). He claims that one explanation lies in the fact that modernity is not only a societal phenomenon, but it entails a world-view in the literal sense of advocating a distinct view of "the world." The religious movements that see themselves as defenders of God or Allah want to bring the kingdom of God to earth. They represent an attempt to restore a sacred tradition as a basis for a meaningful social order, which is one effort among others to preserve or achieve a certain cultural authenticity in the face of a universalizing global culture. Participants in such movements also become important actors on the global scene; thus a reaction against modernity has global implications. In this way, the changing global condition is not only a context and target of fundamentalism; it also serves as its primary precipitating factor.

Whereas several sociologists of religion have emphasized the religious reaction to globalization, others have focused more empirically on the global aspects of many religious traditions. Some have pointed out that several old religions, such as Christianity, Islam, and Buddhism, have always represented global cultures. One example is the Roman Catholic Church. From the beginning, its aim was to be the one, universal church. However, until the twentieth century, it was primarily a European institution and a transplanted European institution overseas. During the papacy of John Paul II, the Catholic Church embraced globalization in the sense of becoming a voice for human rights across the world, and there was a drastic increase in transnational Catholic networks and exchanges worldwide (Cava 2001; Casanova 2001; Romero 2001). Other religious traditions have also become increasingly global, such as Pentecostalism, Charismatic Christianity, and Sufism. Furthermore, the global outlook has been a distinct feature of several new religions and new religious movements, as well as "New Age" proponents (Hexham and Powe 1997; Rothstein 2001).

Globalization theory has been met by critique. According to David Lehmann (2002), a fundamental weakness in contemporary theoretical accounts of religion and globalization is the assumption that the spread of global capitalism is taken to be the model for all globalization. As a result, several scholars perceive globalization as the spread of rationalized, homogeneous, standardized "modern" culture. Furthermore, they tend to assume that a reaction to such globalization is the assertion of local religious identities. Lehmann claims that these perceptions about globalization tend to be simplistic, because they are based on a limited perception of religion. Rather than seeing religion as a symbolic system that confers identity and marks out social, ethnic, and other boundaries, they assume that modern religion is a rational religion. Lehmann argues that several forms of religion, rational as well as popular forms, often exist at the same time. For him, globalization does not form everything into a single homogeneous whole, but it may create local identities and diversity, even if similarities across social and spatial distances also can become more evident.

5.4 Secularization – a multi-dimensional concept

Modernization of society does not necessarily mean secularization. French sociologist Yves Lambert (1999) believes that the emergence of modernity may have four effects on religion: decline, adaptation and new interpretation, conservative reaction, and innovation. Only the first effect can be said to categorically include secularization.

The concept of secularization has several interpretations, so many in fact that some sociologists have proposed that the term be purged as a sociological term. Nonetheless, secularization is a concept that tends to pop up in several contexts. Hence it is necessary to include it in social scientific debates, but as we do, we should bear in mind that it must be defined.

Historically, secularization was first used about the transfer of church properties to state ownership in countries that had been through the Protestant Reformation (Dobbelaere 2002: 22). The concept was not commonly used in sociology until the 1900s. In the sociology of religion, the term is used to indicate that religion in various ways becomes more marginal and is less important. We shall examine how this term has been understood in sociology, but first it is necessary to mention that religious people, such as theologians, have not categorically perceived secularization as a negative phenomenon. Many religious persons will, needless to say, lament their religion's declining position in society, but others see such a change as a liberation of religion. They will argue that now that religion is released from a compromising interweaving of religious interests and secular political power, they can focus on the core of religion. Sociologist Talcott Parsons (1966) supports this view. Through functional differentiation in modern society, religion has lost several functions, but is therefore able to discharge its primary functions better. Niklas Luhmann may also be interpreted in the same vein. Religion has lost a great deal of influence on other systems, but continues to have a strong position when it comes to reducing uncertainty in life (see Section 4.2 on Luhmann). By looking at these examples, we see that views on secularization vary according to the ways in which religion is defined. We have mentioned in Chapter 2 that some sociologists use such a broad definition of religion that secularization, by definition, becomes virtually impossible. Thomas Luckmann (1967) defines religion as a search for one's identity in a wider context. Hence religion becomes a human constant, as it were, and Luckmann argues that organized religion is undermined and marginalized. The debates on secularization theories have nevertheless been based on substantive definitions of religion, connecting religion to something super-empirical.

Sociologist Larry Shiner (1966) provides a classic review of various secularization concepts. He distinguishes between six main interpretations of secularization:

- Religion is undermined because formerly accepted religious symbols, dogmas, and institutions lose their prestige and importance.
- Religion changes content because attention is diverted from the supernatural and the hereafter towards "secular" issues, so that in its content, religious commitment, becomes more like other social commitments.
- Society becomes less religious when religion becomes more inwardly focused, devotes itself to purely spiritual matters, and ceases to affect social life outside the religion itself.
- Religious faith and institutions lose their religious nature and are transformed into non-religious ideas and social institutions. Institutions that previously were seen as religious institutions of creation become secular human institutions.
- The world is de-sacralized. Human life, nature, and society are explained and spoken about from the premise of reason, and not as the result of the actions of divine powers. This is what Max Weber called the "disenchantment" of the world.
- An obligation based on traditional values and actions is replaced by a utilitarian and reasonable rationale for all choices and actions.

It is easy to see that the six interpretations overlap in parts. We also see that secularization sometimes has mutually conflicting meanings. Secularization may mean that religion becomes more secularly oriented, but also that it withdraws to a "purer" spiritual–religious sphere.

Belgian sociologist Karel Dobbelaere (1981, 2002) has attempted to systematize the use of the secularization concept. He recommends a distinction between societal secularization, organizational secularization, and individual secularization. This is also called secularization on the macro, meso, and micro levels. The following discussion is based on Dobbelaere. The organizational level refers to how religious institutions may change in the direction of inner secularization. Dobbelaere's categorization is useful because it leads to a more precise use of the concept, and his approach also opens up the way for questions regarding possible relationships between secularization on various levels. Society and social institutions may be quite secularized even if the majority of individuals are not necessarily atheists. Below, we will begin by examining societal secularization before we turn to organizational and individual secularization.

5.5 Extreme and moderate theories of secularization

The social theories of the nineteenth century tended to be rationalist and optimistic on behalf of science. They were often evolutionary, that is, assuming that society would develop through phases. One secularization theory representative of its time is attributed to Auguste Comte, the French philosopher who introduced the concept of sociology early in the century. He formulated a law on how the ideas of society historically passed through three stages. During the theological stage, events are explained as the result of the activities of gods and spirits. The world then develops into a transitory stage, the metaphysical stage, where philosophical principles replace religious explanations. One example of a valid explanation during the metaphysical epoch is the inherent purpose of nature. Comte believed that he was witnessing the appearance of the positive stage, where explanations became worldly and strictly empirical-scientific. During this epoch, theologians and philosophers must yield to the men of science. Comte as developmental optimist envisioned the future role of the sociologists. He believed that sociologists would act as social engineers and have a major effect on social development. The social laws would gradually be exposed and society could thus be governed on the basis of true knowledge (Thompson 1976).

This form of extreme secularization theory has often been combined with an optimistic belief in scientific progress, and the ways in which such progress would provide a basis for individual world-views. Today, few sociologists envision the disappearance of religion. The most rigid secularization theories are hardly relevant in contemporary sociology of religion. The debate is now between what we may call moderate secularization theories of religion's diminishing importance in society, and theories that question these predictions.

5.6 The secularization of society and its fundamental forces

It is difficult to distinguish clearly between the fundamental forces of secularization, secularization itself, and the effects of secularization. A number of adherents of moderate secularization theories nevertheless point out that secularization primarily means that religion has a diminishing importance for the development of society. The young Peter L. Berger defined secularization as a societal phenomenon: "the process by which sectors in society and culture are removed from the domination of religious institutions and symbols" (1967: 107). Another supporter of secularization theory, Bryan Wilson (1992), repeatedly emphasizes that his theory concerns social frameworks and social schemes, not individual faith. According to Wilson, secularization means that the social functions of religion are undermined. It appears reasonable to speak of secularization when religion no longer legitimates political power and legislation in the same ways it once did, plays a lesser role in the socialization of children, has less domination over cultural life, and is no longer used for interpretation of world events. In brief, secularization means that religion becomes less important for the functioning of the social system.

One must admit that religion in the Western world has lost power and influence in social institutions. In several countries, the state welfare system has taken over the functions of the church deaconate. This is the main trend, even if more recent liberal policies have led to a greater need for private care. State schools have removed instruction in religion or changed its focus toward inter-faith knowledge and dialogue. The influence of religion and the church has also been withdrawn from the legal courts, the military, and penal institutions. Even if publicly financed army chaplains and prison chaplains may still be found in some Western countries, they normally do not participate in formulating war strategies or reaching verdicts. The fact that they still may legitimize the political system is another matter.

In several fields, scientific explanations and legitimations have replaced religious explanations. For centuries, art and literature took their cues from religion, but references to religious traditions are relatively rare today. Religious leaders also have far fewer opportunities than they once had to exercise authority over other areas in society.

The young Peter L. Berger and Bryan Wilson have been mentioned as supporters of moderate secularization theories. Both are heavily indebted to Max Weber, who argued that the decline of religion was related to a general process of rationalization in modern society. According to Weber, attitudes informed by religion and values were replaced by attitudes informed by rationality and goal-orientation. He related this change in attitudes to the emergence of capitalism and industrialization, and to the development of a bureaucracy based on reason and regulations, which was becoming a form of government in every social institution.

Weber did not welcome the "disenchantment of the world." Instead, he was concerned when he described bureaucrats as "specialists without spirit" and rationality as an "iron cage." He nevertheless described the rationalization of society as a fairly inexorable process, even if he allowed for the possibility that religion might have some effect in times of instability and that irrational counter-reactions may occur (Ekstrand 2000). Weber saw no possibility for religion to have a central role in modern society, the role he ascribed to Protestantism during early capitalism.

Weber's outline of the dominance of rationality in modern society is, strictly speaking, merely a description. He does not provide a systematic analysis as to why reason and instrumentality have become prevalent. However, there is little doubt that one explanation is found in the growth of industrialization and bureaucracy. The economy is the first sector to lose its religious ethos. Among the secularization theorists following Weber, many emphasize similar explanatory factors, such as industrialization, capitalism, differentiation, urbanization, and the emergence of science. These factors constitute more materialist explanations of societal secularization than those often found in religious groups. They tend to emphasize spiritual and ideal conflicts that appear in public debates and the school system, and they will often accuse secular authors and the media of undermining religion. Sociological explanations argue that changing material and social conditions will alter individual experiences that, eventually, will affect their world-views.

In his secularization theory, Thomas Luckmann (1967) focuses on the differentiation of society. This is also a major issue for Berger (1967). Their similarity does not come as a surprise, as these two sociologists worked closely together in the 1960s (see Section 4.4). The idea is that various sectors of society gradually extricate themselves from religious control. Economic life acquires its own laws, where rational strategies and calculations govern actions. A sign of this development is that the ethical–religious ban on usury under Catholicism and Luther gives way to an economic-functional idea that money can also be traded at a price. The sciences develop their own ideas and research strategies, where God eventually has no place. This development is reflected in the fact that theology ceases to have a dominant position at European universities. Separate faculties are established for medicine, law, and various natural sciences. In time, politics is also secularized, at least day-to-day politics, while wars continue to be shrouded in a great deal of religious rhetoric. In modern society, each social institution functions according to its own logic. In the economic field revenue is to be earned, in politics power is to be sought, in the courts the truth is to be found, and this logic leaves no room for divine powers.

Peter Berger outlines similar perspectives, not least in his book *The Sacred Canopy* (1967). A canopy here is the arch of a four-poster bed, and Berger's metaphor explains how people in the holistic Christian culture during the medieval era lived within a religious framework that virtually enveloped them from the cradle to the grave. Whatever your personal religious piety and moral rectitude, if you chose to be outside the religious circle, for all intent and purpose, you were also outside society. Berger then describes how this canopy cracks and falls apart, so that today in many societies religion is something you either choose or reject.

The inspiration from Weber is evident when Bryan Wilson speaks of *societalization* as an important underlying force of secularization. Society has become more impersonal. Personal bonds of loyalty, trust, and dependency have largely been replaced by indirect relationships and limited contacts between people who function according to relatively restricted roles. The personal bonds have yielded to abstract expert systems. This development has in itself a secularizing effect, because religion traditionally has been based upon small fellowships and bonds of loyalty between people (Wilson 1982). The content of religion is also influenced by this societalization. It is difficult to maintain faith in a personal God in a society with so few personal bonds. Religion becomes a private matter. The area for religious validity and relevance as moral guidelines and world-views is restricted to the private sector and recreational preferences, and it becomes a widespread belief that politics, government, and religion must remain separated. Religion also becomes a private matter in the sense that an individual's beliefs should be a private concern, and any attempt by other individuals, groups, or social institutions to influence individual religiosity will be taken as an intervention in one's private life.

Urbanization is also at times mentioned as an independent force behind secularization. The idea that cities have a secularizing effect is based on the notion that people escape from the tradition-preserving social control of their rural district. It may also be claimed that the city-dweller is surrounded by manmade creations. This places the individual at the center as the creator, closing the door on world-views that see the human being as a creation of God and at the mercy of forces beyond human power. However, urban life also offers practical advantages for religious communities, as the population is larger and members live in close proximity. In this way, urbanization might stimulate the formation of religious organizations.

In the sociology of religion, it seems that the type of fundamental force selected to account for secularization is related to the theory used to explain religious involvement. This is apparent in the use of deprivation theory to explain why individuals become religious; that is, the theory maintains that when individuals are in a situation of deprivation they seek comfort and compensation in religion (see Section 7.1). Based on this idea, secularization will occur if the deprivation situation is remedied. When the financial situation or social integration in society is improved, poverty and loneliness will become less of a problem and the reasons for seeking religious meaning will thus diminish.

Bryan Wilson (1982) stresses that modern science has had a secularizing effect. Through a lengthy process, atheist explanations have displaced religious ones. This is an argument that might raise objections. Religion has often dealt with topics other than science. A comprehensive biological explanation of what happens to the body when a person dies does not necessarily mean that we accept the reality of death. Moreover, there have been numerous attempts through the centuries at harmonizing religion and science. Nonetheless, it is difficult to ignore the fact that scientific explanations have reduced religion's field of application – from cosmology to psychology, to borrow one of Peter L. Berger's (1967) apt formulations.

5.7 The debate on moderate theories of secularization

The debate on the old secularization theory had a major impact on the sociology of religion. Social anthropologist Mary Douglas was an early critic of the idea that modernization necessarily leads to secularization. Inspired by Durkheim, she believes that as long as a collective ethos and social relationships exist, there will be religion, rituals, and myths, because religion is created in social relationships. Religion will change but will not disappear through modernization. She strongly opposes the view that science has reduced the explanatory powers of religion. Instead, she argues that people understand that religion and science address different problems and thus do not constitute a mutual threat (Douglas 1982a: 8).

Mary Douglas also rejects the idea that people have less contact with nature and therefore have become less religious. Her view is that our questions regarding nature have rather been fortified by the scientific discoveries in our time (Douglas 1982b). Another issue in Douglas' critique is that secularization theorists tend to draw an exaggerated religious picture of the past; they have an "uncritical nostalgia." There is no evidence to support the idea that the masses in ancient times were completely focused on the spiritual or that people's emotional and intellectual lives were so well integrated by religious frameworks (Douglas 1982a: 5).

Other scholars have subsequently developed many of Mary Douglas' objections to secularization theory. Secularization theory became the center of debate among sociologists of religion in the 1980s, partly due to *The Sacred in a Secular Age*, a collection of articles edited by American sociologist Phillip E. Hammond (1985). The emergence of many new religious movements unceasingly spotlighted by the media in the 1970s and 1980s led to doubt as to the validity of secularization theory.

The representatives of the old theory have voiced different responses to these objections, offering various forms of geographical restrictions related to the validity of the theory. Peter L. Berger has exercised substantial and humorous self-criticism upon his earlier works, and has restricted the validity of the moderate secularization theory to Europe, which appears to be a secular island in an otherwise religiously vital ocean (Berger 1999). British sociologist David Martin (1996) has also suggested that Europe is an exception in the world, not least when we consider the studies of charismatic religiosity in a Latin America that is undergoing modernization. One of

Martin's students, Grace Davie, offers the same idea in her book with the descriptive title *Europe: The Exceptional Case* (2002). However, she adds that there is still much respect for established religious institutions in Europe, even if organized religious activity is low and declining.

Yves Lambert (1999) offers an interesting observation when he distinguishes between two "thresholds" of secularization: (1) independence in relation to religious authority, and (2) the potential for all religious symbols to become obsolete. Lambert claims that generally the first threshold has been crossed, but not the second, with the exception of some fields (science and economy) and in a minority of the population. In explaining why secularization has not crossed the second threshold, Lambert maintains that, in part, religions have adapted to modernity, have experienced fundamentalist reactions, and have developed new forms.

Needless to say, many scholars have pointed out that Islamic regimes outside of Europe and America do not at all lend credibility to a general secularization theory. In response, Steve Bruce has stated that his defense of secularization theory does not apply to the entire globe, but rather to the regions of the world – generally Western countries – that have gone through historical processes of pluralization and egalitarianism. However, he has a problem when it comes to explaining the situation in the United States, as do other proponents of moderate secularization theories. In the 1960s, Thomas Luckmann (1967) resolved the "USA problem" perhaps too superficially. Confronted with the contention that from the premises of modernization and secularization theories a far more secularized United States could have been expected, he argued that a form of "inner secularization" had occurred in the many religious communities in the United States. Being a member of such a religious community satisfied more social functions and status than the real religious functions, Luckmann claimed. Peter L. Berger (1967) offered similar ideas when he referred to the term "basketballization" of church life in the United States. This argument may not be entirely legitimate, in the sense that it introduces demands for a high level of sincerity and depth of religious commitment. Berger's claim is not easy to test empirically, either, and one is also left wondering if European religious communities are always brimming with existential gravity.

Steve Bruce's approach to American religion is slightly different. He admits that American religious life is vital, even if a substantial over-reporting of religious activities has been found in studies based on questionnaires (Bruce 2002). He also points to the importance that ethnicity has for religious vitality in the United States, which has been a country of immigration for more than two centuries, and continues to be so. In a nation that to a great extent is composed of ethnic minorities, one should not be surprised that ethnic groups are drawn together to maintain ethnically based traditions, including their religious heritage. In the nineteenth and early twentieth centuries, European immigrants kept their religious traditions alive, and today this continues within other immigrant groups. Hence Bruce argues that the United States constitutes an exception from a general secularization trend in the Western world, an exception that is explained by the role that ethnicity plays in a nation of immigrants. A possible delimitation of this reasoning is that European immigration generally occurred a number of generations ago, and that the importance of ethnicity among Euro-Americans is insignificant in the contemporary United States (Alba 1990).

When it comes to the validity of secularization theories outside liberal and Western regions, we find different views. There are some attempts at controlling whole societies theocratically according to Muslim principles, as seen in Iran and Afghanistan during the Taliban regime. Yet these examples overshadow the more common process that takes place in several Muslim countries of a gradual and quiet liberalization and privatization of Islam. A picture of Islam as a theocratic religion is certainly a major exaggeration.

On a more theoretical level, Steve Bruce (2002) and others have criticized the rationalistic and individualistic picture of man upon which rational-choice-inspired theories of religion are based (see Section 7.3). To claim that individuals at all times seek that which is most advantageous for them, as if they are on a wild and continual comparative religious shopping spree, is to underestimate the social and cultural limitations that exist for the choice of religion. According to Bruce, only a society where religion no longer has any importance can find such a theory of religious change to be true. Whatever the case, religion certainly has more implications for identity and culture than the brand of refrigerator we buy. These social and cultural limitations apply to those who demand religion as well as those who supply religion. The Ford Motor Company dropped its Edsel car model when people no longer wanted to buy it. The Christian Church cannot simply drop the Holy Spirit because it loses ground in a popularity poll.

5.8 Religious diversity, competition, and secularization

Peter L. Berger believes that secularization is self-reinforcing once the holistic "sacred canopy" has started to fall apart and contesting world-views exist side by side. When several prophets preach at the same time, and each one claims to represent the truth, doubts arise as to the truthfulness of all of them.

This is a central idea in the works of Karl Mannheim, the sociologist of knowledge, especially his major work *Ideology and Utopia* (1936). Here, Mannheim describes how the fundamental doubt in the validity of thought and faith begins to take hold after the clergy has lost its intellectual monopoly. Intellectuals who live in separate communities may have different ideas and be thoroughly convinced of their truthfulness. However, once they compete in the same market and become aware of each other, doubt and critique of self will arise, and the result will be a growing interest in interpretation and theory of knowledge. How do we know that we know? Mannheim argues that after the breakdown of the medieval holistic system, the criticism between conflicting disciplines ruined people's confidence in human belief and thought. Though one result was tolerance and dialogue, another result, Mannheim suggests, was the Fascism that emerged around the time he wrote this book, which he saw as a result of individual confusion and passivity.

Peter L. Berger (1967) reasons in similar ways: when there are several truths vying for attention, people become relativistic and are less willing to commit to holistic world-views. Plurality has a secularizing effect in and of itself. In a situation where several alternative world-views are available, the uncomfortable idea emerges that we have chosen God rather than He has chosen us.

In addition to the fact that diversity causes doubts and erodes certainty, diversity may also have a secularizing effect in a more indirect way. Several countries have achieved religious freedom and tolerance, not as a result of the struggle for liberal secular reform, but as a result of competition between religious groups that were convinced they were in sole possession of the truth. When several religious groups compete, and none of them has any realistic prospect of attaining dominance in a given society, a common strategy is to fight for free competition or weaken the link between state authorities and religious leadership. (This process has been described in early American history by Finke (1990) and for several countries by Bruce (1990).) Hence a statutory religious tolerance is introduced. In time, the same tolerance results in a privatization of religion, as religion is to be kept separate from political institution. A legally imposed tolerance will also tend to lead to a trivialization of individual religious choice. People get used to the idea that one can only fight for one's own religious views within certain legal limitations, and only specific means are acceptable in this struggle. In this way, religion is no longer an issue of life and death. Thereby the intensity in the religious involvement is weakened, especially the tendency to proselytize.

Scottish sociologist of religion Steve Bruce is today one of the most ardent proponents of classical secularization theory. Here, he follows Weber, the young Berger, and Wilson. He emphasizes how diversity has a secularizing effect when society is liberal and egalitarian. In an anti-hierarchical, tolerant, equality-oriented, and democratic society, it is difficult to impose religious discipline from above. Religious life must be chosen, and often it is not chosen at all (Bruce 2002).

Some American sociologists have proposed an opposite view. They claim that religious diversity and competition between world-views do not lead to secularization, but to religious vitality and a greater religious mobilization. Organized religion thrives and flourishes best in an open-market system characterized by competition (see also Section 7.3). Two principal promoters of this view, Roger Finke and Rodney Stark (1988), maintain that the more pluralism, the greater religious mobilization in the population.

The concepts of diversity, competition, and religious growth are linked in slightly different ways. First, the liberal economic belief that competition raises the level of activity and quality is applied, while monopolies and subsidies are seen to have the opposite effect. This school of thought is relatively new in the sociology of religion, but it has classical roots. It is more than a curiosity when Rodney Stark and James McCann quote Adam Smith himself, who in 1776 wrote in *The Wealth of Nations* that state-funded and dominant faiths lack eagerness and industry in their supporters. In such a situation, the clergy rests on its privileges, and because of its own indolence, it has neglected to stoke the fire of belief in the majority of people (Smith 1937/1776). The Nordic state churches have often served as deterrent educational examples among sociologists who favor diversity. In the Nordic countries, the large national churches receive funding and privileges from the state, whereas few people actually attend church on a regular basis. Finke and Stark argue that the incentive to work hard is far stronger for religious suppliers when they are unable to lean on state funding and instead operate freely in a market without legal obstacles. The argument that competition leads to a more concerted effort is applied to religious leaders as well as regular church members.

The theorists who combine diversity with religious growth also argue along a different line of reasoning: when the demand is varied, a wide range of products will lead to higher total consumption. Target groups for marketing are divided according to age, ethnicity, gender, class, and perhaps even taste in music and level of intellectualism. Diversity and competition provide specialization in such a way that there is something for every taste. The support for religion in a local community will be greater when there is greater freedom to choose. In this way, the conservative, the cool, the intellectual, and the informal person will find something that suits her or him. The choice is not between one particular religious profile and passivity. Rather the idea is that the more religious alternatives that are offered, the more consumption of religion will take place.

As noted, some American sociologists frequently present these arguments (Finke and Stark 1988; Finke 1990). Less attention has been devoted to a possible link between sociological conflict theory and the theory that diversity leads to religious growth. In a pluralistic situation, religious movements may become more conflict-oriented in the sense that they define themselves in opposition to and different from other movements. This approach may produce vitality, as it motivates the participants to struggle for their cause. A study of American conservative Evangelical Christians supports this line of reasoning. Christian Smith and his co-workers (1998) argue against the so-called enclave theory that states that conservative religion in the United States only survives because it has isolated itself and sought refuge in counter-cultural communities, isolated from the larger society. These movements flourish precisely because they are visible in the public sphere and they challenge religious and cultural pluralism. They appeal to those who link pluralism to moral decay and a harsher society.

Based on the theoretical argumentation and the existing empirical research, it is still difficult to conclude with absolute certainty in favor of the old or the new theories of religious diversity. It is possible that a higher level of precision will make both theories more useful. It might be that in cases where different religious groups oppose each other, frustration and doubt increase, whereas in situations where similar religious groups are in competition, this leads to overall religious growth. In the latter case, the religious groups will unite on some ideas, for example, Christian, fundamentalist beliefs, and reinforce them. Swedish sociologists of religion Eva Hamberg and Thorleif Pettersson (1994) emphasize another condition for religious diversity to produce growth. They contend that diversity leads to growth only in situations where there is a complex religious demand that fans out in different directions. Thus, diversity must be present on both the supply side and the demand side for competition to stimulate religious growth.

Peter L. Berger has adjusted his old theory. He retains the idea that modern pluralism causes individual perception of reality to lose its self-evident status, becoming a matter of choice. However, he now claims that this does not necessarily lead to secularization: "To say that religious beliefs are chosen rather than taken for granted is not the same as saying that these beliefs are no longer held. Put simply, I would propose that pluralism affects the how rather than the what of religious beliefs and practice – and that is something quite different from secularization" (Berger 2001: 449).

Berger has been criticized for his old idea that diversity leads to relativism and doubt. His critics argue that his view is based on a too cognitive and intellectual understanding of religion. For Berger, religion is a puzzle that provides meaning to existence in an intellectually satisfying way. However, it might be pointed out that religion is also about moral issues and the desire for community and belonging.

5.9 Secularization and its limitations

Criticism has been directed against the old secularization theory's postulation that the Western world had been fundamentally secularized over the past three centuries or so. The critics have questioned the theory's image of history and the contemporary period, as it implies a romantic and empirically unfounded picture of a golden age. Instead, they argue that the European medieval era was not only a period of a blooming religious culture, but also of a great deal of religious indifference. When people attended church it was often because they were forced to do so. The medieval era was one of religious apathy more than an era of faith, Lawrence Iannaccone claims (1997: 41). Stark and his colleagues criticize the image of a strongly religious America two hundred years ago, followed by a subsequent religious decline (Finke and Stark 1992). Proponents of what has occasionally been called "the new paradigm" (Warner 1993) point to the empirical fact that the old secularization theory was unable to explain: the contemporary United States appears to be the technologically most advanced society in the world, yet religion is still vital. The new paradigm paints a picture of contemporary religious movements as active, influential, visible, aggressive, modern, and expansive (Finke and Stark 1992).

Rodney Stark and William Sims Bainbridge (1987) have formulated a so-called dialectic secularization theory, where the idea of secularization as a self-limiting process is a key. At the heart of their secularization theory is a general theory of religion based on "rational choice" theory. According to Stark and Bainbridge, individuals seek rewards or advantageous solutions for themselves, and they attempt to avoid costs in doing so. However, in some instances, they must satisfy themselves with compensation for rewards because these are not always available. One example is that people will always see death as a problem and want to obtain eternal life, although this is an unobtainable reward. However, religious communities may offer compensation through a *promise* of eternal life. In areas where the rewards are available, individual actors will search for solutions where the rewards are higher than the costs. In areas where rewards are unobtainable, those who can deliver the best compensation (promises, assurances) gain the most adherents.

Stark and his colleagues argue against the idea that Western societies have experienced a declining interest in religion. They nevertheless concede that secularization proponents are right on one issue. The large mainstream denominations have shown a decline in the United States and Europe. Stark and Bainbridge's explanation is that mainstream religious communities have lost members not because they have failed to keep up with modernity, but because they have adapted too much to modern society and have thus lost their appeal as suppliers of transcendent promises. As these religious communities decline, the market is open for religious movements that offer more specified assurances, or for groups that offer religious compensation. As long as death is an inescapable reality, people will always demand religious compensation. When the mainstream churches no longer satisfy their expectations, people go elsewhere. The decline of churches nourishes religious revivalism and gives birth to different forms of religious experimentation in a stimulated religious market. Religious development in a society is a cyclical or dialectic process. In this way, secularization is a self-limiting process with a far shorter horizon than claimed by Weber-inspired secularization theories.

There is one valid aspect of the critique of the moderate secularization theories. The most deterministic secularization theories allow virtually no room for the "supply side" of the religious field. Their focus is solely on how the modernization process undermines the demand for religion. The new theories stress how religious strategies and organizations make a difference. This is not only a comforting idea for people struggling with religion, but it also contributes to sociological theories of religion. As it relates to the dialectic secularization theory, it may easily end up with a deterministic character, as is the case with all phase theories, whether they outline a cyclical or a linear development. The sum of religion is hardly constant, and it appears too simple and mechanical to say that those who advertise the greatest promises gain the most believers.

Another related theory proposes that when established religious traditions fade away, the path is open for the establishment of new traditions. Individualism and reflectivity may threaten traditions, at least if tradition is defined as something one complies with fairly automatically. Traditions may nevertheless also be considered as an object of choice. As noted, new traditions may also be created. The lighting of candles at gravesites and professional concerts in church are examples of relatively new traditions in the Nordic countries, traditions with strong or weak links to established church life. This approach does not necessarily impart the idea that the human need for tradition is constant. Religion scholar Ninian Smart (1998) contends that throughout history, man has created and changed traditions. "The only thing perhaps that we can change is the past and we do it all the time," he writes (1998: 79), emphasizing that intellectuals with access to historical documentation tend to overestimate how old and durable traditions are. Many traditions are quite new. For the general public, the revival of certain traditions and reconstructions of the past is easily believed because people do not generally remember that far back, nor have they read all that much history: "If you can assume that what is passed on downward through the generations is forgotten, you can shape it as you want." According to Smart, we are not living in a time particularly dominated by de-traditionalization; "Rather we are as as busy as ever retraditionalizing" (Smart 1998: 86).

5.10 Secularization on the organization level: Religion as a source of secularization

We mentioned earlier that Karel Dobbelaere (1981, 2002) structures the discussion by placing secularization on three levels: society, organization, and individual. When he discusses the organizational level, he focuses on the question of whether the source of secularization is to be found within the religious traditions themselves. Richard Fenn (2001) argues that religion is demystifying in itself because it organizes and reduces the uncertainty that human beings experience. Hence, he says, religion constitutes the first stage of a secularization process. People declare something sacred and, thereby, they gain a form of control of a reality that is otherwise chaotic, fluid, and threatening. In this way, secularization and sacralization become two sides of the same coin.

A similar view is found in the writings of Peter L. Berger. Inspired by Weber, he points out that secularization in the Western world partly grows out of religion itself, that is, specific features found in the Judeo-Christian tradition (1967). Berger returns to the prophets and their critique of the Israelites, as expressed in the Old Testament. Prophets such as Amos and Isaiah chastise the local fertility religions and attempt to form an ethical monotheism where God is elevated above the world. In this Jewish prophetic religion, God is the creator of the world, but the world in itself is secularized – it is not divine. The lofty and elevated God of the prophets wanted individuals to act according to moral notions of fairness, and not engage in sacrifices and temple prostitution. Man is assigned the world as an ethical playground. In this, Berger sees the seeds of secularization because humans can continue to act with a focus on the world without maintaining contact with God.

In a simplified historical presentation, Berger mentions the incarnation dogma in Christianity as a new link where God and man come closer to each other again. The form of Christianity that develops up until the 1500s is characterized by continual contacts between human and divine affairs. Local saints and stories of miracles, angels, adulation of Mary, regular religious duties – all of these factors create open channels between the individual's everyday life and the divine. In Berger's simplified church history, the Reformation becomes a new revival of the prophets. Again, everyday life is cleansed: Protestantism labels Catholic miracles, magic, and mysticism as superstition and heresy. Once again, monotheism is promoted, now with slogans such as "the Scriptures only." There is only one bond between God and man, that is, God's word, and this bond can be broken. Martin Luther distinguished between a sacred and a secular regiment, and the secular regiment becomes a realm of reason. According to Luther, God rules the secular regiment, too, but He will only use secular lords to ensure order, justice, and safety. In everyday life, God is removed from this realm. Berger characterizes Protestantism in terms of "an immense shrinkage in the scope of the sacred in reality" (Berger 1967: 111). He claims that this analysis explains why countries dominated by Catholicism appear to be less secularized than Protestant countries.

Steve Bruce (1990) supplements and advances Berger's analysis of Protestantism. Ever since the Reformation, Protestant disciplines have stressed dogmatic correctness, which has created irreconcilable disputes between different branches. This process has, in and of itself, in keeping with Berger's theory of diversity and secularization, undermined the credibility of the religious communities in the mind of the general public. In this context, the ambiguity of religious revivalism can also be mentioned. Revivals tend to encourage intense faith and a high level of activity among those who participate, but they may also take people in an opposite direction. Those who previously have seen themselves as religious without closer scrutiny may perhaps begin to reconsider their own status. When they see that the participants in the revival introduce stricter demands on lifestyle and on faith, they may reject these notions and move away from religion. In this way, revival and secularization also become two sides of the same coin.

This approach represents a contrast to the theory of Stark and Bainbridge (1987). They claim that movements with a definite profile will appeal more to people than vague, liberal religious communities. The latter tend to lose their appeal because their individual characteristics have disappeared in their attempts to adapt to contemporary society. Christian Smith and his colleagues (1998) argue along the same line in their study *American Evangelicalism.* They claim that religious orthodoxy thrives and is not weakened when its proponents are clear and committed. When orthodox individuals struggle together in an urban and pluralist context, they tend to develop strong internal bonds of loyalty. With clear references to Berger's work, these authors claim that "Instead of hiding under an overarching *sacred canopy*, the evangelicals carry 'holy umbrellas' – small worlds of relationships that enable them to be involved in the pluralism of modernity while they remain orthodox" (Smith et al. 1998: 89).

Steve Bruce (1996) outlines a nearly insoluble dilemma for religious organizations in contemporary modern liberal society. One alternative is to adopt a strict and fundamental approach. This strategy may appeal to some, whereas others will abhor it and make the group an object of ridicule. For example, preaching about the pains of hell might be a strategy for the maintenance of religion in the old authoritarian society, but in today's anti-authoritarian society such a strategy will alienate the large majority from religion. The alternative strategy is to adopt a more liberal approach. However, if a group's religious identity is extremely diffuse, few will see reasons for joining. If a person wants to get involved in environmental issues or politics, there are excellent organizations she or he can join that have few or no religious ties. Bruce argues that religious movements also are gradually losing the battle for attention to the entertainment market. In addition, Bruce points out that the liberal churches are losing an important source of recruitment: many people who grew up in a more sectarian Christian tradition sought refuge in the more tolerant and liberal mainstream churches. But as fewer people are recruited to sectarian Christianity, he believes that this flow of disillusioned revivalist Christians will taper off (Bruce 2002).

Bruce points out some dilemmas that religious leaders undoubtedly experience, although his alternatives are perhaps somewhat extreme. People not only demand dogma, social commitment, or entertainment; they are also interested in other types of meaning, not least in belonging and togetherness. Between fundamentalism and a totally self-effacing liberalism, there are perhaps other alternatives for religion than the ones Bruce pictures.

Peter Berger's claim that the lofty God in ethical monotheism is vulnerable to secularization may lead us to reflect on other religious traditions than the Christian faith. As a monotheistic religion, Islam is vulnerable to secularization as well. However, Islam is also a lifestyle religion, where religiously based customs and rituals tend to dominate the everyday life of the believers. Such a connection between religion and everyday life might give Islam more of a protection against secularization than is the case for Christianity.

An argument against these various theories on the underlying forces of secularization is that they are too religiously myopic and fail to consider societal factors. The dynamics of secularization occur in an encounter between traditions of faith and social development. Thus, explanations of secularization can hardly stand alone.

5.11 Secularization on an individual level?

We have seen that a number of scholars claim that secularization addresses the grasp that religion has on society, which does not necessarily mean that individuals no longer are religious. Their major issue is that religion is losing its power and significance in society, and that religion has a more limited role in the private lives of individuals.

It is possible to propose a secularization theory that includes all three levels, that is, society, organizations, and individuals. Such a theory would argue that society is less dominated by religion, that the religious institutions have a very weak orientation towards the transcendent, and that religion has little meaning to individuals. However, our argument above was that the relationship between individual and societal secularization is not necessarily that close. Some scholars claim that societal secularization may lead to individual secularization, especially in the situation when socialization institutions do not promote religion. Other scholars argue that when the state withdraws from the religious sphere, a religious market will emerge and add greater vitality to organizational and individual religious life.

Here, it is useful to distinguish between a weakening of religion on an organizational level and on an individual level. One might agree that religion largely has lost power in society and that religious organizations are less popular than they once were. One might also claim that individual religiosity is as vital as ever, even if it is more detached from the authority of the churches and the religious leaders. We will discuss individual religiosity in more detail in Chapter 7. There, we will also discuss how detached is individual religiosity from established traditions.

5.12 Several great narratives

In 1979 French social theorist Jean-François Lyotard published his book *The Postmodern Condition* (English translation 1984). An oft-quoted claim from this book is that the great narratives are dead. This statement refers to a notion where overarching, holistic interpretations of society and existence no longer have vitality and credibility in an increasingly fragmented world. In this chapter, we have presented a number of great narratives, in the sense that they paint quite ambitious pictures of social and historical developments by stressing only a few characteristic features. Perhaps we can claim that the great narratives are still here, but that they are competing for credibility. Perhaps we can also claim, just to harmonize a little, that they describe various aspects of reality, where one or more features may occur at the same time. For empirically oriented sociologists, it is hardly advisable to choose one favorite story and cling to it at all costs. Instead, the great narratives should provide a basis for more empirical analyses that will help to develop these theories further.

6
Religion in the public sphere

Since the founding of sociology as a discipline, attempts have been made to under-stand the relationship between religion and the secular world. We have seen that many sociological classics took it for granted that processes of industrialization and modernization would eventually lead to secularization, or to religious differentiation, decline, and privatization (see Chapter 5). There was relatively widespread consensus within the sociology of religion over the privatization thesis until the late 1970s and early 1980s, when there was a sudden eruption of religion into the public sphere, not only in Europe but in Latin America, Asia, and the Middle East. Only then did many realize that differentiation did not necessarily mean that religion would remain in its assigned place in the private sphere and not enter the public arena.

There has been a widespread agreement in sociology that religion played an important role in traditional societies. Disagreement emerges regarding the analysis of religion in the public sphere in modern societies. One theoretical tradition, here represented by Max Weber, the early Peter L. Berger, Jürgen Habermas, and Steve Bruce, claims that with the spread of modernization, traditional religious institutions will decline or disappear and religion will become a private affair for the individual. Berger has, however, changed his position regarding this issue and supports a view that is closer to another tradition, here represented by Robert N. Bellah and José Casanova, who argue that religion can be a force for collective action, social unity, and political mobilization, even in modern societies.

The notions of the "public" and the "private" spheres refer here to the traditional dichotomous model of social relations that posits a separation between the domestic sphere of the individual, the family, and leisure, and that of dominant institutions, such as economic, legal, and political institutions. When this chapter is discussing religion in the public sphere, focus is primarily directed on the political sphere, including collectives that operate at different levels, such as the nation, the state, and civil society.

Below, we present five forms in which religion is expressed in the public sphere, that is, as the official religion of the state, civil religion, religious nationalism, public religion, and religious legitimation of political power. But before we do so, we will see how some sociologists have analysed the relationship between religion and politics in traditional and modern societies.

6.1 The diminishing role of religion in the public sphere

Marxist and liberal traditions in sociology have tended to agree that with the spread of modernization, religion would be removed from the public sphere, and this Western experience would eventually be replicated in other areas of the world. These notions, which depict relatively unilinear historical trends, were found in Marx, although Weber developed them in more detail.

In *Economy and Society*, Weber discusses the relationship between religion and politics by raising the problem of state legitimacy. He understands every social sphere to be influenced by structures of domination, which he defines as "the probability that certain specific commands (or all commands) will be obeyed by a given group of persons" (1968/1922, I: 212). According to Weber, all forms of domination require legitimation or self-justification whereby the rulers successfully uphold a claim that they govern by right in accordance with law, tradition, or a similar basis. He proposes three types of legitimate domination: traditional, charismatic, and rational–legal (see Section 8.7). Weber suggests a historical trend from traditional to rational types of authority. He claims that the consequence of rationalization and secularization is that the modern state is stripped of any metaphysical or religious legitimacy. He views secular legitimacy to be in a crisis, as modern society is left in a vacuum that formal rational law cannot fill (Turner 1991: 193).

Following Weber, Peter L. Berger in his early work analyses the relationship between religion and politics in traditional and modern societies in terms of the problem of legitimation. For him, legitimation has to do with the task of justifying the social order in such a way that institutional arrangements are made meaningful or plausible for the individual. In his book *The Sacred Canopy* (1967), Berger argues that religion historically has been the most widespread and effective instrument of legitimation. In this analysis of modernity, he focuses upon the de-institutionalization of meaning that he believes accompanies modernization. Modern Western societies are characterized by a process whereby religion has altogether retreated from the public sphere and into the private sphere. We have seen that whereas Berger offers a view of secularization in *The Sacred Canopy* (1967) that is more or less pervasive and historically inevitable, he later suggests that modernity can even create conditions that are favorable to religious resurgence or to counter-secularization (Berger 1999: 6).

Jürgen Habermas also follows Weber's theory of the inevitability of rationalization and secularization in many ways (see Section 4.1). For Habermas, the emergence of undistorted communication is a fulfillment of the Enlightenment ideal. Although discourses can include talk about the truth and rightfulness of religion, religion will not serve the emancipated communicative action in any fundamental way (Habermas 1984: 49–52). In order to achieve cultural modernity, science, morality, and art must be split off from traditional world-interpretation (Habermas 1982: 251). Thus, religion seems to be relatively unimportant for the communicative competence.

In *Politics and Religion* (2003), Steve Bruce argues that religion continues to be an autonomous force in contemporary politics. However, he attempts to show that this is not so much true for the modern, industrialized countries in the West, which are largely secular, but more so for other parts of the world and in religious traditions other than modern, Western Christianity. Rather than generalizing about all religions, Bruce attempts to demonstrate that the relationship between politics and religion differs according to the religious tradition in question. He compares several different religious traditions and shows that at least four factors are important for the ways in which religions have political consequences.

The first factor Bruce analyses is the nature of the divine. According to him, monotheistic religions, such as Christianity, Judaism, and Islam, are more rigid than the polytheistic religions, such as Hinduism, Sikhism, and Buddhism, which are more tolerant. The second factor has to do with the reach of the religion. He argues that religions that claim universal applications, such as Christianity and Islam, will often be readily attached to imperial ambitions. Yet, whereas Christianity has become so fragmented into nation-states where citizens have developed loyalties to their particular nation-states, such loyalties are weaker in most Muslim countries. For this and other reasons, Islam has retained a global consistency that Christianity lacks. The third factor Bruce discusses is the way the religions deal with religious diversity (especially religious practice). He claims that religions that control religious behavior, such as Islam, tend to be more conservative, strict, and also inhumane than religions that do not impose such control, as for example Christianity. The final factor Bruce analyses has to do with the relationship that a religion has with the state. He claims that there has been a closer relationship between Islam and the state than between Christianity and the state because Christianity recognizes a secular sphere apart from the religious sphere, which Islam does not.

Bruce believes that most conventional religions are incompatible with liberal democracy. However, the specific trait of modern industrial societies of the West is that they are largely secular. He argues that the Protestant Reformation was a vital component in the rise of liberal democracy because it played an important part in the rise of capitalism, it encouraged individualism and egalitarianism, and it created a context of religious diversity. This weakened religion and allowed the growth of secular societies and cultures. Bruce concludes that although religious cultures have contributed a great deal to modern politics, there are important differences in the political consequences of the major world religions. However, these causal relations rest on unintended consequences. It was, for example, not the intention of the Protestant reformers to contribute to the formation of liberal, secular democracies. Therefore, no representatives within any of the religious traditions can be blamed or honored for past events.

Weber, the early Berger, Habermas, and Bruce view religion in the West as bound to abdicate to the force of rationality and at length to retreat to a private sphere set apart from science and politics. Whereas Weber, Berger, and Bruce are concerned about the development they describe, Habermas' task is to protect Enlightenment culture not only from colonization by the institutions of money and power, but also from conservative traditions. In this way, Habermas celebrates the diminishing role of religion in the public sphere in Western societies.

6.2 The continued role of religion in the public sphere

Robert N. Bellah and José Casanova, in contrast to Weber, the early Berger, Habermas, and Bruce, claim that religion has and will continue to play a public role in modern societies. Bellah belongs to the tradition from Durkheim to Parsons, whose aim is to explain social unity in modern, specialized societies. He has developed a theory of religious evolution based on differentiation, postulating that religion has developed through five historical stages: primitive, archaic, historic, early modern, and modern (Bellah 1964). One of Bellah's assumptions is that society rests upon a moral religious understanding (Bellah 1975: ix). He regards society as a totality and the function of religion as to give meaning and motivation to the total system. For that reason, religion is a universal phenomenon. Even where prevailing religious symbol systems are rejected, the solutions of individuals and groups to fundamental problems of orientation and identity may be viewed as religious (Bellah 1972). Thus, he considers unbelief to be impossible (Bellah 1971).

Bellah discusses the relationship between religion and politics in terms of the problem of legitimation, which he defines as "the question whether existing political authority is moral and right or whether it violates higher religious duties" (Bellah 1980: viii). He postulates that in early modern or modern societies religion in the public sphere will take the form of a civil religion. Civil religion is a shared religious factor that is differentiated from church and state. According to Bellah, it consists of a set of transcendent ideals by which society is judged, integrated, and legitimated (Bellah 1967). Within a civil religion there are some societal ideals, as for example each individual's rights, which all members of society support. These ideals provide legitimation for the political institution, and they can also be used to criticize political leaders. Bellah claims that it offered legitimation for political institutions in early American history and carries the potential for renewal of this function in the modern United States. He also maintains that civil religion is a universal phenomenon, so that all societies will have some form of a civil religion (Bellah 1975: 3).

A more recent study of religion in the public sphere is conducted by José Casanova (1994). In his book, *Public Religions in the Modern World*, he begins with a critique of secularization theories, as postulated by Weber and the early Berger. He agrees with the notion that an irreversible historical process of religious differentiation has taken place in the West, but he questions whether institutional differentiation necessarily must result in the marginalization and privatization of religion. Instead, he argues that only empirical studies will demonstrate whether this is so. On the basis of historical sociological studies of public religion in Spain, Poland, Brazil, and the United States, he argues that since the 1980s a widespread process of "deprivatization" of modern religion has taken place throughout the world.

Casanova sees the fusion of the religious and the political as incompatible with the modern principle of citizenship. For him, established churches are also incompatible with modern differentiated states. By drawing on two different traditions in sociology, the comparative sociology of religion and theories of the public sphere and of civil society, he attempts to develop a new analytical framework. He uses the tripartite division of the modern democratic polity into state, political society, and civil society. Since each of these levels corresponds to a different form of public sphere, he argues that there can be in principle public religions at all three levels. He concludes that only public religions at the level of civil society are consistent with modern universalistic principles and with modern differentiated structures (Casanova 1994: 219). Casanova claims that the public interventions of religion in the public sphere in modern civil societies can no longer be viewed as antimodern religious critiques of modernity. Instead, they represent new types of normative critique of specific forms of the institutionalization of modernity. In this way, Casanova argues that the potential of religion raises questions for Habermas' secularist theory of modernity.

The sociologists discussed here differ fundamentally on at least two issues. Regarding the question of the public role of religion in modern societies, Weber, the early Berger, Habermas, and Bruce, on the one hand, maintain that because of advanced differentiation in modern societies, religion cannot offer legitimation for a total society, as Bellah claims. On the other hand, Casanova and the later Berger question whether institutional differentiation necessarily must result in the privatization of religion. Their approach is that this question must be a subject for empirical studies, not a priori theoretical assumptions. The second issue is related to the normative approach taken by some of these sociologists. Whereas Weber, the early Berger, and Bruce describe a development that they do not necessarily see as desirable, Habermas believes that the diminishing role of religion in the public sphere benefits modern societies. In contrast, Bellah calls for the normative aspects of civil religion. Furthermore, Casanova wants to advance the forms of public religion that exist on the civil society level. He believes that these forms of modern public religion will encourage the development of "the common good."

In the following, we will see that the assertion that religion was disappearing from the public sphere did not conform to the development that has taken place over the past two decades. The role of religion in the public sphere is a complex phenomenon that may be expressed in a variety of ways. Below, we will give an overview of this variety and examine the different ways in which religion appears in the public sphere – as the official religion of the state, civil religion, religious nationalism, public religion, and religious legitimation of political power.

6.3 The official religion of the state

Interactions between the state and established majority religious organizations are commonly discussed in terms of "church–state" relations. The concept of church is derived from the context of European established Christian religions. The modern understanding of state as a nation-state is rooted in European post-Reformation history. In discussions of church–state relations, there is often an implicit assumption that there exists a single relationship between two unitary but separate entities. However, the Christian assumptions in this dichotomy create problems when discussing non-Christian contexts. In the Muslim tradition, for example, a mosque is not a church. Whereas a church is a religious organization with registered members, a mosque is primarily a place of prayer and teaching. The closest approximation to "state" is the word *dawla*, which means a ruler's dynasty or his administration (Haynes 1998: 9; Norcliffe 1999: 157–8). Also, some religions, such as Hinduism, do not have ecclesiastical structures and, therefore, cannot pose a clerical threat to the secular state of India. In spite of this fact, Hinduism has still affected elections, political parties, and movements in India (Frykenberg 1993; Smith 1990: 39–42). For these reasons, the traditional conceptual framework of church–state relations is difficult to apply in several African and Asian countries (Haynes 1998: 8–9).

With these conceptual difficulties in mind, we may say that there are a number of church–state relations in the contemporary world. In this section, we will focus on the situation where there is one official religion of the state, in the form of either a confessional state or a state religion. In the case of the confessional state, one dominant religion has ecclesiastical authority over secular power and the religious leaders seek to shape the world according to their interpretation of God's plan. Although confessional states have been relatively rare in the twentieth century, religious leaders in some Muslim countries have attempted to build such states, as found in Saudi Arabia (Esposito 1999: 75), Sudan (Haynes 1998: 112–14; Mayer 1993), Iran, and Afghanistan during the Taliban regime (Esposito 1999: 264–5). In Iran, the Islamic revolution of 1979 led to the remaking of the political order into a Shi'ite theocracy. Since 1906, the country has had a constitution and a parliament, and the Pahlavis had established a bureaucracy on the Western model that divided governmental functions and the separation of powers. After the overthrow, Iran was declared an Islamic Republic. The Fundamental Law of 1979 explicitly established a theocracy by making sovereignty and legislation the exclusive possession of the One God and by firmly rejecting the separation of religion and the political order (Arjomand 1993). Whereas some Muslim countries have succeeded in building confessional states, others have opted for a secular state, as in the case of Turkey (Demerath 2001). However, the majority falls into a middle position.

The situation where there is an officially established faith in an otherwise secular state is found in Britain and the Nordic countries. We will take a closer look at Norway here. The church–state relations were first established during the Reformation as a dictate through a royal decree. In the 1600s, the fusion of political and clerical powers was strengthened, as state and king were perceived to be "of God's grace" and the church was under the power of the king. The new democratic constitution, introduced in 1814, changed the relations between people and the crown, but it did not introduce changes to the church–state relations. Indeed, it stated that "the Evangelical Lutheran faith is the religion of the state" and that the crown was the head of the church.

A religious liberalization took place during the nineteenth and twentieth centuries, which increased the independence of the church and transferred the power of the clergy to appointed councils or councils elected by the church members (Repstad 2002). Recently, issues relating to the integration and rights of non-Christian minorities, especially that of a fast-growing Muslim minority, have surfaced in Norway as in several other European countries. In 1969 a new law secured for all registered religious communities an equal amount of public funding, based on their number of members. Thereby, Muslim communities receive as much public support per member as state church parishes. On the basis of the argument that all citizens of Norway should have equal opportunities and rights to practice religion, suggestions have been made to separate church and state. These issues are not unique to Norway: recently, church and state separated in Sweden (Demerath 2001). The challenges posed by religious minorities making claims for equal opportunities are also pertinent in other European countries with a state religion, such as Britain (Beckford and Gilliat 1998).

One would assume that if church and state were separated, church–state relations would be relatively unproblematic. However, American sociologist of religion Nicholas Jay Demerath (2001: 36–7) points out that there has been a recent growth in church–state tensions in the United States. Issues of state intervention in the affairs of religious groups, and an increasing tendency among some religious groups to put forward claims in the public sphere, have caused controversy (Robbins 1989). Thus, in secular societies with a state religion, such as Norway, the national church is far from dominant. In the United States, where church and state are separated, church–state separation is far from absolute. In both cases, church and state continue to challenge each other.

6.4 Civil religion

The concept of civil religion has its origin in the eighteenth century when it was first posited by the French philosopher Jean-Jacques Rousseau (1981/1762), who believed that every society needed "a profession of faith which is purely civil" in order to integrate members into society. The sociological debate on civil religion appeared in the late 1960s when Robert N. Bellah (1967) suggested that there was an American civil religion, or a common religious factor that existed independently of church and state in the United States. An intense debate on this issue appeared among sociologists of religion in the 1970s and 1980s.

The religious dimension in the public sphere in the United States had been described by several American scholars, but Bellah was the first to develop a sociological theory of civil religion. He argues that because the processes of modernization imply that social and cultural sectors are no longer dominated by traditional religion, civil religion emerges as an alternative way by which modern societies are provided with identity and meaning. He defines civil religion as "a set of religious beliefs, symbols and rituals growing out of the American historical experience interpreted in the dimension of transcendence" (Bellah 1968: 389). In his studies of historical documents, such as the Declaration of Independence and the US Constitution, he cites several references to religion, and the frequent use of the analogy of God, who had led his people to a new land. References to a deity are also made in the inaugural addresses of American presidents. For example, George Washington spoke of "Great Author of every public and private good," John Adams used expressions like "Fountain of justice," and Jefferson talked about "that Being in whose hands we are." Bellah interprets these references as indicators of the beliefs and values of American civil religion (1972: 171–88).

Bellah argues that civil religion has several functions: it offered legitimation in early American history and carries the potential for renewal of this function today (Bellah 1980). Civil religion also has a potential for both integration and division (Bellah 1976), and it has the function of prophecy, referring to its normative aspects. According to Bellah, there is an understanding in American civil religion that society is responsible to a higher moral order. Following this notion, Martin E. Marty (1974) distinguishes between a "prophetic" version of civil religion, which calls the nation's attention to its offenses against the idealizations for which it stands, and a "priestly" version, which glorifies the nation and is a form of religious nationalism (see below).

Bellah (1975: 3) maintains that civil religion is a universal phenomenon. On this basis, a number of comparative studies have been conducted (Bellah and Hammond 1980; Harmati 1984, 1985; Liebman and Don-Yehiya 1983). Some scholars found legitimations for the state or the nation by reference to a transcendent reality (Baily 1986; Layendecker 1986), whereas others concluded that they did not find such legitimations (Hammond 1980). In the Nordic countries, with their state or national churches that include the majority of the population, some have claimed that if civil religion exists, it will do so more in connection with these churches than outside them (Furseth 1994; Repstad 1995a; Sundback 1984).

Bellah's theory of civil religion resulted in a scholarly controversy. His theory posed problems for empirical studies regarding the characterization of civil religion as a social phenomenon, and its distinction from other similar phenomena. Numerous participants in the debate focused on this question, and attempted to find a satisfactory definition of the concept (Gehrig 1981a, 1981b; Richey and Jones 1974). Also, his hypothesis led to controversies over operationalizations (Thomas and Flippen 1972; Wimberley 1979). In addition, his theory was disputed. The critics, who often belonged to the Weberian camp, were skeptical of Bellah's theoretical assumptions. American sociologist of religion Richard Fenn was one of the most severe critics. First, Fenn attacks Bellah's Durkheimian premise that the basis for society is a moral order. He argues that modern societies are characterized by differentiation. As a result, there is no common religious basis for moral order in society, but there is a plurality of meaning systems (Fenn 1970). Second, Fenn criticizes Bellah's analysis of civil religion's functions at different levels, that is, an individual level and a societal level. Fenn argues that religion cannot have a macro-cultural function, but that it can have functions for each individual (Fenn 1972). Finally, Fenn disagrees with Bellah that civil religion provides the basis for social integration. He believes that there cannot exist a total ideology in modern societies that the whole population will support. Therefore, there is no normative civil religion that will influence a whole nation (Fenn 1976). American sociologist Michael Hughey (1983) also points out that civil religious values cannot achieve transcendence and stand apart from and above the nation itself and its institutions. In spite of the controversies, the theory generated numerous historical and empirical studies of civil religion (see Mathisen 1989).

6.5 Religious nationalism

In contrast to Bellah's concept of civil religion as a transcendent universal religion of the nation, which legitimates but also criticizes the nation, religious nationalism represents a world-view in which the nation is glorified and idolized. In this way, religious nationalism is similar to what Marty (1974) terms "the priestly form of civil religion," which celebrates a nation's achievements, greatness, and superiority.

As noted, the modern sense of "nation" emerged in seventeenth- and eighteenth-century Europe, and several theories of modern nationalism have been proposed (Calhoun 1997; Smith 1983). One important theoretical distinction in a definition of the concept of nation is that between essentialism and constructivism (this distinction is also important regarding ethnicity and gender, see Chapters 10 and 11). Essentialism reduces diversity in a population to some single criterion held to constitute its "essence" or its most crucial character. Language, ethnicity, and religion may form such criteria. This is often combined with the claim that the essence is unavoidable or given by nature. It has been assumed, for example, that people are born with some inherent traits that make them part of a particular nation. Constructivism emphasizes the ability of people to define the world from their viewpoint. In the case of nationalism, constructivism focuses on the historical and sociological processes by which nations are created.

According to American sociologist Craig Calhoun (1997: 3), nationalism can also be termed, among other things, as what Michel Foucault (1972, 1977b) calls "a discursive formation," a way of speaking that forms consciousness. Nationalism is a way of thinking about questions such as collective identity, social solidarity, and political legitimacy that helps to produce a nationalist self-understanding and recognition of nationalist claims. In this sense, nations are "imagined communities" (Anderson 1983: 16), and nationalism is a distinctive form of "imagining" collective identity and social solidarity.

Although many nations do not form homogeneous groups, but consist of various ethnic, linguistic, cultural, and religious groups, the rhetoric of nationhood tends to treat the nation as an integral unit or as a type of group. Belonging to a group has an external definition, or a mark that identifies "we" and "them." Belonging to a group involves acknowledging this mark. In the case of a national group, such a mark can be, among others, a common territory, the nation as an integral unit, and a common descent and history. Religion can clearly be an element in many of these features (Ramet 1984: 149).

Territory is usually one of the most important aspects of nationalism. The nation-state has given its citizens a special way to look at the land, which in some cases becomes a kind of sacred space. The case of Jewish nationalism can serve as an illustrative example here. In the pre-modern form of Jewish nationalism there was a close connection between religion and nationalism. Their claim to the land derives from the idea that God gave sanction to the Prophet Samuel to establish a monarchy for the Israelites. However, the political movement that led to the formation of the state of Israel, Zionism, was thoroughly secular and represented a revolt against Jewish religion. Zionism was closely connected to socialism, and its goal was to establish in Israel an ideal society based on social equality, social justice, and productive labor. Since the mid-1950s a new emphasis on Judaism and Jewish tradition as a basis for collective identity emerged, and the combination of religion and ethnicity became increasingly important. Since the Six Day War of 1967 there has been a rise of militant religious groups who combine messianic theory and nationalistic politics. One such group is the religious ultranationalists, Gush Emunim or "bloc of the faithful," whose strategy has been to set up illegal settlements in the Occupied Territories. By revitalizing notions about the tie between the Jewish nation and the soil, which was also prevalent in secular Zionism, they provide religious legitimacy for expansionist policies (Biale 1983; Juergensmeyer 1993; Liebman and Don-Yehiya 1983).

Nationalism also draws upon its past and its future. The importance of history can clearly be seen in the formation of several European nation-states, where the writing of history became part of the nation-building process. In the course of a struggle for independence and freedom, there is also a strong interest in the future. One example is Afghanistan, where Islam became a significant ingredient in nationalist struggles and resistance movements in the 1980s (Esposito 1999: 264–5). The mujahidin were seen as freedom fighters who declared holy war (*jihad*) against the Soviet occupational forces, and their program was to replace the humiliations of Russian dominance with a new Islamic order.

According to the British professor of religion Ninian Smart (1983: 18–19), another important element in nationalism is the national hero, who might be a historical figure or a living person, and who must perform some act or acts that are assumed to be positive for the nation. There has been a resurgence of religion and nationalism in the former Yugoslavia (see Ignatieff 1993 and Ramet 1984), and in Serbia; for example, the role of "Emperor" Lazar is an illustrative example of a national hero. The Serbs claim to descend from the soldiers that Lazar led into battle in Kosovo in 1389. This area had been part of the contested frontier between Christian Europe and the expanding reach of Islam and Ottoman rule. In 1389 Lazar was killed here in a battle with the Turks, and Lazar and his men became symbolic heroes of the battle of Christianity against Islam on European soil. In the nineteenth century this battle became the founding myth of the Serb expansionist project and was a significant element in the Serb nationalism in the 1980s and 1990s. Even before the Yugoslav Federation collapsed, the Serb Orthodox Church marked what they perceived to be the territory of "Greater Serbia" by carrying Lazar's remains across "Serb land." After being actively nurtured by Serb leaders, the memory of these heroes became a firebrand used to legitimate attacks on Bosnian Muslims 600 years later (Ivekovic 2002: 524).

Although religion might be an element in nationalism, religion might also pose a threat to nationalism. Many nationalists find competition in loyalties to other groups, such as family and religious groups. This was one reason why Hitler had as his ultimate goal to abandon the Catholic Church (Lease 1983: 81). Furthermore, nationalism is not a universal religion, but can perhaps be viewed as more akin to a tribal religion (Smart 1983: 27). For that reason, those who belong to universal religions, such as Christianity, Buddhism, or Islam, will often remain ultimately skeptical about nationalism. One example is the two radical Islamic organizations, the Muslim Brotherhood of Egypt and the Jamaat-i-Islami (Islamic Society) in the Indian subcontinent, which appeared in the 1930s and 1940s. They were hostile to Arab nationalism as a secular ideology and viewed it as incompatible with the universalist mission of Islam (Esposito 1999: 67). Although religions can be used as reinforcements of nationalism, they can also be a source of opposition to nationalism.

6.6 Public religion

Whereas the notion of civil religion has struck some as representative of a "top–down" governmental development, the concept of "public religion" has been seen as a "from-the-bottom-up" proposal (Marty 1998: 393). In the literature, there are primarily two different meanings of the concept: first, as a form of civic faith, and second, as expressions of religion in the public sphere.

The term "civic faith" stems from a phrase coined by one of the founding fathers of the United States, Benjamin Franklin. In 1749 Franklin wanted to form an academy in Philadelphia, Pennsylvania. During a discussion about history, he claimed that studies of history are a good because they will "afford frequent Opportunities of showing the Necessity of a Publick Religion." Franklin meant that a public religion was useful "to the Publick," and that it would create "the Advantages of a Religious Character among private Persons" (Wilson 1979: 7). According to American historian John F. Wilson (1979), Franklin's claim that the necessity for a public religion to influence the realm of public life was due to its role in forming the public life of the nation. Franklin and the other founding fathers believed that unless moral values were present in society, the Constitution would be ineffective. They looked out on the thirteen colonies with their various denominations: although these denominations were different, they all were concerned with the common good. This common good was to be part of the public religion, which was to be demonstrated in the education system and in citizens' voluntary actions (Marty 1998: 393–4). The role of religion was, then, to help form good citizens and shape the common life.

The second meaning of the term "public religion" refers to one side of the traditional "public" and "private" distinction in social analysis. Public religion has to do with expressions of religious faith or behavior in the public sphere made by individuals, communities, voluntary associations, or governmental agencies (the state). An important study here is Casanova's (1994) comparative empirical study of five cases of varieties of public religion: Catholicism in Spain, Poland, Brazil, and the United States, and Evangelical Protestantism in the United States. In his study, Casanova analyses different patterns of separation of church and state. He divides each society into three levels – the state, political society, and civil society. As mentioned above, Casanova argues that since there is one public religion at each level, there can in principle be public religions at all three levels, but that this is not necessarily true for all societies. In his analysis, he gives examples of public religions at all three levels. We will here briefly mention some of these examples.

One example of public religion at the state level is the established Spanish Catholic Church. During the Second Spanish Republic (1930–36), the church was separated from the liberal state, which the church violently resisted. During the Franco regime which overthrew the Republic, the church used violence to reassert its status as the established church of a Catholic state. The final break between church and state in Spain came in the 1970s. Casanova thinks that public religion at state level often tends to be oppressive in the same way as the Spanish Catholic Church was. He does not believe that this type of public religion will survive in modern democratic societies.

Casanova found several forms of public religion in the political society. Some public religions at this level were religious movements resisting disestablishment, for example, the above-mentioned mobilization of Spanish Catholicism against the liberal revolution in the 1920s and 1930s. Other public religions in the political society have been religious groups that were mobilized against other political parties (as in Christian Democratic parties). Casanova also argues that the mobilization of religious groups in defense of religious freedom (which happened in Poland) is another form of public religion. So are some religious institutions that have demanded protection of civil rights (Catholic churches in Brazil).

If we are examining public religions at the civil society level, Casanova distinguishes between two types. One type is civil religion, for example Protestantism in nineteenth-century America. This type represents a unified understanding of society and is hegemonic. Another type of public religion at the civil society level is the public intervention of religious groups, such as the anti-abortion movement or the Catholic bishops' Pastoral Letters. The Pastoral Letters, which have spoken on issues such as peace, economic justice, and nuclear warfare, have been presented as the bishops' contribution to a public debate over these issues. This type of public religion represents one of several views on what the good society is and should be. It contributes in the public sphere with normative statements, and it contributes to the public debate. Since they are not hegemonic, public religions at the level of civil society are consistent with modern democratic societies (Casanova 1994: 219). Whereas several studies of public religion have a tendency to assume that there is only one public religion in each society, the strength of Casanova's study is that he differentiates between various public religions at different levels. In addition, he does not assume that every public religion has the same function in all societies, but he analyses how various public religions function in extremely different ways.

6.7 Religion and political power

Whereas the power of religion to legitimize the political sphere can be more or less indirect and implicit in the forms discussed above, there are situations where established religious institutions provide explicit legitimizations of the political power apparatus.

One example of this is the role played by the Orthodox Church in Serbia in the 1990s. We have mentioned above that the Serb Orthodox Church supported the Serb expansionist project even before the Yugoslav Federation collapsed. Indeed, the church came to play an important role in legitimating the Milosevic regime, as members of the church hierarchy and several priests took an active part in the wars in Croatia and Bosnia (Ivekovic 2002: 525–6). For example, Patriarch Pavle and several bishops toured the territories controlled by Serb forces and encouraged other Serbs to defend "their ancestral lands." Priests also justified blowing up mosques, and blessed war leaders who were publicly known as war criminals. One bishop, Filaret, even wore a military uniform and carried a Kalashnikov. When Milosevic signed the Dayton Peace Agreement in November 1995, a split appeared in the church. The militant faction of the clergy denounced Milosevic as "a traitor to the national cause" and became more nationalistic than the regime itself. They also demanded the resignation of Patriarch Pavle, because he did not support them. A more moderate faction, led by Pavle, sought a kind of accommodation with the Milosevic regime. As the policies of the Milosevic regime led to a series of disasters, the Serbian Orthodox Church continued to disagree as to which political leader to defend. Whereas some continued to support Milosevic, others supported the victorious candidate of the election in 2000, Vojislav Kostunica, who was a known Orthodox believer (Ivekovic 2002: 525–6). In this case, the Serb Orthodox Church became highly politicized and divided on the issue of which political leader to support.

6.8 Suggestions for research

The last three decades of the twentieth century witnessed a political revitalization of traditional religions in various parts of the world. This resurgence of religion in the public sphere challenged many of the assumptions of the sociological literature on religion and modernization, as found in the work of Weber, the early Berger, Habermas, and Bruce. Although Bellah proposed that religion would continue to play a public role in modern, specialized societies, the major problem with his theory is his functionalist assumptions, which led him to presuppose that religion is a necessity in modern societies. A more fruitful approach comes from Casanova and the later Berger, who argue that the question of the role of religion in the public sphere must be a subject for empirical studies, not a priori theoretical assumptions.

We have seen that the role of religion in the public sphere can take various forms: as part of the state apparatus, as a civil religion independent of the state and the established religious institutions, as an integral part of nationalism, as part of the public discourse, or as an explicit legitimization of political powers. The role of religion in the public sphere is a complex phenomenon. Therefore, it is questionable whether a single theory or approach can fully account for this. Instead, it is important to investigate in which cases and in which forms religion appears in the public sphere, and which conditions are conducive to its presence or absence. Another significant issue is to look at the effects of the fusion of politics and religion. Whereas it seems that religion in some cases promotes unity, in other cases, it becomes part of a society's fundamental conflicts (see Chapter 9).

Another problem for much sociology of religion when discussing religion and the public sphere is that it tends to be Western-centered. This is problematic in analyses of the role of religion in non-Western countries. It also poses difficulties as non-Western religious traditions, such as Islam, experience growth in the West and challenge accepted notions that religion no longer belongs in the public sphere. Altogether, there seems to be a need for better theories of the intermingling of public and private spheres, as Casanova (1994: 7) argues. We need to reconsider the changing boundaries between the various spheres, the possible roles that religion may have within those spheres, and the role religion may have in challenging these boundaries.

7
Individual religiosity

Sociology is not only engaged in attempts to explain group dynamics, social structures, and social change; it also focuses on the individual. A fundamental question in sociology is: why do social actors act the way they do? Another topic frequently found in recent sociological theory is the individual's view of self and how this view is formed, maintained, and changed. The sociological study of the individual emphasizes that ideas, pictures of self, and actions are affected by the social context. For example, sociology will argue that an individual's view of self is based on her or his interaction with others. A classical theorist here is George Herbert Mead (see Section 3.6).

A key question in the sociology of religion is: why do people become religious? Four different theories have attempted to provide an answer:

- Deprivation theory
- Socialization theory
- Rational choice theory
- Theory of the search for meaning and belonging.

As we present and discuss these theories, we will not make a sharp distinction between the individual religious commitments that are expressed in organized contexts, and more private and individual religiosity. The topic of our discussion will be various forms of individual religious commitment. We will examine how different social experiences support and weaken religious commitment. In doing so, we will focus on the relationship and tension between organized religion and individual religiosity. In more recent sociology, some have argued that individual choice is increasing in contemporary society, particularly in the area of cultural and religious ideas and actions. These ideas are also found in the sociology of religion, and they tend to interpret the individual as a free and searching agent who chooses her or his identity and world-view. Without doubt, several features suggest a growing individualism in contemporary society. We will attempt to diversify this picture and point out that there still are social factors that affect individual religiosity, even individualistic religiosity. Towards the end of the chapter, we will focus on religiously committed individuals, and briefly discuss secularization on the individual level.

7.1 Deprivation theory: Grievances create a need for religion

Deprivation theory maintains that religious commitment is a result of the compensation that religion provides in situations where individuals meet obstacles in life and search for alternative goals. The concept of deprivation in the study of religion can be traced back to Karl Marx. As noted, Marx claimed that religion would fulfill the needs of those near the bottom of the social hierarchy; that is, religion serves as a source of comfort and it takes the form of protest and reaction against injustice and misery (see Section 3.1). This idea, which made the transition into more current sociology almost intact, found support and was developed by numerous sociologists of religion during the twentieth century, most notable by American sociologist Charles Glock (Glock and Stark 1965).

Glock distinguishes between five forms of deprivation: economic, social, organismic, ethical, and psychic. Economic deprivation occurs when one has a difficult financial situation or is poor. Social deprivation implies that one has little access to the types of goods and qualities that are highly appreciated in society. If being male, white, young, and academically successful brings power and prestige, the deprived are found among women, non-whites, the elderly, and the academically unsuccessful. It also appears reasonable to interpret Glock to mean that loneliness and social isolation constitute forms of social deprivation.

Organismic deprivation means that some are in a worse situation than others due to sickness or physical disabilities. Ethical deprivation is the individual's experience of conflict between their personal value system and society's value system, and the discovery that the personal value system is not accepted by society, for example, when an individual or group of people feels, either directly or through the media, that they are in the middle of threatening moral decay. The last form of deprivation is, according to Glock's list, psychic deprivation, which occurs when individuals do not have the appropriate interpretation system to orient themselves in the world.

Norwegian sociologist of religion Jon P. Knudsen (1994) claims that a sixth type of deprivation should be added: existential deprivation. He argues that an individual may be rich, powerful, successful, popular, and in good physical and mental health, and still feel unhappy when it comes to existential questions on the meaning of life. Some would claim that Knudsen's proposal is included in Glock's form of psychic deprivation. Yet, if mental deprivation is interpreted more in terms of poor mental health, it may be justifiable to include existential deprivation as a distinct form of deprivation. Yet, if we do so, we must be aware that we use a fundamentally different understanding of religion than Glock does, that is, where religion no longer is seen as a response to deprivation, but as a quest for meaning. We will return to this understanding of religion later.

It is common to distinguish between absolute and relative deprivation. Absolute deprivation is also called objective deprivation, meaning that absolute standards, such as income, are used to make judgments regarding the deprivation of a group or a person. Strictly speaking, deprivation cannot be absolute in the sense that it is self-evident for all individuals in a given society. Some forms of agreement must be established, for example, among scholars, on how deprivation is to be measured and where the distinction lies between those who are deprived and those who are not. Relative deprivation refers to the subjective feelings and judgments an individual or members of a group have when they compare themselves or their social situation with others and find that their situation is worse. The idea is that people do not use absolute standards when they make such judgments, but they use relative standards or frames of reference. In an affluent society, for example, it may feel like a burden to have a visibly lower standard of living than the average, even if there are no acute needs for food, clothing, and housing.

A key notion in deprivation theory is that people who meet obstacles in their lives or are in unsatisfactory situations will search for alternative goals to compensate and that religion offers such compensation. The compensation may be religious in a restricted sense or more "earthly" in the sense that participation in a religious community provides a form of gratification or reward. Often these two sources of compensation are interwoven. The disabled person may have a religious hope of resurrection with a new body, and at the same time, experience care given by fellow believers. The bereaved, poor, or desperate person may seek comfort in the religious promise that they will meet loved ones in the afterlife, and at the same time feel that their pain is easier to bear through the sharing of grief and loss in a group setting. Likewise, the outsider may find support in a religious community that preaches the equality of everyone before God, a community where they are seen and included. Perhaps some may even have a smug feeling that they have joined a movement that has God on its side, which provides a contrast to the rulers of this world.

In the 1970s, deprivation theory was met with severe criticism that followed two lines: empirical and theoretical. Glock's claim that "It is those who are less gifted, the elderly, women and those who do not lead normal family lives, who are often the most involved in the church" (Glock and Stark 1965: 256) has been contradicted by innumerable empirical studies. These studies show that the lower economic strata fail to dominate established religious communities, and that the middle classes constitute the majority membership of established churches and new religious movements (Barker 1995; Hoge and Roozen 1979; Roof and Hoge 1980). This critique is relevant, although it must be borne in mind that Glock operates with several different forms of deprivation, not only financial poverty. Some empirical studies also provide support for deprivation theory. A Swedish study of people who increased their church attendance showed that they reported more problems than other church-goers when it came to self-purpose, marriage, and money (Pettersson et al. 1994). However, it is important to be aware of the fact that the tendency for personal difficulties to lead people to religious involvement is more likely to take place if these individuals went through a relatively strong religious socialization as children. Religion must be present in a person's mind as a possibility, something to return to in difficult times. Thus, socialization theory might be the real explanation for the increased religious activity in this case, a theory we will discuss in more detail below.

The theoretical critique of deprivation theory argues that it does not provide an adequate explanation of why some deprived people turn to religion whereas others fail to do so. Large groups of people are deprived but far from all of them opt for religion. A second critique claims that the theory tends to focus only on factors that create a demand for religion and ignore the activities that the religious communities initiate to attract new followers. A third argument is that religious commitment, as other forms of commitment, is a result of an individual's resources, not lack of resources. A person's most basic needs in life must be met in order for that person to pose questions about existence, and, even more so, get involved in organizational activities (Bibby and Brinkerhoff 1974).

Religion is a complex and multi-faceted phenomenon. It is naïve to assume that one factor will explain all forms of religiosity. Indeed, the reasons that lead one individual to join a religious movement may not be the same that encourage the same individual to maintain their commitment over time (Beckford 1975). Moreover, there are several forms of religious communities. Some stress their difference from society and protest against what they perceive to be contemporary decay. Other religious communities have a more harmonious relationship to society. Deprivation theory might be more useful in explanations of revival movements that demand individual or social change than in explanations of established faith communities. However, as we pointed out above, even new religious movements do not primarily find their recruits among the deprived.

7.2 Socialization theory: Long-term training teaches individuals to be religious

The fundamental idea in all socialization theory is that we think or act the way we do because we have been raised to do so during our upbringing. We speak of upbringing here in a wide sense, since it refers to more than the verbal teaching given by parents and teachers. Children also learn by watching what others do, not just by what they say. Parents, teachers, and other adults in their lives are important role models. In sociology, the concept of role implies the sum of expectations directed to a person in a particular position. Today, this concept is part of everyday language. We speak of gender roles, teacher roles, and so forth. Socialization is often defined as the process whereby individuals gradually grow into societal roles and learn to comply with the expectations that are directed to these roles. Roles may be more or less determinate for behavior. They prescribe the various tasks an individual must do, and often the ways in which each of them must be done. Roles offer some leeway as they relate to role behavior; for example, in Islam, different imams will fill their role in various ways, as long as they fulfill the most basic prescribed tasks. However, in all sociological role theory and socialization theory there is a premise that the individual largely thinks and acts in ways that are controlled by the expectations of others, which they eventually internalize and make their own. Successful socialization will result in individuals who form a social identity that creates commitment to specific norms and world-views, for example, religious world-views.

It is common to distinguish between formal and informal socialization. The decisive factor is whether the *sanctions* are formal or informal. Sanctions may be positive or negative, and are given as rewards or punishment for behavior, depending upon whether the prescribed norms are complied with or not. In situations where the prescribed norms are adopted and internalized by the great majority, a sanction system is hardly necessary. However, it is far more common that agents of socialization, such as parents and schools, employ sanctions to make socialization more efficient. The state and its representatives have strict formal sanctions, or penalties, at their disposal; for example, people can be arrested, though not arbitrarily in liberal and democratic societies. In some situations, the state has the right to take the custody of children away from their parents. The state also rewards certain initiatives and actions through monetary stimuli, or good grades, or public praise from people of authority. In a family, socialization commonly takes place through more informal sanctions, from a mother's friendly nod to the clever child to a hands-on feedback from a big brother to a troublesome little brother. The use of *negative* sanctions is often called "disciplining," while, if we discuss political opinions, the use of strict sanctions in this case is often labeled "indoctrination."

Socialization theory is relevant in a debate on religious growth. Several empirical studies show that religious parents have a far greater chance of having religious children than non-religious parents do. Of course, it is not difficult to find opposite examples where children oppose and leave their parents' religious faith and practice. However, this seems to be more prevalent in the history of literature than in statistics. The exceptions serve to remind us, though, that the human being is not a machine. A number of negative sanctions will often not lead to the desired behavior, but to rebellion, defiance, or spitefulness.

So far, the examples have centered on parents who are teaching their children. The literature on socialization often distinguishes between primary and secondary socialization. Primary socialization normally occurs during the first years of a child's life. This process points to the child's adjustment to social life, whereby the child develops from an instinctual being to a competent and disciplined social actor who has learned to take the expectations of others into consideration. Primary socialization includes, for example, the learning of language, the learning of relatively controlled behavior, and the learning of the ability to give and receive trust. This form of socialization takes place in primary groups, for example, a family. A primary group is often defined as a group with close and diffuse relationships. The group members know each other as whole persons, and their relationships are close and emotional, although not necessarily free of conflicts. The concept of secondary socialization is used to describe groups characterized by more targeted and limited social relations in, for example, schools, the workplace, and volunteer organizations. Secondary socialization often takes place in secondary groups, which provide more limited knowledge and skills that are used to fulfill specific social roles. In these groups, socialization is generally more formal, even if secondary groups also offer a great deal of informal learning. Besides receiving instruction on how to do their job according to the work description, the newcomer in the office also must learn, for example, where to sit during the lunch break, in order to keep up with the role they have been assigned.

In this area, there is a difference between sociology and at least some disciplines within psychology. Some schools of psychology have emphasized the effects that primary socialization have for our choices later in life. Parts of Sigmund Freud's theory of religion can serve as a good example (see Section 3.5). Several sociologists will argue that socialization during the adult phase has a great effect. This view will allow us to claim that not only do parents socialize their children, but children also socialize their parents. For example, many religious parents have changed their views on issues such as marriage and morality, especially cohabitation and homosexuality, and the agents of socialization have often been their own children.

In the history of sociology, socialization and role theories tend to be related to functionalism. Functionalist theory will argue that in order for society to achieve and maintain order and harmony, new members must be socialized into certain roles (see the discussion on Talcott Parsons, Section 3.7). Over time, concepts of roles and socialization have gained more widespread support than functionalism, and they have been adopted into general social psychology and sociology. (Socialization theory is described in most introductions to sociological theory – a good general introduction to socialization theory can be found in Giddens 1989.) However, socialization theories have continued to cause controversy. An oft-quoted criticism was offered by sociologist Dennis Wrong (1961), who opposed "the over-socialized picture of mankind" presented by socialization theory. He claimed that the descriptions of internalization of norms were too harmonious. They disregarded the fact that a person might have inner conflicts during the socialization process. Furthermore, the individual is more calculating and goal-oriented than socialization theory suggests, which paints the picture of the individual as a being without willpower. Wrong also criticized socialization theory for interpreting conformity as internalization of norms and refusing to admit that conformity can be the result of coercion or force. He also maintained that socialization theory tends to exaggerate the idea that the individual seeks acceptance by others, and thus unilaterally considers human action to be a result of the expectations of others. Even if a fundamental notion in sociology is that the individual thinks and acts in the context of other people, it is deterministic to assume that individual ideas and actions are fully determined by the expectations of other individuals. A general weakness of socialization theory is that it lends itself far better to explaining continuity than change.

Socialization theory can still be relevant as an explanation of some forms of religiosity. It is particularly useful in the situation where individuals have grown up within established and taken-for-granted religious frameworks. In some cases, these frameworks include entire societies, as in a unified religious culture. In other cases, they are based on close networks and relationships that take place in a religious subculture, often isolated from secular society. In the latter case, it is reasonable to explain individual religiosity as a form of adaptation and learning.

Some theories supplement and expand socialization theory. Scholars who study ethnicity, nationalism, and religion will tend to argue that if all of these elements support a similar world-view, they constitute an extremely strong socialization factor (see Chapters 9 and 10). Another socialization factor is the local community. American sociologist of religion Wade Clark Roof conducted a study, *Commitment and Community* (1978), which showed that people with strong ties to their local communities had a higher religious commitment than people with looser communal ties and a stronger national and international orientation. To be valid, such "localism theory," as it was called, assumes that the local community is relatively dominated by religion. However, there are examples of members of small religious minorities who virtually have to turn their backs on their local communities to maintain their religious commitment, and who instead seek support in large gatherings that draw people from a variety of areas.

In modern times, society no longer offers a total religious world-view. Some local communities are able to stimulate religious socialization, as found in Roof's (1978) study. However, the family seems to constitute the most important religious vehicle of socialization. Parents, grandparents, and siblings are, in some instances, religious role models. Close family members tend to stay in touch, particularly when they live close to each other, but this is often true even across relatively long distances. In this way, the family of origin seems to continue to be important for the development of religious commitment, even if social and geographic mobility will tend to weaken this influence. In addition, choice of spouse seems to affect religious commitment. For example, mixed-religion marriages tend to result in religious passivity. Religion seems also to be a factor that has less importance in choice of spouse than it used to have (McGuire 1997). This fact can be seen both as a cause and an expression of secularization.

The validity of socialization theory tends to be questioned in a religiously diverse society. Diversity implies the visibility of various forms of faiths and world-views in the media and in everyday life. Some sociologists argue that diversity increases individual reflection and choice awareness (see Giddens, Section 4.7). Thus, diversity creates difficulties for maintaining a theory that argues that the individual acts without reflection, but according to roles and socialization. Below we will present a theory that claims that individuals are goal-oriented and act according to their calculations of potential risks and rewards. This theory is applied to religious commitment. Later, we will introduce a more inclusive perspective on religious commitment, which retains the premise that the individual is goal-oriented, but expands the notion of the types of goal the individual may have.

7.3 Rational choice theory: Calculated benefits lead to religion

Rational choice theory has been introduced as a new paradigm in the sociology of religion (Warner 1993). Inspired by economic theory on how individuals act in the economic market, it expands this notion to all aspects of life, such as friendship, love, and religion. According to rational choice theory, social actors will always seek to obtain their goals with the least amount of risk and cost involved. They will assess the situation in a rational way and attempt to obtain the best possible overview of alternative actions. They will tend to choose what maximizes their rewards and minimizes their costs. Rational choice theory has found a growing amount of support in the sociology of religion over the past twenty years, and the most influential scholar within this tradition is American sociologist Rodney Stark.

Rational choice theory argues that individuals turn to religion because they see that it gives them some sort of benefits or rewards. They will join the religious groups and movements that will give them the most rewards. As a consequence, religious movements that have a definite profile and offer a greater amount of rewards will achieve more support than religious movements with a more diffuse profile and fewer rewards (Iannaccone 1994). The introduction of rational choice theory into the sociology of religion has led to heated debates, where sociological reasoning has tended to be fused with views on church politics. Sociologists with ties to conservative and Evangelical Christian communities tend to claim that strict, conservative faith communities will have more appeal, whereas sociologists who support more liberal mainstream churches tend to claim that strict religious movements will repel large groups of people in modern, religiously diverse societies (Kelley 1978).

Rodney Stark and his collaborators, as proponents of rational choice theory, argue that all human beings want eternal life. The religious movements that offer the most convincing promises of eternal life will consequently win the greatest amount of adherents (Stark and Bainbridge 1987). However, the notion that individuals design their religiosity based on the rewards they gain can also be used to argue against the idea that whoever promises the most appeals the most. If rational action is to reach a goal with a minimum of cost, one could argue that individuals will tend to live a decent and good life without religious involvement, because they assume that God will accept them as they are and not ask much more of them. Hence, rational choice theory can also be used to explain the fact that there are large groups of people around the world who demonstrate a relatively low level of religious involvement. However, the proponents of rational choice theory have presented the strict, conservative religious alternatives as the most attractive. When they attempt to explain why participants in movements that demand a high level of religious commitment devote so much effort to their religious practices and accept the strict discipline that such movements enforce, they argue that the participants have paid such a high admission fee that they want to reap the benefits that their involvement offers. High investments yield strong commitments. They also claim that it is rational for the movements to set high standards for involvement and accept a lower number of participants, as they do not benefit from free riders (Iannaccone 1994).

The arguments against rational choice theory in the sociology of religion are the same as in general sociology (Young 1997). Steve Bruce provides a summary of the critique in his book *Choice and Religion* (1999). The critics voice doubt that individuals always have clearly defined and stable preferences. They argue that individuals' preferences and goals shift over time, and that they tend to harbor a great deal of ambivalence. The field of religion is in and of itself an arena where the comparison of alternatives may pose a great amount of difficulties.

Many scholars question the idea that social actors are as oriented towards their self-interests as the theory assumes. A genuinely sociological argument is that the theory is too individualistic because it assumes that social actors are disconnected from social and cultural contexts. It is also difficult to explain every established social structure from the premise of individual choices made by millions of people. One does not have to defend a deterministic view of social structures even if one admits that social roles, traditions, power structures, and political institutions seem to act as independent factors. Although these factors can be changed, they are difficult to change, at least from a short-term perspective.

Some critics also ask if social actors always are as calculated as the theory assumes. Proponents of socialization theory will argue that if their theory has an over-socialized image of a human being, rational choice theory's image – that of the economic human – is under-socialized. Some sociologists also claim that individuals do not necessarily aim at maximizing their own benefits, but they are often content with a sense of satisfaction: if there is an alternative that is good enough, individuals will tend to settle for that (Perrow 1986).

In spite of this critique, rational choice theorists have made a valuable contribution to the sociology of religion by bringing the supply side into the academic debate on why people become religious. We have seen that deprivation theory only deals with the ways in which religious demands or needs arise. Socialization theory also attempts to explain how people – relatively unconsciously – demand religion. In contrast, rational choice theory argues that the use and management of resources by providers of religion make a difference. Of course, this argument can be taken too far, to the point where one assumes that a high level of activity automatically will lead to success. It is perhaps not a coincidence that this theory has found support in evangelical groups that favor church growth. This theory is clearly more encouraging for a religious activist than a more deterministic secularization theory. A number of recent empirical studies also confirm that there is a relationship between effort and result. A Swedish study shows, for example, that congregations that offer a greater variety and frequency of church services also witness an increase in church attendance (Pettersson 1994).

Rational choice theory can in many cases shed light on important matters that those involved in an activity have been reluctant to examine. For example, in religious contexts, people with religious power often express unselfish ideals and rationales. It may then be revealing and liberating to remind them that unselfish rhetoric does not necessarily mean one has genuinely noble reasons for one's actions. However, used as a complete and generally valid interpretation key, the rational choice perspective becomes too single-minded and constraining in relation to human practice. The perspective seems to be more relevant in connection with selling and buying than in connection with individual religious life. We still do not choose our religion with the same type of rationality we use to choose detergents. As claimed by Steve Bruce (1999), rational choice explanations of religion will only be valid in a society where choosing religion has become unimportant and trivial. We have not come to the stage where people change religion as easily as they switch to a new brand of car. It might also be tempting to add that even the brand of car is occasionally chosen according to the norms found in the social and cultural context.

It appears reasonable to argue that the rational choice perspective describes the world of men better than the world of women. Several studies conclude that women tend to be more focused on responsibility and care for others than men. A sociologist might want to add that these gender differences are due to social and cultural traditions and relationships of power rather than inherent biological differences. Clearly women also can act in an instrumental way motivated by self-interest.

It is not by chance that this theory primarily has emerged in the United States, although it is controversial there as well. The United States tends to be more dominated ideologically by individualism, liberalism, and competition than other regions of the world, and it has never had the type of strong and dominating central state power as found in several European countries. These historical facts are reflected in the field of religion. The United States has never had a strong state church that was interwoven with political power, but its church history is characterized by competition among several denominations. It is therefore easier to find support for rational choice theory in American studies than in European studies.

The explanation of individual action as a calculated choice to maximize benefits or rewards seems to be more relevant in urban, individualistic societies than in traditional, stable societies. A possible strength of this perspective is that it describes a type of action that has become increasingly common in capitalist societies. Here, we have reached a point where sociology should take a step back and reflect morally on the possible social consequences of its analyses. If we explain all actions as results of selfishness, we may promote a self-fulfilling prophecy.

7.4 Religion as a search for meaning and belonging

An important aspect of rational choice theory is that it maintains the idea that the social actor is rational, which constitutes a contrast to social deterministic theories that tend to argue that actors are passive, irrational beings. Yet, we have pointed to one of the limitations of this approach, namely that it has a fairly restricted view of the types of goals actors have. As we continue to present different attempts at answering the question of why people become religious, we will maintain the idea that the individual is goal-oriented and reasonably rational, but we want to expand the notions of individual goals and purposive rationality. On this basis, individual religiosity can be seen as an expression of a search for meaning and belonging. Here, we will first focus on the search for meaning.

This section deals with the field of sociology that has been called phenomeno-logical, interpretative, and hermeneutic sociology. Whatever the term, this field of sociology opens up the idea that the individual has the ability and consciousness to set meaningful goals. The individual does not automatically respond to the impulses from the environment, but is a conscious being. In order to understand human action, the social scientist must understand the actor's motives, goals, and intentions. Individuals act on the basis of the social context in which they find themselves. Their actions are based on their perceptions and interpretations of the context, on the basis of the meaningful frames they construct. If we take a look at Max Weber's (1968/1922) action theory, we find that he distinguished between four forms of action. Traditional action is controlled by habit and tradition and is more or less conducted automatically. This form of action is easily associated with socialization theory. Affective action is controlled by emotions. Vindictiveness is an example of an affective force, which the actor will not necessarily want to admit. The third form of action is value-rational action, which is action motivated by moral values or ideals. The fourth form of action is purposive-rational action. In this case, the social actor chooses means and goals from the premise of purposive-rational calculations of what will lead to the desired goal. It is inherent in Weber's theory that purposive-rational goals are not necessarily selfish. To clarify the difference between value-rational and purposive-rational action further: some actions may appear to be rational based on purposive rationality, but they are rejected for moral reasons. For example, a scientist may see that the testing of new medication may help humanity in the long run, but she or he may reject the experiments because they will harm the research objects. Thus, value-rational action tends to include more duty ethics than consequence ethics.

Max Weber is a classical sociologist within interpretative sociology. Some contemporary sociologists have continued his understanding of social action in the area of general action theory and the sociology of religion. It is particularly important to explore what we take for granted on an everyday basis in our interpretation of reality. Our perceptions of reality are generally dependent on what Peter L. Berger (1967) calls a plausibility structure, where common perceptions are developed in a continuous negotiation process regarding reality, through social interaction and conversation. Major portions of the perceptions of reality are taken for granted and are not thematized or negotiated. For most of human history, religion has been an important supplier of meaning and order to interpretations of the world. The individual is a being who searches for meaning and order. However, sometimes new and different social experiences bring credibility crises to old and inherited perceptions of reality, religious and secular.

The explanation of individual religiosity as a quest for meaning has come under attack. The argument is that it is based on a cognitive and intellectual understanding of religion (Hamilton 2001). Nevertheless, Weber argues that the need for meaning is both intellectual and emotional. He claims, followed by Berger, that the need for meaning is even more important when the individual faces suffering and evil. Religion has traditionally been an important supplier of theodicies. The term "theodicy"derives from Christian theology, but it is given a broader meaning by Weber and later by Berger (1967). A theodicy is a religious explanation and legitimation of experiences that threaten the meaningful order. Examples of such experiences are accidents, suffering, evil, injustice, and death. One form of legitimation is, for example, the notion that innocent and good people will be compensated for their suffering later in this life or in the next life. Another form of legitimation is the idea that the mighty and unfair will receive their punishment in due course.

Secularization theory (see Section 5.5) deals largely with the decreasing importance of religion in modern society as a supplier of meaning. An illustrative example is found in a survey among members of the Church of Norway (Høeg et al. 2000). When the respondents were asked if Christianity gives meaning to their lives, the most popular response was "Christianity tells me something that gives meaning in some situations."

The sociological focus on meaning and interpretation as a tool to understand social life has become relatively popular during the last thirty years or so. This is part of a general trend in the social sciences and the humanities that emphasizes language, interpretation, and meaning. This development can be seen as a reaction to Marxist and other structurally oriented analyses that tended to stress social structures as stable and determinate factors that control people's lives. However, a one-sided focus on meaning and interpretation represents a problematic scientific idealism. When keywords such as social class, technology, work, and production are replaced by identity, meaning, and symbol, there is a chance that fundamental material and economic structures as well as power structures are ignored. Perhaps it is a banal argument, but no less important, that there are very real barriers and hierarchies in the world that cannot simply be interpreted away through increasing individual awareness.

We mentioned that the meaning perspective has been criticized for its intellectual view of religion. As a result, a common argument is that religion must be understood as a quest for both meaning and belonging. In Meredith McGuire's (1997) introduction to the sociology of religion, she proposes that we must view meaning and belonging as equal factors in our attempts to understand why people become religious. People not only seek what is meaningful; they also seek community and belonging. Needless to say, one person may want to stand alone and find God, whereas another person may want to enjoy the religious community without giving much thought to its ideological content. Yet these two aspects will tend to be closely intertwined and reinforce each other. If people share a common faith, they will often find it attractive to be with like-minded people, and this sense of belonging will tend to strengthen the credibility of the religious universe.

7.5 How embedded? How individualized?

A major theme in contemporary sociology and social theory is the individual disconnection from social and cultural structures. This trend is expressed in several ways. On the one hand, the modern self has far more freedom than previous generations did when it comes to choosing beliefs and practices. On the other hand, the modern self cherishes individual choice as a value more than the older generations did. Social anthropologist Marianne Gullestad (1996) found in her analysis of autobiographies of ordinary people that there is a generational transition from the ideal of "being useful" to "being oneself."

Contemporary Western societies witness a wide range of diversity regarding interpretations and forms of life. Even conservative and traditional individuals must choose their approach as one of several alternatives. According to Peter L. Berger (1979), human beings have gone from "destiny to choice." Sociologist Robert Wuthnow (1998) describes American religiosity as a shift from *dwelling* to *seeking*. This shift implies that loyalties to religious communities have been undermined. Robert Bellah and his colleagues also describe this trend in their book *Habits of the Heart* (1996). Here is told the story of a young nurse from California, Sheila Larson, who describes her own highly individual religion: "It's Sheilaism. Just my own little voice." It is hardly possible to be more individualized than Sheila when it comes to religion. She creates her own religious traditions as she freely chooses some elements she finds in contemporary culture and religion and rejects others.

Another aspect of religious individualism is the subjectification of religion. This trend includes a strong skepticism in regard to authority. The individual's own feelings constitute the criterion for truth, not an external religious authority. Therefore, it is considered more valuable to be "on a path to truth" than to have found all the right answers. This approach rejects the right of religious leaders to dictate the content of one's faith and also tends to label all religious and moral admonitions as fanaticism.

The transition from dogma presented from the top down to the individual search for truth is not unique to religion. We find skepticism towards authorities in contemporary art, culture, and politics. Religious individualism can also be traced within certain religious traditions themselves, such as Protestantism. Martin Luther has been described as a pioneer of Christian individualism, with his critique of papal hierarchical authority. This may be true, even if there has been a tendency for liberal Protestantism to modernize Luther. Peter L. Berger (1967) argues that the Age of Enlightenment, along with Pietism, constitute the historical roots of religious individualism and subjectivism. Pietism in the 1600s and 1700s was admittedly often combined with dogmatic orthodoxy. However, since it placed a major emphasis on the subjective experience as a criterion of true religiosity, it laid the groundwork for religious individualism and critique of authorities. Religious experiences do not easily lend themselves to regulation and standardization – even if a sociologist would be tempted to claim that perceptions and emotions do not derive from an empty social space.

It is important to point out that even conservative religious traditions do undergo change. The Christian revival movements of the 1800s voiced a critique of contemporary societies and cultures. At the same time, they were expressions of the religious individualization that characterized this time period. Several contemporary sociologists of religion claim that this trend is taken even further today, as there is a tendency to shift from a focus on authority to a focus on authenticity.

The demand for authenticity or sincerity regarding one's world-view has been important in different traditions. It appears in revivalist movements and their emphasis on individual conversion, as well as in leftist circles and their ideal of honesty and courage. In contemporary Islam in the West, there is also a search for a "true" form of Islam, devoid of cultural baggage. It is possible that today, in what some call the postmodern era, these demands for sincerity are no longer as severe as they once were. Perhaps it is more legitimate today to enter various religious communities, and even take part in their rituals, without fully supporting the official dogma or even having a definite faith in them. It seems that some people participate in rituals with an attitude of playfulness and experimentation, with an eye to aesthetics, and with a sense of humor, and that their lack of total dedication is not labeled superficial or hypocritical. To some extent, aesthetic attitudes seem to characterize contemporary private religiosity, and they also seem to affect organized religion.

The following descriptions can constitute useful hypotheses in studies of religious change in the contemporary Western world:

- A diminishing emphasis on God's power and strength, and a growing emphasis on God's love and presence.
- A transition from personal to impersonal images of God, with a focus on the power and the energy of the divine.
- Anthropological and functional arguments for becoming religious. A turn from dogmas of redemption and damnation to mental well-being.
- A more optimistic view of the human being, with a change from self-denial to self-realization.
- A more optimistic view of the world, with a change from the world as sinful to the world as a gift from the divine to mankind.
- Increasing emphasis on narratives, symbolic actions, and metaphors, with decreasing emphasis on cognitive and dogmatic verbal statements.
- A transition from cognitive claims to expressions and experiences.

These issues are relevant in studies of people who belong to very different religious traditions, such as Christians, Muslims, Buddhists, and Hindus. They are even more relevant in studies of New Age religious movements. British scholar of religion Paul Heelas (1996) calls New Age, for example, a self-celebrating religion that sanctifies modern life.

So far, we have argued that the religion practiced by the large majority of people in the West tends to be critical of tradition, critical of authority, subjective, eclectic, and focused on identity and self-realization. The image of the contemporary religious person found in the media depicts a person who is on their own path, freely searching for meaning and spirituality. Perhaps this image exaggerates religious individualism. Scholars who study religion are also part of contemporary society and affected by it. Their picture may be colored by the fact that they belong to social groups that tend to emphasize individuality and spirituality. Their picture may also occasionally correspond to their own sympathies toward religious diversity. Therefore, we will offer four objections against the use of a general thesis on religious individualization:

- Such a thesis tends to overlook the fact that individual religiosity is often passed on through social interactions. Individual religiosity should be understood on the basis of its social context.
- Such a thesis tends to conceal the variety in which religion is expressed within different social strata and groups in society.
- Such a thesis fails to capture the fact that the individual's religious universe is continually constructed in a dialogue with established religious traditions.
- Such a thesis conceals the fact that large groups of people continue to be highly involved in established religious communities.

Below, we will continue to elaborate on these issues, particularly the relationship and tension between individual religiosity and organized religion.

7.6 The social basis of individual religiosity

As noted, we must bear in mind that even individual religiosity is passed on through social interactions. It is simply not true that individuals invent their own world-view in a void. Private religiosity and religious individualism are constructed on the basis of social experiences. The ability to cherish freedom of choice and self-realization does not come out of the blue – it is learned. It is reasonable to assume that the ideal of the individual's search for their own world-view will find support in societies that are characterized by a relatively high degree of individualism. Some sociologists take this argument further and describe contemporary individualism as a result of the economic system that increasingly dominates the world, namely the capitalist market economy. As consumers, we are asked to choose freely among goods and services brought to the market, and we are encouraged by advertising and the media to choose the right item just because we "deserve it." It would be strange if this pick-and-choose approach to life did not affect the area of culture and religion (Lyon 2000).

Because people live in different social contexts and have a wide variety of experiences, sociology will argue that their interpretations of life are colored by these experiences. This is not a novel idea. Max Weber (1964/1922) provided an outline of the variety of religion in different social classes that makes for fascinating reading. His theory is somewhat simplistic, and we must keep in mind that he does not propose a deterministic relationship between social class and religion. According to Weber, the religious needs of a group are affected by the nature of their interest situation and their position in the social structure. A society that suffers from an acute struggle to survive will have a religion that primarily serves as support for survival, and it will be oriented toward practical matters. Economically and politically advantaged groups assign to religion the primary function of legitimizing their own life-pattern and situation in the world. Underprivileged groups are more inclined toward religious ideas that promise future compensation for present unhappiness. Furthermore, Weber thinks that peasants have a general tendency to believe in magic and animistic magic or animism because they are dependent upon uncontrollable forces of nature. The middle class is inclined to embrace rational, ethical, inner-worldly religious ideas. Some groups are not very religious at all. Warriors are too proud to subject themselves to a God. Bureaucrats are not much given to emotion, so they generally embrace a rational form of religion. Businesspeople are practical materialists, and the working class is characterized by indifference to or rejection of religions common to large groups of the modern bourgeoisie. Religious specialists, priests, are more intellectual than magicians, so they will tend to develop a more ethical faith in God.

Weber did not suggest that ideas are purely reflections of social class interests. Instead, he argues that ideas must be available in the social and religious context. An additional factor is religious intellectuals, such as charismatic prophets, who play an important role in the diffusion process of specific ideas. Once these ideas are established and have gained acceptance, they tend to become important social factors in and of themselves. For Weber, ideas are able to play a significant role in times of uncertainty and instability. Nevertheless, the diffusion of new religious and ethical ideas is dependent upon a social basis.

Social anthropologist Mary Douglas (1982b) has introduced an interesting but controversial theory on the relationship between world-view and social position. Her argument is that a person's world-view is greatly affected by their experiences. Therefore, it is relatively easy for individuals who live in hierarchical contexts to subjugate themselves within stable hierarchical religious systems. Individuals who are powerless and rejected by the majority will have a tendency to become fatalists and believe that their lives are controlled by unknown powers. People who live in a market economy will become religious individualists, preoccupied with self-realization, critical of authority, and unfaithful to traditions. Finally, those who grow up and live in conflictual contexts will spend their energy on discussing what is accepted and what is not.

This is an extremely schematic theory. Douglas has been criticized for her deterministic picture of religion. For her, religion is a passive reflection of society. Nevertheless, she discusses four categories of social positions and corresponding religious forms in contemporary society, not just religious individualism. In this way, she presents a more nuanced picture than the unambiguous and massive religious individualization discussed by several other scholars.

In addition to social class, gender is also an important differentiating factor in religion. Specifically, empirical analyses show that women tend to score higher on most measures of religiosity than men do. We will discuss gender and religion in more detail in Chapter 11.

7.7 Popular religiosity: A continual discourse with established religious traditions

Sociological surveys on religion have often been criticized because they tend to measure individual religiosity as belief in the official doctrines of particular religious traditions. Questionnaires often list established institutional patterns of behavior, such as prayers, and established religious doctrines, such as belief in God, as alternatives. Furthermore, the religious profiles of the respondents have been measured on the basis of the distance between their responses and that of the official doctrine or established form of proper religious behavior. This critique is absolutely relevant. If individual religiosity is measured on the basis of categories provided by established religious institutions, the picture of an individual's religiosity will be incomplete and misleading. This is particularly true in modern times when individual religiosity often exists outside and independent of established institutions.

However, it is easy to move too far in the opposite direction, overlooking the fact that individual religiosity tends to develop as a discourse with established traditions and institutions. Needless to say, various societies reveal different patterns. In the Nordic countries, empirical studies suggest that the Lutheran tradition has had a greater impact in Finland, Norway, and Iceland than in Sweden and Denmark (Botvar 1993). On the other hand, Danes and Swedes score higher on measures for alternative religiosity than do the inhabitants of the other countries.

This is a difficult field due to problems of measurement. At what point is it reasonable to conclude that a respondent "believes in" reincarnation or astrology? The ways in which the questions are posed will have a major impact on the outcome. It is also misleading to focus on new findings and new trends and overlook the long-term trends. In a Western context, a growing support for alternative religiosity or relatively new minority religions, such as Islam, Hinduism, or Buddhism, may lead a scholar to exaggerate the support for these traditions and overlook the fact that the large majority still supports the Christian tradition. What does it mean to "believe in," anyway? In some contexts, to believe in something implies a strong and dedicated commitment. As it relates to alternative religions or New Age religions, it seems that people's attitudes are more characterized by openness and curiosity than finding a deep personal faith. It might be exciting to read this week's horoscopes in a magazine, but few will choose a boyfriend or a college based on the position of the stars. Moreover, it is possible that the media exaggerate the support for alternative religions and new religious movements in the Western world. The media are generally negative to such movements, and news on this issue provides exotic material which the media relish.

Even if most people in the West continue to draw on Christianity when they construct their own faith, it is not likely that they will accept or swallow every part of this tradition. This seems particularly to be true as it relates to dogma. Several European surveys show that belief in heaven receives a far higher score than belief in hell, and that the sharp dualism between redemption and perdition is waning (Barker et al. 1992). The idea that Christianity is the only true religion has been considerably undermined. In fact, it is quite common, even for active church members, to state that Christianity is true for themselves and, at the same time, say that other religions also hold elements of truth. Again, we see the tendency towards subjective and functional validation of religion. There are of course also several examples of persons who turn away from religion. However, studies show that their negation and discourse on religion continue to be colored by the dominant religious tradition (Furseth 2006).

A common European pattern seems to be that the majority of the population belong to one or two dominant churches and use them for rites of passage, whereas only a fraction actually attend church services on a regular basis, a pattern described by British sociologist of religion Grace Davie in *Religion in Modern Europe* (2000). Inspired by French sociologist of religion Danièle Hervieu-Léger (2000), Davie considers religion to be a form of collective memory. Specifically, consider all the churches and cemeteries with Christian symbols to be found all over Europe. Even if the churches are far from full, they have not disappeared either. Based on this situation, Davie introduces the concept of "vicarious religion" to describe Europe, arguing that Europeans are just as religious as other groups of people, only in a different way. Europeans have a collective memory of dominant churches, often linked with political powers. Therefore, the churches are viewed as a public good. It is nice to have them, but they should not be too intrusive in everyday life. Most Europeans are content with the fact that the churches take care of religious matters on behalf of the population, and they connect with the religious "chain of memories" in critical or solemn situations. It is striking how the dominant churches take control of public grief in the event of major accidents or disasters, even in countries that are seemingly very secular.

Several Europeans view the church as an anchor in their lives, even if they do not attend on a regular basis. Swedish sociologist Per Pettersson (2000) conducted interviews that support Davie's argument. He found that church membership provides a feeling of security and identity, as it creates a sense of belonging to the Swedish culture. Church members also reveal a combination of individualistic and collective orientations. In contemporary sociology of religion, the individualistic orientation and the ritualistic orientation are frequently posed as opposites. Pettersson attempts to explain the relationship between the two. He argues that people tend to use different time-scales when they seek, on the one hand, private and individual religion, and, on the other hand, collective rituals. In the case of individual and private religion, they use a short time-scale, and they find that the established churches are relatively distant as they try to satisfy their religious needs. In the case of collective ritual religion, people use a long time-scale that encompasses their whole life spans. They reveal a desire to have a sense of continuity that transcends their own lives. Pettersson concludes that, in research on the individualization of contemporary religion, the collective dimension has been underestimated.

7.8 Rituals and music as carriers of religiosity

Religious rituals have a variety of functions. In some instances, they function as indicators of rank and exclusivity. One example is found in Greek Orthodox Church services, when the priest is the only person allowed to move behind the iconostasis. Pierre Bourdieu tends to interpret rituals in this way, as a means of affirming differences of power (see Section 4.5). In other instances, rituals are inclusive in the sense that they preserve elements from the collective religious tradition intact, even in situations where people create their own individual world-views.

Rituals are standardized interaction patterns with symbolic content that are carried out in specific situations. The function of rituals is often to create order and maintain meaning and belonging. However, rituals are multi-faceted phenomena. A symbol is something that represents something else, and the relationship between symbol and reality tends to be ambiguous. To participate in or observe a ritual is, in some instances, an emotional experience, because rituals imply a bodily involvement. At the same time, the ambiguity inherent in rituals opens the possibility for multiple interpretations that do not necessarily correspond to the official definition of the ritual. For example, several Christian rituals are compatible with numerous different denominational creeds. Eating a symbolic meal while kneeling in a semicircle, walking in a procession, throwing dirt on a coffin which is lowered into the ground – none of these rituals contains only one interpretation. This fact might constitute one reason why the popular support for rites of passage seems to be consistent, even in relatively secular countries. The combination of the personal and at the same time the non-committed ambiguity provides baptism, confirmation, weddings, and funerals with a broad appeal. The increasing popularity of pilgrimages and tourist visits to churches can be analysed in the same way. A mixture of tourism, interest in cultural history, and spiritual reflection seems to function as an act of devotion with a low level of commitment that appeals to a growing number of people in the West.

All the rituals mentioned above are called rites of passage, as they symbolize and bring about a transition in social status or phase of life. French folklorist Arnold van Gennep (1960/1908) was one of the first to analyse rites of passage, and Victor Turner (1969) developed Gennep's perspective. These scholars believed that they had detected a threefold sequence that characterizes rites of passage in every culture: pre-liminal separation, liminal transition, and post-liminal reintegration into society. Gennep adopted the term "liminal" from Latin *limen*, which means threshold or border. It is not difficult to find examples of the three phases, for example in burial rites. Other scholars have criticized Gennep and Turner's theory and argued that it is too mechanical, in the sense that not every ritual follows the pattern these scholars have outlined. An alternative approach to the analysis of religious rituals and roles can be found in Erving Goffmann's sociology (see Section 4.3). In modern society, there are several examples of old rituals that are used on a regular basis. Nevertheless, the participants may still feel distant from different aspects of the ritual. In one example, funerals, the participants sing psalms diligently and with great enthusiasm. Yet, at the same time, the same psalms have a "role-distancing" effect, to use Goffman's word, in the sense that they create a distance from that which is actually taking place.

Music has a similar effect to that of rituals, namely building a bridge between a religious tradition and the members. Music shares some of the same traits with rituals. Music appeals to emotions, often also to the body. Yet music contains ambiguity. It moves us, even if the direction is difficult to predict. American sociologist Andrew Greeley (1975) attempted to detect what it was that awakened religious experiences in individuals. In his study, listening to music received the highest score. The following are "triggers" mentioned by more than 40 per cent of those interviewed: listening to music, prayer, beautiful nature, moments of reflection, attending a religious service, and listening to a sermon. This study is old, and listening to music might have received an even higher score today. Meredith McGuire (1997) claims that various forms of music, not least religious hymns, serve as important means of maintenance for religiosity, and that the importance of music tends to be underestimated by scholars who are too intellectual in their approach and not easily moved by emotion.

7.9 When religion becomes important: On religiously committed individuals

Even if modern times are characterized by religious individualism and skepticism of institutions, we must not forget that large groups of people seek a religious community on a regular basis and that this participation is important to them. Commitment to fundamentalist movements is dealt with elsewhere in this book (see Section 9.3). Here, we will discuss religious commitment by introducing some perspectives on religious conversion.

In contrast to the concept of recruitment, which tends to have associations with organized activities, the concept of conversion suggests that "inner" changes have taken place in a person's identity and meaning system. A conversion is often accompanied by a new lifestyle and social context. The typical convert will put behind them "the old life" and "the old friends" and search for a new community.

Sociologists have argued that even if a person's conversion often is expressed in a single event, for example, a confession in a group setting, it is useful to view conversion as a process. This is particularly evident in the situation of returnees, or adults who return to the religious community or tradition in which they were raised. Some individuals who received religious socialization as a child leave this tradition as adolescents or young adults, but decide to return later in life. In this case, the conversion has the character of a non-dramatic consolidation – a "returning home."

Conversion is a concept that is found in academic as well as religious discourses. As pointed out by Meredith McGuire (1997), there are different discourses or rhetorical recipes for conversion that are available and used by the convert and the other participating actors. One form of rhetoric is rhetoric of choice, which pinpoints the pain of choosing and the joy of having chosen. Another form is rhetoric of change, which stresses the break with the past (often painted in drab colors) and the start of an entirely new life. A third form is rhetoric of continuity, as exemplified in the statement "I was always troubled" or "the longing was always there."

In sociology and social psychology, there are two dominant approaches in explaining conversion. Up until the 1970s, a common approach was to view conversion as a pathological phenomenon. Explanations tended to either emphasize various forms of crises and internal tensions in the person who converted, or argue that the converted was a passive, irrational object of massive pressure and manipulation, or a combination of the two. Such a psychopathological approach can be seen as an expression of the majority's desire to monopolize the definition of rationality. Keeping with the general trend towards a more actor-oriented sociology, contemporary research reveals how recruits actively are *converting*, acting on their own volition and making their own decisions (Richardson 1985).

Some conversions are socially invisible, in the sense that they take place as a voiceless self-examination. Other conversions are socially visible, at least for close family and friends. Sometimes a religious conversion implies a breach with family and friends. However, a far more common pattern is that pre-existing social networks, such as family, neighbors, and friends, stimulate and encourage conversions. Indeed, research has shown that connections to social networks that have links to the religious group are crucial in the conversion process (Barker 1984; Beckford 1975; Bromley and Shupe 1979). Such networks provide credibility of the religious ideology and social support for joining.

One part of the conversion process is the restructuring of the definition of the convert's identity. The internal restructuring of one's identity ("I once was blind, but now I see ...") is often accompanied by external, visible, and ritual signs of the new identity: the wearing of a hijab, attending prayers in the mosque, speaking in tongues, and giving testimonies. Erving Goffman's perspectives (see Section 4.3) on the dramaturgical aspects of social interaction are relevant here. Several religious communities operate with more or less openly stated scripts that prescribe proper behavior for new converts. They are often expected to create a distance from their previous lives, show visible joy over their conversion, and change their behavior in symbolically important fields. We have seen that Goffmann also argues that prescribed roles can be used to achieve certain advantages. At the same time, the participants in the social interaction are expected to behave in specific ways to avoid embarrassing situations. This "soft" understanding of the role can be useful in an analysis of the new convert: she or he is expected to behave in a more or less prescribed way, but if the behavior is *too* outwardly and visibly phony, it is likely that the group will be disappointed.

The community the converted person enters also must play by certain unwritten rules. During the early phase after the convert has joined, fellow believers are expected to provide warm care and love. They are also expected to provide training in the group's formal ideology and informal rules of behavior. Some converts find that the process of reinterpreting their experiences in the light of a religious narrative is like entering a new and fascinating landscape where minor and major issues in life are seen in a new light.

The ability to maintain a deep religious commitment over a long period of time poses difficulties. This is particularly true if the group expects the participants to live a life characterized by extraordinary religious experiences and few personal problems or issues. The turnover rate in new religious movements and revivalist campaigns is often high. Several newcomers join, but they tend to drop out after a while. Those who are "religious professionals" constitute a special category: they have religion as their profession. In many cases, they will face difficulties if they want to withdraw from organized religious activities. Role expectations, prestige, financial interests, and lack of available comparable opportunities in the secular world will be factors that tend to push them in the direction of remaining in the religious role. The rank-and-file participants will usually not face these kinds of factors.

Some close-knit religious groups will tend to withdraw from society at large. This strategy will primarily be employed by groups characterized by a restricted interaction with "this world" and a tendency to mix work and piety in such a way that life becomes highly regulated and ritualized. However, some movements whose participants work and take part in society also place normative restrictions on their participants to limit their interaction with outsiders, their use of mass media, and so forth. The "world out there" is often described by using derogatory terms. Nevertheless, it is a risky strategy for a group to paint a dark picture of the world in order to maintain the group. If the leaders tell the participants that individuals outside their flock are dissolute and unhappy, and they find out that this hardly is the case, the credibility of the religious leaders is threatened.

Several religious movements attempt to maintain a high level of commitment among the participants by publishing ideological outlines and apologies in books, magazines, videos, DVDs, and so forth. Commitment is also maintained through direct social contact, at meetings and conventions. In some instances, a high level of commitment is maintained by referring to the movement's growth and success in recruitment. A participant's identity will be strengthened when other seekers choose the same path. However, the strategy of focusing keenly on quantitative growth can be risky, especially if the leaders do not provide an adequate explanation as to why the group experiences decline rather than growth. This is also true when it comes to movement activities. On the one hand, they will tend to have a positive effect by keeping commitment alive. On the other hand, they may cause attrition and burnout.

Meredith McGuire (1997) points out three factors that often cause a high level of religious commitment to decline. One factor is increasing contact with the outside world; the second is the experience of discrepancies between ideology and the practice of movement leaders; and the final factor is a movement's experiences of an obvious fiasco. As it relates to the first factor, geographic mobility has a potential for religious redefinition. When individuals move from one area to another, they will experience a loosening of old ties and loyalties and the formation of new ones. If the connection to a church or religious group has been weak or problematic, moving will tend to result in religious withdrawal.

The process of exit from a religious movement or withdrawal from a high level of religious commitment implies a restructuring of identity and world-view, and, in some instances, a change of social community. The more important role religion played in an individual's life, the more difficult is the process of detachment. There has been a tendency among ex-participants or members to report conflicting emotions regarding their exit. On the one hand, they report a feeling of relief from the pressures to conform to the standards and the views of the group. On the other hand, they speak of loss and loneliness, particularly if most of their social lives took place within the movement (Repstad 1984).

7.10 Secularization on the individual level?

Even if there are groups of people who experience dramatic conversions and practice intense forms of religiosity in contemporary Western societies, the large majority seem to have a much lower degree of commitment and perhaps more of a searching attitude. On this basis, is it reasonable to argue that there is a general trend of secularization on an individual level? Does religion mean less than it used to, and for a smaller group of people? Several indicators suggest that participation in organized religious activities has declined, at least in Europe. In several European countries, the graphs depicting religious participation showed a downward turn that began in the 1970s (Dobbelaere 1993). A study of the American baby-boomer generation revealed that even if some have returned to organized religion, the majority seem to be religiously privatized (Roof 1993). Nevertheless, it is too misleading to speak of an unambiguous secularization when it comes to individual attitudes toward institutional religion. In Europe, large groups maintain a form of cultural Christianity (Davie 2000), which often can be seen in the use of church rituals. Seen from a long-term historical perspective, it is difficult to escape the idea that individual secularization is a main trend for Europeans, at least if religious activity is used as an indicator.

Conversely, if we take a look at individual religiosity in general, it is difficult to draw definite conclusions. Even if it seems that the majority of Europeans are more distanced from organized religiosity than they used to be, this does not necessarily mean that they are less religious than their parents' generation. Here, it is relevant to ask how important religion is for most people. For a minority of deeply religious individuals, religion constitutes an important framework for interpreting their realities and practices and for understanding themselves. For the large majority, religion is a resource that is dipped into and used whenever necessary. Based on the idea that individual identities are related to the private sphere, such as family, religion, and leisure activities, some sociologists will argue that religion therefore contributes to an understanding of self and identity. However, this position is debated. Other sociologists will claim that the family has gradually been drained of functions, and that individuals in contemporary society will base their identities on their positions in the work sphere. And here, religion tends to be fairly marginal.

Can we conclude that there is secularization on the individual level? Different scholars provide various answers to this question. If we consider individual religiosity in general, all we can say is that it is changing. We are unable to conclude with general validity the trend in these changes.

8

Religious organizations and movements

8.1 An interest in typologies

Religious commitment can be highly individual and private, especially in modern times. Yet it often experiences growth within or in a critical discourse with established religious organizations. In sociology, an organization is defined as a group with one or more goals and a certain minimum of formal structure. The clarity of the goals and the formality of the organizational structures vary. A central theme in the history of the sociology of religion has been the distinction between various forms of religious organizations. The two German intellectual giants, theologian Ernst Troeltsch and sociologist Max Weber, introduced a classical typology of organizations about one hundred years ago that was developed and refined later by, among others, American theologian H. Richard Niebuhr. Their typology will be described in more detail below. Thereafter, we will take a look at the various ways in which it has been used, for example, in attempts to understand change in religious organizations. We will also examine in more detail how power and authority are exercised in religious organizations, based on yet another typology taken from Max Weber.

The last section of this chapter introduces some sociological theories on religious movements, including new religious movements. In particular, we will examine theories on the recruitment and socialization of participants in such movements. Finally, we will briefly address some methodological issues that are relevant in studies of religious movements and religious minorities.

8.2 Church, sect, and mysticism

It is important to bear in mind that the terms "church" and "sect" do not always mean the same in a sociological context as they do in everyday language. Not all churches that label themselves a church are in fact a church in a sociological sense. Sect is a term that initially was used by sociologists to capture various forms of religious organization outside the church. Even if the term initially was meant to be descriptive, it proved to include certain hidden assumptions about these groups and their participants. The term also came to have such a negative connotation in everyday language that sociologists now speak of religious movements and organizations, rather than sects. However, we will use the term in our outline of traditional theories on sect and church.

German theologian Ernst Troeltsch was a major figure in German theology in the early 1900s. In addition to his contribution to systematic theology and philosophy of religion, he is known for his contribution to church history, particularly his major work *The Social Teachings of the Christian Churches* (1960/1912). It is primarily here he describes the characteristic traits of churches and sects. Troeltsch developed his understanding of the relationship between church and society in collaboration with Max Weber, who for a period of time was his colleague and closest neighbor in Heidelberg. Weber had already given an outline of the distinction between church and sect when Troeltsch wrote his book. For Weber, the distinction was related to individual joining, either through birth or through individual choice respectively.

According to Ernst Troeltsch, the distinction between church and sect had to do with the organization of the religious community. Troeltsch belonged to a liberal theological tradition and he considered the message of Jesus and the early Christians to center on personal devotion and not religious organization. However, during the early history of Christianity the issue of organizing the religious community soon surfaced:

> From the very start three main types surfaced in the sociological development of the Christian idea: the church, the sect and mysticism. The church is an institution that has been endowed with grace and redemption. ... It can accept the masses and adapt to the world because it to some extent may allow itself to disregard the need for subjective holiness. (Troeltsch 1960/1912: 993)

The church is thus an institution that objectively controls the means of redemption that everyone needs. Therefore, it claims unconditional validity and truth, while also allowing itself to be tolerant and adaptive. Troeltsch argues that the church must be able to adapt if it is to form a framework around the lives of all individuals in a society. Here, he formulates a familiar paradox: the church wants to control the world, and is therefore controlled by the world.

In many ways, a sect is the counterpart of a church. It shares a feature with the church in that it claims to own the truth, but in contrast to the inclusive ambition of the church, the sect has an exclusive self-understanding. For the sect, the ownership of the truth in this sinful world is an insight admitted only to a few:

> The sect is a voluntary association, composed of strict and decidedly believing Christians, bound together by the fact that they have all experienced the "rebirth". These believers live separately from the world, are limited to small groups, emphasize the law more than grace, and within their own circles they set up to a varying degree the Christian order based on love. All this is done in preparation and expectation of the coming realm of God. (Troeltsch 1960/1912: 993)

These concepts of church and sect have remained more or less intact throughout the history of the sociology of religion, even if they have been redefined and supplemented. American theologian H. Richard Niebuhr examined Troeltsch's church–sect distinction in his book *The Social Sources of Denominationalism* (1975/1929) and he concluded that the distinction did not fit the American situation. In the United States, numerous denominations lived side by side in relatively peaceful competition. None of them dominated society as a whole, and they were far from the exclusive and closed communities often associated with the sect concept. Niebuhr argued that church and sect can be considered as two extremes of a continuum, and he introduced a third category, the denomination. This is an intermediate form between church and sect that is more ecumenical than both of them in the sense that it accepts that other religious communities also embody important elements of truth. The denomination usually lies somewhere between church and sect when it comes to size. It does not include "the whole society," but is larger than a small group. The denomination also represents an intermediate category as it relates to member commitment. It is less based on sacraments than the church Troeltsch described, and it has a stronger focus on the activity of members during religious events. The denomination is also far more moderate than the sect regarding member compliance and devotion.

A major issue in Niebuhr's book is revealed in its title, *The Social Sources of Denominationalism.* Niebuhr was a theologian who was engaged in the social agenda of his time, and he disliked the fact that the American denominations tended to develop along socio-economic strata. He writes about how the formation of denominations,

> ... represents the accommodation of Christianity to the caste-system of human society. It carries over into the organization of the Christian principle of brotherhood the pride and prejudices, the privileges and prestige, as well as the humiliations and abasements, the injustices and inequalities of that special order of high and low wherein men find the satisfaction of their craving for vain glory. The division of the churches closely follows the division of men into the castes of national, racial and economic groups. It draws the color line in the church of God; it fosters the misunderstandings, the self-exaltations, the hatreds of jingoistic nationalism by continuing in the body of Christ the spurious differences of provincial loyalties; it seats the rich and poor apart at the table of the Lord, where the fortunate may enjoy the bounty they have provided while the others feed upon the crusts their poverty affords. (1975: 3)

We include this lengthy quotation to demonstrate how sociological classical texts frequently have constituted a part of the contemporary social and political debate.

The concept of another form of religious organization, the cult, was introduced in 1932 by sociologist Howard Becker. According to him, a cult is a fairly loose association of individuals with a private and eclectic religiosity (Becker 1932). This description fits some of the new informal and alternative religiosity, so this category has gained increasing academic relevance. Again we must bear in mind that the use of terms may vary between academic and everyday language. Religious cult is sometimes used about cultus or god worship. In the 1970s, it carried the same meaning as sect.

Several sociologists of religion have attempted to develop further the typologies of religious organizations. In order to organize a broad social reality, some have constructed four-field typologies. Such typologies tend to simplify reality in such a way that relevant factors are excluded from their frameworks. This will be evident as we present some categories of religious organizations below. A common feature in these typologies is their attempt to focus on dimensions that are important for society.

Sociologist Roland Robertson's (1970) typology of religious organizations is organized along two dimensions (see Table 8.1). The first dimension is related to the organization's legitimacy. Here, he distinguishes between organizations that claim to be the sole representative of the truth so that all other organizations are fundamentally wrong (unique legitimacy) and organizations that admit other groups to have ownership of the truth (pluralist legitimacy). The second dimension distinguishes between inclusive and exclusive principles of membership. We recognize from Troeltsch the question of how demanding an organization is on its members when it comes to fulfilling specific norms, whether they pertain to morals, dogmas, or activities.

Table 8.1   Robertson's typology of religious organizations

	Unique legitimacy	**Pluralist legitimacy**
Exclusive membership principle	Sect	Institutionalized sect
Inclusive membership principle	Church	Denomination

Here, Robertson introduces a new concept, the institutionalized sect. He uses the Salvation Army as an illustrative example. Institutionalized sects are organizations that have a more open attitude when it comes to cooperation with other religious organizations than sects typically have, at least with organizations that do not entirely differ from them regarding their religious faith. At the same time, the institutionalized sect demands a high level of commitment and activity on the part of their members.

A similar approach is found in the work of British sociologist Roy Wallis (1976). He also uses the dimension of legitimacy and asks whether an organization considers itself unique or as one among several groups that has ownership of the truth (see Table 8.2). The second dimension in his typology is related to the larger society's perceptions of the religious group.

Table 8.2   Wallis' typology of religious organizations

	Unique legitimacy	**Pluralist legitimacy**
Deviant	Sect	Cult
Respectable	Church	Denomination

Here, Wallis includes the cult as one form of religious organization. He considers the cult to be a movement that is open to various world-views, including those that are different from its own. At the same time, it is deviant as it relates to prevailing norms in society. As we see, sociologists use different definitions of cult. If we were to use Wallis' concept of cult to describe new religious movements in contemporary society, we would say that they share some of society's dominant values, but that they use alternative methods. For example, health and well-being are often important values in cults, as they are in society at large. The deviant aspect lies in the fact that cults are critical of established religion and academic medicine, and that they seek alternative ways of attaining the same goals though healing, alternative medicine, meditation, astrology, and self-development.

We will not attempt to contrast these four-field typologies. Instead, we will argue that they represent mutual supplements to each other. To summarize, the concepts of church, sect, denomination, and cult have been used in sociology in the following way.

The *church* is a religious organization that demands to represent the truth exclusively. The classical statement is: "Outside the church there is no salvation." The church includes everybody or virtually everybody in a society. Recruitment takes place through childbirth: new generations are born into the church. The church adapts to some extent to the fact that it must embrace everyone. Therefore, it tends to be oriented towards compromises with the prevailing culture and the political sphere. Hence, the church is relatively moderate in its demands on its members. Most people will also consider the church to be respectable.

The *sect* also perceives itself as a unique owner of the truth. However, it constitutes a minority in a given society. Recruitment takes place through conscious individual choice. Once an individual has joined, the sect requires a high level of commitment and activity. Members are expected to support the teachings of the sect and to comply with its lifestyle, which may be strict and ascetic. Life as a sect member constitutes a major contrast to the lives of people in society. Therefore, the sect and the larger society harbor mutual suspicions towards each other. Sects tend to depict society as a place full of dangers and moral and religious decay. Any compromise with such a society is not an option. Society, for its part, often represented by the media, depicts sects as strongly deviant and problematic.

The term "institutionalized sect," which was introduced by Robertson, refers to a group that maintains the expectation of active support by its members, but it has relinquished its self-understanding as the only dispenser of religious truth. Behind this concept lies the idea that once a sect is established and has experienced growth for a few years, it will tend to develop a more relaxed attitude to its surroundings.

The *denomination* represents yet another step away from the sect. In contrast to church and sect, the denomination is oriented toward cooperation, at least as it relates to other similar denominations. People join through an individual and voluntary choice, although the most important form of recruitment in established denominations takes place through childbirth. The demands for activity and compliance are moderate, and there is a relatively harmonious mutual relationship between the denomination and the larger society.

In contrast to church, sect, and denomination, the *cult* has a pluralist legitimacy. Many cults will emphasize that questions are more important than answers, that the quest is more significant than what is found, and that each individual must find their own way. Hence, it is legitimate to join several different cults, where the turnover tends to be high. The structure and demands on membership are looser compared to the other types of organization; perhaps it is more accurate to speak of clients, consumers, and customers than of members. Courses, seminars, and consultations are important vehicles of socializing, and bookshops and magazines provide arenas for establishing contact. Critics of cults have claimed that they tend to have a commercial character. This may well be true, although the difference in this area to other religious organizations should not be exaggerated. Churches, sects, and denominations also have financial interests.

By emphasizing the loose and individualist feature of cults, we again approach the third form of religious community found in Troeltsch's work, namely mysticism. Having a clearly skeptical attitude towards dogmas, Troeltsch favored mysticism:

> Mysticism implies that the world of ideas that had petrified into formal worship and dogmas is being transformed into purely personal and inner experience. This leads to the formation of groups on a purely private basis, without any permanent form, which also contributes to reducing the importance of the forms of religious services, dogmas and the historical element. (Troeltsch 1960/1912: 993)

It is interesting that Troeltsch labels mysticism a "refuge for the religious life in the educated classes" down through history. Here, he reveals his slightly elitist academic liberal theology. He argues that when mysticism gains a following in sections of the population that are "untouched by science," it will lead to "extravagant and emotional forms of piety." Troeltsch points out that mysticism easily develops into a purely religious individualism, which may end in resignation. From a normative premise, Troeltsch also criticizes sects for losing the general ethical perspective that the church had during medieval times. According to him, sects have become "uncultivated and insignificant" (Troeltsch 1960/1912: 993). Again, we see that the classical typologies have inherent values derived from the social and political context in which they were formed.

8.3 Some specifications and critical notes

What is the purpose of these and other typologies of religious organizations? The church–sect typology has been criticized from many camps, and several different arguments have been raised against it. One objection is that it tends to paint a static and essentialist picture of religion in the sense that religion is organized either this way or that way. Considering this argument, it is important to bear in mind that Weber viewed such typologies to be ideal types, meaning that they were helpful in analysing religion even if they did not exist in their pure form in the real world. In this sense, typologies are useful maps that must not be mistaken for the terrain. At the same time, if the map is glaringly imperfect, its use must be questioned. The revisions of Weber and Troeltsch's typologies throughout the 1900s may be seen as attempts to ensure contact with the terrain. Perhaps the scholars should have drawn intersecting axes rather than cells in a four-field table to point out that the typologies constitute extremes on continuous lines rather than separate entities. The various organizational forms also become more interesting when we use them dynamically and examine how specific religious organizations move between different forms over time. We will return to this issue below.

As noted, the term sect has a negative connotation in everyday language that implies irrational behavior, narrow-mindedness, strange world-views, and brainwashed individuals. An argument against the use of this concept is that scholars should refrain from using terms that carry a different meaning for the general public, due to misunderstanding. Some sociologists of religion oppose this view and claim that sect is an established academic term and that scholars should not give in to an uninformed public. Nevertheless, most sociologists of religion refrain from using the term and speak of religious movements and religious minorities. James A. Beckford (1975) has also attempted to show that in academic contexts the term sect has often been used to describe organizations in a diagnostic way, suggesting that they in some ways are deviant and bizarre.

The church–sect typology is also criticized from a theoretical point of view. The argument is that it is purely descriptive, with no explanatory power in and of itself. There is some truth to that, even if good typologies can prove to be useful. They are helpful in organizing and systematizing an otherwise huge and chaotic mass of information. Therefore, some typologies may contribute to the development of hypotheses. The church–sect typology can, for example, be useful in an analysis of the power and socialization that dominate each organizational form, or in a study of the possibilities that each form has for survival in various social contexts. Although typologies do not replace explanations in the social sciences, they can be a useful step on the way.

Another form of critique against the use of typologies of religious organizations points out that they are based on Western or Christian ethnocentrism. Indeed, the concepts of church and sect derive from a Christian tradition. Is it even possible to envision churches outside a Christian context? If we were going to attempt to do so, it would be necessary to keep in mind the sociological features that constitute the basis for these concepts. From that premise, it could be meaningful in a Muslim context to describe how religious, cultural, and political boundaries coincide and are more or less the same, so that "defecting from" Islam also means defecting from society. In some Muslim countries, such as Saudi Arabia, religion could perhaps be described by using the term "church" in a sociological sense, even if the term is hopelessly ethnocentric, and even if the mosque in part has other functions than the church.

Another related critique is that these typologies are outmoded, even in Western societies. This critique is particularly aimed at church and sect. It seems that these terms are most useful in a Christian holistic culture where insurgents emerge and experience growth, that is, the period from the age of Enlightenment until the nineteenth century. Today it is quite appropriate to ask if there are any churches left in a sociological sense at all, for example, in Europe. The closest unity of church and nation in contemporary Europe seems to be in Greece. The Greek Orthodox Church has continued to count virtually all Greeks as members, and it represents a strong influence in several social institutions, including state schools. In most other European countries, this is a situation of the past. This is also true for the Nordic countries. Here, the dominant Lutheran churches comprise a large majority of the population, who continue to use the church for rites of passage. In situations of crises and disasters, the churches take the initiative to arrange shared national rituals. The fact that many members are baptized as infants, combined with the civil religious role of the churches, would lead us to believe that these majority churches are churches in a sociological sense. This notion is also supported by the fact that these churches put few demands on their members regarding participation. Nevertheless, these churches have far too peaceful ecumenical relationships to other religious communities to be sociologically classified as churches. It is more reasonable to claim that practically every major religious community in contemporary Europe resembles a denomination, including the national churches in Britain and the Nordic countries.

Yet another objection to the church–sect typology concerns its limited relevance. The typology has too narrow a focus on *religious* organizations and it tends to exaggerate the difference between religious organizations and other forms of organization. As a result, the study of religious organizations becomes separated from the sociological study of organizations. If the sociology of religion goes too far in developing its own language and analytical strategies, it will become isolated from general sociology. Such a development is unfortunate, because it will reinforce the trend that general sociology has little interest in contemporary religion, even if the classical sociological theorists demonstrated such an interest. Therefore, a more fruitful approach involves an exchange between the sociology of religion and general sociology. In the study of religious organizations, the sociology of religion has much to gain from using organizational theories found in general sociology.

An argument against this objection could possibly be that conflicts between exclusive and inclusive trends in organizations are not limited to religious organizations alone. Similar trends are also found in political organizations, and, in studies of medical institutions, attempts have been made to use the terms church and sect. For example, one study argues that the dominating medical-faculty system has church-like characteristics, in contrast to more sectarian movements found within alternative medicine (Freund and McGuire 1995).

Nevertheless, it is an inescapable fact that the typology of religious organizations stems from and is dominated by a religious context. This typology's usefulness depends on how distinctive one perceives religious organizations to be. One may say that they are more unusual than some general organization theorists think, but less so than many religious leaders claim. Perhaps one argument for the use of the church–sect typology is that religious organizations are value-based organizations where truth is an important question of principle for many members. This explains why the question of the monopoly on the truth is a fundamental differentiating feature between these forms of religious organizations. However, it is important that general sociological classifications relevant for organizations are used in the study of religion. We will return to some of these, but before we do so, we will examine how churches, sects, and other religious organizations develop over time.

8.4 The dynamics of religious organizations

Max Weber focuses on the question of how social and religious movements survive once the first generation of dedicated enthusiasts is gone. He concludes that movements will develop over time into structured organizations or be institutionalized. Following Weber, H. Richard Niebuhr gives an outline of the development of sects. According to him, sects will eventually become more like churches and, thus, become denominations. "By its very nature the sectarian type of organization is valid only for one generation," he writes (1975/1929: 19). His idea is that the next generation is born into the sect, and will therefore not maintain the same high level of commitment as the first generation did. Niebuhr also draws on Weber's theory that ascetic Christianity will lead to financial affluence. He argues that a higher social mobility among sect members will result in a greater emphasis on economic prosperity and social respectability. As a result, the sect will tend to diminish its conflicts with society and increase its willingness to adapt to the world. The world will also consider sect members with greater acceptance. The outcome is a stronger social integration of the sect into general society. Finally, Niebuhr claims that every organization that attempts to survive over time must develop a certain division of labor. Bureaucratization will eventually take place, and this development is a result of the sect's contagious contact with general society. Experts in the religious community will, among others, begin to compare their conditions with those of experts outside the religious community.

It is not difficult to find empirical cases where sects have become more adapted to their surroundings and have developed into denominations, for example, the Quakers and the Salvation Army. Nevertheless, British sociologist Alan Aldridge (2000) has criticized Niebuhr for describing the path from sect to denomination as a mechanical and deterministic process. Aldridge argues that a strong socialization within a sect can result in a high level of commitment for several generations, and he points to Jehovah's Witnesses as an example. He uses the same example as he claims that even if a sect hires full-time employees, it does not automatically develop a harmonizing relationship with the larger society. Instead, employees in the Jehovah's Witnesses help keep sectarianism alive by providing members with a flow of information on the group's ideology and activities. Furthermore, Aldridge points out that not all sects move up the social and financial ladder. The Amish people in the United States are an illustrative example. They have upheld their anti-modern farming technology, which does not make them particularly rich (2000: 36–7).

Several examples mentioned by Aldridge deal with sects that tend to isolate themselves from society. However, most sects in modern societies tend to be far more integrated into society. The children will often attend public schools where they meet other children, and the adults will interact with outsiders in the work sphere. Niebuhr's prognoses are perhaps more correct for sects that have a relatively high level of interaction with general society. Nevertheless, Niebuhr's construction of a social law on sects that is expected to have general validity resembles deterministic sociology.

American sociologist of religion Thomas O'Dea (1961) has a somewhat more open approach than Niebuhr. He has pointed out a number of dilemmas that religious movements will face over time. First, O'Dea believes that once a religious movement is established, the participants' motives for involvement will become more diverse. Even the most devout will begin to desire prestige, financial security, and the chance to show off their skills. This will cause conflict with those participants who are "pure of heart," those who want to hold on to the original ideals. In addition, the movement's symbols will tend to change, engendering yet more conflict. The same symbols that expressed the participants' religious experiences in the beginning often achieve a fixed status later. For example, in some movements, speaking in tongues becomes a form of religious practice that achieves high prestige among the participants. Later, the same practice represents a problem for those participants who are unsuccessful in speaking in tongues. O'Dea also points out that as the movement is formalized, practical and effective solutions tend to develop, such as a form of bureaucratization. Yet this development will often result in an erosion of the movement's strong fellowship that was originally based on a shared religious experience. If the movement goes through a high membership growth, some of these dilemmas and problems will also tend to intensify.

Furthermore, O'Dea adds that ideological changes tend to take place. As the need to teach the ideology appears, the ideology itself will become more structured and, in some cases, more legalistic. This process might have dire consequences for a movement that is based on a burning care and compassion. As these strong features are undermined, one is left with a fairly petty ascetic conformism.

Finally, O'Dea argues that the institutionalization of power represents a dilemma. The introduction of organizational authority and hierarchical structures will pose problems for movements that previously were egalitarian. This is particularly true if the leadership develops self-interests that present a conflict with the movement's original aims and ethos.

So far, the reader is perhaps left with the impression that the main direction of the dynamics of religious movements is from sect to church. However, this is a much too one-sided picture. Several historical cases show how sects have originated in churches as one or more church members have felt that the church has moved too far from its original ideals. American sociologists Rodney Stark and William Bainbridge (1987) have also outlined almost a general theory that postulates a dialectical relationship. They argue that churches and denominations will tend to be oriented toward compromises, which again create a fertile ground for the formation of new cults and sects.

Even if it is possible that denominations develop in a sectarian direction, it is far more common that denominations produce sectarian splinter groups. Steve Bruce (1990) has in several contexts described how Protestant, conservative communities tend to face a risk of splintering. The heavy focus on correct dogma combined with strong leaders results in a situation where unifying compromising solutions are difficult to find.

All these theories on religious organizational changes over time are interesting and inspiring. Nevertheless, rather than perceiving them to be theories with absolute predictive powers, a more useful approach here, as elsewhere in sociology, is to consider them as "sometimes-true-theories."

8.5 Religious organizations as active entities: Resource mobilization theory

The traditional approach to religious sects has implicitly assumed that people who join sects have some sort of problem, or they have been manipulated into joining. The contemporary approach considers participants in religious movements as active, rational individuals who have specific goals and strategies. A parallel change of approach has taken place within the study of conversion, which is now considered to be an active process (see Section 7.9).

The new approach, frequently called "resource mobilization theory," appeared in the 1960s and 1970s within the study of social movements (Zald and Ash 1966) and was later adopted by sociologists of religion and used in studies of religious movements (Bromley and Shupe 1979). Resource mobilization theory shifts the focus away from the mental state of the participants and turns to the movements' access to resources and their ability to capitalize on them. It analyses the movements' resource situation and various contextual factors that create barriers or opportunities for mobilization. Contextual factors might be legal and political opportunities for forming organizations in a given society. Relevant resources are money, people, pre-existing social networks, communication networks, and media access. Whereas the traditional sect theories tended to focus on individual motivation for joining a religious movement, resource mobilization theory emphasizes the recruitment strategies that a religious movement uses to win new members and the socialization processes it uses to keep them. In a comparative study of several religious and political movements in Norway during the 1800s, one long-term success factor that proved to be important was, for example, the movement's ability to offer roles for the entire family (Furseth 2002).

The transition from viewing the participants in religious movements as passive, manipulated persons burdened with problems to active, goal-oriented participants did perhaps not just represent a shift in theory, but a change in the actual social composition of several religious movements in the Western world. Whereas the large revivalist movements in the 1800s and early 1900s gained most of their popularity in the lower middle class and the working class, a striking feature of new religious movements has been the absence of working-class members, the majority being relatively well-educated middle-class (Barker 1985; Hannigan 1991). Perhaps the change of approach is also related to the distance between the sociologists of religion and their object of study. It is easier to give participants who are socially and culturally distant from the sociologist a diagnosis as passive and manipulated individuals than it is to do so to well-educated participants.

Traditional deprivation theory and resource mobilization theory deal in part with different issues. The first approach asks "why" people seek religious movements; the latter asks "how" movements access available opportunities and mobilize a following. Yet these approaches do not just supplement each other. They also contradict each other on important issues, such as their views on the participants' active and passive roles and the relationship that the religious movement organizations have to the context.

8.6 Organizations characterized by coercion, utilitarianism, and normative commitment

As in all organizations, the structures of religious organizations vary from firm hierarchies to loose networks. Some are democratic, whereas others are authoritarian. Some are strictly hierarchical and others are egalitarian, or they shift structures depending on the projects they are involved in at any time. Some organizations use professionals or bureaucrats to fulfill specific roles and others have a more ad hoc division of labor. As in all organizations, the correspondence between the formal structure of authority and the informal structure may be strong or weak. As in all organizations, gender is an important dimension. Certain positions are formally or informally reserved for men, whereas other positions are reserved for women.

We could continue along the same line. Clearly, general organizational sociology is relevant for the study of religious organizations. In the following, we will present two typologies that are frequently used in the study of organizations in general, and that can be particularly useful in the study of religious organizations. The first typology has been developed by the American sociologist Amitai Etzioni. The second brings us back to the classical sociologist Max Weber.

Amitai Etzioni (1964) has formulated a useful typology of organizations that deals with the relationship between the members and the organization. He distinguishes between coercive, utilitarian, and normative organizations. In coercive organizations, the term "members" should possibly be put in quotation marks: the participants are in the organization because they have to be there. By using a more or less legitimate coercive force, the leaders coerce the members to obey. Prison is the classical example of an organization with a legitimate use of coercion. The military also appears to have, at least for the enlisted soldier, many of the features of a coercive organization.

In utilitarian organizations, the membership is based on a system of rewards and punishments. The most important basis for the relationship is self-interest, which is often financial. In the work sphere, we provide our labor and in return we receive pay. In this form of organization, the leadership will use financial and material rewards as means to control and motivate members.

In normative organizations, members participate because they have the same normative commitment as the organization. The organization is thereby able to dominate its members merely by creating and maintaining a commitment. The members continue to be involved in the organization as long as the activity and the purpose continue to be meaningful to them.

Etzioni's categories are ideal types. Most organizations constitute intermediate forms in real life. For example, some interactions in a prison are characterized by voluntary friendliness, not just coercion. Also, many persons are motivated to work because they like their work and find it meaningful, not just because they are paid for it. Some extreme religious organizations do exercise force upon their members. However, most modern religious organizations have elements of utilitarianism. They often hire people to work in their organizations, and these employees are just as interested in the amount of pay they receive as most other employees.

Nonetheless, most organizations tend to vary between these different forms. In modern, pluralistic, and liberal societies, for example, most religious organizations are primarily normative organizations. The members can rarely be coerced – at least not as adults – because they would respond by leaving. Although some employees who harbor doubts about the organization will remain just to retain their livelihood, the large majority participate because they find the organization's goals and activities to be meaningful. Thus the leaders generally have normative means of control of members at their disposal. They can inspire their members, or at least give them such a modicum of meaning and social belonging that they choose to remain.

This fact has implications for the power wielded by leaders in normative organizations. Normative means of control are relatively weak in a liberal and pluralist society. If the leaders of a religious organization enforce strict discipline and move the organization in a sectarian direction, they might retain some faithful members by appealing to their loyalty. Nevertheless, such a religious organization will easily become less attractive to its environment. In societies characterized by a widespread skepticism towards authority, the media will tend to describe strict religious organizations in terms of sarcasm and ridicule, which is hardly favorable for organizations attempting to recruit new members (Repstad 2003b).

Etzioni's typology can be useful in analyses of religious organizations. As with other ideal types, it is helpful in detecting characteristic features of specific organizations, including features hidden behind the facade and the public image. In a religious context the latter could, for example, be the organization's financial interests or its use of force to maintain commitment and loyalty among members.

8.7 Forms of domination in religious organizations

A number of Max Weber's concepts are still operative in contemporary sociology, for example, his sociology of legitimate domination, where he distinguishes between traditional, charismatic, and legal–rational domination (Weber 1968/1922). Weber uses the German term *Herrschaft*, often translated in English as "legitimate domination" or "authority," meaning the use of power that is perceived as justified and acceptable by those subjected to that use of power. Thus authority is different from the exercise of power based on coercion, threats, and force, and from the use of power based on monopolistic control of economic resources in the market-place. Weber uses these concepts for organizations in general, not only for religious organizations.

Traditional authority is based on habit and the absence of reflection upon alternative forms of domination. In stable societies, the source of authority tends to be tradition. The authority to rule is inherited, for example, from father to son. It has "always" been this way, and no one envisions that it could be any other way. In modern societies, the clergy's authority is also based on tradition to a certain degree. The clergy simply "belongs" on certain occasions. Nevertheless, Weber points out that few have such a presumed source of domination in a modern, differentiated society. Here, authority usually has a different source.

Charismatic authority constitutes a personal source of domination. The holder of charismatic authority is ascribed special powers and a special mandate by their followers. In a religious context, the charismatic aspect is often characterized by a divine calling and mission. The charismatic leader has an unusual magnetism, but from a sociological perspective charismatic authority is not solely based on personal qualities. Even more important is the relationship between the leader and the followers who ascribe to the leader this authority. Therefore, charismatic leaders are more in demand in some situations than in others. In times of rapid and unsettling changes, a demand for a strong leader may grow. In such situations, the creation of myths and idealizations can elevate fairly insignificant personalities into charismatic leaders.

According to Weber, modernization will produce a continuously more rational and "demystified" world (see Section 3.3). He describes the discomfort of modern society as "the iron cage of rationality," and he believes that in times of rapid change this discomfort will result in the formation of social movements controlled by charismatic leaders. Modern mass media may make such leaders even more popular, even if the media often tend to present a sarcastic slant to leaders with a pompous self-image.

Legal–rational authority is the form of domination that Weber primarily relates to the emergence of modernity. This concept is dual and embraces different forms of authority. The legal aspect refers to the fact that the domination rests on a legal basis, whereas the rational aspect refers to knowledge. Altogether, legal–rational authority is based on the fact that the authority figure has a mandate and can invoke the idea that this mandate has been assigned by a widely accepted procedure. By developing Weber further, we propose that there are three categories of authority within the legal–rational concept. The first is the bureaucratic authority, where the bureaucrat's power is delegated in accordance with laws and authorizations. Bureaucrats primarily interpret rules given by others, and their authority is based on the interpretations of given guidelines in individual cases. The bureaucrat's decisions are accepted as legitimate, if there is a sense that the decisions have been made on the basis of a reasonable interpretation of a set of rules. The second category is related to professional authority that is based on expert knowledge. We listen to advice from a doctor or plumber because we believe they act with authority in the particular area of expertise. A third category is democratic authority, which is also legally based, in the sense that it is derived from a constitution. In some instances, a democratic authority represents a corrective to other forms of domination. For example, in a political context, majority decisions may be made into law against the advice of bureaucrats and experts, if the constitutional rules of play indicate that this is a case that must be decided by majority vote. Sometimes, democratic authority represents an ideological critical edge over both bureaucrats and experts. This happens when people's common sense conflicts with narrow-mindedness and sectorial thinking.

As noted, Max Weber discussed how movements were able to survive after the first generation. This is particularly the case for movements led by charismatic leaders. In his analysis, he introduced the concept of the routinization of charismatic authority. A more commonly used sociological term for the same phenomenon is the institutionalization of charismatic authority. A movement will improve its opportunity to survive if it is successful in bringing the personal charismatic authority of the founder into a more formal leadership position, or perhaps office. The classic example, also offered by Weber, is the transfer of the personal authority of Peter the Apostle to the papal office. According to the New Testament, Peter received his authority as leader of the church directly from Jesus, and the Catholic Church has later attached great importance to the so-called apostolic succession – the fact that popes have succeeded each other in an unbroken chain all the way back to the master of the church. Thus the authority is tied to the position of the leader, and it is not threatened even if a pope is elected who has little personal charisma.

Weber's model of different forms of domination has come under critique for being too intellectual and pedantic. Pierre Bourdieu (1987) accuses Weber of engaging in abstract debates on legitimacy. Bourdieu's understanding of power assigns more importance to the idea that people unconsciously tend to internalize ideas and behaviors based on their social context and experiences. Therefore, Bourdieu argues, relationships of dominance need not be justified with references to forms of legitimate or rational reasons. A common and efficient form of exercising power occurs without reflection and without the understanding that it has to do with the use of power at all. When something is considered (or overlooked) as a natural and self-evident matter, power is at its zenith (see Section 4.5). Over the last thirty years or so, sociological theory on power has expanded its concept of power to the degree that it can be invisible and not linked to actors with specific intents. Discourse power, definition power, and anonymous power are terms often used in connection with a wide understanding of power. These wide concepts of power have doubtlessly pointed out important phenomena in social life, but if the concepts of power are too wide they may cloud the fact that some actors actually have more power than others. Theories that argue for the presence of invisible power make change virtually impossible. They are too deterministic and can easily become self-fulfilling prophecies, as in "If changes are impossible, what is the point of trying?"

A critique of Weber's theory of authority closely related to Bourdieu's argument is that Weber draws a very harmonious picture of organizations. With its emphasis on the importance of legitimate domination, Weber's analysis veils the underlying raw and more tangible forms of power. For example, when bureaucratic rules are not respected, the police and the courts will apply a legitimate use of coercion. Nevertheless, Weber's focus on legitimate domination is still useful. One example can be found in religious contexts that harbor ethical ideals of liberty and equality, where there will be very definite demands for justification of the use of power.

All concepts of domination are intellectual categories or ideal types. In this area, reality usually offers a mixture of forms. Does the clergy's or the imam's authority have its source in personal qualities, an office with routinized charisma, legal authorization or traditional inherited respect? Perhaps the clergy and the imam also have some tougher means of persuasion in waiting, and are able to make life uncomfortable for others. The clergy's and the imam's power usually consists of a mixture of these elements, which also tend to vary according to different contexts. The world is not as orderly and well defined as the categories might suggest. Nevertheless, typologies may help us organize an otherwise relatively chaotic reality.

The typology of authority may be used to distinguish between different types of religious organizations according to their prevalent form of domination. It can also be used to gain a better understanding of tensions and conflicts in such organizations. A classic contrast, also described by Weber, is between personal and institutionalized charisma, that is, between the prophet who brings new revelations and the clergy who dispenses the old ones. Tensions may also arise between those who want to emphasize democratic forms of leadership in a religious community, and theologians and others who want to stress the idea that religious truths cannot be changed by a majority vote. The sociological interpretations of such disagreements vary a great deal. Some sociologists see religious leaders' argument that religion cannot be managed democratically as a subjectively honest defense. More critical sociologists will see professional self-interest, for example from theologians, behind such concern for the truth.

8.8 Sociological studies of religious movements and minorities

There are many sociological analyses of religious minority movements. The research consists largely of several case studies, and discrepancies flourish when it comes to conclusions. From an academic point of view, it is somewhat depressing to admit that a recurrent feature of social scientific research on religious minorities is that, regardless of the question, it appears that research can supply very different and in part mutually exclusive answers. This is particularly true as it relates to studies on new religious movements. The different conclusions refer to recruitment, internal matters, and societal significance.

As far as recruitment is concerned, some scholars find that participants in sects and cults are marginal and deprived while other scholars argue that they access several types of resources. Charles Glock is one of the most ardent spokespersons for the deprivation theory in the sociology of religion, and he thinks that people are attracted to sectarian movements because they have a sense of something missing from their lives. If a person is poor, lonely or of little regard in this world, the sect will provide compensation by promising rewards in the afterlife and embracing the acolyte in a safe and tight-knit community where they become important (Glock and Stark 1965: 256). Bryan Wilson notes in his critique of deprivation theory that one can easily find people who live miserable lives but who do not join sects, as well as examples of resourceful people who have joined sects. Wilson argues that various types of sects have different recruiting bases. Sects that attempt to change the lives of individuals, for example, tend to expand in modern, individualist, and partly secularized societies. Revolutionary and miracle-oriented sects that predict dramatic changes across the world in the near future will tend to expand in traditional societies undergoing painful transitions in their encounters with modernity. Wilson also warns against the assumption that simple explanations of sect membership can be found (Wilson 1970; 1990: 47).

British sociologist James A. Beckford (1975) conducted a comprehensive empirical study of members of the Jehovah's Witnesses in Britain. He found that several recruits had grown up in a Christian environment but later dropped out of religion. Their embrace of the Jehovah's Witnesses can be interpreted as a revival of old yearnings. Some of Beckford's findings provide support for the deprivation theory. According to his study, several recruits lived in some degree of social isolation. In particular, he pointed to small nuclear families who lived relatively far away from larger family networks and who worried about their children's environments.

Beckford's study focuses on an established religious minority and was conducted a few decades ago. More recent studies of new religious movements show that their participants tend to be young and middle class (Barker 1985; Hannigan 1991).

When it comes to the social role of new religious movements, scholars present different views. Most emphasize the social powerlessness of these movements (Beckford and Levasseur 1986; Wilson 1990), whereas a small minority regard them as the spearhead of a new religious golden age. The emergence of new religious movements has been described as the result of a contemporary appetite for experimentation in a time of affluence, and a renaissance of magic in times of declining economic expectations (Robbins 1988). Some have applauded new religious movements as a virtually definite proof that secularization theory has failed. Others have viewed them as a sign of secularization, because religion is pushed to the margins of society (Turner 1991; Wilson 1990). They have been alternatively described as an expanding phenomenon, or at the point of stagnation and withering away.

Thus the study of new religious movements is characterized by a relatively high degree of scholarly disagreement. It seems unlikely that empirical research alone will end all disagreement on interpretation. However, debates on interpretation would have a firmer basis if more comparative studies were conducted that analysed various religious movements in different social contexts. There has been a tendency in this field to speak in terms of far-reaching conclusions when the empirical basis consists of only a few case studies. Indeed, case studies of individual movements or communities are useful, but the danger in this approach lies in the exaggeration of some individual features of these particular cases and the lack of consideration of other features that could be just as significant or interesting.

Several scholars have chosen, for practical reasons, to conduct case-study analysis based on observation. Studies of individual communities are more manageable and cost-effective than larger comparative studies of several communities. Nevertheless, perhaps participant observation of single communities should dominate future research to a lesser degree. This form of research seems to have a hidden romantic tendency to exaggerate the idea that religious movements are isolated, locally contained, small communities in large modern societies. As Bryan Wilson (1990) has pointed out, modern religious movements are often integrated in large national and international networks which have their own religious bureaucracies and career ladders. In some instance, surveys of members can be a more appropriate research strategy than case studies based on participant observation.

Furthermore, research seems to suggest that recruitment to institutionalized new religious movements culminated at the end of the 1980s, and that New Age ideas are nowadays communicated more through books and brochures than through strong organizations (Melton 1998). Norwegian scholars of religion have used the expression "religion spread as a thin layer" to describe this development (Alver et al. 1999: 8). The expression suggests that several different religious ideas appear in contexts not traditionally associated with religion, such as popular culture, fashion, advertising, therapy, and tourism. If customer or client roles have become more important than member roles in some parts of religious life, scholars must apply relevant methods to select informants and speak with them on the importance of religion in their lives. If the religious field is no longer clearly demarcated, participant observation is not a useful method of study. And if it is true that various religious ideas mostly exist as individuals' private views, a more appropriate research strategy would be the use of surveys, even if this method can give a somewhat superficial form of knowledge. At least it is useful if we want to gain knowledge about the prevalence of such views in the population.

It is not surprising that sociologists and social anthropologists have tended to harbor a negative view on popular non-sociological explanations of conversions to religious sects, that is, the so-called brainwashing models. These models explain members joining by arguing that effective propaganda techniques seduce potential joiners, whereby they lose control of their own lives. Sociologists have largely rejected this form of explanation, pointing in part to the ideological conditions when they were formulated, namely as American theories about Communist indoctrination during the Cold War.

From an academic point of view, it is more interesting to analyse which groups of actors might benefit from using the brainwashing model (Repstad 1995c; Richardson 1993). First, these models have satisfied the media's insatiable need to cover the exceptional and the sensational within the framework of a battle between good and evil. The story of brainwashing is a story about evil persons who attack unsuspecting and innocent victims. For former members of religious movements, as well as their close friends and relatives, blaming one's actions on brainwashing is a way for all actors to save face. Since participation in a religious movement in some instances implies a breach with family and friends, this explanation shifts the attention away from possible familial problems that could be seen as reasons for the family breakdown. The idea is that family order is re-established once the brainwashing has worn off.

For more or less professional helpers, models of indoctrination by force have opened up and legitimized new therapeutic markets, where various forms of deprogramming are offered. Finally, some competing religious organizations have their own religious version of a brainwashing discourse, in the form of possession by demons or similar. For example, conservative Evangelical Christian groups often attack new religious movements for being the instruments of demonic or satanic forces. Competing movements also often offer a mixture of spiritual and psychological explanations, suggesting that devoting oneself to such forces is dangerous because it is easy to lose self-control.

A majority will readily turn to intentional explanations when they look at familiar phenomena, but they will often use stereotypical descriptions of irrational (or brainwashed) behavior when they look at deviating minority movements. In cases where the movements are exotic, the majority might be tempted to claim that the leaders have poor morals and extreme manipulative powers. None of these explanations appears very honorable, whether one is apathetically programmed by a sect culture or consciously plans a strategy to one's own advantage. Leaders of religious movements are often ascribed all kinds of ignoble motives, for example, personal desires for power mixed with sexual or economic motives. We believe that this does occur, but it is important to bear in mind that our standard explanations, our stereotypes, are easily available when we consider those who are different and exotic.

Scholars may easily fall into the methodological and unethical trap where they juggle between various forms of explanation and treat the statements of some informants in a diagnostic way while uncritically accepting the statements of others. Indeed, social research explanations should be supported by empirical data if possible. How authoritarian are power structures in a given movement is an empirical question, even in movements where we dislike the ideology.

9
Religion, social unity, and conflict

This chapter discusses the ways in which religion contributes to social unity as well as social conflict. Whereas many sociologists of religion have focused on the role religion plays in creating social integration, religion's contribution to conflict has been perceived to be more problematic. The 1970s and 1980s witnessed an increase in conflict and controversy as religious groups experienced growth in the United States, Europe, Latin America, and the Middle East. This religious resurgence was commonly termed "fundamentalism." Although most forms of fundamentalism were peaceful, others have engaged in terror and religious violence.

In this chapter, we will first analyse how religion contributes to social unity, before we examine its role in social conflict. We will continue by focusing more specifically on fundamentalism, the definition of the concept, its common features, and the ways in which this phenomenon has been explained in the sociological literature. Then, we will take a look at religious violence, before we discuss whether the sources of religious conflict are purely social or related to the nature of religion.

9.1 Religion and social unity

An important topic in sociological theory is the bonding of individuals into society. From before the inception of sociology, philosophers have been asking themselves what it is that makes society possible. What integrates society as a whole? What integrates different groups at various levels of society? Which forces hold members of a group in interaction over a given period of time?

Within so-called integration theories, as represented by Émile Durkheim, Talcott Parsons, and Robert Bellah, social cohesion is secured through the presence of specific institutions (family, religion, economy, the legal system) that promote the complementary and coordinated activity of other sub-systems of society. Durkheim, Parsons, and Bellah emphasize that religion helps the social system to sustain stability and equilibrium. Since religion is perceived to be an institution of integration, religion is by these sociologists viewed as a prerequisite for every society in order for it to survive.

Religion can clearly be an important contributing factor in social cohesion. We have seen that religion can be an element in a unifying nationalism, and Bellah found civil religion to provide integration in various periods of American history (see Section 6.4). There are also examples from modern history where religion has played a contributing role in creating social cohesion, for example, in Poland before the collapse of Communism in late 1989. Historically, Catholicism had played a complex but significant role in preserving Polish national identity and preventing the full assimilation of the nation into its neighbors' societies. In the early 1970s, the Catholic Church in Poland was criticized for its caution towards the Communist regime. A shift appeared in the mid-1970s when the church began to voice a defense of human rights and to cooperate with various opposition forces. The accession of a Polish pope, John Paul II, in 1978 made that cooperation all the more important. In the 1980s, nearly 90 percent of the population were members of the church and religious practice was relatively widespread. Although a secularization of beliefs had taken place and it was well known that a large proportion of the population ignored the church's positions on moral issues such as abortion, the grip of the church over the Polish population remained quite firm. The explanation for this was found in the role of the church as the guardian of national values.

From the early 1980s, the Solidarity movement, the largest opposition movement, drew on this tradition by incorporating national sentiments and religious symbolism. The leader of Solidarity, Lech Wałęsa, decorated his jacket with the picture of the Black Madonna of Częstochowa, a Catholic shrine and object of pilgrimage for Polish Catholics (Kennedy and Simon 1983). The relationship between Solidarity and the church changed over time, as Solidarity became increasingly secular and left its roots in the church behind. After the Communist regime collapsed in 1989, the socio-political power of the church also diminished (Haynes 1998: 93–4). Today, the church struggles to find its place in a modern democracy, the main ideological battle being between Catholicism and liberalism (Casanova 1994: 109–13). Although religion undoubtedly did contribute to social integration during a period of Polish history, its role is still not quite clear-cut, as other factors also contributed to such cohesion.

Due to the complexity of modern societies, most do not have one single religion, but have competing religions, or large groups that do not participate in any religious community. In these cases, religion can provide social cohesion in parts of the social structure. The case of Judaism in the United States can serve as an example here. Jews do not form a single racial or ethnic group, so Judaism is not the religion of a single people. There are also many forms of Judaism, such as Reform, Orthodox, Reconstructionist, and Conservative, and within Orthodox Judaism there are many subdivisions as well. In addition, there are many American Jews who do not identify being Jewish with being religious. Nevertheless, the American professor of religion and theology Jacob Neusner claims that it is still accurate to claim that "Jews are a people with a single religion" (Neusner 2000: 108). The reason is that among the nearly 6 million Jews in the United States, about 4.5 million define being Jewish as a matter of religion. Although religion has contributed to some sort of social cohesion among American Jews, the differences between the various forms of Judaism have also created conflict. Furthermore, American Jewish sociologists have debated the future of American Jewry and its ability to preserve its distinctive Jewish religious culture. Some, frequently called the "assimilationists," hold a pessimistic view and assert that American Jewry is assimilating culturally and declining numerically. They see modernization as incompatible with the maintenance of strong ethnic and religious loyalties. Others, called the "transformationists," acknowledge that the United States has modified Jewish life, but they argue that this does not threaten

Jewish continuity. For them, the modernization process has changed but not attenuated Jewish identity (Shapiro 1997: 152–4).

Furthermore, religion may be an important factor providing cohesion in a society characterized by so-called "pillarization." The notion of "pillarization" describes the structuring of society into organizational units, which may be political or religious, that provide social functions and activities for their members (Dobbelaere 1998b). A common example of such organizational units is the early nineteenth-century labor movement, which provided its members with a number of different services, such as unions, insurance, banking, newspapers, leisure activities, schools, and so forth. Because such sub-systems strive towards self-sufficiency, problems in a society arise when the attempt is made to create an overall integration in spite of these different pillars or sub-systems. In some cases, a shared religious tradition may be a source of cohesion in spite of these differentiating factors and may thereby contribute to limiting conflicts in a given society, for example, a religious community that manages to find support across different social classes and ethnic groups.

Also, there are situations where religion seemingly provides integration, but where authoritarian leaders impose an apparent social cohesion upon society's members. One example is Afghanistan, where the mujahidin victory over the Soviet occupational forces led to civil war. Seemingly out of nowhere, a group of students (*taliban*) appeared in 1994 and within two years imposed a new regime of strict Muslim morality and order. Initially, they were portrayed as young students whose successful war of liberation had created peace and social unity. However, the reality was that they had introduced a totalitarian regime (Esposito 1999: 264–5). Due to their extremely conservative interpretation of Islam, they banned all women from the public sphere. They imposed cruel oppression of anyone deviating from their interpretation of Islam and the Shi'ite minority, whom they viewed as heretics (Benard 2002). This type of imposed religious cohesion brought on by pervasive oppression is relatively unusual in recent history.

9.2 Religion and social conflict

We have mentioned that there has been a tendency among many sociologists of religion to emphasize the role of religion in creating social cohesion, and to view conflict as a deviation. However, other sociologists have claimed that both social cohesion and conflict are integral parts of social life.

Although there are several conflict theories in sociology, we will focus on two traditions here. One tradition, which derives from Marx, sees conflict as the basic force of social change (see Section 3.1). According to Marx, class struggle is the fundamental struggle of society, and religious conflict is merely the expression of the underlying struggle between the different social classes. Since religion is understood to be part of the superstructure, this approach tends to undermine the independent role that religion might play in producing conflicts.

Another tradition is based on Georg Simmel's (1971: 70–95) work on social conflict. He views conflict as a form of human interaction and one form of association. He believes that some conflicts are positive and constructive whereas others are costly and tragic. American sociologist Lewis Coser (1956), who is a structural functionalist, draws upon Simmel and emphasizes that social conflicts can have the negative function of weakening society, but they can also have the positive functions of binding groups together and maintaining the social structure. Following this tradition, some conflicts will have stabilizing effects whereas others have disruptive effects. Meredith McGuire (1997: 198–9) argues that "conflict is the obverse of cohesion." This means that cohesion at one level can produce conflict on another level, and conflict from the outside can contribute to internal cohesion. By reviewing the literature on religion and conflict, we find that there are numerous examples of conflicts both between and within religious groups, and connections between religion and social conflict.

Conflicts between religious groups can take place at different levels, within a continent or a region, within a nation, or a local community. Here, we will take a look at a more recent conflict that has emerged in Europe and the Western world, namely the conflict between a rapidly growing Muslim minority and the Christian majority. Today Islam is the second largest religion in several European countries and the third largest religious community in Britain and the United States (Esposito 2000: 180). This growth of Islam is primarily the result of migration from the Middle East, Asia, and Africa to the West, which for many years was so insignificant that it went unnoticed until the late 1960s and 1970s. In the United States, the Muslim presence is less visible than in Europe, due to the fact that many Muslims have kept a low profile and attempted to blend in. In Europe, tensions between religious identity, secularization, and privatization have been growing. These tensions rose to the surface in the 1980s, due to two events: the "Salman Rushdie affair" and the "headscarves affair" in France. The latter event has continued to cause conflict.

The publication of Salman Rushdie's novel *The Satanic Verses* in 1988 resulted in the *fatwa* issued by Ayatollah Khomeini in February 1989, which stated that Rushdie had insulted the Prophet and Islam, and that he should be assassinated. Demonstrations were held in several European cities, followed by international repercussions. The second event, the "headscarves affair" in France, began in 1989 when, in contravention of a new regulation, three Muslim girls at a secondary school insisted on wearing headscarves during school hours. Since the separation of church and state in France in 1905, a ban had existed on overt expressions of religious practice in public schools (Esposito 1999: 249–52; Kepel 1997: 126–46, 184–95; Nielsen 1995: 158–66). In 2004 the French Assembly passed a bill banning Islamic headscarves in public schools. The ban on religious attire in classrooms, which also included Jewish skullcaps and large Christian crosses, led to protests in several European cities.

At the time when these events began to cause conflict, immigration was becoming a more overtly political question in several European countries. In the 1980s and 1990s, a heated debate on the extent of religious freedom was raging. Those who favored stricter immigration policies and assimilation of immigrants into European culture used the "Rushdie affair" as a scare tactic, calling it a frightening portrait of future events and developments if Muslims were allowed to freely practice their religion. The issue for the Muslim communities, on the other hand, is that the same public status and respect should be granted to their religion as to that of the Christian churches. The presence of Islam is continuing to challenge most Western countries regarding the rights of minority religions and the presence of religion in the public sphere (Esposito 2000; Shadid and van Koningsveld 1991, 1996; Vertovec and Peach 1997).

In situations of sacralization of political or social institutions, religion can contribute to social conflict. Sacralization is here defined as "the process by which the secular becomes sacred or other new forms of the sacred emerge" (Demerath 2003: 214). Although sacralization can take many forms, we are here talking about situations where political and/or societal institutions are considered to be sacred or seen as a result of divine will. In situations where large groups of people believe that their political and social institutions are sacred, such a belief might strengthen their support of the institutions in question. In these situations compromises are often difficult to find. One reason may be that leaders get caught up in their own absolute rhetoric: it is not easy to meet the opponent halfway if one has characterized the opponent as a tool of Satan. It may also be difficult to change view on issues one has described as God's order of creation. In extreme cases, violence is used, based on the belief that it will lead to eternal blessing or other religious rewards.

Although religion undoubtedly can lead to conflict, its role is complicated, as other factors often contribute to the conflict as well. In some instances, the claim for a priority of religious identity can clash with other types of identities, such as nation, race, class, and gender, and thus result in conflict. One example is the Indian subcontinent, where the religious conflict between Hindu and Muslim communities has split the nation and become the basis for competing nationalisms (Juergensmeyer 1993). A similar example is found in Northern Ireland, where ethnicity, religion, and politics are so tied together into total identities that segregation is a result (Ignatieff 1993: 216).

In addition to these intergroup conflicts, there have also been several intragroup struggles. Protestantism has frequently experienced conflicts among its many churches and denominations. For example, in the 1970s and 1980s, the so-called "New Christian Right" emerged in the United States, advocating a moral traditionalism in public policy. This movement confronted what they perceived to be "secular humanism" and voiced opposition to pornography, changing sex roles, abortion, and gay rights. On several of these issues, they came into conflict – and continue to come into conflict – with more moderate and liberal Christians (Ammerman 1987, 1991; Wald 1990).

Within the Orthodox churches, after the Soviet Union collapsed and Ukraine achieved its independence, conflicts appeared between the Russian Orthodox Church and the Ukrainian Orthodox Church. The struggle is over the Kiev monastery in Ukraine, which carries different symbolic meanings for Russians and Ukrainians. Kiev is the fountain of Russian Orthodoxy – in 987 Kiev's Prince Vladimir married the daughter of the Byzantine emperor in Constantinople and converted to Christianity. The remains of the monks, who had lived in the monastery before the conversion of Vladimir, are there embalmed in coffins and this is a site of pilgrimage for Orthodox believers. Since Ukraine became independent, a Ukrainian Orthodox Church has sought exclusive jurisdiction over the monastery. For Ukrainians, the site symbolizes the beginning of Ukrainian national consciousness. For Russians, the loss of Ukraine represents also the loss of their own symbolic origins (Ignatieff 1993: 116). This example shows that even in situations where there is a shared religious tradition, conflicts among the adherents of the same tradition may develop.

Finally, social conflicts can also spill over into religious communities and lead to conflicts within the communities, for example, the effect of the women's movement in the 1960s and 1970s, which spawned debates over the role of women in churches. The presence of women clergy has increased in several parts of the world. Women clergy are now common within the Lutheran churches in the Nordic countries, with the exception of a few smaller free churches, and within nearly all mainstream religious organizations in the United States women clergy have been ordained (Carroll et al. 1983). Female bishops have also been ordained in several Western countries. In addition, the women's movement is having its effects on Islam, where the role of women is now frequently debated (Mir-Hosseini 2000; Roald 2001).

More recently, the gay and lesbian movement has led to divisions and strife within churches. In Norway, as in several other countries, the debate has centered on the issue of whether gays and lesbians have the right to be ordained to service in the church. The Church of Norway distinguishes between homosexual orientation and practice, and has only given the right to be ordained to gay and lesbian clergy who refrain from sexual activities. A minority of the bishops have, however, given practicing gay and lesbian clergy who live in stable registered partnerships the right to be ordained. Only a few years back, the view among the church leadership corresponded to the one found in the population. However, the general public is no longer concerned with the distinction between orientation and practice, which has left the church leadership in a conservative camp out of touch with the larger population (Repstad 2002: 70–71).

As we have seen, religion can be a source of conflict. Below we will see how religious communities initiate agendas that often produce conflict. We have mentioned that in the 1970s and 1980s there was a religious resurgence, often called "fundamentalism." During the 1990s and early twenty-first century, the world has also witnessed an increase in religious violence. It is to these issues that we shall now turn.

9.3 Fundamentalism

The term "fundamentalism" originated in the United States in the 1920s, where a series of publications on "The Fundamentals" of the Christian faith served as a point of reference for groups of American conservative Protestants. The purpose was to protect what they saw as the core of Protestant truth against the liberal views of that era. Later, the term "fundamentalism" was broadened to refer to the most conservative expression of some religious bloc, for example, conservative Catholics. In the 1970s and 1980s, it was often used to describe any group that took its religion seriously or that made claims on public policy to reflect their religious views. At this point, the term often had a negative connotation, implying that "fundamentalists" were emotional and irrational extremists or that fundamentalism represented an archaic form of religiosity of the culturally backward (Bruce 2000: 10–12). This led some to reject the term altogether. Other scholars, such as the American church historians Martin E. Marty and R. Scott Appleby (1991: viii–x), who led a larger research project called *The Fundamentalism Project* in the mid-1990s, suggested that there are enough common features in many fundamentalisms to continue using the term.

Although there are numerous understandings of fundamentalism, Scottish sociologist of religion Steve Bruce (2000: 13–15) has in a recent outline of the essential issues and background of this phenomenon pointed to at least five features that many scholars view as common among various fundamentalist groups. First, Bruce points out that fundamentalists tend to claim that one or more sources of ideas, such as a religious text, is free from error and complete, for example, Protestant Christians who view the Bible to be "the word of God" in the sense that its revelation is complete and that it is correct in every detail. Another example is Muslims who see the Qur'an as "God's literal and eternal word." An additional text in Islam is the Hadiths or "traditions," which are narrative stories or preserved accounts about the Prophet's sayings and actions. Each Hadith must be evaluated according to its authenticity, since the original sources are meant to provide a perfect guide.

Second, fundamentalists tend to reach back to real or presumed pasts and claim the existence of ideal original religious conditions. Although they present their vision of the past as whole and pure, they tend to be selective in their view of their past, employing those features that will fit their present agenda. Since this agenda often is to advocate a return to the past, this means for Christians, for example, a return to early Christianity or to earlier versions of Christianity.

The third feature Bruce mentions is that fundamentalists emerge in traditional cultures but one cannot say that they are simply traditional. Fundamentalists not only adhere to a tradition that has survived, but deliberately attempt to regenerate tradition and make it socially significant again. This means that fundamentalists do not just represent the past continued, but they are provoked by change and rework the past for present purposes. The creation of radical revisions of the past and efforts to change the present represent a feature of the modern world. In this way, fundamentalists are affected by the perceived threat to tradition and their efforts to fight back or to resist such threats.

The fourth feature of fundamentalists is that they tend to appeal to marginalized groups in society, such as groups with an ambivalent or insecure socio-economic status. These are groups that are either excluded from power, or are upwardly mobile groups that are prevented from fulfilling their newly raised aspirations (see "deprivation theory" in Section 7.1). However, Bruce's notion seems to give a somewhat simplified picture at this point. French historian of religion Gilles Kepel, who has studied religious fundamentalism over a long period of time, has also emphasized in his earlier work that support for Christian and Islamic fundamentalist movements was primarily found among marginal groups and the educated youth, mainly in the applied sciences, whose parents had migrated from the rural districts to the cities (Kepel 1994: 137–8). In his later work, Kepel (2002) continues to point out that the support of radical, political Islam is found among the marginalized urban poor and the educated youth. However, he also argues that in several instances fundamentalist Islamic movements spread to the devout middle class. Political leaders also used this broader social basis to provide legitimacy. This indicates that the relationship between fundamentalism and social class is more complex than Bruce suggests.

Finally, Bruce points out that many fundamentalists tend to adopt and use modern technology. For example, the American Christian Right has made widespread use of tele-evangelism and built Christian cable television networks. They have also used computerized direct mailing lists to sell their products. In Iran, Ayatollah Khomeini spread his message by using tapes, and we have seen that the communication network within Al Qaeda was primarily built upon an extensive use of the Internet, fax machines, and cellular phones.

Other scholars have, of course, outlined additional features of fundamentalism. Martin E. Marty (1992) includes, for example, that fundamentalists seek authority, offend and cause scandal, resist ambiguity, create sharp divisions between "us" and "them," and are potentially or actually aggressive. Others emphasize the mythical aspects of fundamentalist ideologies, one of which is an expectation of a coming utopian golden age (Nielsen 1993). American sociologists of religion Anson Shupe and Jeffrey K. Hadden (1989: 111) found a common feature among many socio-political movements to lie in their resistance to the global institutional differentiation process. This renders religious institutions and belief systems marginal to culture, and these movements have a desire to bring religion back as an important factor in public policy. This aspect is also important in the American *Fundamentalism Project* (see Marty and Appleby 1991, 1993a, 1993b, 1994, 1995). Although the literature on fundamentalism is extensive and there are numerous ways to define the phenomenon, it seems that most scholarly analyses include several of the features outlined by Bruce.

Most empirical analyses of fundamentalism have focused on a limited number of fundamentalist manifestations found in Christianity, Islam (Kramer 1993; Sivan 1992), and Judaism (Friedman 1992; Hertzberg 1992). In addition, studies have been conducted on fundamentalism within Hinduism (Frykenberg 1993), Buddhism (Tambiah 1993), and Sikhism (Oberoi 1993). One example of a frequently studied fundamentalist movement is the New Christian Right that emerged in the United States in the 1970s. This movement interpreted America as a country in moral decline because it had turned its back on the religious values that had made it great (see among others Hadden 1989; Johnson and Shibley 1989; Wilcox 1996). The movement sought a return to tradition or orthodoxy, as found in their view of the "traditional" family, "traditional" church music, and "traditional" ways of organizing religion. Yet their view of the past was based on ideas, images, and practices that were prevalent in the late nineteenth century (Ammerman 1991). The independent Baptist pastor Jerry Falwell, the leader of an organization named "Moral Majority," began in the late 1970s to mobilize people who were concerned about America's moral decline. For the next decade, Moral Majority managed to mobilize conservative voters, so that their legislators were elected. The greatest success of the Christian Right in the 1980s was its contribution to the presidential election of Ronald Reagan. Yet, as the religious right became active in the political arena, it was exposed to the rules governing that arena. Their politicians had to take part in the public debate, where they often did not do very well. The result was that the movement experienced declining support in the 1990s, and it also failed to achieve any significant victory regarding its agenda. Nevertheless, the Christian Right experienced renewed growth and vitality through the election and re-election of George W. Bush, and a strong political alliance exists between the Christian Right and the Republican Party.

By taking a look at the sociological explanations of the resurgence of fundamentalism during the last three decades of the twentieth century, we find that these can primarily be grouped into two broad categories: crisis theory and resource mobilization theory (Sahliyeh 1990: 3–16). Within so-called crisis theories, religious resurgence is viewed as a result of the crisis of modernization. Various crisis theories emphasize different aspects of modernization that they believe will lead to religious resurgence. This may include the erosion of traditional morality and values, issues of identity, problems of legitimacy and political oppression in several countries, and widespread socio-economic grievances. Several scholars who have analysed fundamentalism belong to this category. Some crisis theories also focus on the disappointing efforts at modernization. One example is an analysis of India, where the argument is that economic deprivation, social exclusion, and political under-representation of the Sikhs in India aroused a militant religious movement (Singh 1990).

Other scholars emphasize crises of legitimacy and identity. Studies of Islamic fundamentalism often point out that several Arab leaders adopted Western socialist ideologies in the 1960s and 1970s and used them to control the state and suppress political and religious opposition. The crisis of leadership in many Arab states was further compounded by corruption and the inability to solve the problems of poverty and unemployment. In addition came the loss of the war against Israel in 1967, which was viewed as a punishment by God for the Arabs' neglect of Islam. Altogether, religious resurgence is explained as a reaction to the policies of the leaders in various countries (An-Na'im 1999; Esposito 2002; Kepel 2002). Some scholars also stress the negative consequences of modernization. Bruce (2000) and Hertzke (1990) argue, for example, that the growth of the New Religious Right in the United States was related to a conservative response among traditional Protestants who opposed the liberal practices in their country (for example, sexual permissiveness). Many of these types of grievances are also found among Muslims in the Middle East, where several Islamic groups claim that the integrity of their social values and institutions is threatened by Western culture (Esposito 2002; Kepel 1994, 2002).

According to these types of crisis theory, religion provides a type of coping mechanism, helping the aggrieved deal with the complexities of life, as religion gives a sense of refuge, guidance, comfort, and discipline. However, a major problem with these types of theory is that religious resurgence becomes a reactive phenomenon, in the sense that it is assumed that people act as they do due to pressures from external factors. These external factors or crises related to processes of modernization cannot in and of themselves explain religious resurgence. There is, thus, a need to explain how religious movements actually mobilize people to collective action.

In contrast to crisis theory, resource mobilization theory argues that collective action is not possible without the presence of opportunities to form organizations and act (see resource mobilization theory, Section 8.5). In addition, the vitality of the movement is dependent upon the presence of a variety of resources, such as people, money, ideology, leadership, organizational structures, and communication networks (Oberschall 1973; Tilly 1978). In this way, resource mobilization theory includes internal factors in its analyses of movement growth. Although Kepel (2002) in his comprehensive analysis of political Islam does not mention resource mobilization theory, he actually points to several factors he believes were necessary for the mobilization of this movement, which are often mentioned by resource mobilization theorists. In order to explain the Islamist upsurge in the 1970s, Kepel focuses on several factors, such as communication networks, ideology, the organizations that took part and the alliances they built, as well as the political opportunities for groups to act. He further analyses the demographic changes that produced a large recruitment pool and the recruitment strategies that were employed. Kepel also includes the financial resources available to Islamic groups through the oil industry and the complex Islamic financial system, which helped to build "Petro-Islam" (Kepel 2002: 62).

Despite these differences between crisis theory and resource mobilization theory, many scholars use a combination of the two, as, for example, Kepel (2002) does. The theoretical contributions to *The Fundamentalism Project* (Marty and Appleby 1991–95) also represented a variety of approaches, linking the dynamics and ideology of movements to their contexts. Due to the complexity of this phenomenon, a comprehensive explanation of the resurgence of fundamentalisms requires the employment of several perspectives.

9.4 Religious violence

Throughout this chapter, we have looked at various types of fundamentalisms, of which most are peaceful. Nevertheless, the distance between civility and violence is short and often swiftly traversed, and several fundamentalist movements have engaged in violence. History provides numerous examples of groups or members invoking the supernatural to legitimate violence. More recently, the world has witnessed how one extremist Islamic network, Al Qaeda, has used the concept of *jihad* (holy war) in Islam as a reason for its violent acts. The attacks on the World Trade Center in New York on September 11, 2001, the train station in Madrid in 2004, buses and trains in London in 2005, and several other places in the world have been justified with reference to this idea.

Sociology supplies several definitions of violence, some of which are relatively wide. One example is that of Pierre Bourdieu, who defines social domination as symbolic violence. Social domination has to do with a domination of the categories of perception, how one evaluates, distinguishes, and perceives phenomena in the world, such as food, art, and music. These perceptions always favor those who are in power, and those who are dominated tend to diminish themselves and their perceptions. This is a condition Bourdieu describes as symbolic violence (see Section 4.5). Johan Galtung (1969) uses the concept of structural violence when regarding every limitation of the human potential that is caused by economic and political structures. Structural violence is thus an invisible form of violence built into the structure of world society. In this chapter, we use a more limited definition of violence. We describe direct violence in the sense that the violence is intended by one or more specific actors, who use physical power with the help of either their bodies or weapons to inflict physical damage on the human body or human property.

Religious violence may take different forms. It may take place in relations between nations (India and Pakistan), between groups and the larger society (the anti-abortion movement in the United States), between groups within a society (Jews and Palestinians in Israel and the Occupied Territories), and between members of a group (male members' oppression of female members). In the following, we will take a look at some of these forms.

One example of religious violence is the abortion clinic bombings, which took place in the United States in the 1980s. In the mid-1980s, there was a drastic escalation in violent incidents directed against abortion clinics, including invasions, vandalism, death threats, bomb threats, bombings, assaults, arson attempts, arson, and kidnapping. In 1985 Revd. Michael Bray and two other defendants were found guilty of destroying seven abortion facilities. Some years later a member of Ray's network of associates, Rachelle Shannon, confessed to a string of abortion clinic bombings. She was also convicted of attempted murder for shooting and wounding Dr. George Tiller as he left an abortion clinic. In 1994 Bray's friend, Revd. Paul Hill, killed Dr. John Britton and his volunteer escort James Barrett as they drove up to an abortion clinic in Florida. Bray justified the violence by claiming that Americans lived in a situation of warfare comparable to Nazi Germany, where the demonic role of the government was hidden to most people. He saw the attacks on abortion clinics and the killing of abortion doctors as defensive rather than punitive acts. He also envisioned a struggle to establish a new moral order and replace the secular government with a biblically based religious politics (Ginsburg 1993; Juergensmeyer 2001: 20–30).

Some studies of religious violence emphasize the processes by which some groups demonize non-members in a manner that facilitates violence. This process is evident in the relationship between militant Muslims and the Western world. Whereas neither the Muslim world nor the West is monolithic, the Muslim world has frequently been presented by the West as the embodiment of oppression, aggression, brutality, fanaticism, and backwardness. Furthermore, the West has been described by several Muslim countries and groups as un-Islamic, atheistic, corrupt, oppressive, and neo-colonialist. Although the causes of terrorism are complex, the long historical cycle of demonization and counter-demonization of the "other" as the hostile "alien" tends to become a self-fulfilling prophecy and can constitute an element in the process that leads to acts of religious terrorism (An-Na'im 1999: 112). According to American professor of religion John L. Esposito (2002: 153–4), Osama bin Laden, Ayatollah Khomeini, and other Muslim leaders have identified specific grievances against Muslim regimes and the United States that are shared among a broad spectrum of Muslims. These are primarily related to American and European foreign policies in the region, especially their relationship with Israel. The Americans and the Europeans tend to overlook the Israelis' brutal policies in the Occupied Territories while meeting the Palestinian leaders with a tougher stand. Bin Laden has addressed these and other issues in his justification of *jihad* (holy war) against the West, which resulted in the attacks on the World Trade Center and the Pentagon on September 11, 2001 and several other places across the world since then.

Within all the major religions, women have been targets of oppression. Patriarchal symbols, myths, and teachings facilitate gender imbalances that in some cases translate into male violence against women (see Chapter 11). Western patriarchal religious traditions have had a tendency to alienate the spiritual, associated with the male, from the physical, associated with the female. Two other traditions within Christianity also contribute to a religious culture of violence against women, namely the support of the patriarchal order as the right order of society, and the glorification of suffering as a path to salvation (Tessier 1999: 1000). The glorification of suffering has functioned as a support for many churches' lack of initiative in dealing with domestic violence: women who live in abusive relationships are told to suffer in silence. However, the tendency to suppress the physical and the sexual is present in all world religions, and so is the view of the patriarchal order as the sanctified cosmic order. These traditions tend to treat women with contempt.

Violence against women has been practiced and justified within many religious traditions, for example, the institutionalized violence of the witch-hunts in Europe during the fifteenth and seventeenth centuries (Levack 1995). In Eastern religious traditions, certain values have degraded women, creating a climate conducive to violence against them. The often religiously supported prioritizing of boys over girls has led to the deaths of more female than male fetuses, and the mortality rate for female children is much higher than that of males in several parts of the world.

A more systematic and institutionalized discrimination and violence against women found a place in Afghanistan during the Taliban regime. In the late 1970s and the early 1980s important steps were taken in this country to improve women's legal status and social positions. Yet the civil war largely defeated the goal of emancipation of Afghan women, and before the Taliban took over, the issue of women's rights became a battle between fundamentalists and reformers (Moghadam 1992). Whereas resistance movements in other parts of the world often recruited women, the Afghan mujahidin excluded women. Women who became too visible or vocal were threatened and sometimes killed. Under the Taliban, women were not allowed to work or attend school. They were not permitted to be seen in the public sphere unless they were accompanied by a man, and they were forced to cover themselves in a head-to-toe covering (*burqa*). Infractions were met with brutal public beatings and women accused of adultery were murdered (Benard 2002).

In studies of religious violence, some explanations focus upon the psychology of those who engage in violence. Other explanations address the social contexts in which violence occurs. A study of religious violence of women will, for example, often outline the patriarchal structure within which such violence can take place. American sociologist Mark Juergensmeyer (2001) takes a cultural approach; that is, he attempts to understand the cultural contexts that produce acts of violence. He focuses on the moral and ideological, as well as the organizational, support that lies behind the violent acts, rather than on the "terrorists" who commit them. He found some common features within several different violent religious groups. One is the perception that their communities are under attack and that their acts are simply responses to the violence that is inflicted upon them. Another feature is the images of cosmic confrontation and warfare that are ties to this-worldly political battles. Furthermore, there are processes of satanization of the "others," often combined with the idea that their group must engage in symbolic empowerment. Although religion does not ordinarily lead to violence, it is not always innocent. We have seen that in some cases religion does play a definite role in justifying violence.

9.5 Social or religious sources of conflict?

In debates over the role of religion in religious conflicts, there is often a tendency to either underestimate religion and reduce all religious conflicts to social conflicts, or overestimate religion and treat it as the dominant cause of the conflict. Regarding the first view, a long tradition in sociology from Marx and Freud sees religion as a surrogate or construct that masks more profound underlying conflicts. Religious liberals may also use the argument that religious conflicts are "actually" conflicts regarding economic, ethnic, or social class issues, because they find it difficult to connect religion to violence. In some cases, religion is indeed related to other social, economic, and political issues. We have seen above, for example, how the strength of religion was related to political opposition in socialist Poland. Poland's Catholic Church gained vitality due to its link to the Solidarity labor movement. When Solidarity left the church to become part of the government and democracy was introduced, the church then faced a new situation of declining religiosity (see Section 9.1).

In other instances, religious cleavages have their sources in societal cleavages. Often religious boundaries overlap with other lines of cleavages, such as ethnicity, race, social class, and political or national loyalties. What appears to be a religious conflict may also be an ethnic and social class conflict. An illustrative example here is the situation in Northern Ireland, which has frequently been described as a religious conflict. Although there is a definite division between Roman Catholics and Protestants, this cleavage also goes along lines of ethnicity, social class, economic interests, politics, neighborhood, and national belonging (Ignatieff 1993). In this way, it is difficult to distinguish the elements of the religious conflict from the other lines of divisions.

Scholars have also pointed out that there are some inherent traits in religions that make them trigger social conflicts and even legitimate the use of violence. Norwegian scholar of religion Torkel Brekke (1999: 123–4) argues that in some instances religion creates radical dichotomies that are useful to justify violent acts. When the distinction between "us" and "them" becomes exceptionally strong, the result may be abuse or holy war. Juergensmeyer (2001: 10) claims that the violence associated with religion is not an aberration but comes from the fundamental structures of the belief system of all major religions. In his study of religious violence, he found that the difference between religious and non-religious terrorism lies in the transcendent moralism that is used to justify violent religious acts, the ritual intensity by which they are committed, and the religious images of struggle and transformation or cosmic battles that are used. Thus, he concludes that there are aspects of all major world religions that can be used to justify violence.

A third position is proposed by American sociologist of religion Nicholas Jay Demerath (2001: 171–80), who calls for a proper midpoint. In his analysis of world politics and religion, he points out that in some cases, religion functions as a trigger and a cause of conflict and violence, whereas in other cases, religion has the role of the surrogate and construct that masks political, social, economic, or ethnic conflicts. Although religion may persist as a vital social and political force, Demerath argues that it is important to study how it fits in with a mix of other cultural and structural considerations.

9.6 Religion as a source of peace?

In this chapter we have seen that religion can play a role in contributing to social cohesion in a society or at different levels of society. We have argued that social cohesion and conflict are both aspects of social life and that social unity at one level often can produce conflict on another level. We have observed the potency of religion in creating conflicts, which also became especially evident in the 1970s and 1980s when several fundamentalisms experienced growth and made their claims in the public sphere. Furthermore, we have seen how religion has played an important role in global events of violence.

Even if religion is a force that can strengthen conflict, religion is also a factor that can help to reduce different types of conflicts. Juergensmeyer (2001: 238) has suggested that one out of several solutions to cure religious terror is that secular authorities embrace moral values, including those associated with religion. If religion could enter the public arena in an undogmatic and unobtrusive way, so that governments could act from the premise of moral integrity, this might make it difficult for religious activists to portray governments as a satanic enemy. Furthermore, Juergensmeyer points out that religion can function, like sport or art, as an escape from turmoil and violence. In some instances, religion has also created a neutral space, where religious leaders meet for mutual understanding. For example, in Israel rabbis and mullahs have met to share ideas. Finally, virtually every world religious tradition has projected images of peace and harmony. In South Africa, for example, the ideas of forgiveness and reconciliation were promoted to try to heal the apartheid years of white suppression, violence, and abuse. Indeed, every world religion upholds moral values that give guidance to peaceful interactions with fellow human beings.

10
Race, ethnicity, and religion

Whereas the sociology of religion has its own conceptual tools to use on the study of ethnicity and religion, we believe that these tools should be integrated with tools derived from ethnic studies. Therefore, this chapter represents an effort to point to classical and current trends in ethnic studies with the hope that this will be of benefit for future studies on race, ethnicity, and religion.

With the exception of Max Weber, none of the founding fathers of sociology paid much attention to ethnicity. The classic figures within ethnic theory are commonly considered to be W.E.B. Du Bois, Max Weber, and Robert E. Park. They provided concepts from which issues such as power, domination, exclusion, and inequality may be understood, and their ideas have been reshaped and reformulated by contemporary scholars. A special interest in contemporary theory is that of changing identities and the creation of new ethnicities. With increasing immigration into Europe and the United States, sociologists of religion have taken up the old tradition within sociology of studying immigrants and the role that religious faith and religious institutions play in their lives. This immigration has also prompted a reassessment of the meaning of citizenship and basic human rights, and challenged theorists and policy planners alike as to how to create societies where racial, ethnic, and religious majorities and minorities experience equal opportunities and equal respect.

This chapter begins by defining some key concepts, before we give a brief outline of classical and contemporary ethnic theory. Then follows an overview of recent research on immigrant religions. Towards the end, issues such as assimilation, pluralism, and multiculturalism are introduced, with some possible implications for the policy debate.

10.1 Concepts of race and ethnicity

Since the sixteenth century, the concept of "race" has been used to describe biologically distinct groups of persons who were supposed to have characteristics of an unalterable nature. The first scientist to develop a hierarchical racial scale based on biological traits was the Swedish botanist Carl von Linné (1707–78), who distinguished between four major racial categories. Later, more detailed distinctions were developed within each category. Over the years, the meaning of the concept "race" has changed several times in line with the ideological need to justify relationships of superiority and exploitation. Modern genetics tends not to speak of races, due to the fact that there has always been so much interbreeding between populations that the boundaries between races are not clear, and that there often are more variations *within* a racial group than *between* groups. Today, social scientists see concepts of race as socially constructed categorizations that are used to identify specific groups. Nevertheless, even if the concept of race is a social construction, it often exists in a real sense in the minds of people. For example, even if social scientists do not believe that race exists as such, it is fully possible to study the social phenomenon of racial categories in different countries. In societies where ideas of race are important, they may be studied as part of a local discourse on ethnicity (Eriksen 1999: 34–5).

The word "ethnicity" derives from the Greek word *ethnos*, which originally meant heathen or pagan. It was used in this sense in English from the fourteenth through the mid-nineteenth century. The American sociologist and social anthropologist William Lloyd Warner was the first to use the term ethnicity in his community studies, particularly in the works on "Yankee City" (Warner 1963/1941–45) and "Jonesville" (Warner 1949). Around the Second World War, the term "ethnics" was used to refer to Jews, Italians, Irish, and other minorities in the United States, and it was usually applied in a derogatory way. In the 1960s the terms "ethnic" and "ethnicity" became common in American and British sociology and social anthropology. They were often used without proper definition, although a common denominator was that they referred to a classification of people and group relationships (Eriksen 1999: 33–4). In sociology, ethnicity often refers to a shared (whether perceived or actual) racial, linguistic, or national identity of a social group. Ethnicity can incorporate several forms of collective identity, including cultural, religious, national, and subcultural forms.

Although ethnicity is often used in relation to a group's assumed racial identity, racial attributes are not necessarily or even usually a feature of all ethnic groups. Sociologists tend to identify social groups on the basis of cultural phenomena, such as shared rituals, language, customs, and so forth. So, even if ethnicity tends to be associated with minority groups, it is important to be aware of the fact that majority groups also are "ethnic." Some scholars think that race and ethnicity should be distinguished and studied separately, whereas others believe that race relations are a special case of ethnicity. A clear distinction between the two can be difficult to uphold. Therefore, it is reasonable to take a more empirical approach and argue that the concept of race may in some instances form part of ideas of ethnicity, and should be studied as such, whereas in some cases it does not (Eriksen 1999: 34–5).

Before the nineteenth century, religion was a primary vehicle used to articulate racist ideas. For example, theology was commonly used in Europe and the United States as a justification for the colonial domination in Africa and the Americas. In South Africa, the white majority used theology to legitimate apartheid as late as the 1980s. The argument was that God wanted the races to live separately to avoid societal chaos. Ironically, during the nineteenth century in Europe, religion was supplanted by science in providing an ideological justification for racial thought. At the same time, religion was increasingly used as a vehicle for attacking racism. The abolitionist movement in the United States, which opposed slavery, was generally based in Protestant churches. In the 1960s religion also played a significant role in the civil rights movement that sought to end segregation. Although many white churches opposed integration at first, most churches opposed racism by the end of this decade

(Kivisto 1998: 400). In the 1980s and 1990s, some European churches also became important participants in the immigration discourse, hosting asylum seekers and calling for more human immigration policies. However, this has only been true for some churches, as the majority have been relatively silent in the discourse on racism in Europe.

10.2 Classical theories of race and ethnicity

A major figure within classical theory on race is W.E.B. Du Bois (1868–1963), an African-American professor in history and economics. Du Bois moved racial explanations from the area of theology and "folk knowledge" and located them within the disciplines of history and sociology. With his focus on issues such as consciousness and identity, he introduced several themes that are particularly relevant in contemporary discourse.

Du Bois adheres to a tradition within race theory, the germ theory of races, which held that races, not individuals, are the significant carriers of values (Stein 1989: 84). Although this racial theory states that social values are primarily biological, Du Bois also outlines a relationship between a group's position in the social structure and the nature and degree of its consciousness. For him, white and black people represent different types of consciousness because they inhabit different social worlds (Dennis 2003: 15–16). In his book, *The Souls of Black Folks* (1968/1903), Du Bois introduces the concept of "double consciousness," which describes the conflict between the dual identities he believes he found among African Americans in the early 1900s. According to Du Bois, because white Americans do not yield black Americans any true self-consciousness, black Americans always have to look at themselves through the eyes of white Americans (1968: 495–6). As a result, Du Bois believes that African Americans have a self that contains competing goals. Their history represents, therefore, a struggle to attain a united self of being both black and American (1968: 496). This does not, however, imply that Du Bois believes that African Americans should assimilate into Anglo-Saxon culture. He argues that they should follow their own original ideals (Stein 1989: 82). In early 1900, Du Bois also studied how race relations were intertwined with religion in the United States. He views religious involvement as a source of ethnic attachment among African Americans as well as European Americans. On that basis, some have argued that Du Bois indeed was the very first American sociologist of religion (Zuckerman 2002).

The one classical sociologist who discusses race and ethnicity is Max Weber. Within the framework of his time, he discusses these topics in relation to class, status, and party. Although race and ethnicity had been defined on the basis of biological and social differences, Weber argues that these differences were not "natural," but socially determined. According to Weber, racial identity is "common inherited and inheritable traits that actually derive from common descent. Of course, race creates a 'group' only when it is subjectively perceived as a common trait" (Weber 1968/1925, I: 385). Likewise, Weber sees ethnicity as a "presumed identity" and ethnic groups are "those human groups that entertain a subjective belief in their common descent because of similarities of physical type or of customs or both, or because of memories of colonization and migration; this belief must be important for the propagation of group formation" (Weber 1968/1925, I: 389). Weber's definition of ethnic groups has subsequently been adopted in most of its basic elements by many scholars in the field.

According to Weber, it is not biological differences alone that constitute an ethnic group, but also its "customs" – clothing, food, housing, division of labor between women and men, and so forth. He also believes that it is not just physical and cultural aspects that are important but the subjective perceptions of these aspects. Ethnicity does not automatically end in group formation, although it facilitates such formation (Guibernau and Rex 1997: 2–3; Stone 2003: 32–3). Weber has a strong sense of the role of history in shaping perceptions about race and ethnicity. He looks at ethnic groups as having memories of a shared past, attachments to a territory, and certain traditions. All of these features may survive for a long period of time even in situations of colonization or migration. He also emphasizes the historical nature of discrimination and prejudice. When he argues against the widespread notion at this time that different races have repulsion against each other, he uses the existence of millions of people of mixed racial backgrounds in the United States as an argument against this view (Weber 1968/1925, I: 385–6). Thereby, Weber argues that discrimination is not naturally given, but historically conditioned.

In his discussions on race and ethnicity, Weber also calls attention to the role of religion. On the one hand, he sees religion as a legitimation used to segregate minority groups from the majority, as exemplified in the case of European Jewry. On the other hand, Weber claims that as in all status groups, the position of a racial or ethnic group will influence its religious orientation (see Section 3.3). According to him, positively privileged groups tend to believe that their human dignity is related to their beauty and excellence, so their "kingdom" is "of this world." In contrast, negatively privileged groups tend to connect their human dignity to the future, so they uphold a belief that "the last will be the first" in the afterlife or that the Messiah will appear and reward them (Weber 1968/1925, II: 934). In this way, Weber attached importance to the question of the role of religion in shaping racial and ethnic relations.

The sociological study of ethnicity in the modern world owes much to the American tradition of immigration and racial studies conducted by Robert Ezra Park (1864–1944) and others at the University of Chicago, where Park was professor in sociology. The Marxist tradition in sociology would argue that social conflicts between racial and ethnic groups is a manifestation of false consciousness, because the fundamental conflict is between social classes and not between ethnic groups. However, Park points to the importance of status groups in an explanation of social conflict. He claims that social conflict is most often the result of the efforts of status groups to enhance or protect their position in the social structure. Therefore, the conflicts between white Americans, African Americans, and recent immigrants to the United States have to do with relative group position, style of life, and beliefs (Lal 2003: 45).

The tradition from Park assumed that immigrants would assimilate into the United States and adopt its culture. Nevertheless, studies from the United States in the 1960s and 1970s demonstrated that several different ethnic groups resisted the pressures of assimilation into white Anglo-Saxon Protestant culture. Instead, they celebrated a revival of ethnic ties. In Europe, however, ethnicity fell into ill repute after the collapse of the Soviet Union and the brutal struggle for territory in the name of ethnicity, nationalism, or ethnic nationalism (see Chapter 9). The growing immigrant ethnic minorities also became the focus of hostility in their countries of settlement. As we will see below, these changes came to affect contemporary theories of ethnicity.

10.3 Contemporary theories of race and ethnicity

In response to the new world that developed towards the end of the twentieth century, several themes emerged among scholars on race and ethnic relations. Some central themes were concerned with the construction of ethnic identity and the origin and dynamics of ethnic groups. Various perspectives characterize the debate on ethnicity among contemporary sociologists and anthropologists, although one major division is that between essentialist and instrumental theory.

The essentialist approach defines an ethnic group by its distinctive common history and culture. The content of the culture, shaped by history, distinguishes one ethnic group from another. Essentialism presents a static and naturalistic view of ethnicity, as seen in socio-biology. More flexible essentialist variations distinguish themselves from biological or naturalistic approaches, and also emphasize historical ties. Here, ethnicity is viewed as a phenomenon that has "objective" cultural roots or is based on kinship established through birth (Horowitz 1985). Whether the essentialist theories emphasize biology or history, there is a tendency within this approach to view ethnicity as a "natural" and stable phenomenon.

The instrumentalists emphasize the socially constructed nature of ethnicity and the ability of individuals to pick and mix from a variety of ethnic heritages. Within this approach, ethnicity is treated as a social, political, and cultural resource for different interest and status groups. Drawing on Weber's notion of "social closure" or the general tendency of social groups to attempt to form monopolies, a new perspective on ethnic group formation opens up. Norwegian social anthropologist Fredrik Barth's (1969) writings on ethnic groups and boundaries represent variations on this theme. Barth claims that ethnic boundaries entail social processes of exclusion and incorporation. These boundaries are not dependent upon an absence of contact with outsiders, but persist despite a flow of personnel across them (Barth 1969: 9–10). In his analysis, Barth emphasizes the perceptions and purposive decision making of social actors. For him, ethnicity is situationally defined and produced in the course of social transactions that occur at or across the ethnic boundary in question. These transactions are of two basic kinds: processes of internal and external definitions. In the first case, actors signal to in- or out-group members a self-definition of their nature or identity. In the second case, one person or set of persons defines the other(s). Thus, the process of identity production is internal and external and takes place at a number of different levels. The post-Barthian social anthropology of ethnicity and communal identity has tended to emphasize the first side of the internal–external dialectic: upon processes of internal definition by groups rather than external definition by surrounding society (Jenkins 2003: 62).

A new approach that builds on some of the insights of earlier theories has emphasized ethnicity as a social construction, and has been referred to by a number of scholars (see Kivisto 1993). Werner Sollors (1989), professor in English and African-American studies at Harvard University, argues that the social construction of ethnicity constitutes a part of the process he calls the "invention of ethnicity." Sollors claims that several categories were previously perceived as "essentialist," such as childhood, generations, gender, region, and history. However, scholars now acknowledge the general cultural constructedness of the modern world (Sollors 1989: x). Sollors uses the category of "invention" to emphasize not so much originality and innovation as the importance of language in the social construction of reality. This concept suggests widely shared, though debated, collective fictions that are continually reinvented. Sollors argues against those instrumentalists who view ethnicity as merely a rational construct of those who use it for political or economic reasons. Although he does not dismiss this instrumentalist position, he does not want to reduce all aspects of ethnicity to such means-to-an-end calculations. Nevertheless, both the instrumentalists and the constructionists regard ethnicity, whether it is viewed as a resource or as a discourse, as a way in which groups organize in order to contest with one another for power. In that way, both see ethnicity as implying social conflict (Avruch 2003: 77). Whereas the instrumentalists tend to see the conflict as one over resources, the constructionists view it as a conflict over control of the dominant discourse of the society.

By calling ethnicity, that is, belonging and being perceived by others as belonging to an ethnic group, an invention, Sollors signals an interpretation in a modern and postmodern context. Postmodernists speak of invention in order to lay bare the textual strategies in the construction of the individual. Some postmodern discourse has gone so far as to let "reality" disappear behind an inventive language that dissembles it. Even if the concept of ethnicity is a social construction accomplished over historical time, it exists in a real sense in the minds of people. In a study of British Pakistani youth, Jessica Jacobson (1998) found, for example, that Pakistani ethnicity, as a basis of identity, was not something that they could shape at will. It was experienced as something given and inescapable. Since the majority of Britons regarded Pakistanis as foreign or alien, the British Pakistani youth maintained essentialist conceptualizations of identity. This shows that there is an inherent tension between the observers of ethnicity and the actors who are involved (Avruch 2003: 72). This does not mean that ethnicity is not socially constructed, but it does imply that there are certain limits to the extent to which individuals can redefine themselves and the groups to which they belong.

In some instances the constructionist approach can swing too far in the direction of emphasizing human agency and not giving attention to structural contexts. Peter Kivisto (1993: 101) has pointed out that the process of invention of ethnicity must be seen in a dialectical perspective, because not only do migrants or indigenous peoples shape ethnic identities and boundaries, but so do other groups, including the dominant groups in society. Often there are two or more competing versions of ethnic identity and group definition. Therefore, differences in political, economic, and cultural power must be considered when analysing the process of constituting and reconstituting ethnicity.

10.4 Immigration and religion

In the United States there is a long tradition of studying immigrants and their religion. W. Lloyd Warner was among the first to analyse the religious roots of various ethnic groups (Warner 1963/1941–45, 1949). In his classic, *Protestant–Catholic–Jew*, Will Herberg (1960) also analysed the transformation of religion that was taking place among immigrants and their children. Herberg predicted that the salience of ethnicity would gradually erode among American immigrants, only to be replaced by a heightened salience in the religious traditions. His thinking, which was common at the time, was premised on an assumption that no significant immigration into the American nation would occur in the near future.

However, the 1960s and 1970s witnessed a wave of immigration into Europe and the United States. These newcomers were overwhelmingly non-Europeans. In Europe, they came primarily from North Africa and Asia; in the United States, most immigrants came from Asia, Latin America, and the Middle East. As a consequence, the ethnic and religious landscapes in Europe and the United States have changed in significant ways. Towards the end of the twentieth century, Islam was the largest minority religion in several European countries and it is the third largest religion in the United States after Christianity and Judaism, and will become the second largest in another decade or so (Esposito 2000: 173).

Documentation on the situation of the new religious minorities in Europe and the United States was sparse until the 1980s. Most social science research tended to focus on issues related to the economics and politics of immigration and ignore the religious dimension of the immigrant and the ethnic minority communities (Yoo 1999: 8–10). This lack of attention clearly reflects the secular assumptions of sociology and anthropology, but the differences in levels of attention can also mirror the reality of religious life in different immigrant communities. For example, the extensive research on the religious life of Koreans in the United States emphasizes the role of Protestant Christianity in their lives, whereas lack of research into the religious dimension of the Filipino-American community can reflect their lack of involvement in American Catholicism (Kivisto 1993: 95).

In 1970s Europe, there were few visible signs of religious worship among the men who had come for temporary work without their families. When family reunification became more common, religious expression became more evident. Towards the end of the 1980s, tensions between religious identity, secularization, and privatization rose to the surface across Europe, especially related to the role of Islam. At this point, it was evident that the non-European workers did not return to their countries of origin in great masses, as had been expected. The children of immigrants grew to maturity and entered the labor market, and some entered colleges and universities. These developments and events placed the subject of Muslims in Western Europe on the academic and political agendas, with the realization that there was a growing religious factor in the social and political processes associated with immigration and ethnic minorities. At this point, scholars began to show a growing interest in new immigrant religions in the West.

Today, there are numerous studies that discuss the relationship between migration and religion. A large body of literature gives primacy to Islam, although some include

Buddhism, Hinduism, and Sikhism. Some provide an overview of the religious minorities that are present in one country, such as the United States (Eck 2001; Haddad et al. 2003). Other studies focus on one religious minority, such as Muslims, and analyse their social, political, cultural, and religious position in Europe and the United States (Bukhari et al. 2004; Haddad 1991; Haddad and Smith 2002; Kepel 1997; Nielsen 1995). Other scholars, again, analyse the different religious traditions found in a broadly defined ethnic group, such as Asian and Pacific Americans (Iwamura and Spickard 2003; Yoo 1999). A common theme is the ways in which migration has transformed the religious values and the organization of the religious community. One study, Yvonne Yazbeck Haddad and Adair T. Lummis' (1987) *Islamic Values in the United States*, analyses how Islamic values are preserved, abandoned, and transformed among American Muslims. On the one hand, religion frequently increases in importance as a result of migration. The situation of diaspora may strengthen the feeling of fellowship and revitalize the religious tradition. Learning the religious ideology becomes important to find a sense of belonging, and religion plays a role in a group's attempts to maintain cultural and linguistic identity. Several immigrant religious communities also provide services they did not deliver in the old country. For example, some immigrant religious communities offer language classes, activities for the children, women's groups, health services, and so forth. On the other hand, the new context in which migrants find themselves and the new discourses to which they are exposed may also transform the religious traditions. For example, the Western discourse on women's liberation and equality may put pressures on religious traditions towards more equality for women and men (Nyhagen Predelli 2004).

There has also been a growth in the number of case studies of specific immigrant religious congregations or groups, especially in the United States. Whereas some studies concentrate on specific communities (Haddad and Smith 1994; Schmidt 1998), others include a series of ethnographies that describe several different immigrant congregations across the nation (Warner and Wittner 1998). Comparative studies of several immigrant religions have also been conducted, and these have tended to be limited to one geographical area, such as Houston (Ebaugh and Chafetz 2000, 2002) or Los Angeles (Miller et al. 2001).

A review of the existing case studies on immigrant religion in the United States suggests a few common topics. A major theme is the role of religion in the maintenance and reproduction of ethnic identity. Stephen R. Warner and Judith G. Wittner (1998) found that a religious identity was highly salient for today's immigrant groups. However, not all immigrants maintain a country-of-origin religious identity, but join convert congregations who have turned away from the dominant tradition of the country of origin. Many Hispanic Protestants and Chinese Christians do this. Furthermore, the most characteristic adaptation of immigrant religious groups is the development of congregational forms and structure. Regardless of how their counterpart institutions abroad are structured, there is a tendency among immigrants to form organizations with a membership, religious leaders, and a number of lower-level organizations and groups. In addition, several immigrant religions also adopt a community-center model, where they deliver secular services to members, such as celebrations of secular holidays, language classes, health services, and recreational activities (Ebaugh and Chafetz 2000; Warner and Wittner 1998).

A major issue in several studies is the role of women in immigrant congregations. Migration tends to change the status of women and men in society, family, and religion, and although immigrant women face many of the same challenges as immigrant men, they frequently face a unique set of problems. On the one hand, they may experience marginalization and a loss of influence on family life. On the other hand, they may enjoy more independence, resources, and secured legal rights than they did in their homelands (Hondagneu-Sotelo 1994). Some immigrant women assume roles in the congregations that were not available to them in their country of origin, and for them, the church or the mosque can prove to be a vehicle of empowerment and integration into society (Haddad and Lummis 1987; Hermansen 1991; Miller et al. 2001; Schmidt 1998). In some instances, women play an increasingly important role in inter-religious dialogues, and women's involvement and knowledge result in new discourses within the religious communities (Jonker 2003). However, it is equally clear that this empowerment has certain limits. Often women are actively excluded from religious life, as the religious community offers the men an arena to reclaim the honor they are deprived of by the immigrant experience. In these cases, the men tend to monopolize the leadership roles in the congregations (Ebaugh and Chafetz 2000; Warner and Wittner 1998).

Finally, when considering religion and immigration, the issue of the children of immigrants becomes immediately apparent. Warner and Wittner (1998) found that whereas the immigrant congregation is a home away from home for the first generation, it often feels oppressive to the second generation. Ebaugh and Chafetz (2000) also concluded that few immigrant congregations are able to attract the children as members and active participants. A growing conflict between immigrants and their children over religious issues has also been noted elsewhere (Schmidt 1998). One finding is a tendency among some immigrant parents to become stricter with their children than is common in their country of origin, especially with their daughters. Such conflicts are, in some instances, related to religion, and in other instances they are related to traditional customs practiced in the old country. The latter type of conflict was apparent in a tragedy that took place in Sweden in 2002, where a young Swedish-Kurdish woman, Fadime, was murdered by her father, due to a family conflict over morality and family honor (Wikan 2003).

A growing number of studies of the children of immigrants have focused on their complex construction of ethnic and religious identities. Although these studies also describe generation differences and conflicts, they emphasize the multiple cultural competence of this generation as they are carving out a space for themselves (Østberg 1998). In her study of Pakistani youth in England, Jessica Jacobson (1998) found that while ethnic identity is largely perceived as a "natural" or "given" fact of life, religion is regarded as more of a matter of personal choice. There seems also to be a trend among European and American Muslim youth to distinguish between their ethnic and Muslim identities. Although many voice a belief in the unchanging and unchangeable teachings of Islam, they search for a more "authentic" form of Islam, free of cultural non-Islamic baggage. The search for a pure form of religion sifted out from the culture is found in several studies (Ebaugh and Chafetz 2000; Jacobson 1998; Jonker 2003; Schmidt 1998). Finally, within some local Muslim traditions, as for example the German and Nordic traditions, young women are in the process of establishing key positions. Some of them are converts. They play an active role in the student, youth, and women's organizations, and they use their knowledge of Islam to negotiate their positions as women within the Muslim community (Jacobsen 2004; Jonker 2003; Roald 2001, 2004; Tiilikainen and Lehtinen 2004; Østergaard 2004).

Much of the migration literature prior to the 1960s assumed that immigrants leave one country to permanently settle and become assimilated into another society. However, more recent studies show that people who cross borders today do not necessarily stay to adopt their new country as their own, but travel frequently between their host country and their country of origin (Ebaugh and Chafetz 2002; Levitt 2001). The image of migrants as transnationals became the metaphor for this new perspective (Ebaugh and Chafetz 2002: 1).

American sociologist Peggy Levitt (2001) conducted the first study focusing on transnational religious ties. She describes the religious beliefs and practices that people from Miraflores, a town in the Dominican Republic, brought from their home country and adapted to the United States. These migrants belong to the Catholic Church wherever they reside, and their home- and host-country religious practices often have much in common. Levitt finds that the Boston community was affected by the religious beliefs and practices the immigrants brought with them from Miraflores. These immigrants came from a strong tradition of lay leadership, which was uncommon in the Catholic churches in Massachusetts, and they introduced their own traditions in this area. Church participation also brought different groups from the Dominican Republic together in the United States, which created alliances that could be mobilized to reach political goals. Later, Ebaugh and Chafetz (2002) studied five congregations in Houston that represented different types of transnational religious networks. They found that immigrants were involved in creating and sustaining transnational religious ties that have changed the landscape of American religion. These transnational ties also prompted change within the traditional religious cultures and congregational structures of their homelands. In this way, the transnational religious networks in which immigrants participate play an important role in the global, transnational world.

10.5 Assimilation, pluralism, and multiculturalism

The end of the twentieth century witnessed a political development that brought about changes in the relationship between ethnic groups and states in the West. The Soviet Union collapsed, the European Union expanded through new member states, and the migration into Europe and the United States continued. These developments raise questions, among others, about the meaning of citizenship, identity, and human and religious rights, which also affect the theories attempting to deal with these issues (Kivisto 2002: 27–42).

Up to the mid-1990s, the theoretical discourse on ethnicity was limited to polemics between assimilationists and pluralists. As noted, Park and other sociologists from the Chicago School believed that assimilation, or the eradication of the cultural heritages of the immigrants and the adaptation of what were deemed to be genuinely

American values, was inevitable. In the 1960s and 1970s the assimilation paradigm came under increasing pressure. Led by the African-American community, claims were being made by various minority groups for a celebration of their ethnic and racial heritage and "roots." Altogether, there was a new appreciation for diversity. By the 1970s, assimilation theory was abandoned and replaced by cultural pluralism, which stated that ethnic differences would persist. Related to the rise of the cultural pluralist paradigm was a growing interest in the social construction of ethnicity, as suggested by Werner Sollors.

In the 1990s, both theories were criticized for being too simplistic, with their focus on identifying one analytical tool in the study of ethnic relations. Assimilation theory was revitalized. Some American scholars claim that assimilation indeed was taking place among the descendants of European immigrants in the United States (Alba 1990). However, other American studies of children of more recent immigrants suggest that they adapt, integrate, or assimilate in different sectors of American society. The process of assimilation into particular subcultures of the host society is called "segmented assimilation" (Portes 1995). Some argue that the potential for assimilation is dependent upon the role played by the state, in the sense that state policies will have a major impact on whether minority groups are incorporated into society or excluded from full inclusion. According to this perspective, assimilation in the sense of civic incorporation can provide a basis for creating a common culture while assuming ethnic diversity (Parekh 2000).

Multicultural theorists, such as Charles Taylor (2003), locate their discussions of ethnic group-belonging in terms of notions of citizenship in pluralist democracies. They consider citizenship as a fundamental mode of identity and basis for social solidarity. Multicultural theory emphasizes action, such as state action, ethnic collective action, and individual action. There is a long debate on the content of the term "multiculturalism," where theorists frequently differ and tend to mix descriptive and normative aspects of the term. A common feature is, however, that multiculturalism addresses the claims made by ethnic groups to maintain a distinctive identity and engage in what Taylor (1992) refers to as "the politics of recognition." This term describes the process whereby ethnic identities are preserved while at the same time finding citizenship as an identity that unites various groups within a polity. Some have criticized multicultural theorists for "essentializing" ethnic group identities by treating ethnicity as a natural given, whereas it is a social construct. Questions are also raised regarding the right and ability of individuals to define their own identities separate from the ethnic group to which they belong, to exit the ethnic group, define themselves different than the group, and so forth. These issues are particularly relevant due to the increase in interethnic and interracial marriages and children.

The role of religion in the public sphere is a controversial issue in several European countries and the United States (see Chapter 6 and Section 9.2). An underlying premise in much debate on assimilation, pluralism, and multiculturalism has been that religion is a phenomenon that belongs to the private sphere. Dominated by the secular assumptions of sociology and anthropology, there has been an expectation among several social scientists and policy makers that communities of immigrant descent would follow a course characterized by the privatization of religion (Nielsen

1995: 157). In this way, there has been an implicit idea that religious minorities would become relatively secularized over time.

In spite of these expectations, several religious minorities in Europe began in the 1980s and 1990s to demand the same public status and respect granted to their religion as that of the majority religion. On that basis, some proposed that a solution was not to be found in the privatization of religion, but rather in a pluralization of the public sphere (Beckford and Gilliat 1998; Parekh 2000). This implies that religious minorities should have equal opportunities to participate in public life and to follow their own cultural practices in public, within the usual conditions imposed for the sake of public order and safety.

The perspectives above all assume that the nation-state is the appropriate unit within which people are to be integrated or excluded. As noted, there are increasingly transnational aspects of modern migration, where many people live and sometimes work in two worlds. Transnationalism is part of the globalization process (see Section 5.3). The consequence of this process is that migrants increasingly define their identities on the premise of their country of origin as well as their destination, and they take part in the social, political, economic, and religious life in both the sending and the host society (Ebaugh and Chafetz 2002; Levitt 2001).

10.6 The policy debate

We have mentioned that the growing migration and the new development with an expanded European Union have led to a debate on the significance of citizenship. In most European countries, rights that were previously given to individuals who were citizens in a particular nation-state have now been extended to apply to individuals who are residents in that nation-state. Indeed, the basis of legitimation of membership has changed. Whereas shared nationality used to be the main source of equal treatment, the rights of individuals are now legitimated by international codes, conventions, and laws on human rights, independent of their citizenship in a nation-state. However, while the legitimation of membership rights has changed to a transnational level, membership itself is organized more or less the same way. On that basis, some argue (Soysal 2003) that there is a need to construct a post-national model of membership to capture the new situation facing several European countries and the United States. Whereas citizenship assumes a single membership, meaning that a person can only be a citizen in one country, the post-national model implies multiplicity of membership, meaning that one can have citizenship in several countries. For example, dual citizenship has become increasingly common. In many countries, political participation and right to welfare services are also guaranteed for all people living within that country's borders. Although the growth of supranational institutions and transnational laws has been a development in most European countries, other countries work in the opposite direction. This is especially true for some of the new states that appeared after the collapse of the Yugoslav Federation, which are going through a nation-building process. These states insist on rights that are exclusively for citizens of the new national state.

Due to the increasing ethnic and religious diversity in most European countries and the United States, several societies have increasingly faced the necessity of adapting their public policies to the presence of new minorities. The growing religious factor in the social and political processes associated with minorities has included a reconsideration of the legal provisions pertaining to the freedom of religion. The idea that varieties of cultural meanings all have claims to equal respect has a long tradition in the United States, but it is relatively new in Europe. It implies that the human groups that share different cultures can claim the same opportunities as other groups to put their cultures into practice. Ideas of equal opportunities have usually been confined to and discussed in relation to spheres such as employment, housing, or health care. However, in several European countries, the notion of equal opportunities has also been extended to apply to religion. This debate has taken place within the public school system, the health system, the social service system, the prisons, and the military (Beckford and Gilliat 1998; Furseth 2001a).

Nevertheless, several scholars have pointed out that the presence of religious traditions that make claims on the public sphere creates tensions for liberal democracies (Kivisto 2002; Richmond 2003). The question is how liberal democracies are to respond to the claims made by religious fundamentalists, whether they are Christian, Muslim, or belong to any other religious tradition, who insist upon imposing their ideas and practices on others by force or by eliminating those who are different. These are critical issues that confront the liberal democracies of the advanced industrial nations.

The twenty-first century is continuing to pose challenges to traditional models of integration. On the one hand, minorities in Europe and the United States experience severe pressures to adapt to their host societies. Their religious institutions continue to change and respond to new circumstances. This process of adaptation is influenced by several factors. There are vast national, ethnic, cultural, and religious differences among the various minorities living close to each other in several American and European cities. There is also social and religious differentiation in the generation of children of immigrants born or raised in Europe and the United States. Whereas some are entering colleges and universities and becoming part of the next generation of leaders within their communities, others are entering the labor market employed in minimum-wage jobs, or growing up into unemployment and marginalization. On the other hand, the host societies increasingly face the necessity of adapting their public policies to the presence of ethnic and religious minorities. Whereas institutional arrangements have slowly changed to accommodate the presence of minorities, the pressures of adaptation on an individual level often weigh most heavily on the minorities and only to a lesser degree on the majority.

Most nations in Europe face the reality of a multicultural future and they confront the task of finding ways of incorporating various ethnic and religious groups into full societal membership. Much is unclear regarding multiculturalism, and many difficult issues confront liberal democracies. Dealing with these issues constitutes some of the challenges facing sociology today.

11
Religion and gender

Over the last decades a large number of studies have been conducted within the field of gender and religion. This chapter is meant to make only a small contribution. We will first consider different images of women and men found in the sacred texts within different world religions. A considerable number of books and articles have appeared on this topic, especially within theology and religious studies (see Sharma 1994; Young 1999). Yet the topic of women and religion is not confined to sacred texts and symbols only, but also to actual lives. What distinguishes the religious experiences of women from those of men? Several scholars have focused on religious institutions and attempted to determine the actual roles women have within different world religions or within various religious communities. Many studies of contemporary religiosity have described women's responsiveness to religion. Social scientists who have analysed the high participation of women in religion have attempted to explain why this is so. Women's religious participation has also been criticized. Feminism has claimed that religious women have "false consciousness." Therefore, we will assess the relationship between feminism and religion. In discussions on gender and religion, a closely related topic is the religious interpretation of sexuality. Religion tends to regulate sexuality, and its directions and proscriptions are often directed towards women and towards homosexuals, lesbians, bisexuals, and transgender people. We will look at these issues towards the end of the chapter.

Analyses of gender and religion often tend to lean towards generalizations. Women vary, as do men, according to social class, education, cultural heritage, ethnicity, race, and nationality. It is also important to remember that women and men, whether they are heterosexual, homosexual, lesbian, bisexual, or transgender, do not constitute single unified groups that have the same interests or are exposed to the same type of treatment or discrimination in every part of the world and at all times.

11.1 The role of religion in interpreting gender and gender roles

As an introduction to the area of gender and religion we will give a brief overview of the images of women and men that are found in the world religions. What do the sacred texts teach about women? What are the symbols of femininity and masculinity? Traditionally, this field of research is conducted by scholars of theology and religious studies. However, living in increasingly multi-religious societies requires that social scientists also have a minimum of knowledge of some teachings of the world religions. Therefore, we will take a quick glance at the ideas regarding gender in Christianity, Judaism, Islam, Hinduism, Sikhism, and Buddhism.

Within Christianity, theologians and philosophers have taught that God is neither male nor female. In the early 1980s the American Christian feminist Rosemary Radford Ruether presented one of the first systematic critiques of Christian theology from a feminist perspective in the book *Sexism and God-talk* (1983). She found that the "God-talk," which is usually presented as objective and neutral, was mostly presented as a male rather than a human experience of God and reality. Whereas the earliest Christian theology drew upon the figure of Sophia, the Goddess of Wisdom, which made for a gender-neutral theology, the establishment of Christianity focused on Jesus Christ as God made flesh in the male sex. As a male he presents a one-sided conception of the deity. Thus, a change took place in Western religion when it became masculine in nature (Arthur 1987). Within this Christian tradition woman has been seen as subordinate to man in both creation and in daily life, though the equality between men and women has always been taught regarding salvation. A number of scriptural passages speak about the subordination of women, especially in St. Paul, which have been used to legitimate the marginalization of women. This view continues to be prevalent in many Christian churches today (King 1993: 47).

Catholicism had provided more room for female religious figures of identification, especially Mary, the mother of Jesus. The new interpretation by Protestantism of the Christian tradition was more ambiguous when it came to the position of women. In many ways, the Reformation represented a masculinization of Christianity. Yet Martin Luther contributed in his theology and way of life to a potential higher respect for women through his positive view of marriage and his critique of celibacy as a Christian way of life. However, Luther also consolidated the strictly gendered role division between women and men in the Christian order of creation.

While the Judeo-Christian religion retained a masculine and hierarchical structure which discriminated against and excluded women, some have argued that there still are feminine aspects within this religious tradition. In the Old Testament God is represented through feminine images, and the wisdom literature on the feminine image of Sophia is important. Furthermore, the doctrine of the Trinity reveals feminine traits in the Father (as a Father and a Mother) and the Holy Spirit (as a Mother who unites the Father and the Son). There is also the figure of Mary, who is perceived as the abode of the Holy Spirit, the place of his presence and his action in the world (Gardini 1987). Others have argued that parts of the New Testament provide positive images of women. For example, a study of the Gospel of Luke concluded that this text views women as vehicles of revelation and voices of theological insight. Women received the blessings of Jesus, they were his followers, they participated in the ritual meal, they were used as teaching material of Jesus, and Jesus used feminine images to describe himself (Via 1987).

Both Jewish and Christian feminists have attempted to reinterpret various sacred texts that they share, one of which is the creation story. Whereas the figure of Eve has had a far-reaching influence in Christianity, one Jewish tradition held that the name of the woman whose creation is mentioned first was not called Eve, but Lilith. Lilith was considered to be Adam's first wife and Eve the third. Lilith insisted on full equality with Adam because of their identical origin. When Adam did not agree to this, she left him. Not even a group of angels sent by God was able to change her mind. Numerous female figures in the Hebrew Bible have been regarded by contemporary women as "foremothers" of the faith. Some are matriarchal figures, whereas some are women of the Exodus and the Promised Land, or women of the times of the prophets (King 1993: 44–5).

The spiritual equality between men and women is also recognized in Islam. The Qur'an states that women and men have been created out of one single soul. Men and women also pray as equals before God. Many Hadiths, traditions of the Prophet, also characterize the female companions to the Prophet in a positive way. For example, Aisha, the wife of the Prophet, enjoys a particularly elevated status as a strong woman who engaged in political disputes. More controversial are the Hadiths that describe the nature of women. One Hadith states that the testimony of a woman is worth half of that of a man because women are deficient in intellect and religion, and it is often interpreted to mean that women are emotional whereas men are rational (Roald 2001: 119–32).

Riffat Hassan (1990: 100–16), an Islamic feminist with Indo-Pakistani roots who lives in the United States, has claimed that the negative attitudes pertaining to women which prevail in Muslim societies are rooted in three theological assumptions: first, that man is the origin of creation; second, that women are defined as temptresses; and third, that women were created as a means for men. The Norwegian scholar on Islam Anne Sophie Roald (2001: 124–5) argues that these views might be more prevalent in the Indian subcontinent than they are in the Arab-speaking sphere. Thus, there are geographical and cultural variations in the interpretations of these issues within Islam.

Whereas the spiritual equality between men and women has traditionally been accepted in Islam, the issue of social equality has been controversial. The question of gender relations is relevant within the family sphere and in a wider social context. We shall look at the family sphere first – gender relations are closely connected to ideas about marriage and family in Islam because of the belief that every Muslim should be married if possible. Thus, the ideal relationship between a man and a woman can only occur within marriage. The Muslim marital relationship is based on ideas of complementarity and not of equality. Although little is said in the Qur'an about gender relations, it does state that men are the breadwinners of the family, and they are the protectors and maintainers of control of women. It even allows the physical punishment of women in certain situations. The Hadiths convey two sides of gender relations which also are evident in the Qur'an: first, that the relationship between husband and wife is one of mercy and tenderness, and second, that the husband has the power. When it comes to the role of women in the public sphere, one Hadith prohibits female leadership (Roald 2001: 145–9, 185–200). The Muslim feminist Fatima Mernissi has in her book *Women and Islam* (1987) made this question a major issue in the struggle for the empowerment of Muslim women. Indeed, several Muslim countries have had female leaders. Other controversial issues have been the right of men to take a second wife, and Islamic female dress. The patriarchal tradition within Islam has come under increasing pressure from the ideology of gender equality, especially among Muslims living in the West, but also within several Muslim countries. One example is contemporary Iran, where an indigenous discourse on these issues is taking place (Mir-Hosseini 2000).

By taking a look at Hinduism, we find that the view on women is ambiguous. In the Vedas, the scriptures of Hinduism, the gods are predominantly male. This reflects a patriarchal society, where gender relations are frequently discussed in terms of the "male caste" and the "female caste." A fundamental distinction that affects gender relations is the distinction between purity and impurity. In Hinduism raw nature is considered impure, whereas culture is pure. Impurity is more connected to women than men. For example, menstruating women cannot cook and they cannot enter the temple. The notions of purity and impurity are used as legitimations for the caste system. The upper caste strives to maintain purity, and in order to achieve this goal it separates itself from the rest of society. The lowest castes remove impurity from the higher castes, but by doing so they remain impure. Only the pure, or the upper-caste man, can reach spiritual freedom (Smith 2002: 21).

Nevertheless, Hinduism has a strong tradition of female goddess worship. Hinduism perceives of the divine cosmic energy, *Shakti*, as a female. In addition, the great Goddess, called *Devi* or "mother," appears in several different forms. She may be the source of all existence. The Goddess is sometimes described as the mother of the universe who pervades all things. The knowledge of the universe is also identical with the forms of the all-powerful Goddess. Festivals are arranged in her honor. The notions of the Goddess also played a role in Indian nationalism as she came to stand for the country and her power (King 1993: 51–2).

Within the International Society for Krishna Consciousness (ISKCON) or the Hare Krishna movement, which constitutes one form of Hinduism that has been particularly popular in the West, the leadership teaches spiritual equality between men and women. The goal is to reach a relationship of loving service to God. Thereby, devotional service, characterized by its attitude of submission, constitutes both the path and the goal, and is open to men and women alike. However, the founder of the movement, Srila Prabhupada, included negative comments about women, viewing women's bodies and maternal roles as more constraining than men's bodies and roles. After his arrival in the United States in the 1960s, he allowed men and women to enter the movement and become disciples. In principle, women can become leaders, take renunciation or be gurus like men, although this has not happened as yet (Knott 1987).

Sikhism has been perceived as one form of Hinduism, although it has become a separate religion. The origins of Sikhism can be traced to Guru Nanak, who was born in India in 1469. In the community of disciples that grew around Nanak, men and women shared equally when it came to labor, cooking, and congregational activities. Nanak was sensitive to discrimination towards women and denounced customs such as *sati* (burning of widows), veiling, and beliefs in menstrual pollution. Altogether, women and men had relatively equal status. In 1699 the Tenth Guru after Nanak founded the Khalsa, an elite brotherhood, which marked a dramatic departure from the past. A new emphasis on masculine features was introduced, which was associated with the strongly militant character of the Khalsa. Nevertheless, the Sikh code of conduct, which was published in 1950, states that women should not veil their faces, infanticide is prohibited, widows are allowed to remarry, dowry and child marriages are prohibited, and there is no prohibition against abortion. Today Sikh scriptures uphold gender equality, although the religion is still affected by its long history of masculine emphasis (Shackle 2001, 2002). A pioneering work of the American scholar of religion Nikky Singh (1993) has attempted to redefine the understandings of gender in Sikhism.

In Buddhism various traditions present different views on women. In contrast to Hinduism, where women could not reach the spiritual freedom of upper-caste men, the Buddha taught that *nirvana* (liberation) was within reach for women and men, rich and poor. The Buddha's view on women was more generous and positive than that of later monks. He preached to women, and he reluctantly allowed them to become nuns. Within two centuries after the Buddha's death, two different aspects of Buddhism developed. Within the Hinayana school, a distinctly anti-woman attitude was common. Women were considered to be ugly, blind, wretched, with enormous sexual appetites, whereas men were viewed as noble, loyal, generous, and holy. Within this tradition, women were viewed as obstacles to the liberation of monks. In the Mahayana school, all human experience, male or female, was considered the ground of enlightenment. There is no division in *Prajna* or wisdom. The supreme wisdom or *Prajnaparamita*, the "Perfection of Wisdom," is a feminine name. She is not worshipped as a goddess, but she rescues people from ignorance and suffering, and faith in her will lead to liberation. In India and Tibet a number of feminine deities arose in the Mahayana school, which was more favorable to women than the Hinayana school. Later, two other schools of Buddhism arose, the Vajrayana and Zen. The Vajrayana originated in Tibet and had a strong inclination toward the equality of women. Nevertheless, there is still no full ordination of women in the present-day Vajrayana school. Zen developed in China and from there to Korea and Japan, and it viewed enlightenment as available to women and men. The Zen school has various practices regarding women, because it spread to such different parts of the world. Probably western Mahayana Buddhism gives the greatest freedom to women. As a contrast, the Theravada school, which grew out of the Hinayana school and spread to South East Asia, still considers women inferior to men (Bancroft 1987).

When comparing writings from different religious traditions and their images of women, the British professor of theology and religion Ursula King found two distinct types of images of women. One is the mother image, which is closely bound to women's fertility and sexuality. The other is a non-material image or a mate-image. Here women are seen as equal and independent or as complementary to males, but not as their subordinates (King 1993: 45). Altogether, many teachings on women within the world religions operate with a dualistic perspective, which divides the body and the mind, nature and spirit, man and woman, as well as earth and heaven. Women are associated with body, nature, and earth, whereas men are associated with mind, spirit, and heaven (King 1993: 47). Many feminist attempts to deconstruct religious language and texts have detected these and similar underlying assumptions.

11.2 Women's and men's religious experiences

The feminist project of discovering how any given experience is gendered has continued to be important in the sociology of religion (Woodhead 2003). Individuals participate in religious organizations and movements as females and males.

Organizations and movements create and maintain structures that continue to reproduce gendered relations.

Research suggests that women and men do experience God and faith differently (see Ozorak 1996: 18). Women tend to emphasize personal relationships with a loving God and with others in the religious community, while men tend to stress God's power and judgment, and their own spiritual discipline. In this, women conceptualize religion in terms of relationship rather than individuation. A study of the rationales offered by women and men returnees to modern Orthodox Judaism finds that they indeed are different (Davidman and Greil 1994). Both women and men in this study return to Orthodoxy. However, their motivations, or their accounts of their motivations, are not the same. Whereas women emphasize issues related to family and personal relationships, men stress ethical and workplace concerns. Women and men also differed in their perceptions of the nature of God. More men than women believed in a personal God, and half the female respondents were uncertain about the nature of God. Just because women and men return to the same religion, they are not necessarily doing so for the same reasons.

It also seems that women value aspects such as connectedness and community when it comes to religious participation. A study of women involved in organized religion concluded that they emphasized the importance of caring and community in their religious experience. They also stressed a view of God as a friend rather than as a cosmic ruler or judge. Although the majority of women were aware of gender inequalities in their religious traditions, they believed that the benefits of religious involvement, such as fulfilling relationships, outweighed the negatives of male-dominated leadership and organization (Ozorak 1996).

In addition to accommodating to traditional forms of religions, women also have created women-centered religions. These are outside the dominant religious traditions, with a small number of participants. Their level of organization also varies. However, they are important as indications of new ways that women form alternative avenues for exploring religion. The women's spirituality movement consists of a number of women-centered ritual groups which support women's ritual authority and are oriented toward female deities and the celebration of rituals. One important theme is the ways in which these beliefs, rituals, and symbols are empowering for women. Women have been creative in forming new rituals and reinterpreting religious symbolism. Some ritualistic practices have as their objective the healing of individuals. American sociologist of religion Meredith McGuire (1988) reports that non-medical forms of healing are rather widespread among educated and economically secure middle-class people. Another type of ritual healing has been practiced among female victims of abuse (Jacobs 1989; Nason-Clark 2003). It is important to know that there are male spiritual movements as well. One example is an American Evangelical movement for men (Barkowski 2004; Brickner 1999; Williams 2001). Here, the rituals have the character of male initiation rituals. At the same time, they also express a transformation of the self. The Promise Keepers emphasize the development of a disciplined masculinity, based on ideals of heterosexuality and authority (McGuire 2003).

Women-centered ritual groups have also emerged within traditional religions, for example, the feminist liturgical movement within Christianity and Judaism (Procter-Smith and Walton 1993). The women who take part are either ordained or lay women who are dissatisfied with the traditional ceremonies and who have chosen to make liturgies that meet their spiritual needs. Since this movement claims women's ritual authority, it usually stands in some degree of tension with the official church or synagogue.

For some, this tension has meant moving into another religious tradition altogether, particularly contemporary feminist reconstructions of ancient goddess-centered religions. This trend in women's spirituality has emerged through the creation of rituals that are designed to provide women with a means to bond with one another while exploring images of female strength derived from ancient symbols of the Goddess. The Goddess movement is a type of modern paganism. Some have claimed that it is very much a part of the postmodern age or that it is a "designer religion," because the adherents have a tendency "to collect, adapt and creatively reassemble an eclectic mix of religious elements from many different living and ancient traditions" (Rountree 2002: 478).

Another movement that grew out of the feminist movement and neo-paganism is Dianic Wicca, a religious feminist witchcraft. American sociologist of religion Helen A. Berger (1998) has given a thorough analysis of Wicca, based on more than ten years of field research. According to Berger, Wiccans trace their origins to a mystical pre-Christian past in Europe and to the work of witches who practiced in the United Kingdom in the early 1900s. Individuals use a complex system of symbols and practices to define personal and collective identity, meaning, and purpose. According to Wiccans, individual and collective spiritual development is achieved by mystical activity that they enact in private and collective domains. The movement has emphasized concern for women's rights, the environment, and gay and lesbian rights. Although witchcraft is a decentralized religion that emphasizes the spontaneity of religious expression, routinization is taking place. The Wiccans are attempting to establish formal structures, professional leaders and administrators. Another interesting introduction to one particular Wicca community, "Reclaiming" in San Francisco, is provided by Norwegian theologian and social anthropologist Jone Salomonsen (2002). Since she not only participated fully in their rituals during the course of her fieldwork, but also requested and received initiation as a Reclaiming Witch, she gives detailed information about their rituals, teachings, and community life.

Feminist witches and women in the American Goddess movement create myths and symbols to shape a framework of meaning and attempt to redefine power, authority, sexuality, and social relations. Although it has been criticized for being a movement for white, educated, middle-class women, some groups recruit a more varied mix of women as regards race, ethnicity, and social class (Griffin 1995). Critique has also been raised against its orientation toward the transformation of self, claiming that it is a narcissistic distraction from political action. However, empirical studies have shown that rates of political participation are high in this group (Finley 1994).

11.3 The role of women in religious organizations

In studies of women and religion, several scholars have analysed religious institutions and the actual roles of women within different religious communities. To what extent do women take part in ritual and religious practice? Do they hold positions of authority, and if so, at which levels? When women are faced with restrictions, how do they negotiate and carve out a space for themselves?

We will first take a look at the Christian tradition. Some studies have examined the role and place of women in early Christianity. American sociologist of religion Rodney Stark (1995, 1996) found that women had played a far more important role in the early Christian church than previously assumed. Women often served as deacons, which meant that they assisted at liturgical functions and administered the charitable activities of the church. They held positions of honor and authority, as they functioned as evangelists and teachers. They enjoyed greater power and status than did pagan women. Women also contributed to growth as they tended to recruit their pagan husbands and provided new converts through childbearing. Stark concludes that women constitute one major factor in explaining the growth and diffusion of early Christianity.

Numerous studies on the role of women in pre-twentieth-century religious movements have also been conducted. In the Nordic countries, there are analyses of women in the Lutheran lay movement (Markkola 2000), Methodism (Furseth 2002), and various mission organizations (Nyhagen Predelli 2003; Seland 2000). In Norway, the early Lutheran lay movement, represented by the Hauge movement of the early nineteenth century, gave a relatively large sphere of action to women, as they functioned as speakers and leaders of local groups (Furseth 1999). However, the missionary movement from the 1880s to 1920 limited the role of women (Seland 2000). The widespread official view during this period was that women should not be speakers or leaders. Nevertheless, women managed to create a sphere for themselves and achieve informal positions. The gender roles within religious organizations were often affected by the greater society. This is evident in a study of Norwegian missionaries in Madagascar (Nyhagen Predelli 2003). The adaptation of male and female missionaries to local cultural conditions in Madagascar led to changes in the relationship between gender and religion at an organizational and individual level. Regardless of the gender roles as they were defined either by society or the religious organizations, these studies show that women carved out a space for themselves and played an important part at different levels in these movements.

Studies of the role and place of women in historic Christian groups in the United States reveal similar findings. In an analysis of the spiritual careers of Puritan and Evangelical women in early America (1600–1850), American historian Marilyn J. Westerkamp (1999) traces the female spiritual tradition to the Puritans, Baptists, Methodists, and Evangelical reformers. Although gender relations changed between 1600 and 1850, the hegemonic ideologies were maintained that consistently defined women as physically, intellectually, and emotionally weaker than men. The women's claim to religious authority within these movements rested upon their connection with the Holy Spirit, which the male leaders attempted to control. By the middle of the nineteenth century, women achieved ordination, worked as missionaries, were lay preachers, established churches, produced sacred texts, and founded new religions. Westerkamp concludes that religion was both an oppressive and an empowering force for women in early America.

If we take a look at contemporary Christian groups and churches, the research has tended to distinguish between traditional and liberal communities, and conservative communities. Within the traditional and liberal communities, focus has been directed on women and the ministry. The ordination of women has been a slow process. In the United States, women accounted for 2.2 percent of the clergy in 1930, compared with 2.9 percent in 1970 and 4.2 percent in 1980 (Carroll et al. 1983: 4). In 1990 they constituted approximately 10 percent (Chaves 1997: 15). Many "mainline Protestant denominations" did not permit ordination of women until the 1950s, 1960s, and 1970s. A broad analysis of the growing numbers of women in the ministry in the United States found that female and male clergy held similar entry-level placements, whereas sharp gender differences appeared when they reached mid-level positions (Carroll et al. 1983). These tendencies have proved to remain consistent, resulting in a "glass ceiling" effect for women who have an interest in leadership positions at a higher level. Although this has been the pattern within European-American churches, similar trends have also been found in African-American churches (Baer 1994: 77). In the Roman Catholic Church women are not admitted to the priesthood. Women cannot act *in persona Christi* (in the person of Christ) because they are not biological men (Farrell 1991: 339). However, in 1965 Catholic women in the United States were admitted to schools of theology for ministerial preparation, and in 1983 doors were opened for the appointment of laity as parish administrators. In the early 1990s, women headed approximately 2 percent of Catholic parishes in the United States (Wallace 1994). In this way, Catholic women have attempted to change the church from within.

Studies of women clergy in other countries show similar patterns to those in the United States. In Norway, a study of women clergy found that women faced problems during the hiring process. Some were ignored and others withdrew their applications due to local resistance against them. However, the majority of the informants reported that once they were hired, they were well received by their colleagues and the congregations. This study also shows that these clergywomen attempted to change their roles so that they would correspond to what they perceived to be more feminine values (Høeg 1998).

There are signs indicating that women and men clergy have a somewhat different profile. A Swedish study shows, for example, that women clergy tend to focus on social relations in their preaching and they often use an everyday language, whereas men clergy attempt to communicate dogmatic knowledge using a theological language (Bäckström 1992). There is, however, no reason to believe that such findings will continue to be true at all times. Since this study was conducted, the number of women clergy has increased drastically in the Nordic countries. It may very well be that women clergy today represent a broader spectrum than the pioneer generation, and that men clergy have been affected by their female colleagues.

If we look at conservative communities, scholars have been puzzled at the large number of female participants in these types of communities. One example is the Women's Aglow International, which is a non-denominational fellowship of Pentecostal (Full Gospel) women. The movement began in Seattle, Washington in 1967 and now has fellowships all over the world, including Europe. The membership is predominantly female. Because they believe that the Scriptures teach that women should be submissive to male authority, each chapter's advisors are men, and women need their husbands' permission to participate. The movement encourages women to be homemakers, so few members work full time (McGuire 1988: 19–20).

A number of studies have appeared which explore why women participate in such a male-dominated type of religion. Early research based on women who had joined communal groups suggested that in times when cultural values seemed to be unstable and in flux, the attraction for women lay in the certainty and stability of traditional roles (Aidala 1985). Later research argues that women believe that they have something to gain from these groups (Brasher 1998; Neitz 1987). Evangelical religion changes the home and recovers the family. It preaches an ideology that can be used by women to domesticate men (Martin 1990: 81–2). Thus, women trade the formal authority and positions for their husbands' increased involvement in the family.

One of the reasons behind the many divisions among Jews today has to do with varying views on women. There is a major line of division between the various Orthodox groups and all the others (Berkowitz 1999: 551). The Orthodox groups have kept women from becoming rabbis and from taking part in liturgical, ritual, and decision-making roles. In the synagogues women are usually separated from men by a partition or gallery. No Orthodox women are allowed to become rabbis. A woman's place is considered to be in the home, where she is responsible for educating the children, preparing and celebrating the Sabbath and other religious holidays. The strong emphasis on tradition and differentiated gender roles among the Ultra-Orthodox has restricted these women even more than Orthodox women. Ultra-Orthodox women do not participate much in the wider society, as their activities are even more centered on the home (Kunin 2002: 148–9). Feminist scholars studying women newly converted to Orthodox Judaism are also asking themselves why women embrace such a restrictive religiosity. Research suggests that women stress issues related to family and personal relationships. The delineation of distinct and conventional roles for men and women and normative patterns for nuclear family life were important elements in the attraction of these groups for potential converts (Davidman and Greil 1994).

Other groups within Judaism have included women at a more equal level. In the past twenty years, leaders within Reform Judaism in the United States have responded to concerns of women in several ways: the ordination of women, ritual naming of daughters, words and songs by women, language about women. In 1972 women were for the first time ordained to become rabbis in the Reform movement. Since the early 1970s, there has also been an increasing popularity of covenant-initiation ceremonies for daughters that are performed at home or in the synagogue during regular Sabbath worship. Furthermore, women's words and songs have been included in the official liturgies (Wenig 1993).

When looking at Muslim women living in the Western world, we find that some choose a relatively secular approach to life. Other women reveal a more conservative or traditional understanding of their role. Those women who see themselves as feminists often define themselves as different than Western feminists. Muslim European and North American women have played important roles in their Muslim congregations and will continue to do so as these communities are experiencing growth. Some women are becoming Islamic scholars (Roald 2001), while other women are the primary instructors in faith and practice of Islam for the women and children in their congregations. Some work in Muslim schools as teachers. Many women also function as board members in the various congregations and are responsible for the congregations' finances (Nyhagen Predelli 2004).

The issue of the Islamic mode of dress has been controversial. Many Westerners have been puzzled at the fact that so many educated middle-class women have adopted this form of dress. Many have searched for one reason or motive behind the new emphasis on Islamic dress and ended up with simplistic explanations. A more reasonable approach is to assume that women have a wide variety of motives for wearing a veil or a *hijab* (scarf), for example, and one woman may also have several motives at the same time for doing so. The scarf may represent a visible symbol of one's acceptance of Islam's social prescriptions. In this case, the scarf represents a new level of religiosity and a desire to adhere to religious prescriptions in one's daily life. It may be that the scarf functions as an identity marker that demonstrates to the world that this woman is a Muslim. Yet another motive may be that wearing Islamic dress secures a woman certain benefits, such as protection against harassment or access to free bus rides to the university, as was the case in Egypt (Kepel 2002). British scholar of religion Linda Woodhead (2002: 346) also mentions that many women in Muslim societies use the scarf to negotiate their way into social space.

Within Hinduism, the leaders in the temples are generally men. This pattern also holds true in a Western context. Here, temple priests are usually men of the Brahmin caste. Nevertheless, women are involved in temple administration at different levels. In the United States, some women hold prominent leadership positions in the larger temples. Women have also innovated new ritual functions, where they take part in processions previously only done by men. We have seen that menstruation is considered polluting in Hinduism, and therefore menstruating women do not go to a temple in India. Because temples often function as community centers and learning institutions in the West and because women often are involved in administration, rules of purity and impurity are more relaxed and left up to each individual. Indeed, there are even some women gurus who periodically tour parts of the world, and some women gurus have founded organizations. In Michigan, there is even a women's monastic movement, Sarada Ashram. Hindu practice in the West is slowly undergoing change to accommodate women (Narayanan 1999).

We have seen that within Buddhism women have been allowed to become monks, but they have always been given an inferior position to the male monks. For example, the nuns have never had the same position to teach, whereas the men have formed several different schools of thought (Bancroft 1987). In some cases, the distinctive gender-role expectations have led to sexual and other power abuses on the part of male leaders. Whereas traditional gender roles within Buddhism have tended to be upheld in several Asian countries, this pattern seems to have changed in the West. In the United States, Buddhist women have begun to take leadership positions. The American Buddhist teacher Sandy Boucher (1988) spoke to more than one hundred influential Buddhist women, and these women demonstrated the wide range of influence Buddhist women have in the West. Some women have voiced strong arguments for gender equality, whereas others have transformed Buddhist monastic vows. There are also Buddhist women teachers.

In the twenty-first century, women are active in every world religion. The impact of women is more evident in liberal Christian communities, in Reform Judaism and western Mahayana Buddhism in the West, than in conservative Christian groups, Orthodox Judaism, the Hinayana school, and more conservative forms of Islam. All of the world religions in the West are undergoing significant transformation in the response to the needs and world-views of their Western adherents. The participation of women in these communities continues to press on with changes in order to meet women's concerns and needs.

11.4 The participation of women in religious groups – different explanations

Women's responsiveness to religion has been described in several studies of twentieth-century religiosity in the Western world. In the United States, census data from 1926 showed that a majority of cult members, as well as members of most mainstream denominations in the United States, were women. The high membership among women in churches continued throughout the century and has been found in study after study (Finke and Stark 1992: 10, 35; Stark and Bainbridge 1985: 237). Many new religious movements that appeared in the 1970s also demonstrated the same pattern of female membership (Howell 1998; Puttick 1999; Stark and Bainbridge 1985: 413–17). Women of all ages have continued to outscore men on most measures of religiosity. Studies from the United States have shown a tendency for women to have a more positive attitude toward Christianity than men (Francis and Wilcox 1998), and they tend to score higher than men on interest in religion, have a stronger personal religious commitment, and attend church more frequently. This pattern appears to hold over the life course, regardless of the type of religious organization in question (see Miller and Hoffmann 1995; Ozorak 1996). This tendency is not only confined to the United States. Findings from the European Value Studies also confirm a higher score on religious values among women than men in Britain, Germany, Norway, and Denmark (Botvar 1993; Gundelach and Riis 1992). Gender differences in religiosity are not limited to the north-western part of the world. British sociologist of religion David Martin (1990: 182–4) found that in Latin America women tended to join the new Protestant charismatic churches before men did.

Attempts have been made to explain why women seem to be more responsive to religion than men. Two main groups of theories have emerged in the social science literature (Francis and Wilcox 1998: 462–3; Miller and Hoffmann 1995: 63). The first stresses social or contextual influences that shape different responses to religion among men and women. This group may be divided into two categories: gender-role socialization theories and structural location theories. Gender-role socialization theories argue that females are taught to be more submissive, passive, obedient, and nurturing than males, and that these traits are associated with higher levels of religiosity (Miller and Hoffman 1995). Structural location theories argue that females are more religious than males because of their structural location in society. Because women tend to have a lower participation in the labor force and more responsibility for the upbringing of children, they will have more time for religious activities (Luckmann 1967). Some also say that women's involvement in raising children leads them to be religiously involved because such activities are related to the well-being of the family (Glock et al. 1967).

The second group of theories concentrates on personal or individual characteristics which differentiate between men and women (Aidala 1985; Francis and Wilcox 1998). This group is more common within the psychology of religion. It may be divided into three categories: depth psychology theories, personality theories, and gender-orientation theories. The last is of most interest for us here. Gender-orientation theories are based on notions of feminine and masculine orientations as personality constructs. This theory has been used to argue that individual differences in religiosity should be affected more by gender orientation than by being male or female (Thompson 1991). Religious experiences should, then, be for people with a feminine orientation, although both men and women may have a feminine orientation.

Critique has been directed against these main groups of theories for either emphasizing alleged characteristic traits of the participants or focusing upon their location in the social structure. The idea is to shift the emphasis from asking "why" women participate in religious movements to "how" movements mobilize women into collective action. By doing so, the focus is shifted away from the qualities of the women toward the qualities of the religious communities (Furseth 2001b). Indeed, some studies have linked the proportion of females in religious groups to organizational factors, such as opportunities and equality available to women. A study of women in black spiritual churches in the United States argued that because men tended to monopolize positions of religious leadership in most African-American religious groups, some women turned to spiritualism because it provided an alternative vehicle to religious leadership (Baer 1994). Likewise, a study of several charismatic communal movements showed that the proportion of women was found to increase when the organizational structure allowed greater freedom and equality for women (Wright 1994).

The first two types of explanations of women's involvement in religious communities emphasize the "demand-side" approach to religion, meaning that it focuses on contextual variables or the character traits of the women involved to explain why they are receptive to religion. The latter explanation is more based on the "supply-side" approach to religion, meaning that it looks at the supply of factors that women find attractive, which in turn will entice them to get involved. Although there has been considerable controversy among those sociologists of religion who support demand-side theories and those who adhere to supply-side theories, our view is that both types of approach can be useful in understanding women's high rate of involvement in religion.

11.5 Feminism and religion

The high religious participation by women has not only been an object of explanation, but also an object of critique. Western feminists have claimed that religiously active women have "false consciousness," meaning that they lack a true understanding of themselves and the oppressive forces of religion. Here, we want to discuss the relationship between feminism and religion. Western feminism has commonly been divided into different phases. We will attempt to look at these different phases and combine them with various trends within the study of religion and gender.

Feminism is commonly divided into at least three waves (Ellingsæter 1999). The first wave dates to nineteenth-century movements for women's rights in Europe and the United States. This wave tended to be gender blind in the sense that equality between the sexes was promoted. On the one hand, the feminist movement at this time tended to be distinct from and in opposition to organized religion. On the other hand, the feminist movement was often intertwined with religious organizations or religiously based organizations in complex ways. For example, early feminism in several European countries and the United States was often closely related to religiously based movements, such as the temperance movement. Women tended to be active in religious movements and had positions in these types of movements long before they took part in political movements. Religious organizations provided, then, organizational models that incorporated women, which the political movements later adopted (Furseth 2002). In this way, religious movements constituted one of several early conditions of the emergence of feminism in the nineteenth century. In other cases, religious movements were also influenced by the secular feminist movement. Several studies of the role of women in religious movements, such as missionary organizations, show that the women were to some degree affected by the feminist movement. This link was hardly direct and their discourse took place within the structures of a religious discourse. In some cases, women in the missionary movement adhered to the traditional roles, whereas in other cases women had untraditional positions of authority and leadership (Nyhagen Predelli 2003).

The second wave of feminism flourished in the 1960s and 1970s. Different types of categories appeared, based on their political orientations. One common theme was the focus on the patriarchy as a concept or theory about gender power and gender difference. This phase came to have a profound effect on the study of religion and gender. Several analyses, especially from female theologians, criticized Christianity and attempted to form a feminist spirituality and theology. This approach stressed fundamental differences between women and men. It emphasized the female nature and sought to elaborate a distinctively female spirituality in opposition to patriarchal dominance (Daly 1978). Linda Woodhead (2003: 69) has pointed to several weaknesses in these forms of analyses of Christianity that appeared during this period. First, they tended to focus on Christian symbolism rather than the religious organization within which women functioned. Second, they used the concept of patriarchy to describe varied and complex phenomena. Third, they tended to look at religiously active women as victims. Finally, several of these studies relied on an essentialized understanding of differences between women and men. Women and men were described as if they were fundamentally different beings, and women usually came out on the positive side whereas men were described in mostly negative terms.

Some of the feminist theologians who rejected traditional religion turned to feminized versions of spiritualities, such as the Goddess movement and Wicca. This interest in feminist spirituality movements and groups is still active (Berger 1998), and some scholars within this field are followers of the Goddess movement (Finley 1994) or are initiated as witches (Salomonsen 2002). Their studies tend therefore to combine a somewhat apologetic approach with a more common social science methodological approach. The weakness in some of these studies is that the scholars do not always clarify how their apologetic approach affects their analyses.

The third wave of feminism, which appeared in the late 1980s and early 1990s, came as a result of the critique of patriarchy and the turn in the social sciences from labor and economy to identity and culture. Numerous critiques were raised against theories of patriarchy. The major critique stated that patriarchy was presented as a universal, transhistorical, and transcultural phenomenon: women were everywhere oppressed by men in more or less the same way. There was a tendency towards biological essentialism, which did not provide a basis to theorize about the enormous historical and contemporary variation in women's situation. The idea of patriarchy often overlooked the complexity of the relationship between gender and religion. There was a leaning towards viewing all religious traditions and practices as oppressive forces, which represented a reductionist view of religion. However, we have seen that several studies show that even in historic religious organizations, where men dominated the structures, women managed to carve a place for themselves and pressured for either informal or formal positions of power.

The third wave of feminism seeks instead to explore gender that is understood to be socially constructed. In this way, gender differences are seen as flexible, complex, multi-faceted, and only loosely connected to the body (Lorber and Farrell 1991). Also, if women are not unified, there cannot be only one feminism for women. There must be several feminisms open to the various possibilities that might make up a future not marked by domination. In the area of religion, the analyses have been directed at the different ways in which religion may benefit those who are involved, both women and men. Instead of viewing women just as victims, their human agency is here restored. Examples are Davidman and Greil's (1994) study of women returnees to Orthodox Judaism and David Martin's (1990) study of Pentecostalism in Latin America. Davidman and Greil show how women are attracted to Orthodoxy because it provides a sense of community and emphasizes family values. Martin found that women joined Pentecostalism because it gave them a more respected role in the home and it domesticated their husbands; that is, the husband stops drinking and abusing. Even if he joins a patriarchal theology, his practice becomes more human and oriented towards equality.

Instead of looking at religion as a purely patriarchal phenomenon, future analysis of gender and religion will benefit from looking at religion as a phenomenon that plays a role in the structuring and restructuring of gender relations. Religion can be oppressive, but it can also provide empowerment and resources to those who are involved.

11.6 Religion, sexuality, and family orientation

Several religious traditions have norms that regulate women's and men's sexuality, and illustrate the often close relationship between sexuality and religion. Many traditions have norms that restrict women's sexuality and condemn homosexuality and bisexuality. Indeed, the traditional family still appears to be the ideal in numerous religious communities today.

If we take a look at classical sociology, an overlooked aspect of Max Weber's (1979: 343–50) work is his examination of the relationship between sexuality and religion. According to Weber, originally the relation of sex and religion was very intimate, as sexual intercourse was often part of orgiastic religion. In this case, ecstasy was considered "sacred." A tension between religion and sex came, however, when the cultic chastity of the priest was introduced. At this point, sexuality was considered to be dominated by demons. Weber claims that religions controlled by prophets and priests regulated sexual intercourse through marriage. As a result of the rationalization and intellectualization of culture, eroticism is pushed into a non-routinized or irrational sphere. For Weber, there are similarities between erotic and mystical experiences. Just as the erotic relation offers a union of two souls, the mystical experience creates a union between the mystic and God. This psychological affinity creates an antagonism between eroticism and religion. Furthermore, Weber points out that ethical salvation religions, such as Protestantism, reject both eroticism and mystical experience. The ethic of religious brotherhood is based on the idea that one person subordinates him- or herself to another person, and this is opposed to erotic love, which is a form of self-indulgence. In this way, Weber believes that the relationship between sexuality and religion is characterized by opposition and tension.

Another theorist who has also noted the close relationship between sexuality and religion is Michel Foucault. According to Foucault, religion is inseparable from questions of the body and sexuality (see Section 4.6). Discourses on religious practice and belief center around the body and what people do with their bodies. Foucault thinks that there is a close relationship between oppressive hegemonic structures of patriarchy and homophobia. His constructivist model of the body and sexuality has inspired a rethinking within theology, religious studies, and the sociology of religion that analyses the relationship between the body, sexuality, and religion (see Carrette and King 1998).

Several feminist writers have provided a more extensive examination of the relationship between the body, sexuality, and religion. Here, we will see briefly how this has been expressed within Roman Catholicism, Islam, and Hinduism. According to Ruether (1990), Roman Catholic traditions have devalued women's dignity or status in nature. The tradition from Thomas Aquinas states that women are inferior to men by nature. Since women and men are not equal, sex is not seen as an expression of love. In contrast, any separation of sexual pleasure from procreation, even within marriage, is viewed as mortally sinful. Protestants initially shared this narrow view of sexuality. Once it was accepted within Protestantism in the twentieth century that the expression of love was a valid reason for sexuality, the traditional arguments against birth control began to break down within Protestantism, but not in the Roman Catholic Church. Homosexuality has also been condemned for some of the same reasons that contraception was condemned; that is, it was sexual pleasure without procreation. In addition, the homosexual act took place outside marriage, so it was fornication. Because it also violated the structure of reproductive sexuality, it was also defined as sodomy. Thereby, Ruether concludes, the Vatican leadership has remained concerned to control women's and men's bodies and fertility by enforcing its teaching on birth control, abortion, and homosexuality.

The Muslim attitude towards sexuality in general is positive, but the Muslim attitude towards women's sexuality is more complex. The Islamic tradition does not see sexuality as the opposite of spirituality, but describes it as a sign of God's mercy. Sexuality is perceived as a divine instrument to create an intimate and loving relationship between woman and man in marriage. However, the pre-Islamic notions of "honor" and "shame" are still common in many Muslim societies today. These concepts are linked to women's chastity and sexual behavior. Thereby, men's "honor" is located in women's sexuality, which is seen as a man's possession. Since women's sexuality is related to men's honor and self-image, it becomes vitally important in Muslim societies to control women's bodies. Riffat Hassan (1990) argues that this control is done in different ways: by denying women access to birth control, by emphasizing a man's right to have sexual relations with his wife at his wish, and by putting a high premium on female fertility. The use of the veil or *hijab* by Muslim women can also be interpreted as a way by which a woman's sexuality is kept under control, says Hassan.

Within Hinduism, traditional attitudes towards women are based on their ability to share a man's life and bear him children, especially sons. Hindu scriptural sources are predominantly androcentric, meaning that they center around the man or the male. This idea has a profound influence in contemporary India, as well. We have seen that impurity is connected to the female body during menstruation and childbirth. Although a mother is worshiped and her fertility is celebrated, her procreating body does not have a high status (Narayanan 1990).

Although many religious traditions attempt to regulate women's sexuality, many contemporary women are involved in the study and interpretations of their religious scriptures, particularly as they relate to women's role and sexuality. When doing so, several women have been involved in attempting to discriminate between the central and unchanging aspects of religious teachings and what has been incorporated as a result of cultural impact. In other words, there is a search for an authentic form of religion, where the cultural aspects are sifted away. From a sociological perspective, one may say that the attempt is being made to reinterpret the religious tradition in a new cultural context, since sociology hardly will accept the idea of a religion that is free from its social context.

Whereas women's sexuality is often not acknowledged and is sought to be controlled, homosexuality and bisexuality are either not recognized or condemned in many religious traditions. Often homosexuality is understood as a flawed or sinful expression of human sexuality, especially within more conservative traditions or churches. Within more moderate or mainstream Christian groups there is often a tendency today to recognize homosexuals and other sexual minorities as persons needing God's grace and the congregation's care at the same level as heterosexuals. Many churches still preach a distinction between sexual orientation and sexual practice, which leaves them with an attitude of "hate the sin and love the sinner." More liberal religious teachings tend to accord homosexual, bisexual, and transsexual persons the right to be fully human and fully homosexual, bisexual, or transsexual. A controversial issue today is admitting homo/bisexual people to the ordained ministry. Whereas many churches will not ordain practicing homo/bisexual people, more liberal churches have openly gay and lesbian ministers. Some churches also practice blessings of unions or marriages of same-sex people.

Some research has addressed how homosexual people negotiate with various religious traditions (see Thumma and Gray 2005). The negative view of homosexuality in conservative circles has led many to view Evangelical Christianity and a homosexual lifestyle as incompatible. Therefore, it is often assumed that gays and lesbians will attend more liberal churches, if any. However, there is a study of one Evangelical group in the United States, which is formed for the purpose of helping persons reconcile their gay lifestyle with their Evangelical religious identity. Through a process of socialization, the members renegotiate the boundaries and definitions of their religious identity to include a positive valuation of homosexuality. For these persons, their core identity becomes a gay Evangelical Christian one (Thumma 1991). Another study focuses on religion in the lives of gay men, lesbians, bisexuals, and transgender people in Los Angeles (Wilcox 2003). Here, the conclusion is that these people are religiously individualistic, despite the fact that most either have been or are involved in a religious community. Religious individualism is perceived as a necessary strategy that the participants use to remain in conservative religious traditions and yet retain a positive self-image.

In most religious traditions, the family has been considered the basic unit of society. As a result, anything that has threatened the family unit has been viewed with suspicion and as a threat against religion. This orientation towards the family is still prevalent within contemporary religions. Although family patterns have changed drastically in the Western world, so that the traditional family consisting of mother, father, and children now constitute a minority, churches and religious organizations tend largely to operate from a basis that their adherents constitute members of traditional families. The result is that large groups in the population, such as single-parent families, families where the parents have previously been married and have children from past and present marriage, families with same-sex parents, same-sex couples, and singles feel like outsiders. However, different groups in contemporary society, whether they consist of women, homosexuals, or persons who live in various types of families, do not necessarily accept their designated place in many religious communities. Instead, they negotiate and create a sphere of action for themselves, accompanied by new roles. In this way, they contribute to religious renewal and innovation.

12

Sociology, theology, and religious faith

12.1 Conflicting perspectives?

In this final chapter, we will address the relationship between sociology, theology, and religious faith. How far-reaching are sociological interpretations and explanations? Are religious faith and sociological interpretations of religion conflictual? This chapter will address these issues. We will also look at the relationship between religious faith and the sociology of religion at a more practical level. What are the pros and cons of having a religious faith when studying religion as a sociological phenomenon? Also, how do churches and other religious organizations use sociology in their activities?

12.2 Methodological atheism: Sociology and its silence on the question of religious truth

What is the relationship between maintaining that something is religiously true and explaining religion as a human phenomenon, for instance, in a social or cultural context? Most sociologists, qua sociologists, consider religion to be a phenomenon that is created by human beings. Few, if any, sociologists explain religious changes as results of God's or Allah's will, or as expressions of an animated cosmos. A sociologist who wants to understand why a religious movement appears at a specific time and place will search to find social conditions that are assumed to be favorable for such movements. One possible hypothesis is that social equality facilitates the emergence of religious movements, whereas social inequality stimulates movements advocating political reform. Another possible hypothesis is that religious trends fluctuate according to economic cycles. By relying on deprivation theory, the argument is that religious movements tend to emerge in times of economic crisis. Other factors are also important in explaining an emerging religious movement. For example, it is important to see if there is a charismatic leader who has the ability to develop a following. Even if it is difficult to provide a sociological explanation of a religious movement, this is not the issue here. Our aim is to point out that sociological explanations emphasize human and social conditions, not divine interventions. Sociology is methodologically atheistic, to use an expression taken from Peter L. Berger (1967). This does not mean, however, that sociology is substantively atheistic. The sociologist may be a Christian, a Muslim, or an atheist, as other interpretations of reality than the sociological one do exist. Yet the sociological interpretation does not include a divine reality in its analysis. A sociologist will remain silent on the issue whether there is a divine reality behind, beyond, underneath, or hidden inside human and social reality. In this way, sociology brackets the question of truth. Hence, this position could be labeled "methodological agnosticism." By using this term, we emphasize that sociology does not claim to know anything about the truth of religion. The term "methodological atheism" stresses that sociology uses immanent, that is, "this-worldly" explanations, and excludes religious explanations. Methodological agnosticism means that sociology is able to provide information about the dimensions and expressions of religion, but it is unable to make any claims regarding the truth of religion.

Peter L. Berger argues that every religion and every aspect of religion can be the object of a sociological analysis. In his book *The Sacred Canopy* (1967), he leaves his earlier attempt to make Christian faith accessible to sociology (Berger 1961). Whereas in his earlier work he was inspired by Karl Barth's theological distinction between religiosity as man's quest for God and Christian faith as God given, he concludes in his later work that the empirical sciences treat Christian faith as any other form of religion. In general, it is easier to accept social and even reductionist explanations and interpretations regarding "distasteful" religious movements than it is to do the same regarding one's own religious faith. This could be one reason why sociology and psychology tend to use more deterministic theories to explain religious sects and minorities than they use to explain religious organizations and churches they favor, which indeed is an unprofessional approach.

Every aspect of religious life and religious institutions can, thus, be made objects of sociological analysis. Nevertheless, the relationship between religion and social context is more easily seen within some parts of the religious traditions than others. An illustrative example is found in the Christian tradition, where morality and the prevalent views on the church institution tend to be colored by social changes. The reason is that morality and ideas about what the church should be are closely related to the conditions under which people live. In contrast, dogmatic issues are further distanced from people's lives and thereby more protected against change. In earlier times, Christian dogma contained several cosmological propositions. After painful encounters with the heliocentric world-view, most of these propositions have been transformed to symbolic statements. Therefore, contemporary Christian dogmas often contain claims that do not easily lend themselves to empirical falsification. Managers of tradition in the churches also tend to protect dogmas from change. Nevertheless, dogmatic changes do take place. One example is found in notions of hell and perdition, which have been toned down in mainstream preaching during the last forty to fifty years. The major reason for this is that more anti-authoritarian societies pose difficulties for legitimating harsh and punishing styles of leadership – even when they come from God.

The analyses suggested above can be more or less well founded, sociologically speaking. Berger's point is that it is just as legitimate for a sociologist to study substantial elements in the Christian faith or any other faith, as it is to study other aspects of religion, such as religious practices or organizational styles. The main issue is that the sociologist cannot make judgments regarding questions of religious truth.

British sociologist and theologian Robin Gill has debated the relationship between sociology and religious belief. He argues that even if one is able to detect the origin of a religious phenomenon, one cannot draw conclusions regarding the truth of this phenomenon (Gill 1975: 20). Saying that Y is caused by X does not say anything about the truth of Y. He sees the confusion of the questions of origin and truth as a generic fallacy, and he presents a provoking example to illustrate this issue. In the 1970s, a story appeared in several newspapers that a scientist claimed to have evidence that Christianity originated as a psychedelic mushroom cult. The first Christians' faith in Christ's resurrection appeared as a vision caused by eating a particular mushroom. The scientist in question has hardly had his name imprinted in golden letters in the history of the sciences, but Gill uses this example for the sake of the argument: imagine that scientists managed to demonstrate, by means of finding new texts from the New Testament time period or otherwise, that this history of psychedelic origin was true! Philosophically speaking, such a finding would not disprove the truth of Christianity. A religion may be true even if it has originated from adherents who were high on mushrooms. Why should God not be able to use such means, one may ask. To use a less strange example: religion may have true value even if it is male-dominated, Western, and so forth.

Logically, there is a lot to be said for Gill's point of view. However, the credibility of religion is obviously affected by such explanations of origin. For example, the credibility of Christianity would be weakened if the mushroom theory were made probable, just like the credibility of Christianity has been shaken again and again in history as its perceptions of the world and human nature have been challenged and altered. Sociology and its relativizing perspectives can become an existential threat to the religious believer. Faith can be challenged when it turns out that what was religiously rejected yesterday (or in the North), is acceptable today (or in the South) or viewed as a gift from God tomorrow (or in the West).

This particular debate is limited to the relationship between sociology and religion. However, it is relevant for all areas in sociology as it addresses the relationship between this discipline and the world-views and understanding of self that participants in sociological studies have. In all human sciences, there are differences and tensions between what social actors think and believe and the scientific interpretations of these thoughts and beliefs. Yet the tension is intensified when the scholars claim that a phenomenon is a social product and the social actors believe that it is a message from God.

This debate is also relevant for disciplines other than sociology. Indeed, it addresses issues that are pertinent to every science that uses this-worldly explanations and interpretations, which in fact includes every science, since this norm has been crucial in the sciences since the Age of Enlightenment. In the history of the sciences, the secularization process was, roughly speaking, completed by the twentieth century. Church historians with a background in theology tended to lag behind, but even the most religious contemporary church historian will hardly be comfortable with religious, trans-empirical explanations. Other parts of theology have also been affected by the secularization of the sciences. This process has been full of controversies and conflicts, but most biblical scholars agree that the origin of the biblical texts must be studied by using the same historical–critical method that is used to study any other historical text. A similar development is taking place within some parts of Islamic theology. It is still controversial, however, to those theologians who presuppose that the holy texts are the result of a direct revelation from God.

Gradually, theology as a discipline has undergone a division of labor. Some theological disciplines examine the history of texts and specific events. In this area, the research rests upon methodological atheism. The aim is to find out the probability that something happened, the intentions of the authors of a text, and so forth. Other theological disciplines, frequently called systematic theology and practical theology, are more explicitly normative. Their point of departure is that divine forces can affect the world. The status of these two disciplines varies according to institutional contexts and faith traditions. Schematically speaking, academic theology must legitimate itself to fellow academics by stressing methodological atheism, whereas church-oriented theology tends to emphasize more explicitly normative aspects. The latter is particularly true for theology within conservative churches. The social context of theology is important, as well. Still simplifying, in situations of social instability, theology will tend to be open towards the intervention of divine powers, whereas in stable societies, theology will be more oriented towards methodological atheism, leaving less room for direct divine intervention.

The same variations are found in other academic theological traditions, such as Islam. In general, Islamic theology tends to be more faithful to the religious explanations of the origins of its classical texts than academic Christian theology is. However, several Muslim theologians and historians also use the social context as an explanatory factor when they attempt to understand the form and content of the Qur'an and other authoritative texts.

12.3 Classical sociologists and their scientific optimism

The use of methodological atheism does not imply that this approach is completely neutral and objective. Instead, the normativity of this approach is more implicit. All forms of research consist of interpretation: it is an interpretation in and of itself when one views religion as a socially determined phenomenon. Even within this approach, several different interpretations are possible, as seen in the example above regarding the emergence of a religious movement. Sociology and the other social sciences have come a long way in the direction of modesty since the Frenchman August Comte (1798–1857) gave the name "sociology" to this discipline. Originally, Comte planned to name the new science "social physics," which reveals his scientific ideals. Since the natural sciences had been successful in detecting natural laws, Comte maintained that sociologists could, by using methods of observation, experiment, and comparison, find the fundamental laws in human life and society. He assumed that society functions in a deterministic and predictable way. His aim was to use this new knowledge of social laws to create a better society. The combination of belief in exact methods, the possibility of detecting how the social machinery works, and the vision of improving society through scientific knowledge has been a vital dimension in much sociology after Comte. Yet some traditions in the history of sociology have been more modest on behalf of the discipline. These traditions have maintained that since human beings are conscious and creative beings, sociology is unable to predict the future, regardless of how advanced the methods one uses and regardless of the amount of data one collects. These hermeneutic, interpretative traditions argue that all we can hope for is a more profound understanding of the different ways in which human beings think and act. Several scientific disciplines underwent a transformation in their understanding of themselves during the so-called critique of positivism that took place at most Western universities during the 1960s and 1970s. Positivism is a term that is used to describe the assumption that exact knowledge about an unambiguous reality and its laws can be obtained through the use of rigorous methods. The critique of this optimistic belief in science hit the social sciences particularly hard. It pointed to the provisional character and the element of interpretation inherent in all sciences. During this process of reflection on the fundamental aspects of science, a renewal took place of the sociological traditions that stress human beings as creative and intentional beings. According to this approach, human and social lives do not simply follow mechanical laws.

The critique of positivism and growing scientific modesty have resulted in a lower degree of conflict between the scientific study of religion and religious faith. The social sciences developed during the nineteenth century were, to a large extent, children of the Age of Enlightenment. Several founding fathers in the social sciences harbored an ambition to explain religion as such. As early as the mid-eighteenth century, Scottish philosopher David Hume attempted to explain why religion existed, in his book with the revealing title, *A Natural History of Religion* (1976/1757). Here, he explained religion as a product of hope and fear: in order to control his fears, man personified frightening natural phenomena. Hume's premise is that religion is a human construct. We find a resembling rationalism and reductionism in the early social anthropology of the nineteenth century. Karl Marx, too, explained religion in reductionist terms, that is, as a symptom of something else than religion. In his work, religion is a protest and a comfort that human beings create when they face social injustice and misery (see Section 3.1). Émile Durkheim's theory of religion can also be seen as reductionist, as religion is basically interpreted as an expression of the social community: society is more than the sum of each individual, and this is expressed in religion (see Section 3.2). If we leave sociology and take a look at psychology, we see that Sigmund Freud's theory of religion is also ambitious in the sense that it attempts to explain why religion exists. He views the origin of religion as a projection based on the experiences of the little child in the family, especially the experiences of the helpless child with a powerful father. Freud also adds a functionalist explanation: religion is a necessary bulwark against uncontrollable instincts, a form of cultural safety belt. At the same time, Freud is critical towards religion. For him, it is a controlling and neurotic bond. In his book, *The Future of an Illusion* (1928/1921), Freud hopes that religion will become superfluous and disappear, as people develop patterns of behavior based on self-insight and reason (see Section 3.5).

All of these scholars perceived themselves as rational, scientific, and objective thinkers. In retrospect, however, we see that their theories are clearly based more on culturally determined presuppositions than pure logic. They were rationalists who were convinced that social life had a dynamic that could be detected through detailed scientific work that sought to establish social laws. Each of them stressed one major factor they believed constituted the origin of religion, be it social injustice, social integration, or neuroses. They also related their ideas of the origin of religion to the question of religious truth. Altogether, these scholars were extremely ambitious on behalf of the sciences, which was common at the time. Methodically, they made widespread generalizations based on a limited amount of empirical data, be it aboriginal tribes or ladies from Vienna with weak nerves. Their merit is a bold desire for a holistic understanding of society, which is more or less lost in contemporary sociology, as it is divided into numerous sectors, sometimes called hyphenated sociology. Nevertheless, these classical theorists must take their part of the responsibility for the fact that religious people still tend to associate the social sciences with a one-sided negative attitude towards religious faith, despite many decades of sociology based on methodological atheism or agnosticism.

Contemporary sociology offers a multitude of trends that will, to a varying degree, provoke religious people and their understanding of themselves and their faith. Hermeneutical sociology, leaving ample room for the actors' own interpretations of the world, is more easily combined with religious faith than a sociology outlining strict causal links between social contexts and religious content. Intention analyses or meaning analyses based on an assumption that people largely act based on their interpretations of the world seem to be more "faith-friendly" than a sociology suggesting deterministic causal propositions, where human consciousness, interpretation, and choice are made invisible in the analysis (Repstad 1995b: 56–61).

12.4 Religion varies in its compatibility with sociology

The collision between sociology and religious faith is not just affected by sociology's explanatory ambitions. Some religious ideas seem to be relatively incompatible with sociological analyses of religion. The stronger the faith is in otherworldly causes of events, the stronger the conflict is with social scientific perspectives. Admittedly, a form of "inner secularization" has taken place in several religious traditions as they have confronted the Enlightenment and rationalism. A subjectivizing process has also changed Christian faith and theology since the seventeenth century. In most churches, Christianity as a total cosmology has been replaced by a faith and a theology that pose moral and existential challenges. The result is that several theologians and active church members reserve a relatively large space for scientific explanations. Similar developments take place within other religious traditions as well. At the same time, there are numerous examples of religious traditions refusing to adapt in this way, as they struggle to uphold an overall religious world-view. Believers who stress God's direct guidance and intervention in the world will have more difficulties with the sociology of religion than believers who find traces of God in the goodness of human beings. Believers who claim that the Qur'an or the Bible is a direct and faultless revelation will tend to view sociological and historical approaches as threats. This is less so for believers who view these holy texts as affected by the world in which they originated and by the people who wrote them.

12.5 Contemporary critique of methodological atheism

More recently, academic critique of methodological atheism has appeared, which is based on a different line of argument than the more constant critique that stems from religious groups with a profound faith in divine intervention.

At the center of the controversy is *Theology and Social Theory. Beyond Secular Reason*, written by British theologian John Milbank (1990). Milbank argues that theological and social scientific discourses are deeply conflictual. Sociology is not only methodologically atheistic. The discipline is simply atheistic, as it does not admit the existence of a divine reality. According to Milbank, a process of "policing the sublime" takes place in sociological discourse: the exalted, sacred, and sublime is being tamed, limited, and disciplined. The divine is either presented as an expression of more real and powerful social conditions, or religion is seen as an attempt to find meaning in personal experiences. Sociology tends to operate with the implicit assumption that these experiences can be more adequately interpreted in other ways. Milbank claims that the sociology of religion represents a liberal meta-narrative that offers religion an extremely limited space and significance. Sociology states that religion is in fact a private matter, and that it belongs to the world of emotions and subjective sentiments. It is taken for granted that religion has little or no influence in the public sphere because sociology suggests that religion only has one function, namely to help people to master anxiety and insecurity, not least in the face of death.

According to Milbank, this is an example of how modern thinking projects its own issues back into history. He argues that historical evidence shows that fear of dying largely is a modern phenomenon that emerged in the eighteenth century. People used to view death more as a natural transition than a threat. In several areas, sociology of religion is a naïve child of its time: when contemporary sociologists of religion argue that social and economic structures are the most fundamental forces in history, such a claim represents an expression of what modern man desires. This is combined with a superficial belief that human beings are the same at all historical times. To conclude, Milbank's critique of sociology of religion is part of a more general critique of modernity.

According to Milbank, there is a profound conflict here: theologians who accept sociological explanations base their thinking on a secular, alternative meta-narrative with just as comprehensive ambitions of explanation as theology. He thinks that it is impossible to create a dialogue and compromise between theology and sociology, because sociology already *is* a theology (or an anti-theology, explaining God away). For Christians, only a theological discourse is adequate. They have to deduct their understanding of society from their Christian view. Milbank is ambitious on behalf of theology. He argues that theology has the ability to describe and shed a complete light on the areas that the social sciences attempt to explain. Theologians must insist that Christianity has the best interpretation and practice, Milbank claims. It is not quite clear whether he leaves room for sociology as a kind of subordinated discipline under theology.

Milbank's confrontation with sociology has been met by critique from theologians as well as sociologists. Theologians have accused him of ending up in a theocratic position, where questions are not asked regarding the truth of theology. Sociologists have argued that he draws an overly reductionist picture of contemporary sociology and that he ignores the challenges sociology poses for churches, theology, and religion: "Could Milbank *really* be suggesting that there were no politics of baptism, ordination and credal formation and of the episcopal or papal power to define and pronounce? Is there really no intelligible social geography of conversion or demographics of dechristianisation?" (Martin 1997:110).

Kieran Flanagan, a Catholic sociologist, presents his view on the relationship between sociology, theology, and religious faith in his book *The Enchantment of Sociology* (1996). In contrast to Milbank, who describes sociology as secular positivism and postmodernism as secular nihilism, Flanagan sees opportunities for a closer relationship between sociology and theology. The reason is that issues of reflection, identity, and understanding are addressed in contemporary sociology. Existential and theological issues are emerging in sociology in an unexpected way, Flanagan says. A postmodern culture has crushed the myth of secularization, and faith in basic secular truths has been weakened. The optimistic idea of progress and other grand narratives has dissolved. Several sociologists deal with issues of meaning, identity, and morality, and some paint a picture of a world characterized by re-sacralization and re-enchantment. According to Flanagan, this new situation enables theologians and Christian sociologists to participate in the dialogue on religious premises, as they maintain their professional integrity.

In a response, sociologist James Beckford (1997) modifies Flanagan's description of contemporary sociology. Admittedly, there has been a growing interest in faith and spirituality in recent sociological theory. Several theorists, such as Bauman, Giddens, and Habermas, include issues such as ethics, philosophy, politics, as well as sociology in their work. However, this is only part of the picture. Along with these trends, rational choice theory has appeared in the sociology of religion as a new paradigm, and here Beckford is unable to find much of mystery and enchantment. Besides, Beckford argues that the majority of these theorists anchor religion in human weakness, not in divine forces. He uses Zygmunt Bauman as an illustrative example. Bauman depicts religious institutions in an extremely conventional way. To the extent that religion flourishes, it does so because it attracts some groups in times of rapid change and high level of insecurity (Bauman 1992).

British sociologist of religion David Martin has somewhat more positive learnings towards Flanagan's agenda. Sociology has rediscovered agency and narrative and thereby brought itself closer to the theological discourse (Martin 1997). Martin agrees with Flanagan that if sociologists are lacking an emphatic understanding of the religious meaning of rituals and institutions, their research is defective. Yet Martin stops there, as his position is methodological atheism. Sociologists cannot use variables "that represent divine action."

Some sociologists are connected to religious organizations, either through their work or through their own world-views. In some cases, the relationship between sociology and religious faith becomes a personal matter. In this group, the large majority still use some form of methodological atheism. This position is not without its problems. It seems somewhat arbitrary to repeatedly state: "Now I speak as a sociologist" or "Now I transcend my role as a sociologist and voice my personal views on this religion." Generally speaking, modern scholars have learned to handle several different perspectives. Most of them conduct research on religion as a human and social phenomenon, as they add that a social scientific perspective does not provide a complete picture of religion. Social scientists who have a religious faith will hardly cease to be uncomfortable with methodological atheism, but the replacement of this position with another theory of knowledge will most likely create more problems than it solves.

12.6 Research from the inside or the outside?

What are the pros and cons of having a religious faith when you study religion as a sociological phenomenon? We have seen that the Age of Enlightenment established a scientific tradition for interpreting religion from the outside, as something other than religion, be it fear of natural phenomena, hope for a better life, or comfort in situations of misery and injustice. During the nineteenth century, some theologians and scholars of religion disputed these outside explanations. German theologian Friedrich Schleiermacher depicted religion as an autonomous phenomenon *sui generis*. According to his view, religion was primarily an emotion, and it was just as real as observed material objects. German theologian and historian of religion Rudolph Otto was an important scholar in this tradition, who wanted to emphasize the distinctive character of religion. He went far along the line of argument that only people who are religious themselves can study religion in an adequate way. Early in his work *The Idea of the Holy* (1958/1917), he addresses readers and asks them to direct their minds to a deeply felt moment of religious experience. Those who are unable to do so, and have no experience in this area, are actually asked to read no longer, for "it is not easy to discuss such questions of religious psychology with one who can recollect the emotions of his adolescence, the discomforts of indigestion, or, say, social feelings, but cannot recall any intrinsically religious feelings" (Otto 1958/1917: 8).

More recent scholars of religion, such as Mircea Eliade (1959), have also claimed that the essence of religion is not grasped unless one is religious. Contemporary Canadian scholar of religion Wilfred Cantwell Smith (1981) is the most definite spokesperson for the privileged position of the insider in religious research: "No statement of Islamic faith is true that Muslims cannot accept. No personalist statement about Hindu religious life is legitimate in which Hindus cannot recognise themselves. No interpretation of Buddhist doctrine is valid unless Buddhists can respond: 'Yes! That is what we hold'" (Smith 1981: 97).

In the following, we will continue to discuss this *insider–outsider* debate as a more practical issue. Do religious scholars produce better or worse research on religion than non-religious scholars do? Here, we will exclude theology and focus on empirical research.

Some arguments for the insider position are fairly practical and down to earth: you have extensive knowledge about your own religion, which will prevent you from committing basic mistakes. Furthermore, you already have a network of people who trust you and who will make sure you access better information than the scholar who comes from outside. Another argument deals with the ability of *einfühlen*, of taking the actor's point of view: only people who have or have had religious experiences are able to understand the meaning of religious commitment. Here, metaphors from music or stained-glass paintings are used to support the argument. An unmusical person or a hearing-impaired person is only able to enjoy music in a limited way. Likewise, stained-glass paintings appear dull and of no interest seen from the outside, but once you see them from the inside, they shine in many colors. These arguments can be persuasive, but perhaps somewhat seductive.

From the perspective of the theory of science, these arguments belong to a scientific tradition that stresses the significance of taking the actor's point of view. If *einfühlen* is crucial in an understanding of religion, the scholar's own faith or lack thereof becomes more important than in situations where the sociology of religion emphasizes structural or institutional factors. For example, the behaviorist considers the religious faith of the scholar to be of little or no significance. This tradition views consciousness as a black box, and the aim of science is to detect regularities, patterns, and causal relations by observing behavior from the outside.

The main objection to the notion that religious people make the best scholars of religion is, of course, that everyone who lives wholeheartedly inside a religious tradition is unable to create the distance deemed necessary to conduct a reliable and valid analysis. This is partly due to intellectual limitations: one is so familiar with one's own tradition that it is nearly impossible to review one's own backyard with a critical eye. One takes for granted that which an outsider will question. It is also a matter of loyalty: one's own commitment can narrow the focus and turn it away from the less attractive aspects of religion. A religious attitude can also blind a scholar to possible connections between the religious expressions and their social context. A sociologist is hardly able to construct an interpretation of a "pure" religion that exists independent of a social context. However, strong loyalties to one religious tradition create difficulties in producing unbiased analyses of other traditions. There are several examples of scholars with a Christian conviction who are unable to describe other religious traditions in those traditions' own terms. Instead, they tend to measure the distance between their research objects and their own religious standards.

Another argument often used to support an insider perspective is that neutrality in research is an illusion. Unbelief is also a form of belief. No inside experience with religion might lead to superficial descriptions. Scholar of religion Eric J. Sharpe addresses this issue in his book *Understanding Religion* (1999). One of his arguments is that several contemporary Western scholars of religion harbor an implicit commitment to religious diversity and openness: they are positive to religion in general, but negative to religious dogma. They are critical towards the dogmatic dimensions of their childhood religious traditions, but at the same time, they reveal openness and curiosity regarding alternative religiosity and other religious traditions. Sharpe argues that there is a trend in Western research on religion, namely to favor exotic traditions and dislike familiar traditions. Although Sharpe might exaggerate, his views can be used as a reminder to apply the same standards to all religions. The home ground should represent neither an advantage nor a drawback.

One possible argument is that the scholar with the best presuppositions to study religion is the one who once was religiously committed, but no longer is so. In this case, the scholar will know religion from the inside, but has the necessary analytical distance. In other words, this scholar will be able to move between empathy and critical analysis. A position as ex-religious will also be beneficial in an analysis of negative aspects of religion. A person who has felt the yoke of a religious organization on their shoulders, or has once been a religious zealot, may obtain a deeper understanding of a form of religion that can seem quite impenetrable and irrational to outsiders. In addition, the ex-religious will be free from bonds of loyalty obstructing the quest for truth. This position requires of the ex-member that they have a relatively relaxed and non-conflictual relationship to the former group. A person with a desire for revenge is hardly the best scholar to interpret the religious movement they have left in a fair and non-judgmental way.

This discussion is becoming become pretty schematic, as the ranking list of the best scholar hardly follows our distinction between insider and outsider. Several other factors affect the quality of sociological analyses of religion. The ability to shift and balance between closeness and critical distance is most likely found among scholars with quite different religious positions. In modern times, most people relate to a multitude of contexts and roles. Several outsiders will feel empathy towards the believer, and many believers have the ability to reflect upon their faith.

It is hardly a relevant option to follow William Cantwell Smith (1981) and let the believer be the final judge of the sociological analysis of religion. Of course, sociologists of religion are, like other social scientists, subject to the ethical codes of presenting the social actors' views in a fair way. Nevertheless, once a scholar produces an interpretation, she or he must present the analysis even if the actors disagree with it. Generally speaking, one important ambition for the social sciences is *transcending recognition*. Competent actors should be able to recognize the social phenomena described, but they should also be offered new insights.

12.7 The sociology of religion as an applied science

In this chapter, we have presented several issues in a schematic way, mostly for pedagogical reasons. Must we choose between sociological interpretations and a religious conviction? Do insiders or outsiders produce the best research? We have modified the alternatives, even if the different views and the tensions between them cannot be completely harmonized. Nevertheless, several examples are found of a peaceful coexistence between sociology of religion and religious organizations. Indeed, several churches have used sociology of religion as an aid in their work. An illustrative example is found in the Nordic countries, where the Swedish, Norwegian, and Finnish national churches have founded institutes for church-related research. In their work, the sociology of religion constitutes the most important approach. During the first half of the twentieth century, several American denominations also used sociological analyses to help them create a society based on Christian values. In this case, sociology became an integral part of what was viewed as a *diaconia* for society. This form of reasoning was behind the Middletown study, conducted by Helen and Robert Lynd (1929), a study that became a classic in American local community studies.

In Europe, French sociologist Gabriel LeBras was a pioneer from the 1930s in conducting detailed empirical analyses of popular religiosity, aiming at vitalizing the Catholic Church. In other countries as well, a similar *sociologie religieuse* was established. In addition, so-called pastoral sociology was developed, especially in Germany, which focused on the role of the clergy and its possibilities to communicate in the world.

Applied sociology of religion has tended to be descriptive and use poor theorizing. In an early article, Peter L. Berger and Thomas Luckmann (1963) described applied sociology of religion as an alliance between archbishops and Gallup pollsters. The main critique has been that the perspectives used are bound up with the concerns and strategies of the church. Thereby, these scholars become too nearsighted. Nevertheless, contemporary applied sociological church research is largely based on methodological atheism. Indeed, some church research also raises critique against the churches. In fact, this form of research may prove to increase the respect for popular religiosity within the church.

The global tendency towards religious and world-view pluralization has been manifested at an organizational level. In 1948, a Catholic organization for the sociology of religion was founded in Belgium, *Société Internationale de Sociologie des Religions* (SISR). Here, we will choose SISR as an illustrative example. Other organizations, such as *Association for the Sociology of Religion* (ASR), have gone through a similar process. During the last fifty to sixty years, SISR has become an international organization for sociologists of religion. Today it is the largest of several such organizations. In the 1950s, SISR opened its organization to non-Catholic members. After a few years, members were no longer asked about their religious affiliation or faith (Voyé and Billiet 1999). The first members with a non-Christian background were Jewish sociologists of religion. Today, the organization also includes members with a Muslim background. Still, the large majority of sociologists of religion, including members of SISR, have a Christian background, culturally speaking. The absence of a broader Muslim sociology of religion has been explained by two factors. First, there seems to be a general tendency for Islam to have a lower degree of acceptance of critique and contextualizing than most modern Christian traditions. Second, sociology of religion is still dominated by a Western and Christian profile, which is evident if we take a look at the use of concepts and empirical illustrations (Hamès 1999). This book, now approaching its end, is also characterized by this situation. It is reasonable to believe that in the years to come, a positive attitude to the sociology of religion will develop among scholars from all religious traditions. Instead, the view on this discipline will most likely differ more among fundamentalist and liberal groups within each religious tradition. The ability to create space for critique and reflexivity regarding faith and science seems to be a precondition for a combination of sociological interpretations and religious faith.

Bibliography

Adams, Bert N. and R.A. Sydie. 2002a. *Classical Sociological Theory*. Thousand Oaks, CA: Pine Forge Press.

—— 2002b. *Contemporary Sociological Theory*. Thousand Oaks, CA: Pine Forge Press.

Aidala, Angela A. 1985. Social Change, Gender Roles, and New Religious Movements. *Sociological Analysis* 46(3): 287–314.

Alba, Richard D. 1990. *Ethnic Identity: The Transformation of White America*. New Haven, CT: Yale University Press.

Aldridge, Alan 2000. *Religion in the Contemporary World. A Sociological Introduction*. Oxford: Polity Press.

Alver, Bente, Ingvild S. Gilhus, Lisbeth Mikaelsson, and Torunn Selberg 1999. *Myte, magi og mirakel i møte med det moderne* [Myth, magic and miracles in encounters with the modern]. Oslo: Pax.

Ammerman, Nancy T. 1987. *Bible Believers: Fundamentalists in the Modern World*. New Brunswick, NJ: Rutgers University Press.

—— 1991. North American Protestant Fundamentalism. In *Fundamentalisms Observed*, edited by Martin E. Marty and R. Scott Appleby, 1–65. Chicago, IL and London: University of Chicago Press.

An-Na'im, Abdullahi A. 1999. Political Islam in National Politics and International Relations. In *The Desecularization of the World*, edited by Peter L. Berger, 103–21. Grand Rapids, MI: Wm. B. Eerdmans.

Anderson, Benedict 1983. *Imagined Communities*. London: Verso.

Arjomand, Said Amir 1993. Shi'ite Jurisprudence and Constitution Making in the Islamic Republic of Iran. In *Fundamentalisms and the State*, edited by Martin E. Marty and R. Scott Appleby, 88–109. Chicago, IL and London: University of Chicago Press.

Arthur, Rose Horman 1987. The Wisdom Goddess and the Masculinization of Western Religion. In *Women in the World's Religions, Past and Present*, edited by Ursula King, 24–37. New York: Paragon House.

Avruch, Kevin 2003. Culture and Ethnic Conflict in the New World Order. In *Race and Ethnicity. Comparative and Theoretical Approaches*, edited by John Stone and Rutledge Dennis, 72–82. Oxford: Blackwell.

Bäckström, Anders 1991. *I Guds tjänst. En profilundersökning av Strängnäs stifts präster 1991*. Strägnäs: Struangnäs stift.

Baer, Hans A. 1994. The Limited Empowerment of Women in Black Spiritual Churches: An Alternative Vehicle to Religious Leadership. In *Gender and Religion*, edited by W.H. Swatos, Jr., 75–92. New Brunswick, NJ and London: Transaction.

Baert, Patrick 1998. *Social Theory in the Twentieth Century*. Cambridge: Polity.

Baily, Edward 1986. Zivilreligion in Grossbritannien [Civil religion in Great Britain]. In *Religion des Bürgers. Zivilreligion in Amerika und Europa*, edited by H. Kleger and A. Müller, 104–20. Munich: Chr. Kaiser.

Bancroft, Anne 1987. Women in Buddhism. In *Women in the World's Religions, Past and Present*, edited by Ursula King, 81–104. New York: Paragon House.

Banton, Michael 1970. The concept of racism. In *Race and Racialism*, edited by S. Zubaida, 17–34. London: Tavistock.

—— 1987. *Racial Theories*. Cambridge: Cambridge University Press.

Barker, D. et al. 1992. *The European Value Study 1981–1990. Summary Report*. London: Gordon Cook Foundation.

Barker, Eileen 1984. *The Making of a Moonie*. Oxford: Blackwell.

—— 1985. New religious movements: yet another great awakening? In *The Sacred in a Secular Age*, edited by Phillip E. Hammond, 36–57. Berkeley: University of California Press.

—— 1995. *New Religious Movements: A practical introduction*. London: HMSO.

Barker, Martin 1981. *The New Racism*. London: Junction Books.

Barth, Fredrik (ed.) 1969. *Ethnic Group and Boundaries*. Oslo: Universitetsforlaget.

Bartkowski, John P. 2004. *The Promise Keepers. Servants, Soldiers, and Godly Men*. New Brunswick, NJ: Rutgers University Press.

Baudrillard, Jean 1983. *Simulations*. New York: Semiotext(e).

Bauman, Zygmunt 1989. *Modernity and the Holocaust*. Cambridge: Polity Press.

—— 1992. *Intimations of Postmodernity*. London: Routledge.

—— 1993. *Postmodern Ethics*. Oxford: Blackwell.

—— 1998a. *Globalization: The Human Consequences*. Cambridge: Polity Press.

—— 1998b. Postmodern religion? In *Religion, modernity and postmodernity*, edited by Paul Heelas, 55–78. Oxford: Blackwell.

—— 1998c. *Work, Consumerism and the New Poor*. Buckingham: Open University Press.

—— 2000. *Liquid Modernity*. Cambridge: Polity Press.

—— 2001. *Community: Seeking Safety in an Insecure World*. Cambridge: Polity Press.

Becker, Howard 1932. *Systematic Sociology on the Basis of the Beziehungslehre and Gebildelehre of Leopold van Wiese*. New York: Wiley.

Beckford, James A. 1975. *The Trumpet of Prophecy*. Oxford: Basil Blackwell.

—— 1992. Religion, modernity and post-modernity. In *Religion: Contemporary Issues*, edited by Bryan R. Wilson, 11–27. London: Bellew.

—— 1997. The disenchantment of postmodernity. *New Blackfriars* 73, (913): 121–8.

—— 1999. Postmodernity, High Modernity and New Modernity: Three Concepts in Search of Religion. In *Postmodernity, Sociology and Religion*, edited by Kieran Flanagan and Peter C. Jupp, 30–47. London: Macmillan.

—— 2000. "Start Together and Finish Together." Shifts in the Premises and Paradigms Underlying the Scientific Study of Religion. *Journal for the Scientific Study of Religion* 39(2): 481–95.

—— and Sophie Gilliat 1998. *Religion in Prison. Equal Rites in a Multi-Faith Society*. Cambridge: Cambridge University Press.

—— and M. Levasseur 1986. New Religious Movements in Western Europe. In *New Religious Movements and Rapid Change*, edited by James A. Beckford, 29–54. London: Sage.

—— and Thomas Luckmann (eds) 1989. *The Changing Face of Religion*. London: Sage.

Bell, Catherine 1992. *Ritual theory, ritual practice*. New York: Oxford University Press.

Bell, Daniel 1973. *The Coming of Postindustrial Society*. New York: Basic Books.

—— 1976. *The Cultural Contradictions of Capitalism*. New York: Basic Books.

Bellah, Robert N. 1964. Religious evolution. *American Sociological Review* 29: 358–74.

—— 1967. Civil Religion in America. *Daedalus* 96: 1–21.

—— 1968. Response. In *The Religious Situation*, edited by D. Cutler, 388–93. Boston, MA: Beacon Press.

—— 1971. The Historical Background of Unbelief. In *The Culture of Unbelief*, edited by R. Caporale and A. Grumelli, 39–52. Berkeley: University of California Press.

—— 1972. *Beyond Belief: Essays on Religion in a Post-Traditional World*. New York: Harper & Row.

—— 1975. *The Broken Covenant. American Civil Religion in Time of Trial*. New York: The Seabury Press.

—— 1976. Response to the Panel on Civil Religion. *Sociological Analysis* 37: 153–9.

—— 1980. Introduction. In *Varieties of Civil Religion* by Robert N. Bellah and Phillip E. Hammond, vii–xv. San Francisco, CA: Harper & Row.

—— and Phillip E. Hammond 1980. *Varieties of Civil Religion*. San Francisco, CA: Harper & Row.

——, R. Madsen, W.M. Sullivan, A. Swidler, and S.M. Tipton 1996. *Habits of the Heart: individualism and commitment in American life*. Berkeley: University of California Press.

Benard, Cheryl 2002. *Veiled Courage. Inside the Afghan Women's Resistance*. New York: Broadway Books.

Bendix, Reinhard 1977. *Max Weber. An Intellectual Portrait*. Berkeley, Los Angeles, London: University of California Press.

Berger, Helen A. 1998. *A Community of Witches: Contemporary Neo-Paganism and Witchcraft in the United States*. Columbia: University of South Carolina Press.

Berger, Peter L. 1961. *The Precarious Vision: A Sociologist Looks at Social Fictions and the Christian Faith*. Garden City, NY: Doubleday.

—— 1967. *The Sacred Canopy: Elements of a Sociological Theory of Religion*. Garden City, NY: Doubleday.

—— 1969. *A Rumor of Angels*. Garden City, NY: Doubleday.

—— 1977. *Facing up to Modernity: Excursions in Society, Politics, and Religion*. New York: Basic Books.

—— 1979. *The Heretical Imperative: Contemporary Possibilities of Religious Affirmation*. Garden City, NY: Anchor/Doubleday.

—— 1986. *The Capitalist Revolution*. New York: Basic Books.

—— (ed.) 1999. *The Desecularization of the World. Resurgent Religion and World Politics*. Grand Rapids, MI: The Ethics and Public Policy Center and Wm. B. Eerdmans.

—— 2001. Reflections on the sociology of religion today. *Sociology of Religion* 62(4): 443–54.

—— and Thomas Luckmann 1963. Sociology of Religion and Sociology of Knowledge. *Sociology and Social Research* 47: 417–27.

—— 1981/1966. *The Social Construction of Reality*. Harmondsworth, Middlesex: Penguin.

—— 1995. *Modernity, Pluralism and the Crisis of Meaning*. Gütersloh: Bertelsmann Foundation.

Berkowitz, Michael 1999. Judaism: Modern Movements. In *Encyclopedia of Women and World Religion*, edited by Serenity Young, 551–3. New York: Macmillan.

Beyer, Peter 1990. Privatization and the Public Influence of Religion in Global Society. In *Global Culture. Nationalism, globalization and modernity*, edited by Mike Featherstone, 373–95. London: Sage.

—— 1994. *Religion and Globalization*. London: Sage.

Biale, David J. 1983. Mysticism and Politics in Modern Israel: The Messianic Ideology of Abraham Isaac Ha-Cohen Kook. In *Religion and Politics in the Modern World*, edited by Peter H. Merkl and Ninian Smart, 191–202. New York and London: New York University Press.

Bibby, R. and M.B. Brinkerhoff 1974. Sources of religious involvement. *Review of Religious Research* 15(2): 71–9.

Blumer, Herbert 1962. Society as Symbolic Interaction. In *Human Behaviour and Social Process: An Interactionist Perspective*, edited by Arnold Rose, 179–92. Boston, MA: Houghton-Mifflin.

—— 1969. *Symbolic Interactionism*. Englewood Cliffs, NJ: Prentice-Hall.

Botvar, Pål Ketil 1993. *Religion uten kirke. Ikke-institusjonell kirke i Norge, Storbritannia og Tyskland* [Religion without church. Non-institutional religion in Norway, Great Britain, and Germany]. Oslo: Diakonhjemmets høgskolesenter.

Boucher, Sandy 1988. *Turning the Wheel: American Women Creating the New Buddhism*. San Francisco, CA: Harper & Row.

Bourdieu, Pierre 1977. *Outline of a Theory of Practice*. Cambridge: Cambridge University Press.

—— 1986. *Distinction. A Social Critique of the Judgement of Taste*. London and New York: Routledge & Kegan Paul.

—— 1987. Legitimation and Structured Interests in Weber's Sociology of Religion. In *Max Weber, Rationality and Modernity*, edited by Scott Lash and Sam Whimster, 119–36. London: Allen & Unwin.

—— 1994. *Language and Symbolic Power*. Cambridge: Polity Press.

Brasher, Brenda E. 1998. *Godly Women. Fundamentalism and Female Power*. New Brunswick, NJ and London: Rutgers University Press.

Brekke, Torkel 1999. *Religion og vold* [Religion and violence]. Oslo: Humanistisk forlag.

Brickner, Bryan W. 1999. *The Promise Keepers: Politics and Promises*. Lanham, MD: Lexington Books.

Bromley, David G. and Anson D. Shupe 1979. *"Moonies" in America*. Beverly Hills, CA: Sage.

Bruce, Steve 1990. *A House Divided. Protestantism, Schism and Secularization*. London: Routledge.

—— 1996. *Religion in the Modern World: From Cathedrals to Cults*. Oxford: Oxford University Press.

—— 1999. *Choice and Religion: A Critique of Rational Choice Theory*. Oxford: Oxford University Press.

—— 2000. *Fundamentalism*. Cambridge: Polity Press.

—— 2002. *God is Dead. Secularization in the West*. Oxford: Blackwell.

—— 2003. *Politics and Religion*. Cambridge: Polity Press.

Bryant, J. and D. Jary (eds) 1991. *Giddens' Theory of Structuration: A Critical Appreciation*. London: Routledge.

Bukhari, Zahid H., Sulayman S. Nyang, Mumtaz Ahmad, and John L. Esposito (eds) 2004. *Muslims' Place in the American Public Square: Hope, Fears, and Aspirations*. Walnut Creek, CA: AltaMira Press.

Calhoun, Craig 1992. Introduction: Habermas and the Public Sphere. In *Habermas and the Public Sphere*, edited by Craig Calhoun, 1–48. Cambridge, MA: The MIT Press.

—— 1997. *Nationalism*. Minneapolis: University of Minnesota Press.

——, Edward LiPuma and Moishe Postone 1993. *Bourdieu: Critical Perspectives*. Chicago, IL: University of Chicago Press.

——, Joseph Gerteis, James Moody, Steven Pfaff, and Indermoham Virk 2002. *Contemporary Sociological Theory*. Oxford: Blackwell.

Carrette, Jeremy R. 1999. Prologue to a confession of the flesh. In *Religion and Culture* by Michel Foucault, selected and edited by Jeremy R. Carrette, 1–47. New York: Routledge.

—— 2000. *Foucault and Religion*. London and New York: Routledge.

—— and R. King 1998. Giving Birth to Theory: Critical Perspectives on Religion and the Body. *Scottish Journal of Religious Studies* (Special Edition) 19(1): 123–43.

Carroll, Jackson, Barbara Hargrove, and Adair Lummis 1983. *Women of the Cloth*. San Francisco, CA: Harper.

Casanova, José 1994. *Public Religions in the Modern World*. Chicago, IL and London: University of Chicago Press.

—— 2001. Religion, the New Millennium, and Globalization. *Sociology of Religion* 62(4): 415–41.

Cava, Ralph Della 2001. Transnational Religions: The Catholic Church in Brazil & the Orthodox Church in Russia. *Sociology of Religion* 62(4): 535–50.

Chaves, Mark 1997. *Ordaining Women*. Cambridge, MA: Harvard University Press.

Clayton, Richard 1971. 5-D or 1? *Journal for the Scientific Study of Religion* 10(1): 37–40.

Cohen, Philip 1992. "It's racism what dunnit": hidden narratives in theories of racism. In *"Race", Culture and Difference*, edited by James Donald and Ali Rattansi, 62–103. London: The Open University.

Coser, Lewis A. 1956. *The Functions of Social Conflict*. New York: The Free Press.

Daly, Mary 1978. *Gyn/Ecology: The Metaethics of Radical Feminism*. Boston, MA: Beacon Press.

Davidman, Lynn and Arthur L. Greil 1994. Gender and the experience of Conversion: The Case of "Returnees" to Modern Orthodox Judaism. In *Gender and Religion*, edited by William H. Swatos, Jr., 95–112. New Brunswick, NJ and London: Transaction.

Davie, Grace 1990. Believing Without Belonging. *Social Compass* 37(4): 455–69.

—— 2000. *Religion in Modern Europe. A Memory Mutates*. Oxford: Oxford University Press.

—— 2001. The persistence of institutional religion in modern Europe. In *Peter Berger and the Study of Religion*, edited by Linda Woodhead with Paul Heelas and David Martin, 101–11. London and New York: Routledge.

—— 2002. *Europe: The Exceptional Case*. London: Darton, Longman and Todd.

Davis, Kingsley 1948–49. *Human Society*. New York: Macmillan.

Demerath III, Nicholas Jay 2001. *Crossing the Gods. World Religions and Worldly Politics*. New Brunswick, NJ and London: Rutgers University Press.

—— 2003. Secularization Extended: From Religious "Myth" to Cultural Commonplace. In *The Blackwell Companion to Sociology of Religion*, edited by Richard K. Fenn, 211–28. Oxford: Blackwell.

Dennis, Rutledge 2003. W.E.B. Du Bois's Concept of Double Consciousness. In *Race and Ethnicity. Comparative and Theoretical Approaches*, edited by John Stone and Rutledge Dennis, 13–27. Oxford: Blackwell.

Dobbelaere, Karel 1981. Secularization: A Multi-Dimensional Concept. *Current Sociology* 29(2): 1–216.

—— 1993. Church Involvement and Secularization: Making Sense of the European Case. In *Secularization, Rationalism and Sectarianism*, edited by Eileen Barker et al. Oxford: Clarendon Press.

—— 1998a. Bourdieu, Pierre. In *Encyclopedia of Religion and Society*, edited by William H. Swatos, Jr., 61. Walnut Creek, CA: AltaMira Press.

—— 1998b. Pillarization. In *Encyclopedia of Religion and Society*, edited by William H. Swatos, Jr., 364. Walnut Creek, CA: AltaMira Press.

—— 2002. *Secularization: An Analysis at Three Levels*. Brussels: P.I.E.–Peter Lang.

Dorrien, Gary 2001. Berger: theology and sociology. In *Peter Berger and the Study of Religion*, edited by Linda Woodhead with Paul Heelas and David Martin, 26–39. London and New York: Routledge.

Douglas, Mary 1982a. The Effect of Modernization on Religious Change. *Daedalus* (Winter): 1–19.

—— 1982b. *In the Active Voice*. London: Routledge & Kegan Paul.

Du Bois, W.E.B. 1968/1903. W.E.B. Du Bois. The Souls of Black Folks. In *Black Voices*, edited by Abraham Chapman, 494–511. New York: St. Martin's Press.

Durkheim, Émile 1966/1895. *The Rules of Sociological Method*. New York: The Free Press.

—— 1982/1912. *The Elementary Forms of the Religious Life*. London: George Allen & Unwin.

—— 1984/1893. *The Division of Labor in Society*. London: Macmillan.

—— 1997/1897. *Suicide: A Study in Sociology*. New York: The Free Press.

Dutcher-Walls, Patricia 1999. Sociological directions in feminist biblical studies. *Social Compass* 46(4): 441–53.

Ebaugh, Helen Rose and Janet Saltzman Chafetz 2000. *Religion and the New Immigrants*. Walnut Creek, CA: AltaMira Press.

——— 2002. *Religion Across Borders*. Walnut Creek, CA: AltaMira Press.

Eck, Diana L. 2001. *A New Religious America: How a "Christian Country" Has Become the World's Most Religiously Diverse Nation*. New York: Harper San Francisco.

Ekstrand, Thomas 2000. *Max Weber in a Theological Perspective*. Leuven: Peeters.

Eliade, Mircea 1959. *The Sacred and the Profane*. New York: Harcourt.

Ellingsæter, Anne Lise 1999. Patriarkatet. Teori og kritikk [Patriarchy. Theory and critique]. In *Om makt. Teori og kritikk*, edited by Fredrik Engelstad, 151–73. Oslo: Gyldendal.

Erickson, Victoria Lee 2001. Georg Simmel: American Sociology Chooses the Stone the Builders Refused. In *The Blackwell Companion to Sociology of Religion*, edited by Richard K. Fenn, 105–19. Oxford: Blackwell.

Eriksen, Thomas Hylland 1999. Ethnicity, race and nation. In *The Ethnicity Reader*, edited by Montserrat Guibernau and John Rex, 33–42. Cambridge: Polity Press.

Esposito, John L. 1999 *The Islamic Threat. Myth or Reality?* New York and Oxford: Oxford University Press.

——— 2000. Islam in the World and in America. In *World Religions in America*, edited by Jacob Neusner, 172–83. Louisville, KY: Westminster/John Knox Press.

——— 2002. *Unholy War. Terror in the name of Islam*. Oxford and New York: Oxford University Press.

Etzioni, Amitai 1964. *Modern Organizations*. Englewood Cliffs, NJ: Prentice-Hall.

Farrell, Susan A. 1991. "It's Our Church, Too!" Women's Position in the Catholic Church Today. In *The Social Construction of Gender*, edited by Judith Lorber and Susan A. Farrell, 338–54. Newbury Park, CA: Sage.

Featherstone, Mike (ed.) 1990. *Global Culture. Nationalism, globalization and modernity*. London: Sage.

Fenn, Richard 1970. The Process of Secularization: A Post-Parsonian View. *Journal for the Scientific Study of Religion* 9(2): 117–136.

——— 1972. Toward a New Sociology of Religion. *Journal for the Scientific Study of Religion* 11(1): 16–32.

——— 1976. Bellah and the New Orthodoxy. *Sociological Analysis* 37(2): 160–66.

——— 1982. *Liturgies and Trials. The Secularization of Religious Language*. Oxford: Blackwell.

——— 2001. Editorial Commentary. In *The Blackwell Companion to Sociology of Religion*, edited by Richard Fenn, 3–22. Oxford: Blackwell.

Finke, Roger 1990. Religious Deregulation: Origins and Consequences. *Journal of Church and State* 32(3): 609–26.

——— and Rodney Stark 1988. Religious economies and sacred canopies. *American Sociological Review* 53: 41–9.

——— and Rodney Stark 1992. *The Churching of America – 1776–1990: Winners and losers in our religious economy*. New Brunswick, NJ: Rutgers University Press.

Finley, Nancy J. 1994. Political activism and Feminist Spirituality. In *Gender and Religion*, edited by William H. Swatos, Jr., 159–72. New Brunswick, NJ and London: Transaction.

Flanagan, Kieran 1996. *The Enchantment of Sociology: A Study of Theology and Culture*. London: Macmillan.

Foucault, Michel 1967. *Madness and Civilization: A History of Insanity in the Age of Reason*. London: Tavistock.

—— 1970. *The Order of Things*. London: Tavistock.

—— 1972. *The Archaeology of Knowledge*. London: Tavistock.

—— 1973. *The Birth of the Clinic: An Archeology of Medical Perception*. London: Tavistock.

—— 1977a. *Discipline and Punish: The Birth of the Prison*. London: Allen Lane.

—— 1977b. *Power/Knowledge: Selected Interviews and Other Writings, 1972–1977*. New York: Pantheon.

—— 1986. *The History of Sexuality, Volume I: An Introduction*. New York: Viking.

—— 1988. *The History of Sexuality, Volume III: The Care of the Self*. New York: Vintage Books.

—— 1999. *Religion and Culture*. Selected and edited by Jeremy R. Carrette. New York: Routledge.

Francis, Leslie J. and Carolyn Wilcox 1998. Religiosity and Femininity: Do Women Really Hold a More Positive Attitude Toward Christianity? *Journal for the Scientific Study of Religion* 37(3): 462–9.

Freud, Ernst and Heinrich Meng (eds) 1963. *Sigmund Freud. Oskar Pfister. Briefe 1909–39*. Frankfurt: S. Fischer Verlag.

Freud, Sigmund 1928/1921. *The Future of an Illusion*. London: Hogarth Press.

—— 1953–74/1930. *Civilization and its Discontents*. Standard Edition of the Complete Psychological Works of Sigmund Freud. Vol. XXI. London: Hogarth Press.

—— 1953–74/1901. *The Psychopathology of Everyday Life*. Standard Edition of the Complete Psychological Works of Sigmund Freud. Vol. III. London: Hogarth Press.

—— 1960/1913. *Totem and Taboo*. New York: Knopf.

—— 1964/1938. *Moses and Monotheism*. New York: Knopf.

Freund, Peter and Meredith McGuire 1995. *Health, Illness and the Social Body. A Critical Sociology*. Englewood Cliffs, NJ: Prentice-Hall.

Friedman, Menachem 1992. Jewish Zealots: Conservative versus Innovative. In *Fundamentalism in Comparative Perspective*, edited by Lawrence Kaplan, 159–76. Amherst: University of Massachusetts Press.

Frykenberg, Robert Eric 1993. Hindu Fundamentalism and the Structural Stability of India. In *Fundamentalisms and the State*, edited by Martin E. Marty and R. Scott Appleby, 233–55. Chicago, IL and London: University of Chicago Press.

Furseth, Inger 1994. Civil Religion in a Low Key: The Case of Norway. *Acta Sociologica* 37: 39–54.

—— 1999. The role of women in the Hauge movement. *Lutheran Quarterly* XIII: 395–422.

—— 2001a. *Muslims in Norwegian Prisons and the Defence*. KIFO Report no. 15. Trondheim: Tapir.

—— 2001b. Women's Role in Historic Religious and Political Movements. *Sociology of Religion* 62(1): 105–29.

—— 2002. *A Comparative Study of Social and Religious Movements in Norway, 1780s–1905*. New York: The Edwin Mellen Press.

—— 2006. *From Quest for Truth to Being Oneself. Religious Change in Life Stories*. Hamburg: Peter Lang.

Gager, John G. 1975. *Kingdom and Community*. Englewood Cliffs, NJ: Prentice-Hall.

Galtung, Johan 1969. Violence, peace and peace research. *Journal of Peace Research* 6(3): 167–91.

Gardini, Walter 1987. The Feminine Aspect of God in Christianity. In *Women in the World's Religions, Past and Present*, edited by Ursula King, 56–67. New York: Paragon House.

Gehrig, Gail 1981a. *American Civil Religion: An Assessment*. Monograph Series. Storrs, CT: Society for the Scientific Study of Religion.

—— 1981b. The American Civil Religion Debate: A Source for Theory Construction. *Journal for the Scientific Study of Religion* 20(1): 51–63.

Giddens, Anthony 1984. *The Constitution of Society: Outline of the Theory of Structuration*. Cambridge: Polity Press.

—— 1985/1971. *Capitalism and modern social theory*. Cambridge: Cambridge University Press.

—— 1989/1973. *The Class Structure of the Advanced Societies*. London: Unwin.

—— 1989. *Sociology*. Cambridge: Polity Press.

—— 1990. *The Consequences of Modernity*. Stanford, CA: Stanford University Press.

—— 1991. *Modernity and Self-Identity. Self and Society in the Late Modern Age*. Cambridge: Polity Press.

Giddens, Anthony 1998. *The Third Way: The Renewal of Social Democracy*. London: Polity Press.

Gilhus, Ingvild S. and Lisbeth Mikaelsson 2001. *Nytt blikk på religion. Studiet av religion i dag* [New perspectives on religion. The study of religion today]. Oslo: Pax.

Gill, Robin 1975. *The Social Context of Theology*. Oxford: Mowbrays.

Ginsburg, Faye 1993. Saving America's Souls: Operation Rescue's Crusade Against Abortion. In *Fundamentalisms and the State*, edited by Martin E. Marty and R. Scott Appleby, 557–88. Chicago, IL and London: University of Chicago Press.

Glock, Charles Y. and Rodney Stark 1965. *Religion and Society in Tension*. Chicago, IL: Rand McNally.

——, Benjamin B. Ringer, and Earl R. Babbie 1967. *To Comfort and To Challenge*. Berkeley: University of California Press.

Goffman, Erving 1959. *The Presentation of Self in Everyday Life*. New York: Doubleday.

—— 1961. *Asylums*. New York: Doubleday.

—— 1963. *Stigma*. Harmondsworth, Middlesex: Penguin.

—— 1967. *Interaction Ritual: Essays on Face to Face Behavior*. New York: Doubleday.

—— 1974. *Frame Analysis*. New York: Harper & Row.

—— 1983. The Interaction Order. *American Sociological Review* 89(1): 1–53.

Greeley, Andrew M. 1975. *The Sociology of the Paranormal*. London: Sage.

Griffin, Wendy 1995. The Embodied Goddess: Feminist Witchcraft and Female Divinity. *Sociology of Religion* 56(1): 35–48.

Guibernau, Montserrat and John Rex (eds) 1997. Introduction. In *The Ethnicity Reader*, edited by Montserrat Guibernau and John Rex, 1–12. Cambridge: Polity Press.

Gullestad, Marianne 1996. *Everyday Life Philosphers. Modernity, Morality, and Autobiography in Norway*. Oslo: Scandinavian University Press.

Gundelach, Peder and Ole Riis 1992. *Danskernes Værdier* [Values among Danes]. København: Forlaget sociologi.

Guneriussen, Willy 1999. *Å forstå det moderne* [Understanding the modern]. Oslo: Tano Aschehoug.

Gustafsson, Göran 1997. *Tro, samfund och samhälle. Sociologiska perspektiv* [Faith, community, and society. Sociological perspectives]. Örebro: Libris.

Habermas, Jürgen 1980. *Legitimation Crisis*. London: Heinemann.

—— 1982. A Reply to my Critics. In *Habermas. Critical Debates*, edited by John B. Thompson and David Held, 219–83. London: Macmillan.

—— 1984. *The Theory of Communicative Action*. Vol. I. London: Heinemann.

—— 1987. *The Theory of Communicative Action*. Vol. II. Boston, MA: Beacon Press.

—— 1989/1962. *The Structural Transformation of the Public Sphere*. Cambridge, MA: The MIT Press.

—— 1994. Struggles for Recognition in the Democratic Constitutional State. In *Multiculturalism. Examining the Politics of Difference* by Charles Taylor. Edited and with an introduction by Amy Gutman, 107–48. Princeton, NJ: Princeton University Press.

—— 2002. *Religion and Rationality. Essays on Reason, God, and Modernity*. Edited and with an introduction by Eduardo Mendieta. Cambridge: Polity Press.

Hadaway, C. Kirk, Penny Long Marler, and Mark Chaves 1993. What the Polls don't Show: a Closer Look at U.S. Church Attendance. *American Sociological Review* 58 (December): 741–52.

Haddad, Yvonne Yazbeck (ed.) 1991. *The Muslims of America*. New York: Oxford University Press.

—— and Adair T. Lummis 1987. *Islamic Values in the United States: A Comparative Study*. New York: Oxford University Press.

—— and Jane I. Smith 1994. *Muslim Communities in North America*. Albany: State University of New York Press.

—— and Jane I. Smith (eds) 2002. *Muslim Minorities in the West. Visible and Invisible*. Walnut Creek, CA: AltaMira Press.

——, Jane I. Smith, and John L. Esposito 2003. *Religion and Immigration. Christian, Jewish, and Muslim Experiences in the United States*. Walnut Creek, CA: AltaMira Press.

Hadden, Jeffrey K. 1989. Religious Broadcasting and the Mobilization of the New Christian Right. In *Secularization and Fundamentalism Reconsidered*, edited by Jeffrey K. Hadden and Anson Shupe, 230–51. New York: Paragon House.

Halévy, Elie 1949. England in 1815. In *A History of the English People in the Nineteenth Century*, Vol. I. London: Ernest Benn Limited.

Hamberg, Eva and Thorleif Pettersson 1994. The Religious Market: Denominational Competition and Religious Participation in Contemporary Sweden. *Journal for the Scientific Study of Religion* 33(3): 205–16.

Hamès, Constant 1999. Islame et sociologie: une rencontre qui n'a pas eu lieu? [Islam and sociology: A meeting that never took place?] In *Sociology and Religions. An Ambiguous Relationship*, edited by Liliane Voyé and Jaak Billiet, 171–82. Leuven: Leuven University Press.

Hamilton, Malcolm 2001. *The Sociology of Religion*. London: Routledge.

Hammond, Phillip E. 1980. The Conditions for Civil Religion: A Comparison of the United States and Mexico. In *Varieties of Civil Religion* by Robert N. Bellah and Phillip E. Hammond, 40–85. San Francisco, CA: Harper & Row.

Hammond, Phillip E. (ed.) 1985. *The Sacred in a Secular Age*. Berkeley: University of California Press.

Hannigan, John A. 1991. Social Movement Theory and the Sociology of Religion: Toward a New Synthesis. *Sociological Analysis* 52(4): 311–31.

Harmati, Béla (ed.) 1984. *The Church and Civil Religion in the Nordic Countries of Europe*. Geneva: The Lutheran World Federation.

—— (ed.) 1985. *The Church and Civil Religion in Asia*. Geneva: The Lutheran World Federation.

Hassan, Riffat 1990. An Islamic perspective. In *Women, Religion and Sexuality: Studies on the Impact of Religious Teachings on Women*, edited by Jeanne Becher, 93–128. Geneva: World Council of Churches Publications.

Haynes, Jeff 1998. *Religion in Global Politics*. London and New York: Longman.

Heelas, Paul 1996. *The New Age Movement. The Celebration of the Self and the Sacralization of Modernity*. Oxford: Blackwell.

—— 1999. On Things not being Worse, and the Ethic of Humanity. In *Detraditionalization. Critical Reflections on Authority and Identity*, edited by Paul Heelas, Scott Lash, and Paul Morris, 200–222. Oxford: Blackwell.

Helle, Horst Jürgen 1997. Introduction. In *Essays on Religion* by Georg Simmel, translated by Horst Jürgen Helle with Ludwig Nieder, xi–xx. New Haven, CT and London: Yale University Press.

Herberg, Will 1960. *Protestant – Catholic – Jew*. New York: Doubleday.

Herbert, David 1996. Religious Traditions in the Public Sphere: Habermas, MacIntyre and the Representation of Religious Minorities. In *Muslims in the Margin*, edited by W.A.R. Shadid and P.S. van Koningsveld, 66–79. Kampen: Kok Pharos.

Hermansen, Marcia K. 1991. Two-Way Acculturation: Muslim Women in America Between Individual Choice (Liminality) and Community Affiliation (Communitas). In *The Muslims of America*, edited by Yvonne Yazbeck Haddad, 188–201. New York: Oxford University Press.

Hertzberg, Arthur 1992. Jewish Fundamentalism. In *Fundamentalism in Comparative Perspective*, edited by Lawrence Kaplan, 152–58. Amherst: University of Massachusetts Press.

Hertzke, Allen D. 1990. Christian Fundamentalists and the Imperatives of American Politics. In *Religious Resurgence and Politics in the Contemporary World*, edited by Emile Sahliyeh, 67–79. Albany: State University of New York Press.

Hervieu-Léger, Danièle 2000. *Religion as a Chain of Memory*. Cambridge: Polity.

—— 2001. The twofold limit of the notion of secularization. In *Peter Berger and the Study of Religion*, edited by Linda Woodhead with Paul Heelas and David Martin, 112–25. London and New York: Routledge.

Hexham, Irving and Karla Powe 1997. *New Religions as Global Cultures*. Boulder, CO: Westview Press.

Hill, Michael 1973. *A Sociology of Religion*. London: Heinemann.

Hoge, Dean and David A. Roozen 1979. Research on factors influencing church commitment. In *Understanding Church Growth and Decline: 1950–1978*, edited by Dean Hoge and David A. Roozen, 42–68. New York: Pilgrim Press.

Holmes, Stephen and Charles Larmore 1982. Introduction. In *The Differentiation of Society* by Niklas Luhmann, xiii–xxxvii. New York: Columbia University Press.

Hondagneu-Sotelo, Pierrette 1994. *Gendered Transitions: Mexican Experiences of Immigration*. Berkeley: University of California Press.

Horowitz, Donald L. 1985. *Ethnic Groups in Conflict*. Berkeley: University of California Press.

Horrel, David G. 2001. Berger and New Testament Studies. In *Peter Berger and the Study of Religion*, edited by Linda Woodhead with Paul Heelas and David Martin, 142–53. London and New York: Routledge.

Howell, Julia Day 1998. Gender Role Experimentation in New Religious Movements: Clarification of the Brahma Kumari Case. *Journal for the Scientific Study of Religion* 37(3): 453–61.

Hughey, Michael W. 1983. *Civil Religion and Moral Order. Theoretical and Historical Dimensions*. Westport, CT: Greenwood Press.

Hume, David 1976/1757. *A Natural History of Religion*. Oxford: Clarendon Press.

Høeg, Ida Marie 1998. *Rom i herberget? Kvinnelige menighetsprester på arbeidsmarkedet i Den norske kirke* [Room at the inn? Women clergy on the labor market in the Church of Norway]. KIFO Report No. 6. Trondheim: Tapir.

—— et al. 2000. *Folkekirke 2000* [Folk Church 2000]. Oslo: Stiftelsen Kirkeforskning.

Iannaccone, Laurence R. 1994. Why strict churches are strong. *American Journal of Sociology* 99(5): 1180–211.

—— 1997. Rational choice: framework for the scientific study of religion. In *Rational Choice Theory and Religion: Summary and Assessment*, edited by L.A. Young, 25–45. New York: Routledge.

Ignatieff, Michael 1993. *Blood and Belonging. Journeys into the New Nationalism*. New York: The Noonday Press.

Inglehart, Ronald 1977. *The Silent Revolution. Changing Values and Political Styles Among Western Publics*. Princeton, NJ: Princeton University Press.

—— 1990. *Culture Shifts in Advanced Industrial Society*. Princeton, NJ: Princeton University Press.

Isbister, J. N. 1985. *Freud. An Introduction to his Life and Work*. Cambridge: Polity Press.

Ivekovic, Ivan 2002. Nationalism and the Political Use and Abuse of Religion: The Politicization of Orthodoxy, Catholicism and Islam in Yugoslav Successor States. *Social Compass* 49(4): 523–36.

Iwamura, Jane N. and Paul Spickard (eds) 2003. *Revealing the Sacred in Asian and Pacific America*. New York and London: Routledge.

Jacobs, Janet L. 1989. The Effects of Ritual Healing on Female Victims of abuse: A Study of Empowerment and Transformation. *Sociological Analysis* 50(3): 265–79.

Jacobsen, Christine M. 2004. Negotiating gender: Discourse and practice among young Muslims in Norway. *Tidsskrift for kirke, religion og samfunn* 17(1): 5–28.

Jacobson, Jessica 1998. *Islam in Transition. Religion and identity among British Pakistani youth*. London and New York: Routledge.

Jenkins, Richard 2003. Rethinking Ethnicity: Identity, Categorization, and Power. In *Race and Ethnicity. Comparative and Theoretical Approaches*, edited by John Stone and Rutledge Dennis, 59–71. Oxford: Blackwell.

Johnson, Benton and Mark A. Shibley 1989. How New Is the New Christian Right? A Study of Three Presidential Elections. In *Secularization and Fundamentalism Reconsidered*, edited by Jeffrey K. Hadden and Anson Shupe, 178–98. New York: Paragon House.

Jonker, Gerdien 2003. Islamic Knowledge through a Woman's Lens: Education, Power and Belief. *Social Compass* 50(1): 35–46.

Juergensmeyer, Mark 1993. *The New Cold War? Religious Nationalism Confronts the Secular State*. Berkeley: University of California Press.

—— 2001. *Terror in the Mind of Go*d. Berkeley and Los Angeles: University of California Press.

Kelley, Dean 1978. Why the conservative churches are still growing. *Journal for the Scientific Study of Religion* 17(1): 129–37.

Kennedy, Michael D. and Maurice D. Simon 1983. Church and Nation in Socialist Poland. In *Religion and Politics in the Modern World*, edited by Peter H. Merkl and Ninian Smart, 121–54. New York and London: New York University Press.

Kepel, Gilles 1994. *The Revenge of God*. University Park, PA: Pennsylvania State University Press.

—— 1997. *Allah in the West. Islamic Movements in America and Europe*. Stanford, CA: Stanford University Press.

—— 2002. *Jihad. The Trail of Political Islam*. Cambridge, MA: Harvard University Press.

King, Ursula 1993. *Women and Spirituality. Voices of Protest and Promise*. London: Macmillan.

Kivisto, Peter 1993. Religion and the new Immigrants. In *A Future for Religion? New Paradigms for Social Analysis*, edited by William H. Swatos, Jr., 92–108. Newbury Park, CA: Sage.

—— 1998. Racism. In *Encyclopedia of Religion and Society*, edited by William H. Swatos, Jr., 399–401. Walnut Creek, CA: AltaMira Press.

—— 2002. *Multiculturalism in a Global Society*. Oxford: Blackwell.

Knott, Kim 1987. Men and Women, or Devotees? Krishna Consciousness and the Role of Women. In *Women in the World's Religions, Past and Present*, edited by Ursula King, 111–28. New York: Paragon House.

Knudsen, Jon P. 1994. *Kulturspredning i et strukturelt perspektiv – Eksemplifisert ved politisk og religiøs endring under moderniseringen av det norske samfunn* [Cultural diffusion in a structural perspective – Exemplified by political and religious change during the modernization of Norwegian society]. Lund: Lund University Press.

Kramer, Martin 1993. Hizbullah: The Calculus of Jihad. In *Fundamentalisms and the State*, edited by Martin E. Marty and R. Scott Appleby, 539–56. Chicago, IL and London: University of Chicago Press.

Kroker, A. and D. Cook 1988. *The Postmodern Scene*. London: Macmillan.

Kuhn, Thomas 1970. *The Structure of Scientific Revolutions*. Chicago, IL: University of Chicago Press.

Kunin, Seth K. 2002. Judaism. In *Religions in the Modern World*, edited by Linda Woodhead et al., 128–81. London and New York: Routledge.

Lal, Barbara Ballis 2003. Robert Ezra Park's Approach to Race and Ethnic Relations. In *Race and Ethnicity. Comparative and Theoretical Approaches*, edited by John Stone and Rutledge Dennis, 43–54. Oxford: Blackwell.

Lambert, Yves 1999. Religion in Modernity as a New Axial Age: Secularization or New Religions Paradigms? *Sociological Analysis* 60(3): 303–33.

Layendecker, L. 1986. Zivilreligion in den Niederlanden [Civil religion in the Netherlands]. In *Religion des Bürgers. Zivilreligion in Amerika und Europa*, edited by H. Kleger and A. Müller, 64–84. Munich: Chr. Kaiser.

Lease, Gary 1983. The Origins of National Socialism: Some Fruits of Religion and Nationalism. In *Religion and Politics in the Modern World*, edited by Peter H. Merkl and Ninian Smart, 63–88. New York and London: New York University Press.

Le Bon, Gustave. 1960. *The Crowd*. New York: Viking Press.

Lechner, Frank J. 1993. Global Fundamentalism. In *A Future for Religion? New Paradigms for Social Analysis*, edited by William H. Swatos, Jr., 19–36. London: Sage.

Lehmann, David 2002. Religion and Globalization. In *Religions in the Modern World*, edited by Linda Woodhead, Paul Fletcher, Hiroko Kawanami, and David Smith, 299–315. London: Routledge.

Levack, Brian. 1995. *The Witch-Hunt in Early Modern Europe*. London and New York: Longman.

Levine, Donald N. 1971. Introduction. In *Georg Simmel: On Individuality and Social Forms*, edited by Donald Levine, ix–lxv. Chicago, IL: University of Chicago Press.

Levitt, Peggy 2001. *The Transnational Villagers*. Berkeley: University of California Press.

Liebman, Charles S. and Eliezer Don-Yehiya 1983. *Civil Religion in Israel*. Berkeley: University of California Press.

Lorber, Judith and Susan A. Farrell (eds) 1991. *The Social Construction of Gender*. Newbury Park, CA: Sage.

Luckmann, Thomas 1967. *The Invisible Religion: The Problem of Religion in Modern Society*. New York: Macmillan.

—— 1983. *Life-World and Social Realities*. London: Heinemann.

Luhmann, Niklas 1979. *Trust and Power*. New York: John Wiley & Sons.
—— 1982. *The Differentiation of Society*. New York: Columbia University Press.
—— 1993. *Risk: A Sociological Theory*. New York: Walter de Gruyter.
—— 1995. *Social Systems*. Stanford, CA: Stanford University Press.
Lukes, Steven 1973. *Émile Durkheim. His Life and Work*. Harmondsworth, Middlesex: Penguin.
Lynd, Robert S. and Helen M. Lynd 1929. *Middletown: A Study in American Culture*. New York: Harcourt Brace.
Lyon, David 2000. *Jesus in Disneyland. Religion in Postmodern Times*. Cambridge: Polity.
Lyotard, Jean-François 1984. *The Postmodern Condition: A Report on Knowledge*. Manchester: Manchester University Press.
Malinowski, Bronislav 1974/1925. *Magic, Science and Religion and Other Essays*. London: Souvenir Press.
Mannheim, Karl 1936. *Ideology and Utopia. An Introduction to the Sociology of Knowledge*. New York: Harvest Books.
Markkola, Pirjo (ed.) 2000. *Gender and Vocation. Women, Religion and Social Change in the Nordic Countries, 1830–1940*. Helsinki: Finnish Literature Society.
Marrett, R.R. 1914. *The Threshold of Religion*. London: Methuen.
Martin, Bernice 2001. Berger's anthropological theology. In *Peter Berger and the Study of Religion*, edited by Linda Woodhead with Paul Heelas and David Martin, 154–88. London and New York: Routledge.
Martin, David 1990. *Tongues of Fire. The Explosion of Protestantism in Latin America*. Oxford and Cambridge: Blackwell.
—— 1996. Religion, Secularization and Post-Modernity: Lessons from the Latin American Case. In *Religion and Modernity – Modes of Co-existence*, edited by Pål Repstad, 35–43. Oslo: Scandinavian University Press.
—— 1997. Theology and Sociology: The Irish Flaneur's Account. *New Blackfriars* 78(913): 105–10.
Marty, Martin E. 1974. Two Kinds of Two Kinds of Civil Religion. In *American Civil Religion*, edited by R.E. Richey and D.G. Jones, 139–57. New York: Harper & Row.
—— 1992. Fundamentals of Fundamentalism. In *Fundamentalism in Comparative Perspective*, edited by Lawrence Kaplan, 15–23. Amherst: University of Massachusetts Press.
—— 1998. Public Religion. In *Encyclopedia of Religion and Society*, edited by William H. Swatos, Jr., 393–4. Walnut Creek, CA, London, New Delhi: AltaMira Press.
—— and R. Scott Appleby (eds) 1991. *The Fundamentalism Project, Vol. 1: Fundamentalisms Observed*. Chicago, IL and London: University of Chicago Press.
—— (eds) 1993a. *The Fundamentalism Project, Vol. 2: Fundamentalisms and Society*. Chicago, IL and London: University of Chicago Press.
—— (eds) 1993b. *The Fundamentalism Project, Vol. 3: Fundamentalisms and the State*. Chicago, IL and London: University of Chicago Press.

—— (eds) 1994. *The Fundamentalism Project, Vol. 4: Accounting for Fundamentalisms*. Chicago, IL and London: University of Chicago Press.

—— (eds) 1995. *The Fundamentalism Project, Vol. 5: Fundamentalisms Comprehended*. Chicago, IL and London: University of Chicago Press.

Marx, Karl 1955/1844. Contribution to the Critique of Hegel's Philosophy of Right. In *On Religion*, by Karl Marx and Friedrich Engels, 41–58. Moscow: Foreign Languages Publishing House.

—— 1955/1845. Theses on Feuerbach. In *On Religion*, by Karl Marx and Friedrich Engels, 69–72. Moscow: Foreign Languages Publishing House.

—— 1975/1844. Economic and Philosophical Manuscripts. In *Karl Marx. Early Writings*. Edited by Quintin Hoare and introduced by Lucio Lolletti. New York: Vintage Books.

—— 1983/1867. *Capital*. Vol. I. Moscow: Progress Publishers.

—— and Friedrich Engels 1955/1845–46. German Ideology. In *On Religion*, by Karl Marx and Friedrich Engels, 73–81. Moscow: Foreign Languages Publishing House.

Mathisen, James A. 1989. Twenty Years after Bellah: Whatever Happened to American Civil Religion? *Sociological Analysis* 50(2): 129–46.

Mayer, Ann Elisabeth 1993. The Fundamentalist Impact on Law, Politics, and Constitutions in Iran, Pakistan, and the Sudan. In *Fundamentalisms and the State*, edited by Martin E. Marty and R. Scott Appleby, 110–51. Chicago, IL and London: University of Chicago Press.

McGuire, Meredith 1988. *Ritual Healing in Suburban America*. New Brunswick, NJ and London: Rutgers University Press.

—— 1997. *Religion. The Social Context*. Belmont, CA: Wadsworth.

—— 2003. Gendered Spiritualities. In *Challenging Religion*, edited by James A. Beckford and James T. Richardson, 170–80. London and New York: Routledge.

Mead, George Herbert 1962/1934. *Mind, Self, & Society*. Edited and with an introduction by Charles W. Morris. Chicago, IL: University of Chicago Press.

Meeks, Wayne 1983. *The First Urban Christians*. New Haven, CT: Yale University Press.

Melton, J. Gordon 1998. The Future of the New Age Movement. In *New Religions and New Religiosity*, edited by Eileen Barker and Margit Warburg, 133–49. Aarhus: Aarhus University Press.

Mendieta, Eduardo 2002. Introduction. In *Religion and Rationality. Essays on Reason, God, and Modernity*, by Jürgen Habermas, 1–36. Cambridge: Polity Press.

Mernissi, Fatima 1987. *Women and Islam: An Historical and Theological Enquiry*. Oxford: Blackwell.

Milbank, John 1990. *Theology and Social Theory: Beyond Secular Reason*. Oxford: Blackwell.

Miles, Robert 1989. *Racism*. London and New York: Routledge.

—— 1993. *Racism and "race relations."* London and New York: Routledge.

Miller, Alan S. and John P. Hoffman 1995. Risk and Religion: An Explanation of Gender Differences in Religiosity. *Journal for the Scientific Study of Religion* 34(1): 63–75.

Miller, Donald E., Jon Miller, and Grace R. Dyrness 2001. *Immigrant Religion in the City of Angels*. Los Angeles: Center for Religion and Civic Culture, University of Southern California.

Mir-Hosseini, Ziba 2000. *Islam and Gender*. London and New York: I.B. Tauris.

Mitzman, Arthur 1971. *The Iron Cage. An Historical Interpretation of Max Weber.* New York: Grosset's Universal Library.

Moghadam, Valentine M. 1992. Fundamentalism and the Woman Question in Afghanistan. In *Fundamentalism in Comparative Perspective*, edited by Lawrence Kaplan, 126–51. Amherst: University of Massachusetts Press.

Morris, Charles W. 1962. Introduction. In *Mind, Self, & Society* by George H. Mead, edited and with an introduction by Charles W. Morris, ix–xxxv. Chicago, IL: University of Chicago Press.

Narayanan, Vasudha 1990. Hindu Perceptions of Auspiciousness and Sexuality. In *Women, Religion and Sexuality*, edited by Jeanne Becher, 64–92. Geneva: World Council of Churches Publications.

—— 1999. Hinduism: Modern Movements. In *Encyclopedia of Women and World Religion*, edited by Serenity Young, 428–30. New York: Macmillan.

Nason-Clark, Nancy 2003. The making of a survivor: rhetoric and reality in the study of religion and abuse. In *Challenging Religion*, edited by James A. Beckford and James T. Richardson, 181–91. London and New York: Routledge.

Neitz, Mary Jo 1987. *Charisma and Community*. New Brunswick, NJ: Transaction.

Nettl, J.P. and Roland Robertson 1968. *International Systems and the Modernization of Societies*. London: Faber and Faber.

Neusner, Jacob 2000. Judaism in the World and in America. In *World Religions in America*, edited by Jacob Neusner, 107–22. Louisville, KY: Westminster/John Knox Press.

Niebuhr, H. Richard 1975/1929. *The Social Sources of Denominationalism*. New York: Meridian.

Nielsen, Donald A. 1998. Émile Durkheim. In *Encyclopedia of Religion and Society*, edited by William H. Swatos, Jr., 145–8. Walnut Creek, CA: AltaMira Press.

Nielsen, Jørgen S. 1995. *Muslims in Western Europe*. Edinburgh: Edinburgh University Press.

Nielsen, Niels C., Jr. 1993. *Fundamentalism, Mythos, and World Religion*. Albany: State University of New York Press.

Norcliffe, David 1999. *Islam. Faith and Practice*. Brighton, UK and Portland, OR: Sussex Academic Press.

Nyhagen Predelli, Line 2003. *Issues of Gender, Race, and Class in the Norwegian Missionary Society in Nineteenth-Century Norway and Madagascar*. New York: The Edwin Mellen Press.

—— 2004. Interpreting Gender in Islam: A Case study of Immigrant Muslim Women in Oslo, Norway. *Gender & Society* 18: 473–93.

Oberoi, Harjot 1993. Sixth Fundamentalism: Translating History into Theory. In *Fundamentalisms and the State*, edited by Martin E. Marty and R. Scott Appleby, 256–85. Chicago, IL and London: University of Chicago Press.

Oberschall, Anthony 1973. *Social Conflict and Social Movements*. Englewood Cliffs, NJ: Prentice-Hall.

O'Dea, Thomas 1961. Five dilemmas in the institutionalization of religion. *Journal for the Scientific Study of Religion* 1(1): 30–39.

Østberg, Sissel 1998. Pakistani Children in Oslo: Islamic Nurture in a Secular Contest. Unpublished PhD dissertation. Institute of Education, University of Warwick, UK.

Østerberg, Dag 1988. *Talcott Parsons sosiologiske essays.* Oslo: Cappelen.

Østergaard, Kate 2004. Muslim women in the Islamic field in Denmark: Interaction between converts and other Muslim women. *Tidsskrift for kirke, religion og samfunn* 17(1): 29–46.

O'Toole, Roger 2001. Classics in the Sociology of Religion: An Ambiguous Legacy. In *The Blackwell Companion to Sociology of Religion*, edited by Richard K. Fenn, 133–60. Oxford: Blackwell.

Otto, Rudolf 1958/1917. *The Idea of the Holy.* New York: Oxford University Press.

Ozorak, Elizabeth Weiss 1996. The Power, but not the Glory: How Women Empower Themselves Through Religion. *Journal for the Scientific Study of Religion* 35(1): 17–29.

Parekh, Bhikhu 2000. *Rethinking Multiculturalism: Cultural Diversity and Political Theory.* London: Macmillan.

Parsons, Talcott 1949/1937. *The Structure of Social Action.* New York: Free Press.

—— 1966. *Societies: Evolutionary and Comparative Perspectives.* Englewood Cliffs, NJ: Prentice-Hall.

—— 1971. Belief, unbelief, and disbelief. In *The Culture of Unbelief*, edited by R. Caporale and A. Grumelli, 207–45. Berkeley: University of California Press.

—— 1974. Religion in Post Industrial America. *Social Research* 41(2): 193–225.

—— 1979/1951. *The Social System.* London: Routledge & Kegan Paul.

——, Robert F. Bales, and Edward A. Shils 1953. *Working Papers in the Theory of Action.* New York: Free Press.

Pettersson, Per 2000. *Kvalitet i livslånga tjänsterelationer. Svenska kyrkan ur tjänsteteoretiskt och religionssociologiskt perspektiv* [Quality in life-long service relations. The Church of Sweden from perspectives of service theory and sociology of religion]. Stockholm: Verbum.

Pettersson, Thorleif 1994. Gudstänstutbud och besöksfrekvens i Svenska Kyrkan [Benefits from church services and frequency of attendance in the Church of Sweden]. *Tro & Tanke* 9: 53–74.

——, Karl Geyer, and Owe Wickström 1994. Gudstänstbesökerna [Church attendances]. *Tro & Tanke* 4: 113–235.

Perrow, Charles 1986. *Complex Organizations – a Critical Essay.* New York: Random House.

Pickering, W.S.F. 1984. *Durkheim's Sociology of Religion.* London: Routledge & Kegan Paul.

Poloma, Margaret M. 1979. *Contemporary Sociological Theory.* New York: Macmillan.

Portes, Alejandro 1995. Children of Immigrants: Segmented Assimilation. In *The Economic Sociology of Immigration*, edited by Alejandro Portes, 248–80. New York: Russell Sage.

Postone, Moishe, Edward LiPuma, and Craig Calhoun 1993. Introduction: Bourdieu and Social Theory. In *Bourdieu: Critical Perspectives*, edited by Craig Calhoun, Edward LiPuma, and Moishe Postone, 1–13. Chicago, IL: University of Chicago Press.

Procter-Smith, Marjorie and Janet R. Walton (eds) 1993. *Women at Worship*. Louisville, KY: Westminster/John Knox Press.

Puttick, Elizabeth 1999. Women in New Religious Movements. In *New Religious Movements*, edited by Bryan Wilson and Jamie Cresswell, 143–62. London and New York: Routledge.

Ramet, Pedro (ed.) 1984. *Religion and Nationalism in Soviet and East European Politics*. Durham, NC: Duke University Press.

Repstad, Pål 1984. *Fra ilden til asken. En studie i religiøs passivisering* [From the fire to the ashes. A study of religious passivity]. Oslo: Universitetsforlaget.

—— 1995a. Civil Religion in Modern Society. Some General and Some Nordic Perspectives. *Kirchliche Zeitgeschichte* (8)1: 159–75.

—— 1995b. *Den sosiale forankring. Sosiologiske perspektiver på teologi* [The social basis. Sociological perspectives on theology]. Oslo: Universitetsforlaget.

—— 1995c. Sociological Methods in the Study of New Religious Movements. In *Studying New Religions*, edited by Margit Warburg, 3–14. København: University of Copenhagen, Institute of History of Religions.

—— 2002. *Dype, stille, sterke, milde. Religiøs makt i dagens Norge* [Deep, quiet, strong, mild. Religious power in contemporary Norway]. Oslo: Gyldendal.

—— 2003a. Has the pendulum swung too far? The construction of religious individualism in today's sociology of religion. *Temenos* 37–8: 181–90.

—— 2003b. The Powerlessness of Religious Power in a Pluralist Society. *Social Compass* 50(2): 161–73.

Rex, John 1986. *Race and Ethnicity*. Stony Stratford: Open University Press.

Richardson, James T. 1985. The active vs. passive convert: Paradigm conflict in conversion/recruitment research. *Journal for the Scientific Study of Religion* 24(2): 119–36.

—— 1993. A social psychological critique of "brainwashing" claims about recruitments to new religions. *Religion and the Social Order* 3B: 75–97.

Richey, Russel E. and Donald G. Jones 1974. *American Civil Religion*. New York: Harper & Row.

Richmond, Anthony H. 2003. Postindustrialism, Postmodernism, and Ethnic Conflict. In *Race and Ethnicity. Comparative and Theoretical Approaches*, edited by John Stone and Rutledge Dennis, 83–94. Oxford: Blackwell.

Riis, Ole 1996. *Metoder og teorier i religionssociologien* [Methods and theories in the sociology of religion]. Aarhus: Aarhus universitetsforlag.

Roald, Anne Sofie 2001. *Women in Islam. The Western Experience*. London and New York: Routledge.

—— 2004. Muslim Women in Sweden. *Tidsskrift for kirke, religion og samfunn* 17(1): 65–77.

Robbins, Thomas 1988. *Cults, Converts and Charisma*. London: Sage.

—— 1989. Church-and-state issues in the United States. In *Encyclopedia of Religion and Society*, edited by William H. Swatos, Jr., 87–90. Walnut Creek, CA, London, New Delhi: AltaMira Press.

Robertson, Roland 1970. *The Sociological Interpretation of Religion*. Oxford: Blackwell.

—— 1987. Church–State Relations and the World System. In *Church–State Relations*, edited by Thomas Robbins and Roland Robertson, 39–51. New Brunswick, NJ: Transaction.

—— 1991. After Nostalgia? Wilful Nostalgia and the Phases of Globalization. In *Theories of Modernity and Postmodernity*, edited by Bryan S. Turner, 45–61. London: Sage.

—— 1992. *Globalization: Social Theory and Global Culture*. London: Sage.

Rocher, Guy 1974. *Talcott Parsons and American Sociology*. London: Nelson.

Romero, Catalina 2001. Globalization, Civil Society and Religion from a Latin American Standpoint. *Sociology of Religion* 62(4): 475–90.

Roof, Wade Clark 1978. *Commitment and Community: Religious Plausibility in a Liberal Protestant Church*. New York: Elsevier.

—— 1993. *A Generation of Seekers. The Spiritual Journeys of the Baby Boom Generation*. New York: HarperCollins.

—— and Dean Hoge 1980. Church involvement in America: social factors affecting membership and participation. *Review of Religious Research* 21(4): 405–26.

Rothstein, Mikael 2001. *New Age Religion and Globalization*. Aarhus: Aarhus University Press.

Rountree, Kathryn 2002. Goddess Pilgrims as Tourists: Inscribing the Body through Sacred Travel. *Sociology of Religion* 63(4): 475–96.

Rousseau, Jean-Jacques 1981/1762. *The Social Contract*. Harmondsworth, Middlesex: Penguin.

Ruether, Rosemary Radford 1983. *Sexism and God-Talk. Toward a Feminist Theology*. Boston, MA: Beacon Press.

—— 1990. Catholicism, Women, Body and Sexuality: A Response. In *Women, Religion and Sexuality*, edited by Jeanne Becher, 221–32. Geneva: World Council of Churches Publications.

Sahliyeh, Emile 1990. Religious Resurgence and Political Modernization. In *Religious Resurgence and Politics in the Contemporary World*, edited by Emile Sahliyeh, 3–16. Albany: State University of New York Press.

Salomonsen, Jone 2002. *Enchanted Feminism: Ritual, Gender and Divinity among the Reclaiming Witches of San Francisco*. New York: Routledge.

Schaanning, Espen 1992. *Modernitetens oppløsning* [The dissolution of modernity]. Oslo: Spartacus.

Schmidt, Garbi 1998. *American Medina. A Study of the Sunni Muslim Immigrant Communities in Chicago*. Lund: Department of History of Religions.

Seland, Bjørg 2000. "Called by the Lord" – Women's place in the Norwegian Missionary Movement. In *Gender and Vocation. Women, Religion and Social Change in the Nordic Countries, 1830–1940*, edited by Pirjo Markkola, 69–111. Helsinki: Finnish Literature Society.

Shackle, Christopher 2002. Sikhism. In *Religions in the Modern World*, edited by Linda Woodhead et al., 70–85. London and New York: Routledge.

—— et al. (eds) 2001. *Sikh Religion, Culture and Ethnicity*. Richmond, Surrey: Curzon.

Shadid, W.A.R. and P.S. van Koningsveld (eds) 1991. *The Integration of Islam and Hinduism in Western Europe*. Kampen: Kok.

—— (eds) 1996. *Muslims in the Margin: Political Responses to the Presence of Islam in Western Europe*. Kampen: Kok.

Shapiro, Edward S. 1997. A time for healing. American Jewry since World War II. In *Religion: North American Style*, edited by Thomas E. Dowdy and Patrick H. McNamara, 147–54. New Brunswick, NJ: Rutgers University Press.

Sharma, Arvind (ed.) 1994. *Today's Woman in World Religions*. Albany: State University of New York Press.

Sharpe, Eric J. 1983. *Understanding Religion*. London: Duckworth.

Shiner, Larry 1966. The concept of secularization in empirical research. *Journal for the Scientific Study of Religion* 6(2): 207–20.

Shupe, Anson and Jeffrey K. Hadden 1989. Is There Such a Thing as Global Fundamentalism? In *Secularization and Fundamentalism Reconsidered*, edited by Jeffrey K. Hadden and Anson Shupe, 109–22. New York: Paragon House.

Simmel, Georg 1971. *On Individuality and Social Forms*. Edited by Donald Levine. Chicago, IL: University of Chicago Press.

—— 1997. *Essays on Religion*. Translated by Horst Jürgen Helle with Ludwig Nieder. New Haven, CT and London: Yale University Press.

Singh, Karandeep 1990. The Politics of Religious Resurgence and Religious Terrorism: The Case of the Sikhs of India. In *Religious Resurgence and Politics in the Contemporary World*, edited by Emile Sahliyeh, 243–61. Albany: State University of New York Press.

Singh, Nikky-Guninder Kaur 1993. *The feminine principle in the Sikh vision of the transcendent*. Cambridge: Cambridge University Press.

Sivan, Emmanuel 1992. The Islamic Resurgence: Civil Society Strikes Back. In *Fundamentalism in Comparative Perspective*, edited by Lawrence Kaplan, 96–108. Amherst: University of Massachusetts Press.

Smart, Barry 1990. Modernity, Postmodernity and the Present. In *Theories of Modernity and Postmodernity*, edited by Bryan S. Turner, 14–30. London: Sage.

Smart, Ninian 1968. *Secular Education and the Logic of Religion*. London: Faber.

—— 1983. Religion, Myth, and Nationalism. In *Religion and Politics in the Modern World*, edited by Peter H. Merkl and Ninian Smart, 15–28. New York and London: New York University Press.

—— 1998. Tradition, retrospective perception, nationalism and modernism. In *Religion, Modernity and Postmodernity*, edited by Paul Heelas, 79–87. Oxford: Blackwell.

Smith, Adam 1937/1776. *The Wealth of Nations*. New York: Modern Library.

Smith, Anthony 1983. *Theories of Nationalism*. London: Duckworth.

Smith, Christian et al. 1998. *American Evangelism: Embattled and Thriving*. Chicago, IL: University of Chicago Press.

Smith, David 2002. Hinduism. In *Religion in the Modern World*, edited by Linda Woodhead et al., 15–40. London and New York: Routledge.

Smith, Dennis 1999. *Zygmunt Bauman. Prophet of Postmodernity*. Cambridge: Polity Press.

Smith, Donald E. 1990. The Limits of Religious Resurgence. In *Religious Resurgence and Politics in the Contemporary World*, edited by Emile Sahliyeh, 33–44. Albany: State University of New York Press.

Smith, Wilfred Cantwell 1981. *Towards a World Theology: Faith and the Comparative History of Religion*. Maryknoll, NY: Orbis Books.

Spiro, Melford 1965. Religious systems as culturally constituted defense mechanisms. In *Context and Meaning in Cultural Anthropology*, edited by Melford Spiro, Glencoe, IL: Free Press.

—— 1966. Religion: problems of definition and explanation. In *Anthropological Approaches to the Study of Religion*, edited by Michael Banton, 85–126. London: Tavistock.

Sollors, Werner (ed.) 1989. *The Invention of Ethnicity*. New York and Oxford: Oxford University Press.

Soysal, Yasemin Nuhoglu 2003. Toward a Postnational Model of Membership. In *Race and Ethnicity. Comparative and Theoretical Approaches*, edited by John Stone and Rutledge Dennis, 291–305. Oxford: Blackwell.

Stark, Rodney 1995. Reconstructing the Rise of Christianity: The Role of Women. *Sociology of Religion* 56(3): 229–44.

—— 1996. *Reconstructing the Rise of Christianity: Adventures in historical sociology*. Princeton, NJ: Princeton University Press.

—— and William Sims Bainbridge 1985. *The Future of Religion*. Berkeley: University of California Press.

—— and Williams Sims Bainbridge 1987. *A Theory of Religion*. New York: Peter Lang.

—— and Charles Y. Glock 1968. *American Piety*. Berkeley: University of California Press.

Stein, Judith 1989. Defining the Race 1890–1930. In *The Invention of Ethnicity*, edited by Werner Sollors, 77–104. New York and Oxford: Oxford University Press.

Stone, John 2003. Max Weber on Race, Ethnicity, and Nationalism. In *Race and Ethnicity. Comparative and Theoretical Approaches*, edited by John Stone and Rutledge Dennis, 28–42. Oxford: Blackwell.

Strauss, Anselm 1965. Introduction. In *On Social Psychology*, by George H. Mead, edited and with an introduction by Anselm Strauss, vii–xxv. Chicago, IL and London: University of Chicago Press.

Strong, P.M. 1988. Minor Courtesies and Macro Structures. In *Erving Goffman. Exploring the Interaction Order*, edited by Paul Drew and Anthony Wootton, 228–49. Boston, MA: Northeastern University Press.

Sundback, Susan 1984. Folk Church Religion – A Kind of Civil Religion? In *The Church and Civil Religion in the Nordic Countries of Europe*, edited by Bela Harmati, 35–40. Geneva: The Lutheran World Federation.

Swatos, William H. and Kevin Christiano 1999. Secularization Theory: The Course of a Concept. *Sociology of Religion* 60(3): 209–28.

——, Peter Kivisto, and Paul M. Gustafson 1998. Max Weber. In *Encyclopedia of Religion and Society*, edited by William H. Swatos, 547–52. Walnut Creek, CA, London, New Delhi: AltaMira Press.

Tambiah, Stanley J. 1993. Buddhism, Politics, and Violence in Sri Lanka. In *Fundamentalisms and the State*, edited by Martin E. Marty and R. Scott Appleby, 589–619. Chicago, IL and London: University of Chicago Press.

Taylor, Charles 1992. *Multiculturalism and "The Politics of Recognition."* Princeton, NJ: Princeton University Press.

—— 2003. The Politics of Recognition. In *Race and Ethnicity. Comparative and Theoretical Approaches*, edited by John Stone and Rutledge Dennis, 373–81. Oxford: Blackwell.

Tessier, L.J. 1999. Violence. In *Encyclopedia of Women and World Religion*, Vol. II, edited by Serenity Young, 1000–1002. New York: Macmillan.

Thomas, Michael C. and Charles C. Flippen 1972. American Civil Religion: An Empirical Study. *Social Forces* 51: 218–25.

Thompson, E.H. 1991. Beneath the Status Characteristic: Gender Variations in Religion. *Journal for the Scientific Study of Religion* 30(4): 381–94.

Thompson, E.P. 1965. *The Making of the English Working Class*. London: Victor Gollancz.

Thompson, K. 1976. *Auguste Comte: the foundation of sociology*. London: Nelson.

Thumma, Scott 1991. Negotiating a Religious Identity: The Case of the Gay Evangelical. *Sociological Analysis* 53(4): 333–47.

—— and Edward R. Gray (eds) 2005. *Gay Religion*. Walnut Creek, CA: AltaMira Press.

Tiilikainen, Marja and Isra Lehtinen 2004. Muslim women in Finland: Diversity within a minority. *Tidsskrift for kirke, religion og samfunn* 17(1): 64–65.

Tilly, Charles 1978. *From Mobilization to Revolution*. Reading, MA: Addison-Wesley.

Toynbee, Arnold 1954. *A Study of History*. Vol. 8. London: Oxford University Press.

Troeltsch, Ernst 1960/1912. *The Social Teachings of the Christian Churches*. Vols I–II. New York: Harper & Row.

Turner, Bryan S. 1990. Periodization and Politics in the Postmodern. In *Theories of Modernity and Postmodernity*, edited by Bryan S. Turner, 1–13. London: Sage.

—— 1991. *Religion and Social Theory*. London, Newbury Park, CA, New Delhi: Sage.

Turner, Victor 1969. *The Ritual Process*. Chicago: Aldine.

Tylor, Edward 1903. *Primitive Culture*. London: John Murray.

Van Gennep, A. 1960/1908. *The Rites of Passage*. Chicago, IL: University of Chicago Press.

Varcoe, Ian 1998. Identity and the limits of comparison: Bauman's reception in Germany. *Theory, Culture and Society* 15(1): 57–72.

—— 2003. Zygmunt Bauman. In *Key Contemporary Social Theorists*, edited by A. Elliott and L. Ray, 38–44. Oxford: Blackwell.

Vertovec, Steven and Ceri Peach (eds) 1997. *Islam in Europe*. London: Macmillan.

Via, E. Jane 1987. Women in the Gospel of Luke. In *Women in the World's Religions, Past and Present*, edited by Ursula King, 38–55. New York: Paragon House.

Voyé, Liliane and Jaak Billiet (eds) 1999. *Sociology and Religions. An Ambiguous Relationship*. Leuven: Leuven University Press.

Wacquant, Loïc J.D. 1993. Bourdieu in America: Notes on the Transatlantic Importation of Social Theory. In *Bourdieu: Critical Perspectives*, edited by Craig Calhoun, Edward LiPuma, and Moishe Postone, 235–62. Chicago, IL: University of Chicago Press.

Wadel, Cato 1990. *Den samfunnsvitenskapelige konstruksjon av virkeligheten* [The social scientific construction of reality]. Flekkefjord: Seek forlag.

Wald, Kenneth D. 1990. The New Christian Right in American Politics: Mobilization Amid Modernization. In *Religious Resurgence and Politics in the Contemporary World*, edited by Emile Sahliyeh, 49–65. Albany: State University of New York Press.

Wallace, Ruth 1994. The Social Construction of a New Leadership Role: Catholic Women Pastors. In *Gender and Religion*, edited by W.H. Swatos, Jr., 15–26. New Brunswick, NJ and London: Transaction.

Wallerstein, Immanuel 1974. *The Modern World-System*. Vol. I. New York: Academic Press.

Wallis, Roy 1976. *The Road to Total Freedom: A Sociological Analysis of Scientology.* London: Heinemann.

Warner, Michael 1992. The Mass Public and the Mass Subject. In *Habermas and the Public Sphere*, edited by Craig Calhoun, 377–401. Cambridge, MA: The MIT Press.

Warner, R. Stephen 1993. Work in progress toward a new paradigm for the sociological study of religion in the United States. *American Journal of Sociology* 98(5): 1044–93.

—— 1998. Immigration and Religious Communities in the United States. In *Gatherings in Diaspora. Religious Communities and the New Immigration*, edited by R. Stephen Warner and Judith G. Wittner, 3–34. Philadelphia, PA: Temple University Press.

—— and Judith G. Wittner 1998. *Gatherings in Diaspora. Religious Communities and the New Immigration*. Philadelphia, PA: Temple University Press.

Warner, W. Lloyd 1963/1941–45. *Yankee City*. New Haven, CT and London: Yale University Press.

—— 1949. *Democracy in Jonesville*. New York: Harper & Brothers.

Weber, Max 1964/1922. *The Sociology of Religion*. Boston, MA: Beacon Press.

—— 1968/1925. *Economy and Society*, Vols I–III. Edited by Guenther Roth and Claus Wittich. New York: Bedminster Press.

—— 1979. *From Max Weber: Essays in Sociology*. Collected and edited by Hans Gerth and C. Wright Mills. New York: Oxford University Press.

—— 2001/1904–05. *The Protestant Ethic and the Spirit of Capitalism*. London: Routledge.

Wellmer, Albrecht 1991. *The Persistence of Modernity*. Oxford: Polity Press.

Wenig, Margaret Moers 1993. Reform Jewish Worship: How Shall We Speak of Torah, Israel, and God? In *Women at Worship*, edited by Marjorie Procter-Smith and Janet R. Walton, 31–42. Louisville, KY: Westminster/John Knox Press.

Westerkamp, Marilyn J. 1999. *Women and Religion in Early America 1600–1850*. London and New York: Routledge.

Wikan, Unni 2003. *For ærens skyld: Fadime til ettertanke* [For the sake of honor. In retrospect of Fadime]. Oslo: Universitetsforlaget.

Wilcox, C. 1996. *Onward Christian Soldiers? The Religious Right in American Politics*. Boulder, CO: Westview Press.

Wilcox, Melissa M. 2003. *Coming Out in Christianity. Religion, Identity, & Community*. Bloomington and Indianapolis: Indiana University Press.

Williams, Rhys H. (ed.) 2001. *Promise Keepers and the New Masculinity. Private Lives and Public Morality*. Lanham, MD: Lexington Books.

Wilson, Bryan R. 1967. *Patterns of Sectarianism*. London: Heinemann.

—— 1970. *Religious Sects.* London: World University Library.

—— 1982. *Religion in Sociological Perspective*. Oxford: Oxford University Press.

—— 1990. *The Social Dimension of Sectarianism*. Oxford: Clarendon Press.

—— 1992. Reflections on a many-sided controversy. In *Religion and Modernization: sociologists and historians debate the secularization thesis*, edited by Steve Bruce, 195–210. Oxford: Clarendon Press.

—— 2001. Salvation, Secularization and De-moralization. In *The Blackwell Companion to Sociology of Religion*, edited by Richard K. Fenn, 39–51. Oxford: Blackwell.

Wilson, John F. 1979. *Public Religion in American Culture*. Philadelphia, PA: Temple University Press.

Wimberley, Ronald C. 1979. Continuity and the Measurement of Civil Religion. *Sociological Analysis* 40: 59–62.

Wittgenstein, Ludwig 1958. *Philosophical Investigations*. 2nd edition. Oxford: Blackwell.

Woodhead, Linda 2002. Women and Religion. In *Religions in the Modern World*, edited by Linda Woodhead et al., 332–56. London: Routledge.

—— 2003. Feminism and the Sociology of Religion: From Gender-blindness to Gendered Difference. In *The Blackwell Companion to Sociology of Religion*, edited by Richard K. Fenn, 67–84. Oxford: Blackwell.

Wright, Sue Marie 1994. Women and the Charismatic Community: Defining the Attraction. In *Gender and Religion*, edited by William H. Swatos, Jr., 143–57. New Brunswick, NJ and London: Transaction.

Wrong, Dennis 1961. The Over-Socialized Conception of Man in Modern Sociology. *American Sociological Review* 26: 184–93.

Wuthnow, Robert 1998. *After Heaven: Spirituality in America Since the 1950s*. Berkeley: University of California Press.

——, James Davison Hunter, Albert Bergesen, and Edith Kurzweil 1987. *Cultural Analysis. The Work of Peter L. Berger, Mary Douglas, Michel Foucault, and Jürgen Habermas*. London and New York: Routledge & Kegan Paul.

Yinger, J.M. 1970. *The Scientific Study of Religion*. London: Routledge.

Yoo, David K. 1999. *New Spiritual Homes. Religion and Asian Americans*. Honolulu: University of Hawai'i Press.

Young, L.A. (ed.) 1997. *Rational Choice Theory and Religion: summary and assessment*. New York: Routledge.

Young, Serenity 1999. *Encyclopedia of Women and World Religion*. New York: Macmillan.

Zald, Mayer N. and Roberta Ash 1966. Social movement organizations: growth, decay and change. *Social Forces* 44: 327–43.

Zuckerman, Phil 2002. The Sociology of Religion of W.E.B. Du Bois. *Sociology of Religion* 63(2): 239–53.

Index